Thinking Skills
Pre-K & UP

Spatial Reasoning

Table of Contents

To parents:

Spatial Reasoning

In this section, your child will develop spatial reasoning skills as such as spatial judgment and visualization of objects from multiple perspectives. This section contains activities like tracing, mazes, coloring, jigsaw puzzles, matching shapes, comparing heights, and others. By completing this section your child will gain the ability to think about objects in relation to space and to draw conclusions based on the information gained from each activity.

Each skill is introduced in a step-by-step manner that allows your child to master it without frustration. Over the course of the section, the difficulty level of these activities increases as your child gains confidence in his or her spatial reasoning ability.

Tracing

Two Paths

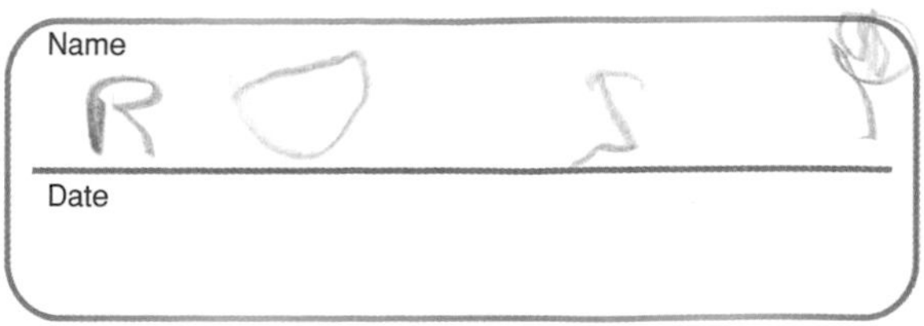

To parents
Guide your child to write his or her name and date in the box above. Do the exercise along with your child if he or she has difficulty.

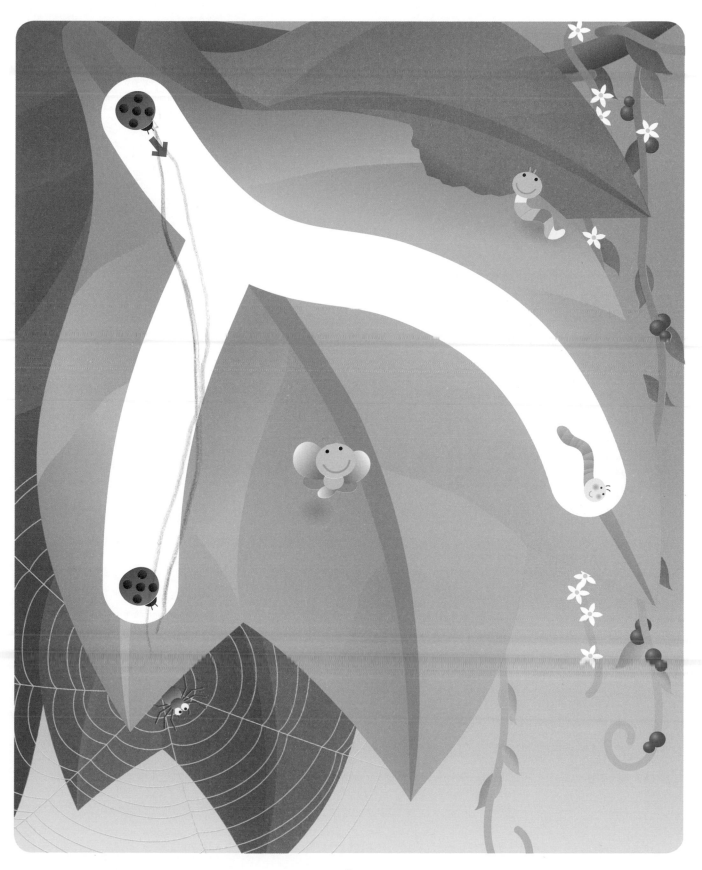

■ Draw a line to the matching animal.

■ Draw a line to the matching object.

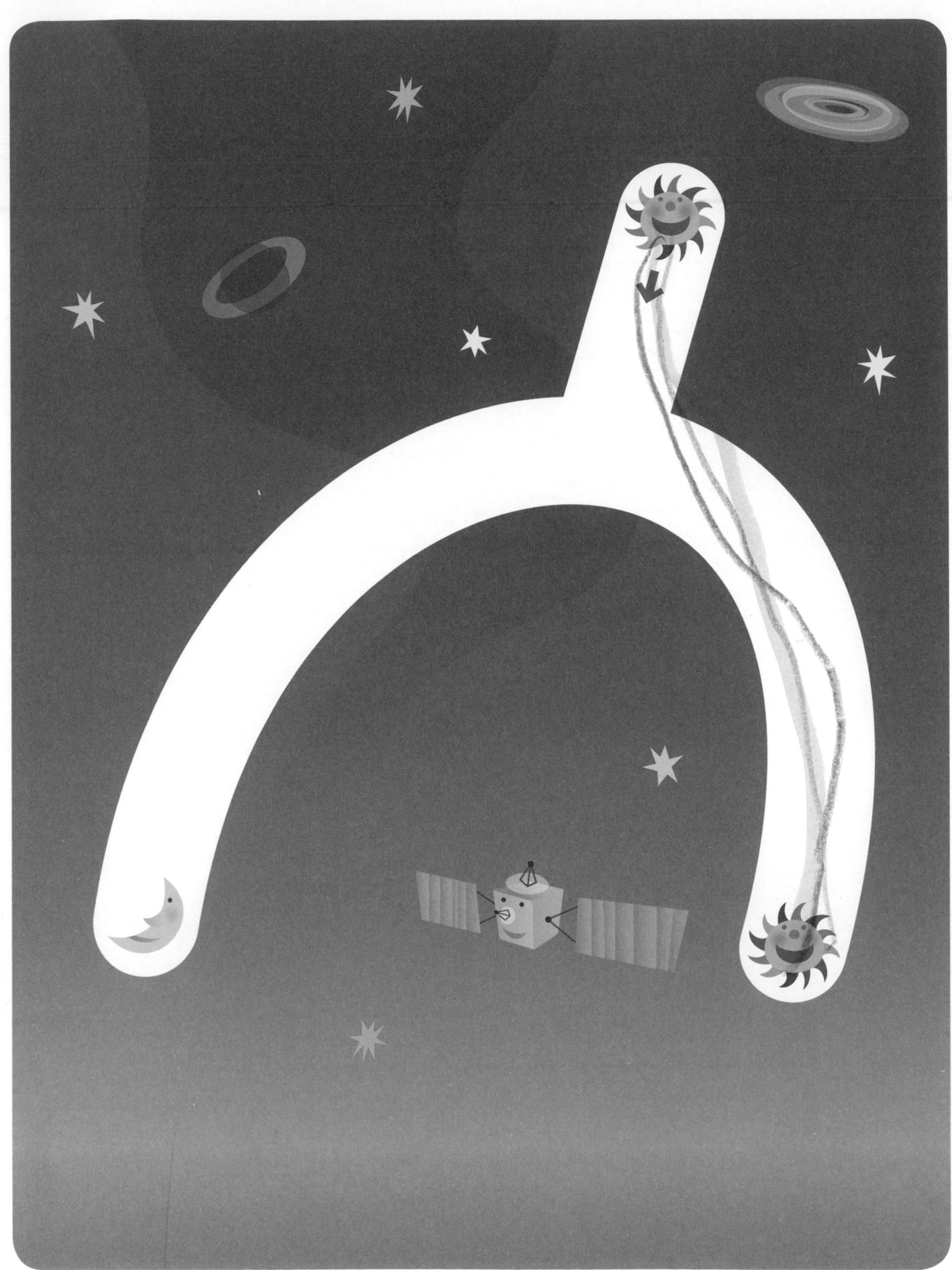

Tracing
Three Paths

Name ROSE

Date

■ Draw a line to the matching animal.

To parents
If your child has difficulty, point to the start and the end of the correct path. Tell your child to draw a line between the matching pictures.

■ Draw a line to the matching object.

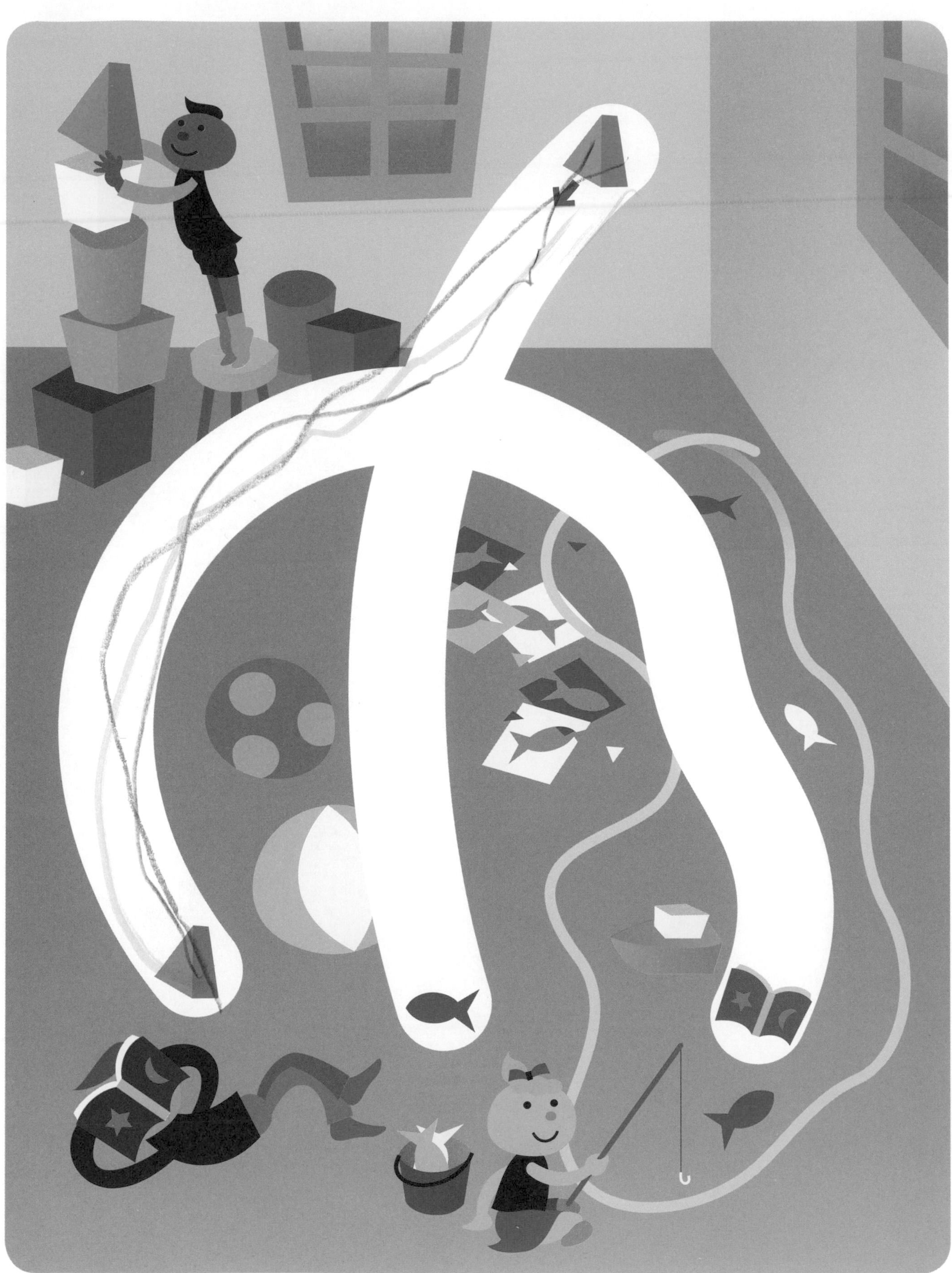

Tracing
Four Paths

Name ROSE HOJE

Date

■ Draw a line to the matching animal.

To parents
These exercises become more challenging as the number of possible paths increases, and as the paths become narrower and longer, little by little. Encourage your child to match the right pictures.

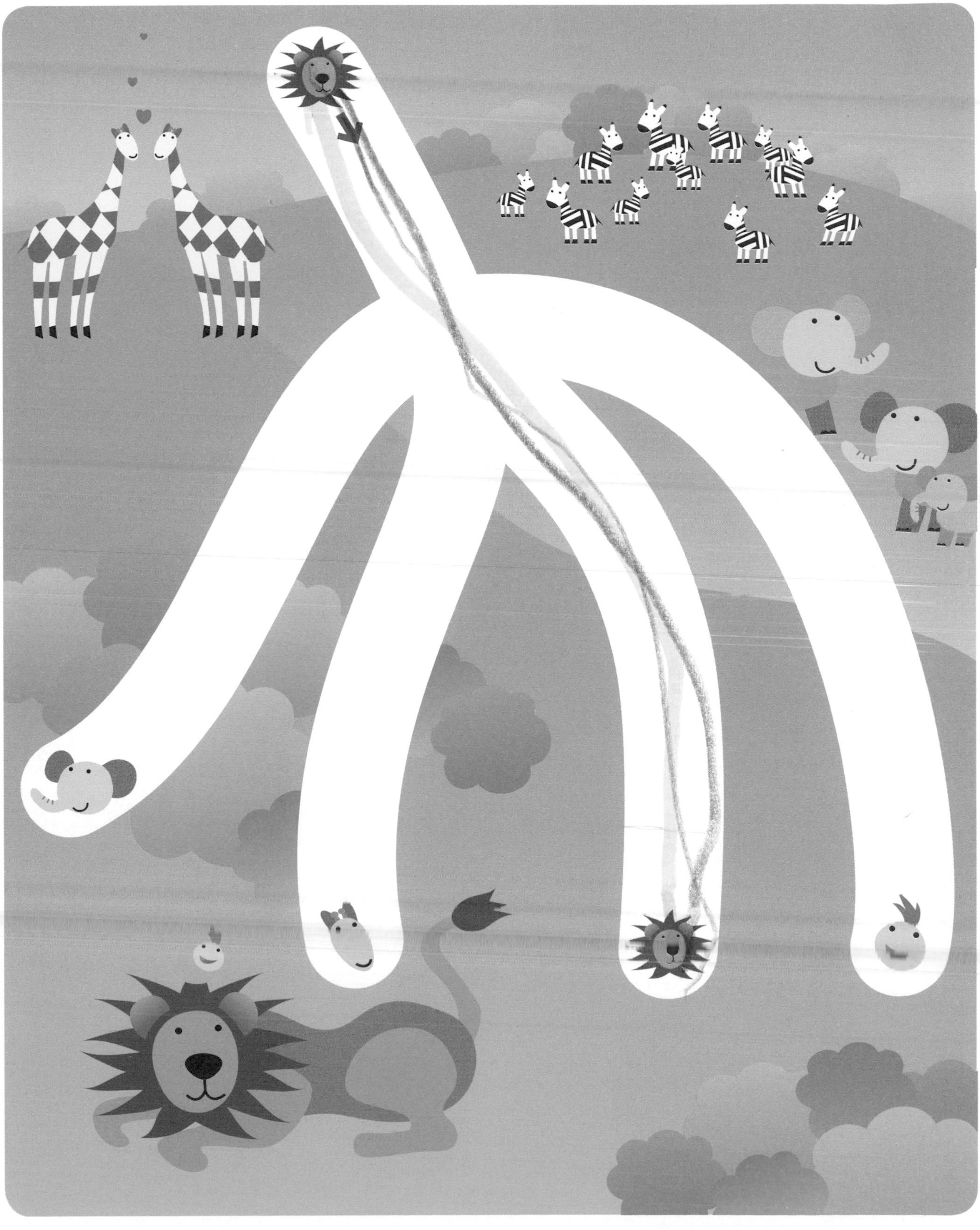

■ Draw a line to the matching object.

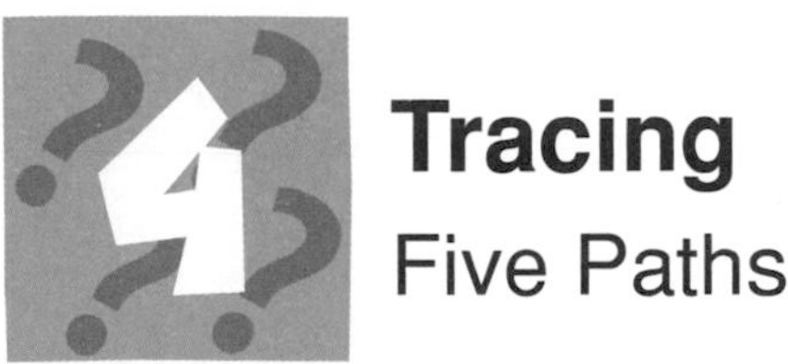

Tracing
Five Paths

Name

Date

■ Draw a line to the matching animal.

To parents
Have your child trace a line with his or her finger before using a pencil, if your child has difficulty.

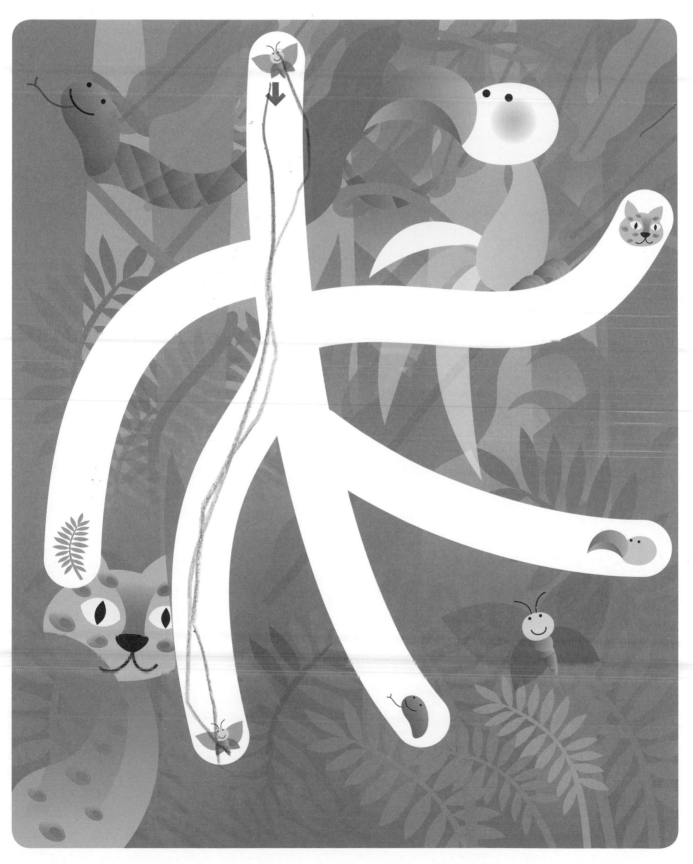

■ Draw a line to the matching object.

Mazes

Level One

Name

Date

■ Draw a line to the matching animal.

To parents
It is okay if your child has trouble staying inside the path. Continue to give your child a lot of encouragement.

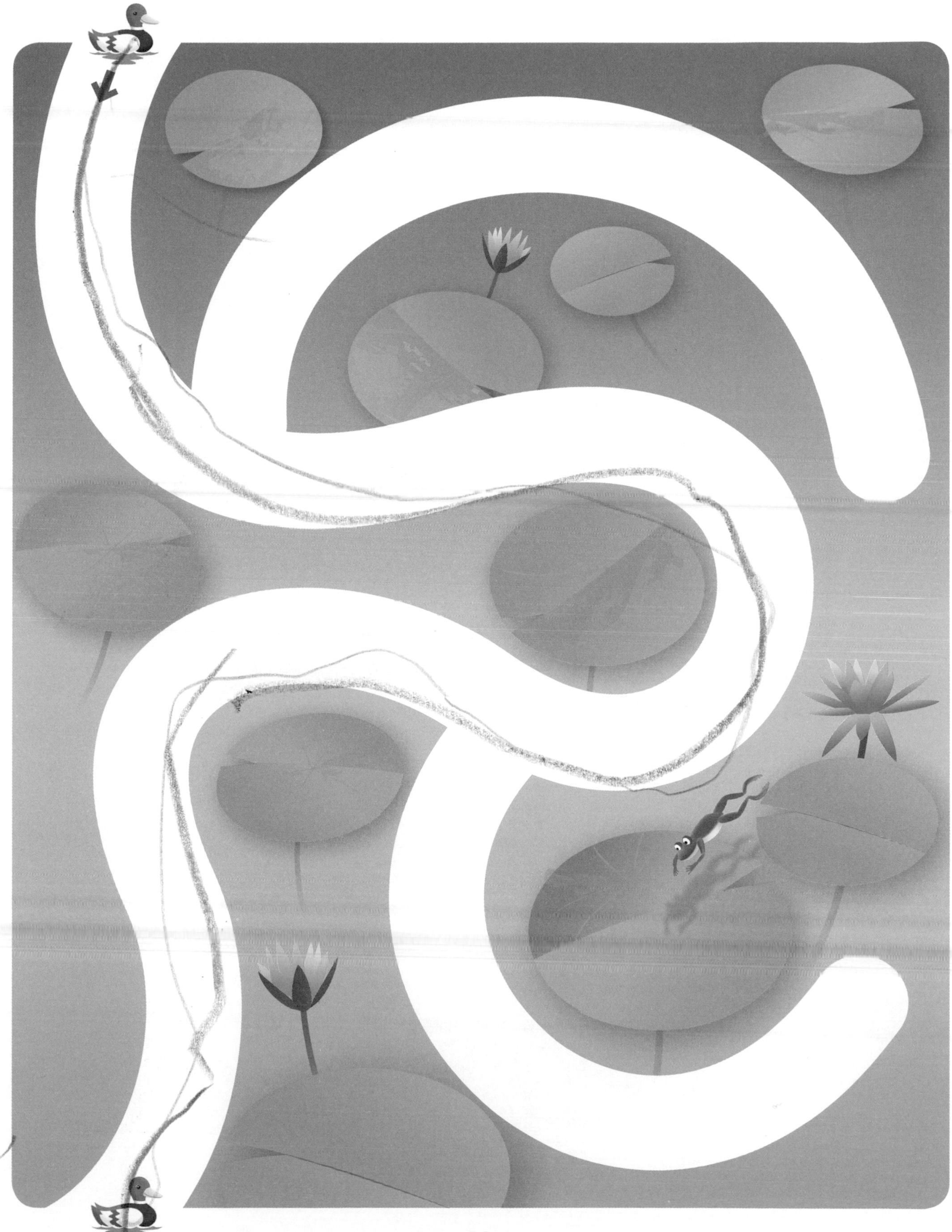

■ Draw a line to the matching animal.

Mazes
Level Two

Name

Date

To parents
If your child comes to a dead end, point to the pictures at the start and the end of the maze. Tell your child to draw a line between the pictures.

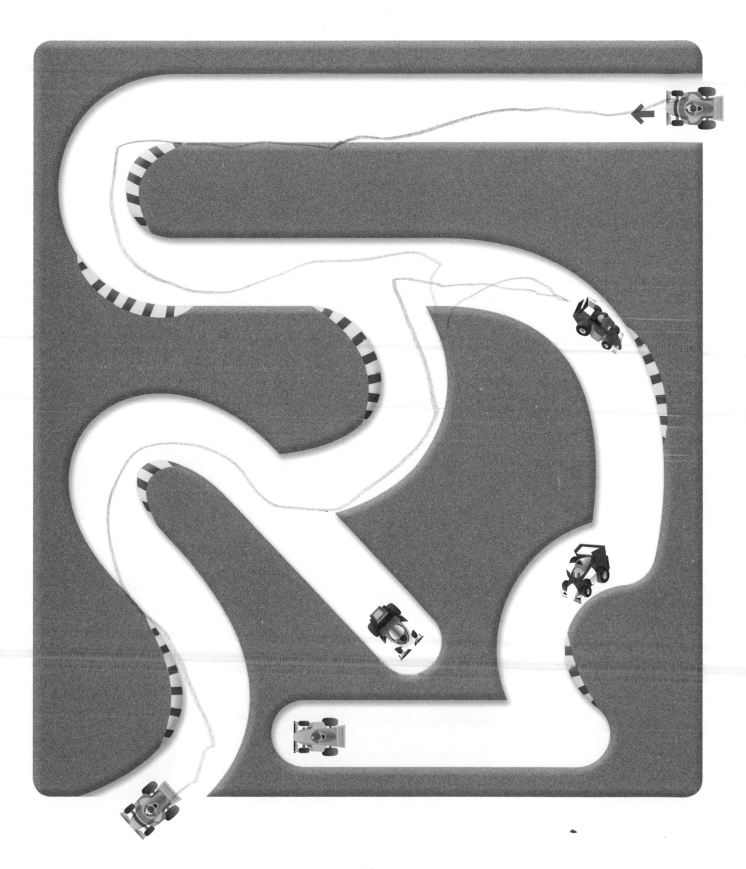

■ Draw a line to the matching object.

■ Draw a line to the matching object.

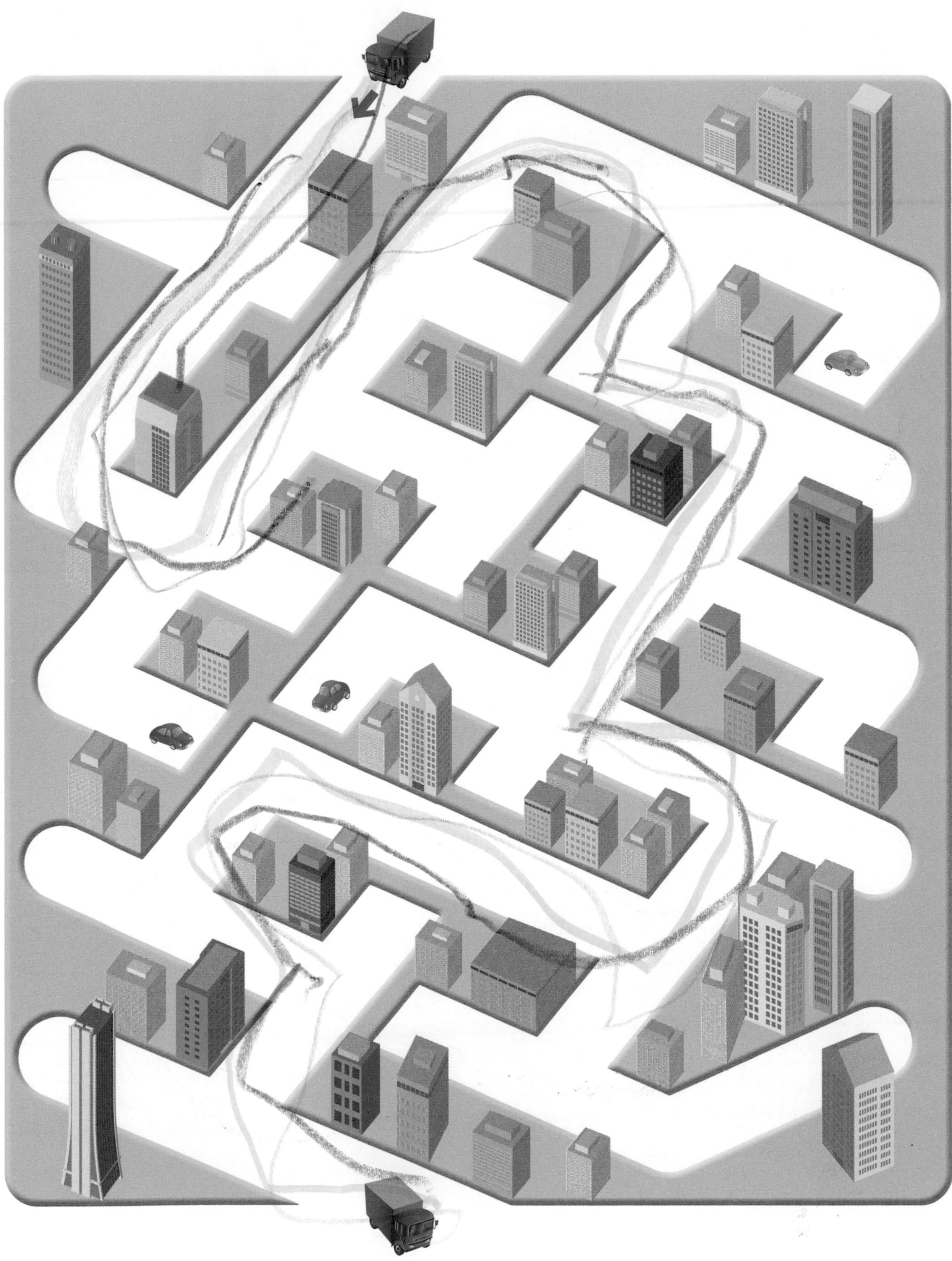

Mazes
Level Three

Name

Date

To parents
It is okay if your child struggles to find his or her way through the maze. Encourage your child to enjoy the activity.

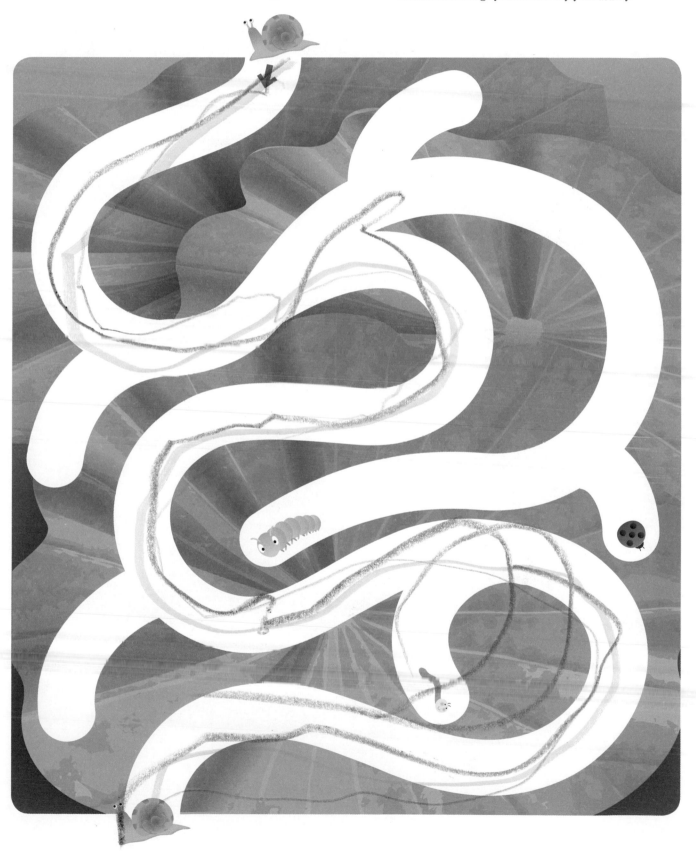

■ Draw a line to the matching animal.

■ Draw a line to the matching animal.

Mazes

Level Four

Name

Date

■ Draw a line to the matching animal.

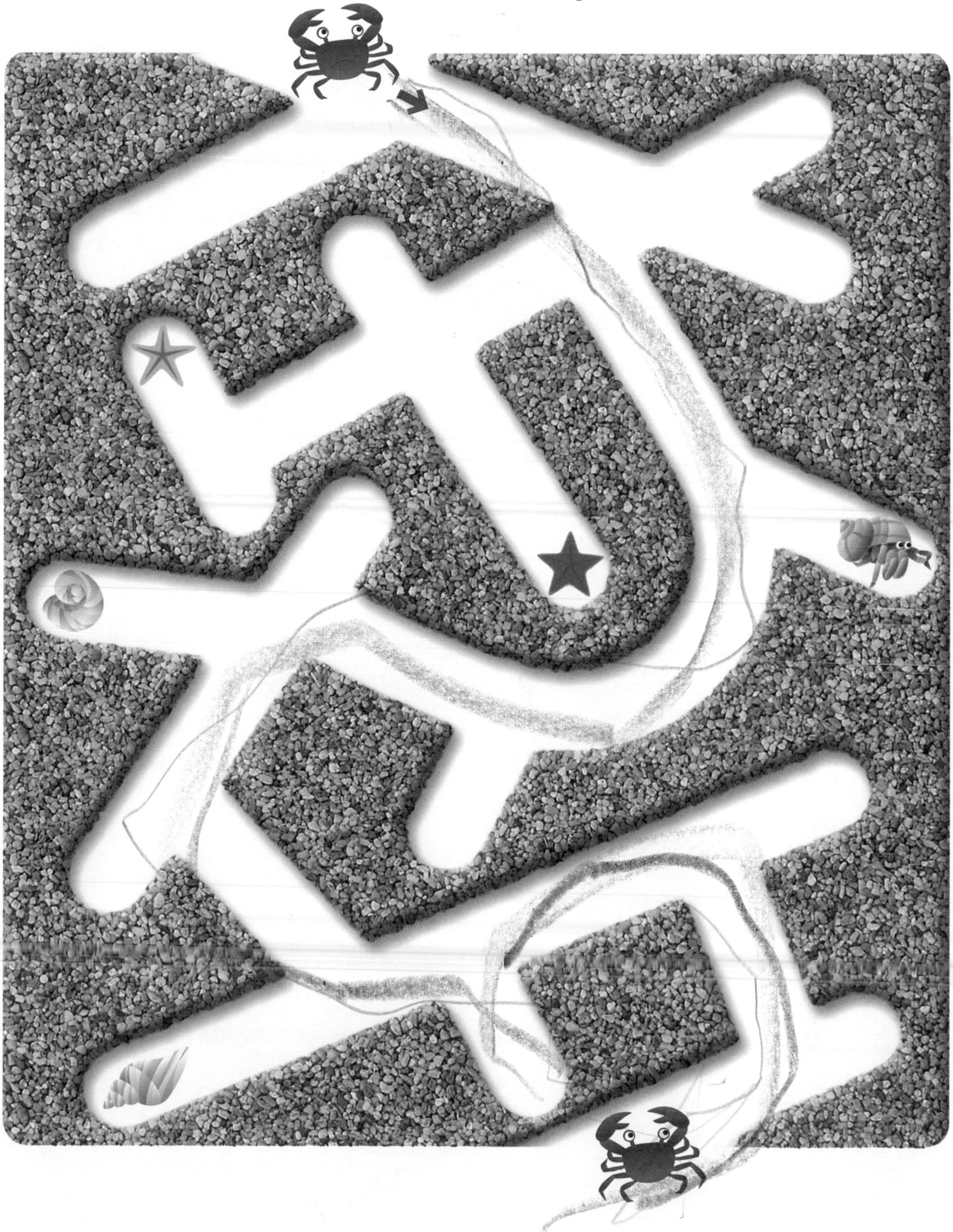

To parents
For extra practice, have your child continue to trace the path using different colors.

■ Draw a line to the matching animal.

Following Directions
Level One

Name

Date

To parents
You may wish to read the directions out loud to your child, step by step. Have your child trace a line with his or her finger before using a pencil, if your child has difficulty.

■ Draw a line by following the directions: Start at the dot (●). Go to the bakery ( ). End at the star (★). Do not turn back on the path.

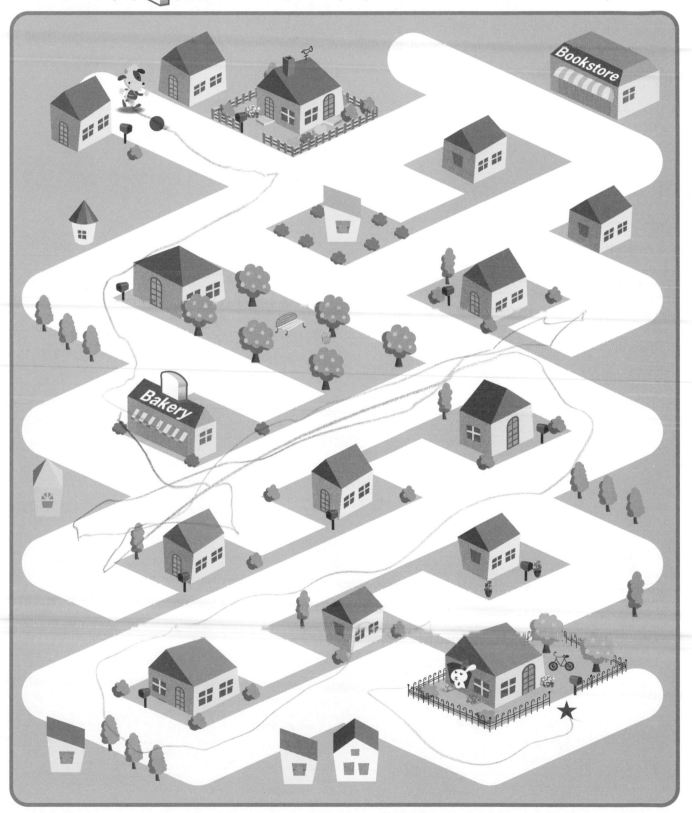

Bookstore

Bakery

■ Draw a line by following the directions: Start at the dot (●). Go to the bookstore (📖). End at the star (★). Do not turn back on the path.

Following Directions
Level Two

Name

Date

To parents
If your child has difficulty, look at the map together before he or she begins. Ask your child to point out some different locations on the map.

■ Draw a line by following the directions: Start at the dot (●). Go to the flower shop ( ). Go to the grocery store ( ). End at the star (★). Do not turn back on the path.

■ Draw a line by following the directions: Start at the dot (●). Go to the park ( ). Go to the mall ( ). End at the star (★). Do not turn back on the path.

Following Directions

Level Three

Name

Date

To parents
Read the directions aloud to your child if he or she has difficulty.

■ Draw a line by following the directions: Start at the dot (●). Go to the shoe store ( ). Go to the pharmacy ( ). Go to the toy shop ( ). End at the star (★). Do not turn back on the path.

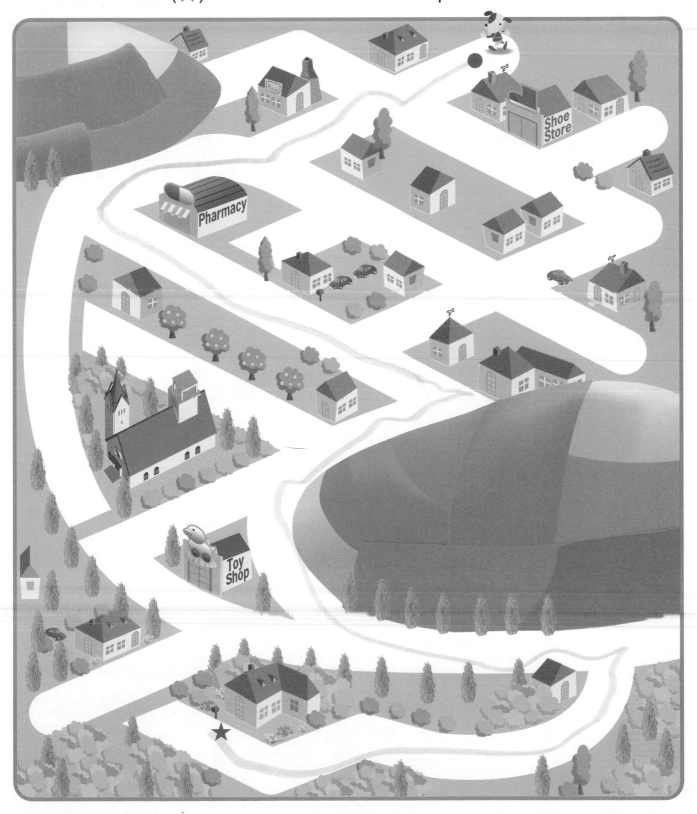

■ Draw a line by following the directions: Start at the dot (●). Go to your grandfather's house ( ). Go to your cousin's house ( ). Go to your uncle's house ( ). End at the star (★). Do not turn back on the path.

Following Directions
Level Four

Name

Date

To parents
It can be challenging to carry out all the steps without turning back on the path. If your child has difficulty, have your child trace each step with his or her finger before using a pencil.

■ Draw a line by following the directions: Start at the dot (●). Go to Chelsea's house ( ). Go to Paul's house ( ). Go to Jayden's house ( ). Go to Ashley's house ( ). End at the star (★). Do not turn back on the path.

Chelsea

Paul

Ashley

Jayden

■ Draw a line by following the directions: Start at the dot (●). Go to Mia's house ( ). Go to Emily's house ( ). Go to Tom's house ( ). Go to John's house ( ). End at the star (★). Do not turn back on the path.

Jigsaw Puzzles
Level One

■ Draw a line to the piece that fits.

Name

Date

To parents
Encourage your child to look at the shapes of the pieces carefully. Looking at the illustrations will also help your child match the correct pieces.

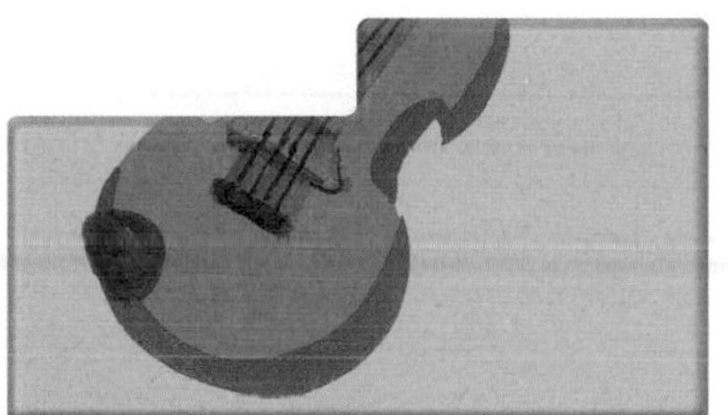

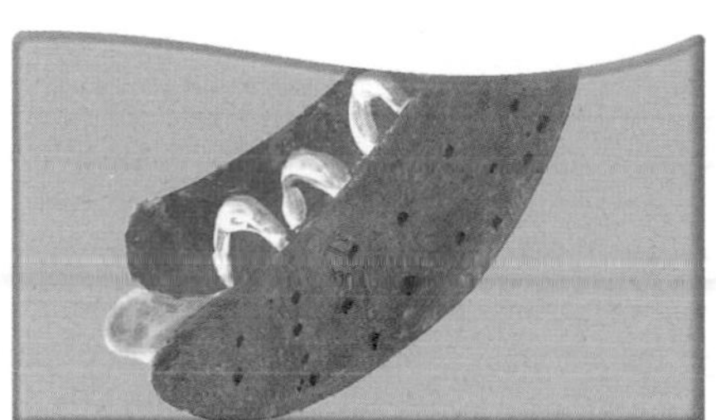

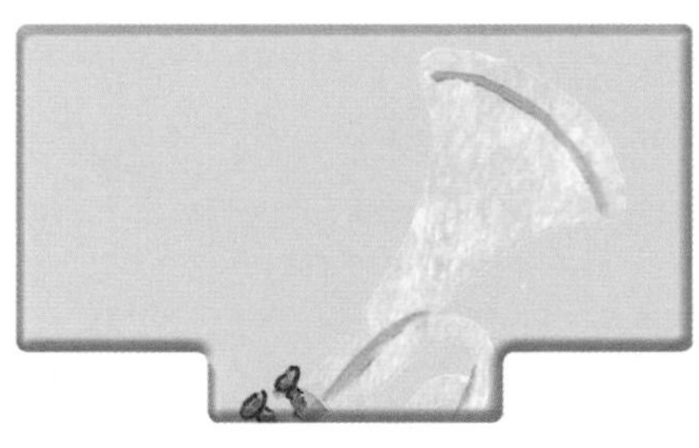

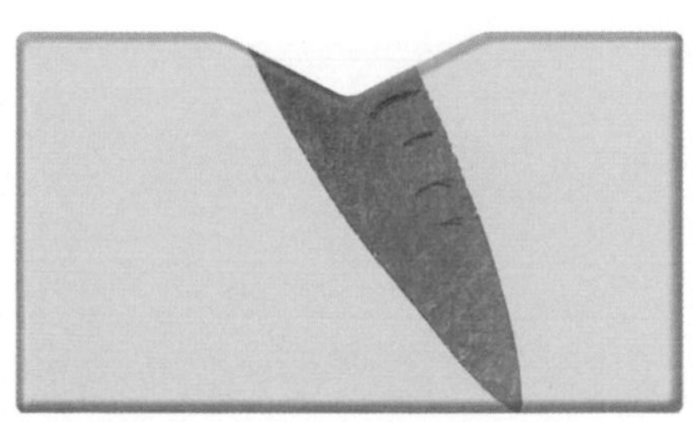

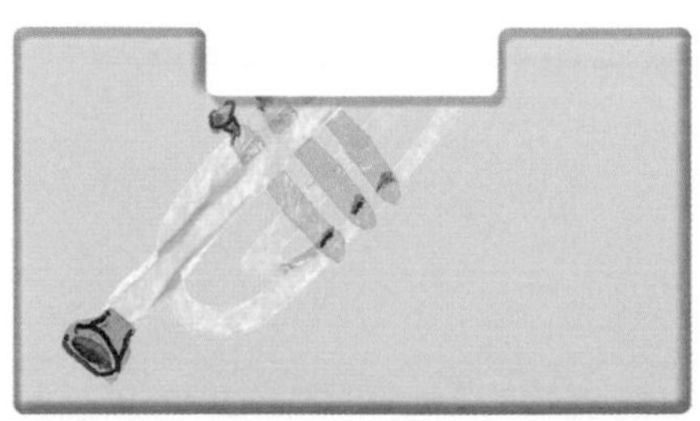

■ Draw a line to the piece that fits.

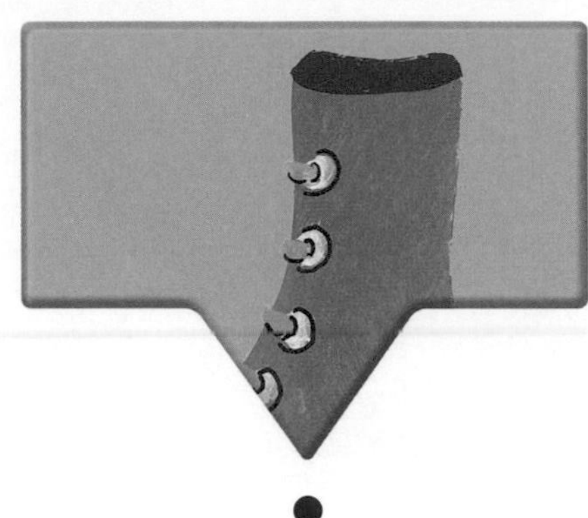

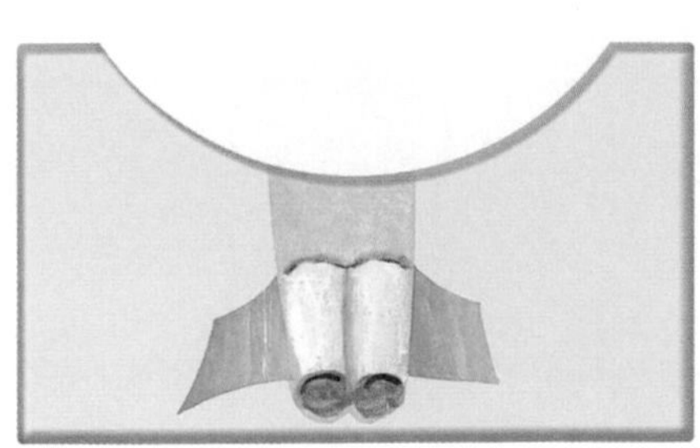

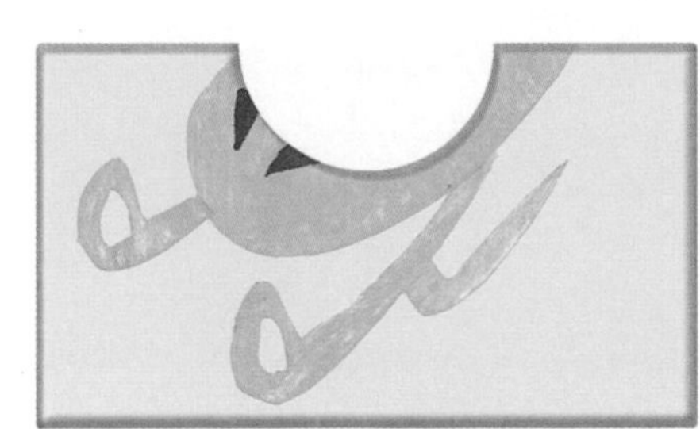

Jigsaw Puzzles
Level Two

Name
Date

■ Draw a line to the piece that fits.

To parents
The two pieces in the bottom row have the same illustration. Encourage your child to look at the edge of each puzzle piece.

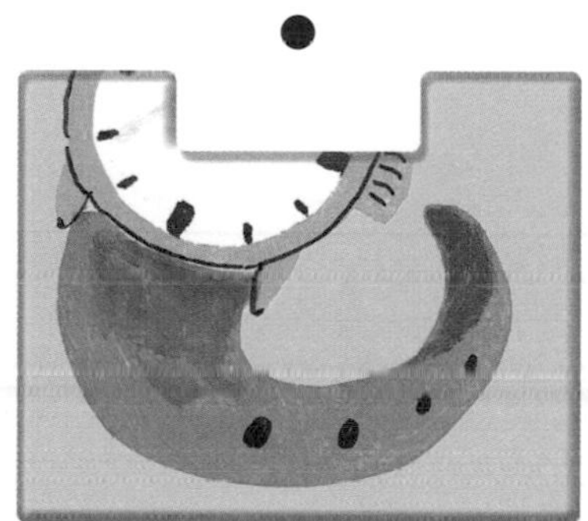

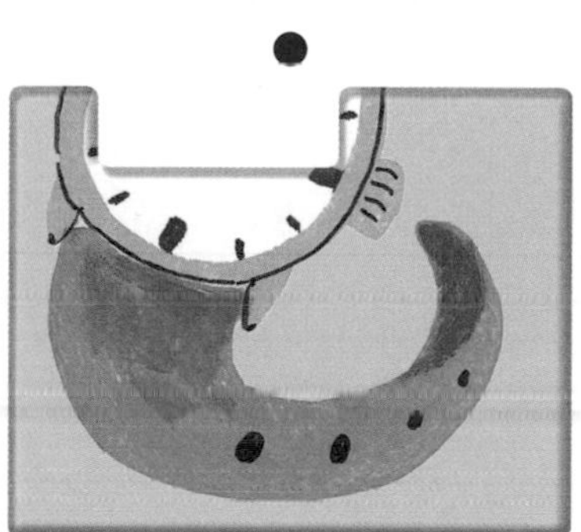

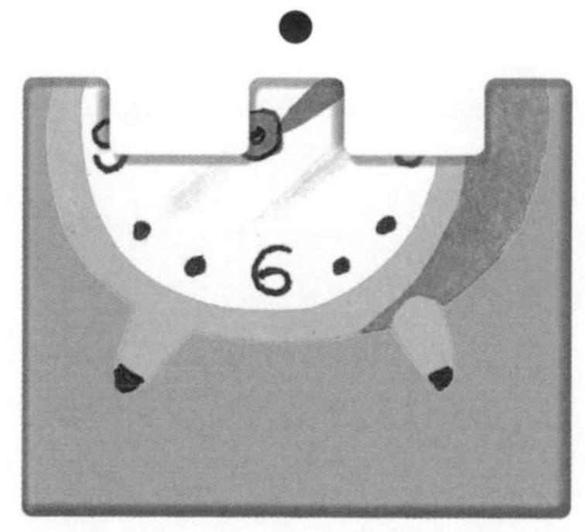

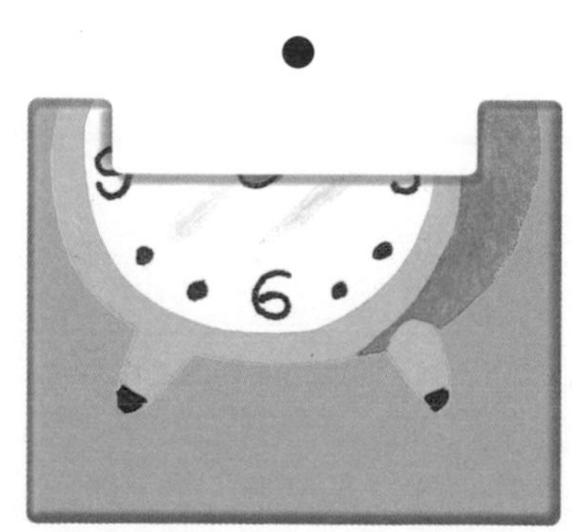

■ Draw a line to the piece that fits.

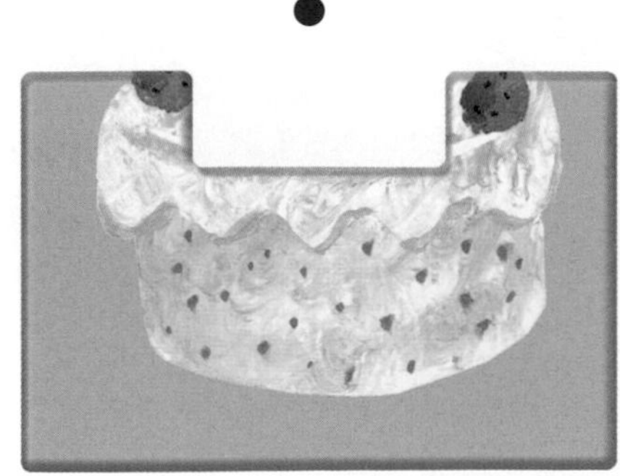

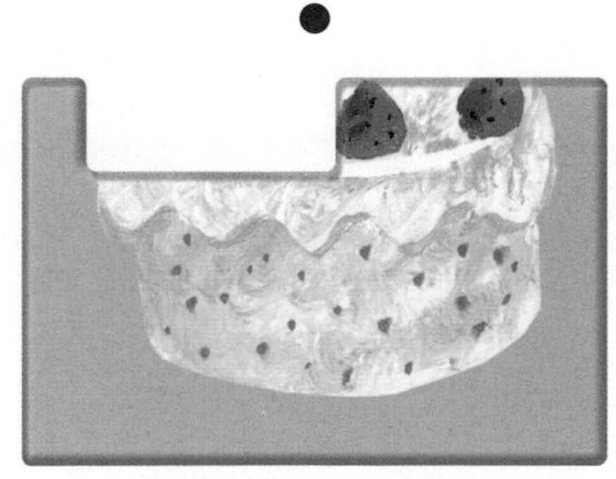

Jigsaw Puzzles

Level Three

Name

Date

■ Draw a line to the piece that fits.

To parents
The number of puzzle pieces in the bottom row has increased. Encourage your child to look carefully at each piece.

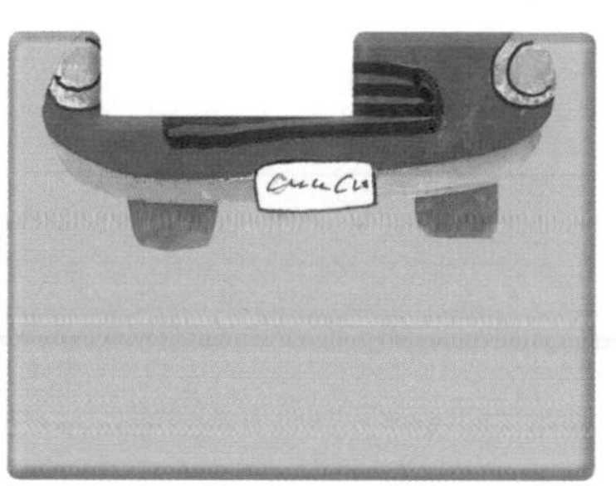

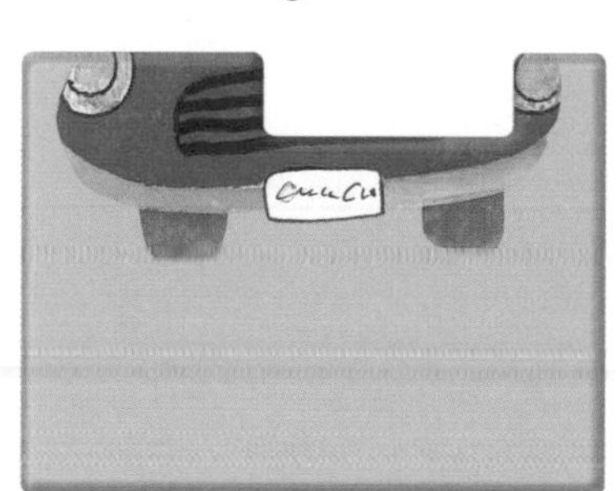

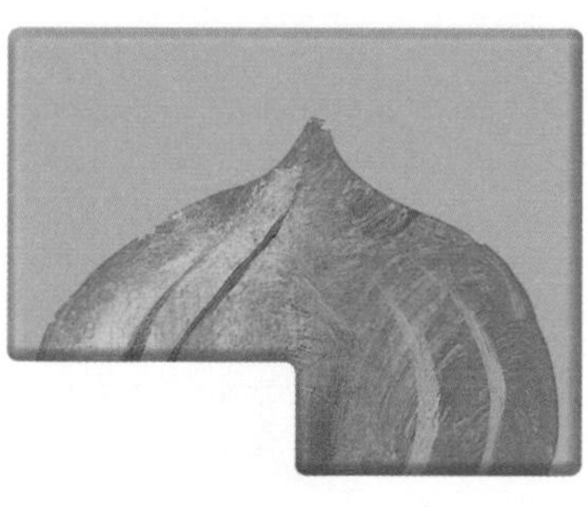

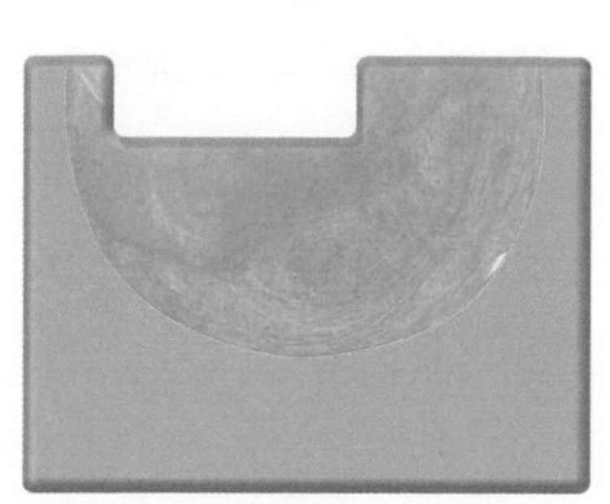

■ Draw a line to the piece that fits.

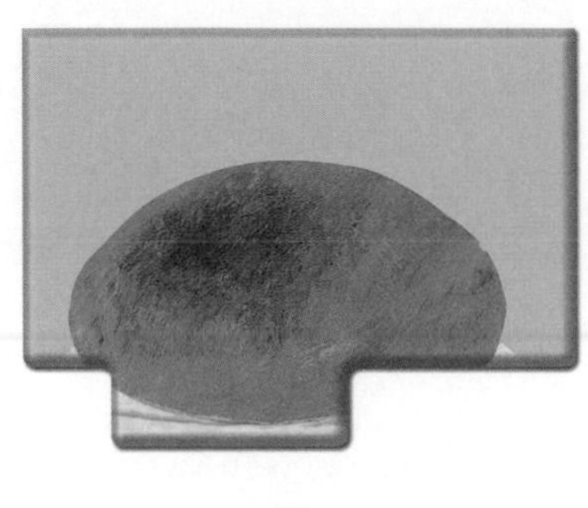

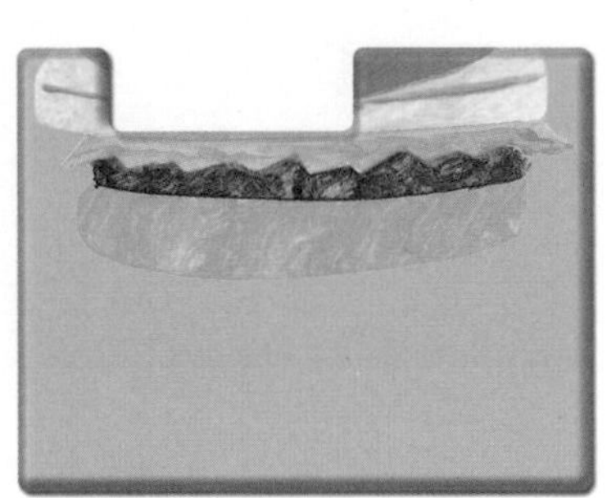

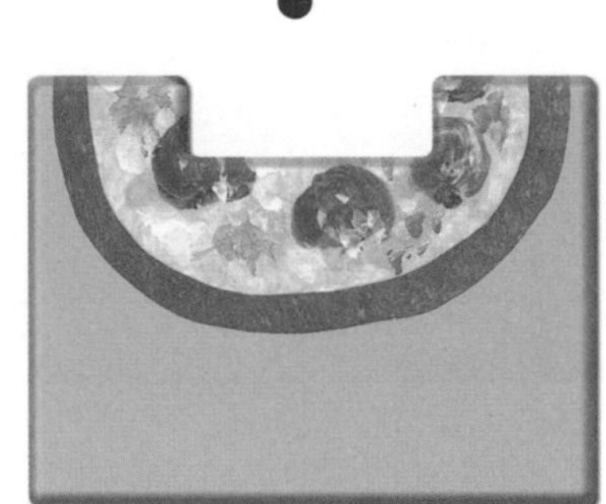

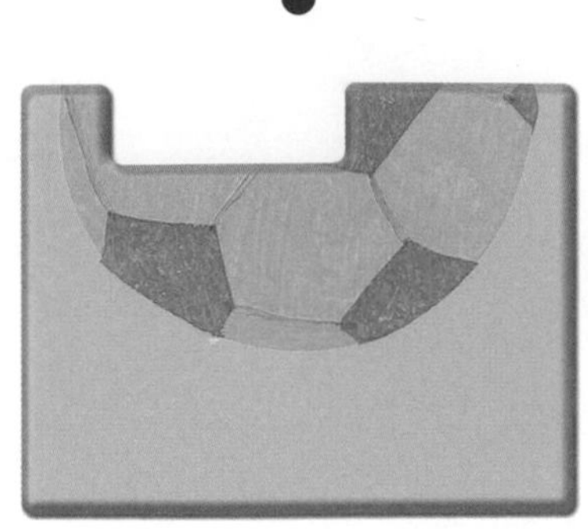

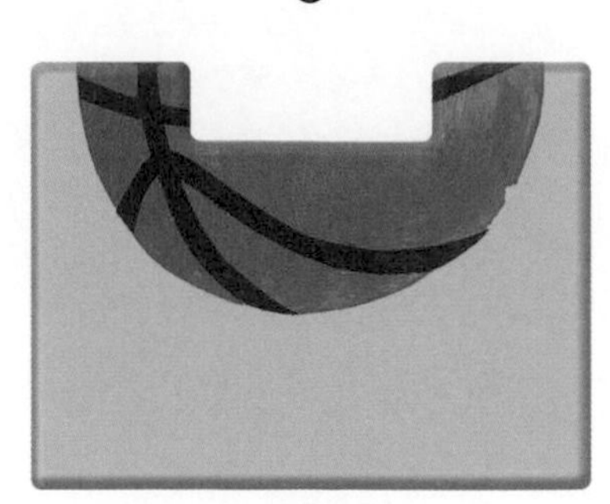

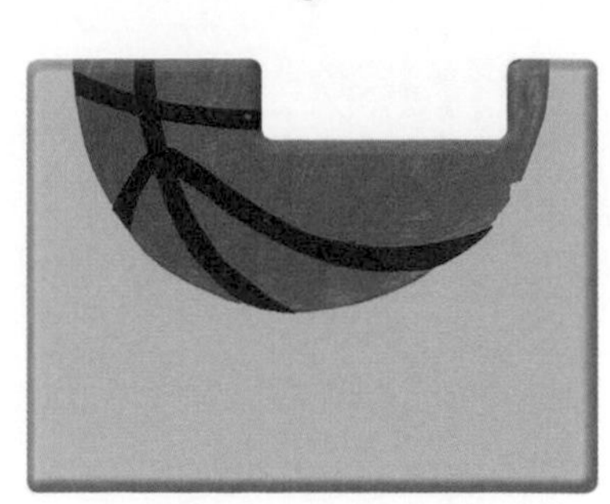

Jigsaw Puzzles
Level Four

Name

Date

■ Draw a line to the piece that fits.

To parents
If your child has difficulty with the activity, look at the edge of each puzzle piece with your child. Together, describe the shapes or patterns that you see.

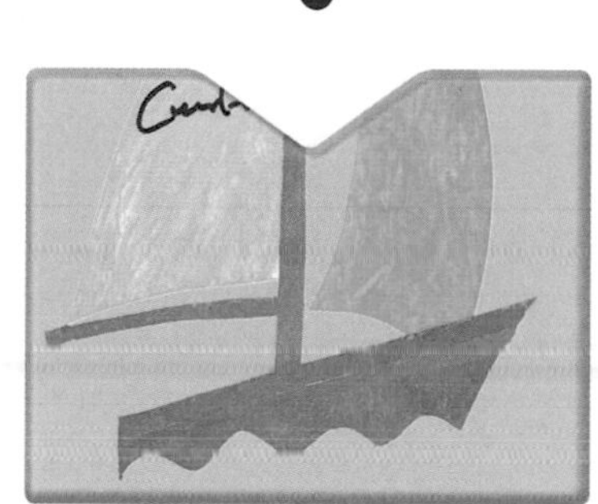

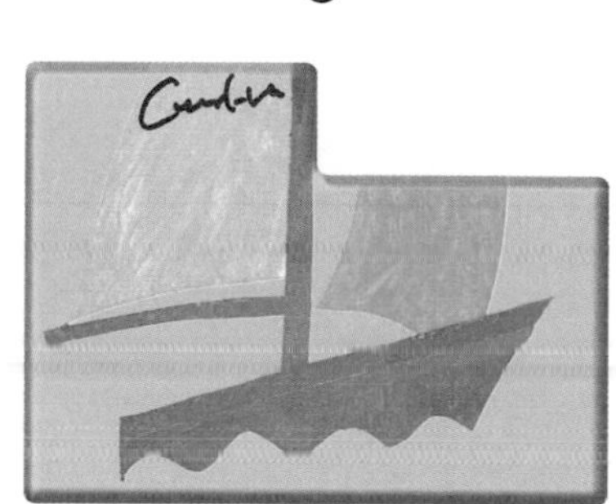

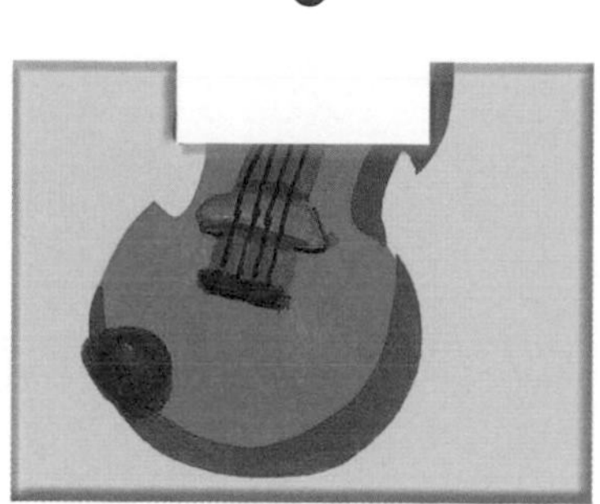

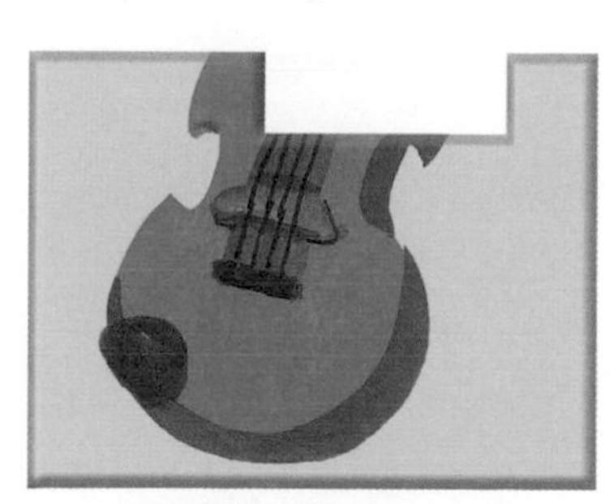

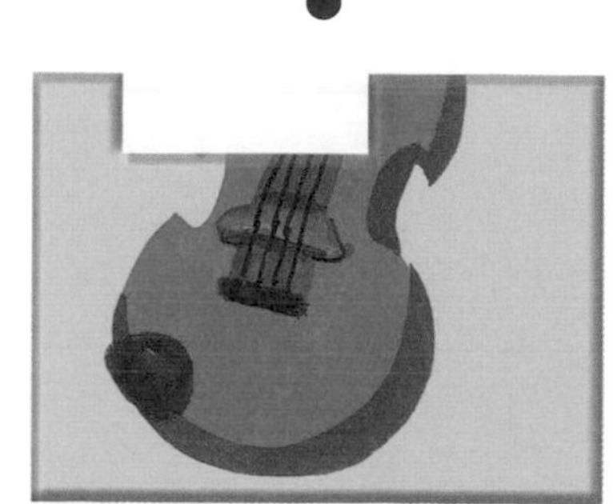

■ Draw a line to the piece that fits.

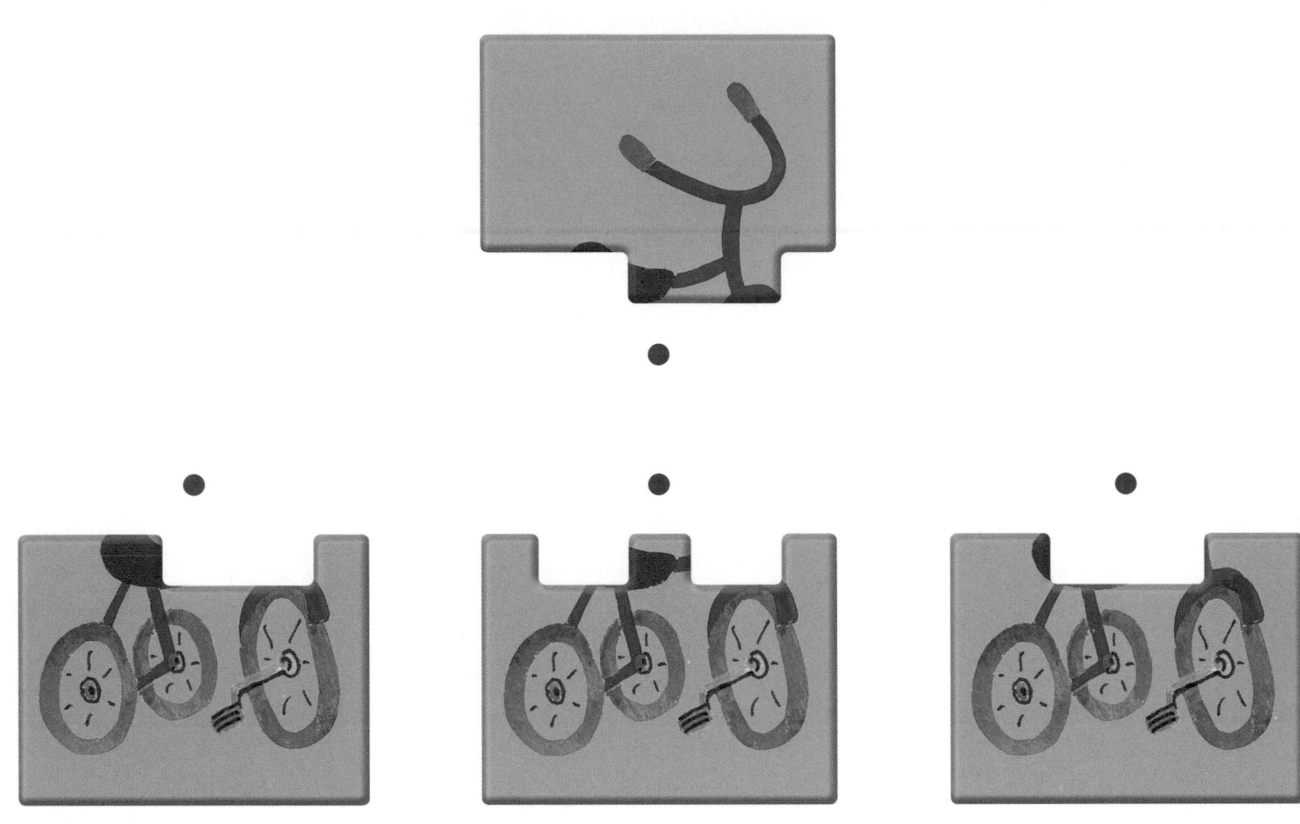

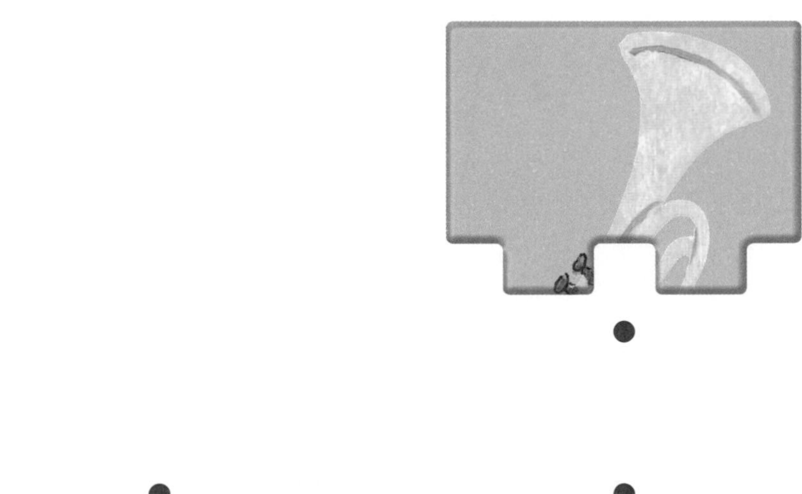

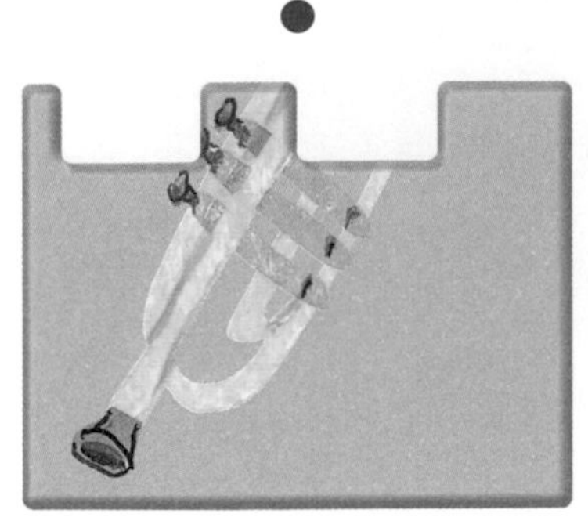

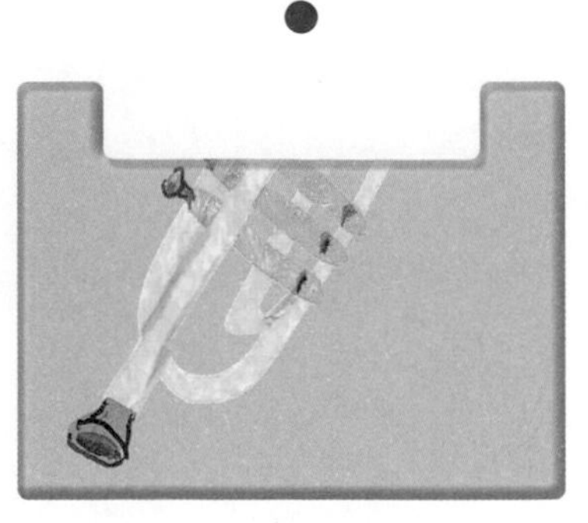

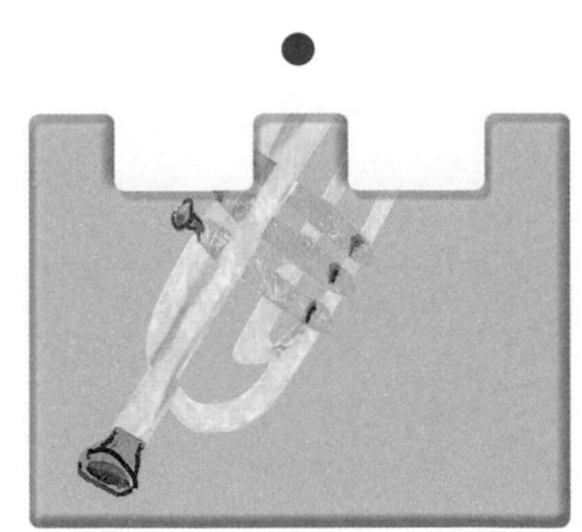

Matching Figures
Level One

Name

Date

■ Draw a line to the matching animal.

To parents
If your child has difficulty with the exercise, look at the silhouette together. Ask your child to describe the features he or she sees such as rounded ears and tufts of fur.

■ Draw a line to the matching object.

Matching Figures
Level Two

Name

Date

■ Draw a line to the matching animal.

To parents
When your child has completed the exercise, ask him or her what the illustration is and talk about the features of the shape.

■ Draw a line to the matching object.

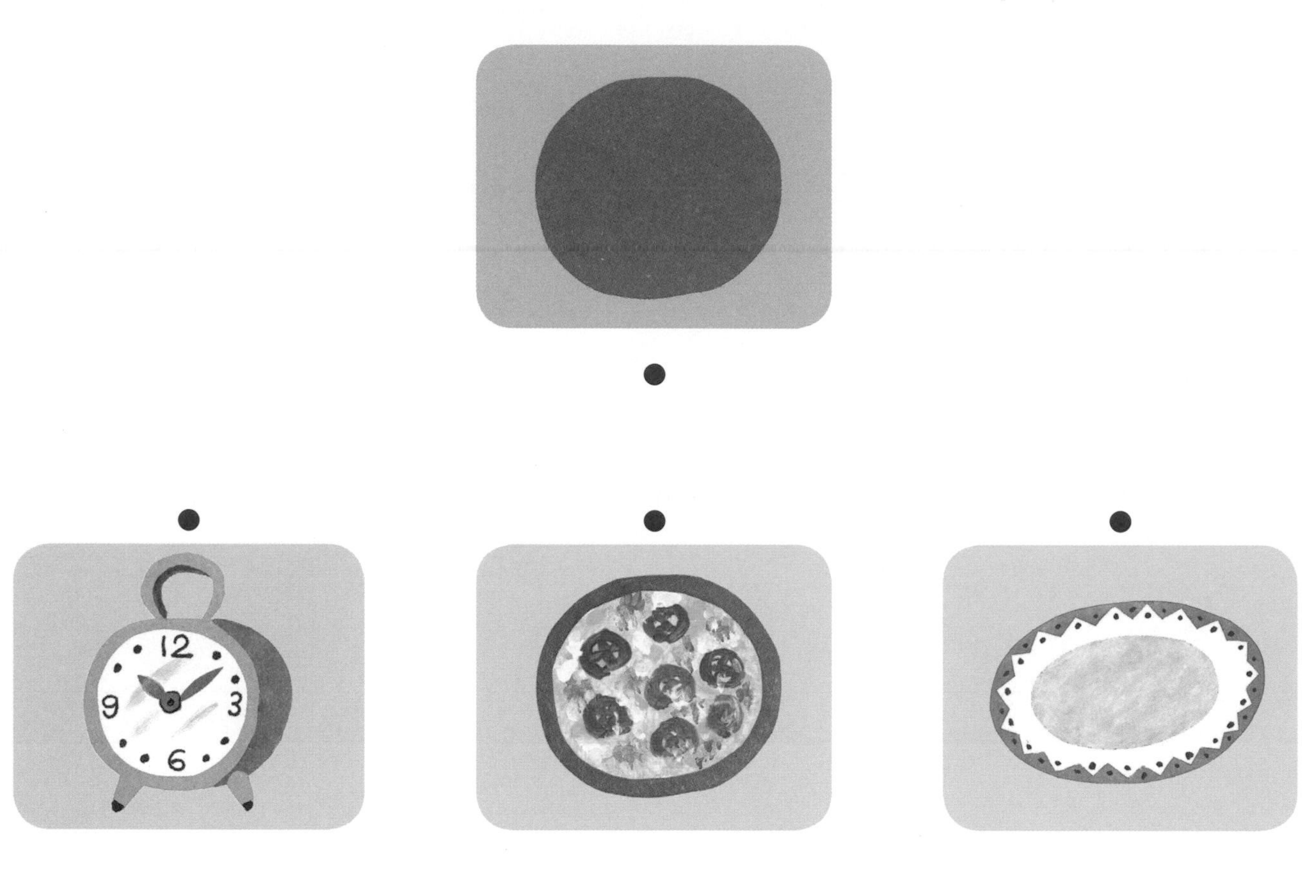

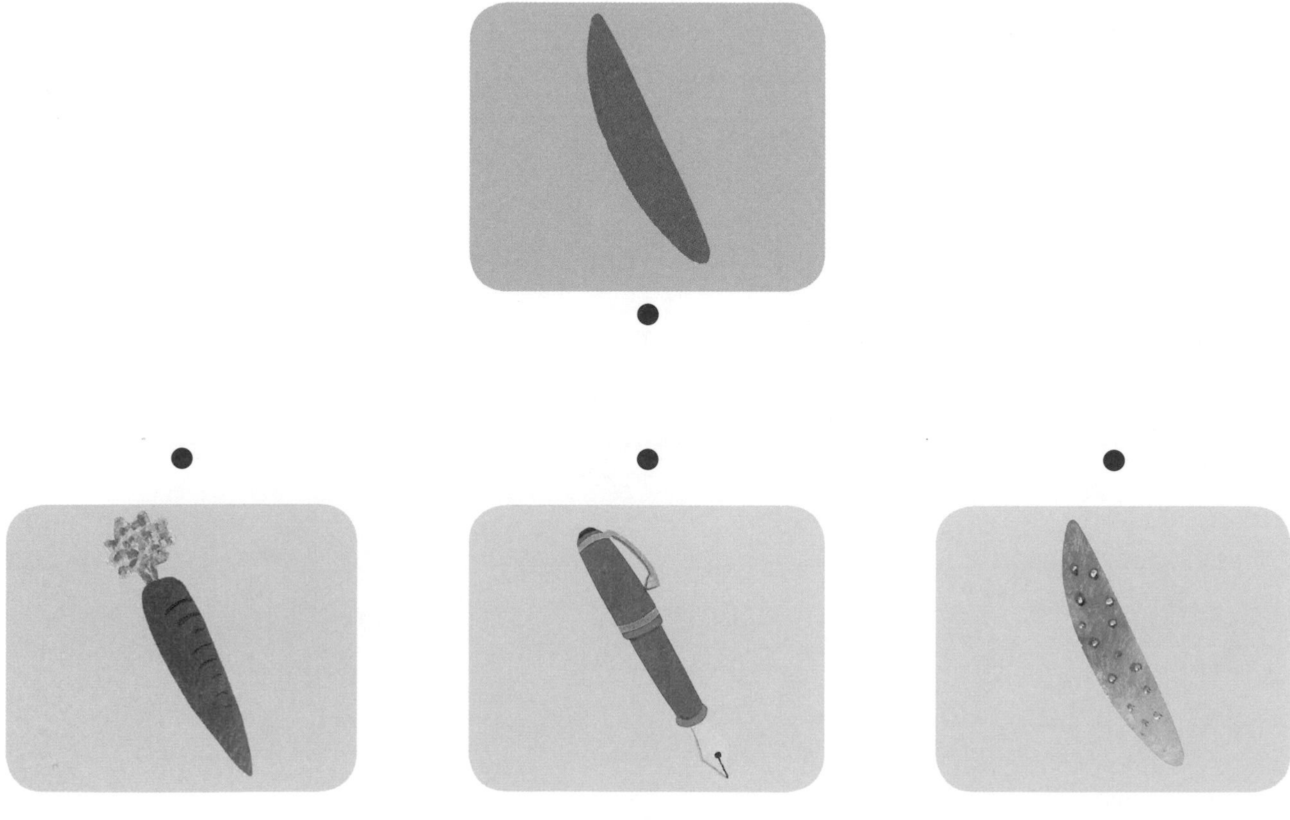

Matching Figures

Level Three

To parents
The number of pictures in the top row has increased. Encourage your child to match the pictures in the top row one by one.

■ Draw a line to the matching animal.

■ Draw a line to the matching object.

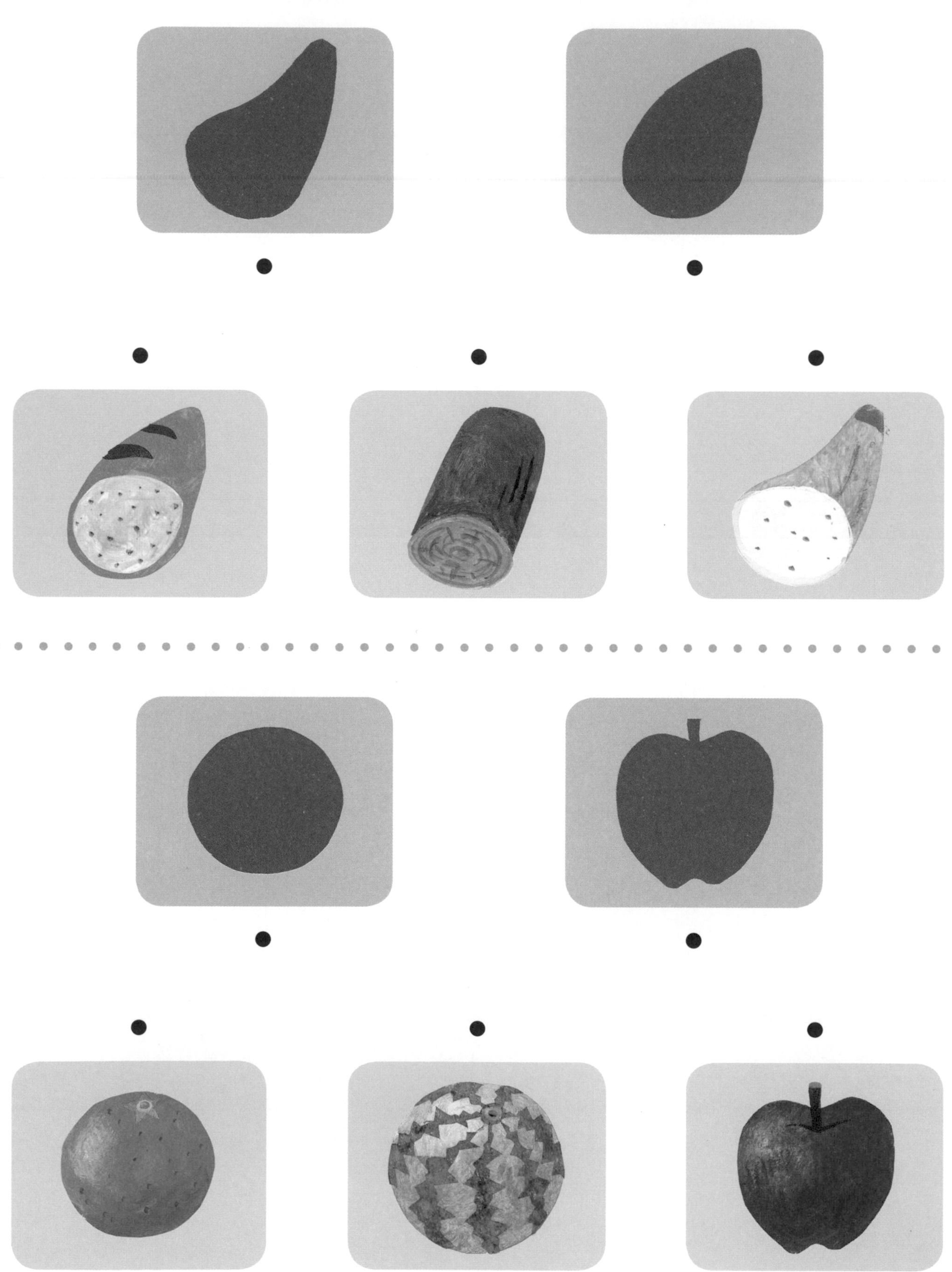

Matching Figures
Level Four

Name

Date

To parents
Encourage your child to notice the details of each silhouette.

■ Draw a line to the matching animal.

■ Draw a line to the matching object.

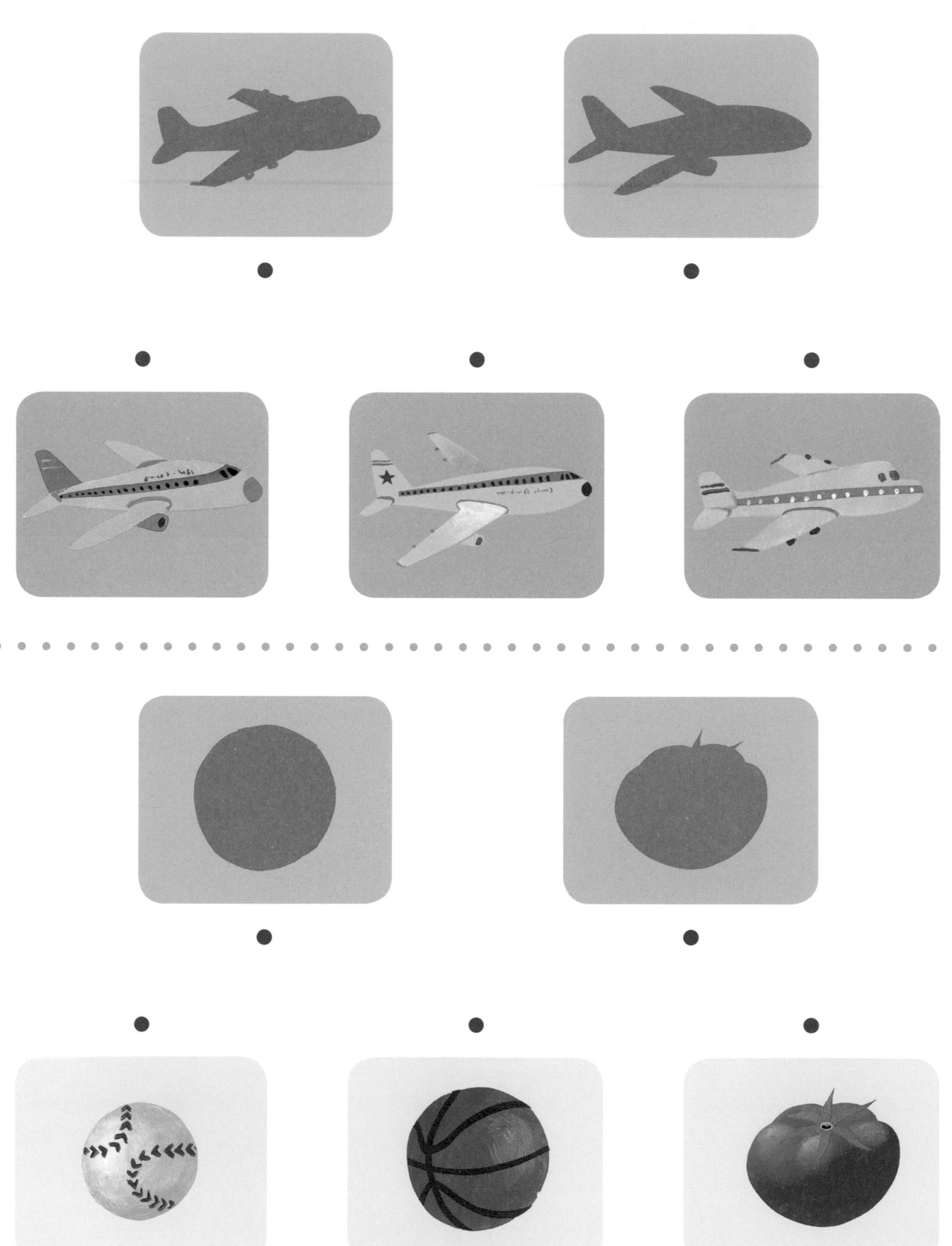

Reasoning with Shapes
Circle & Triangle

Name

Date

To parents
If your child has difficulty, encourage him or her to check if the illustrations in the right column have a triangle.

■ Choose which picture shows the two shapes put together. Write a check mark (✓) beside the picture.

(✓)

( )

( )

■ Choose which picture shows the two shapes put together. Write a check mark (✓) beside the picture.

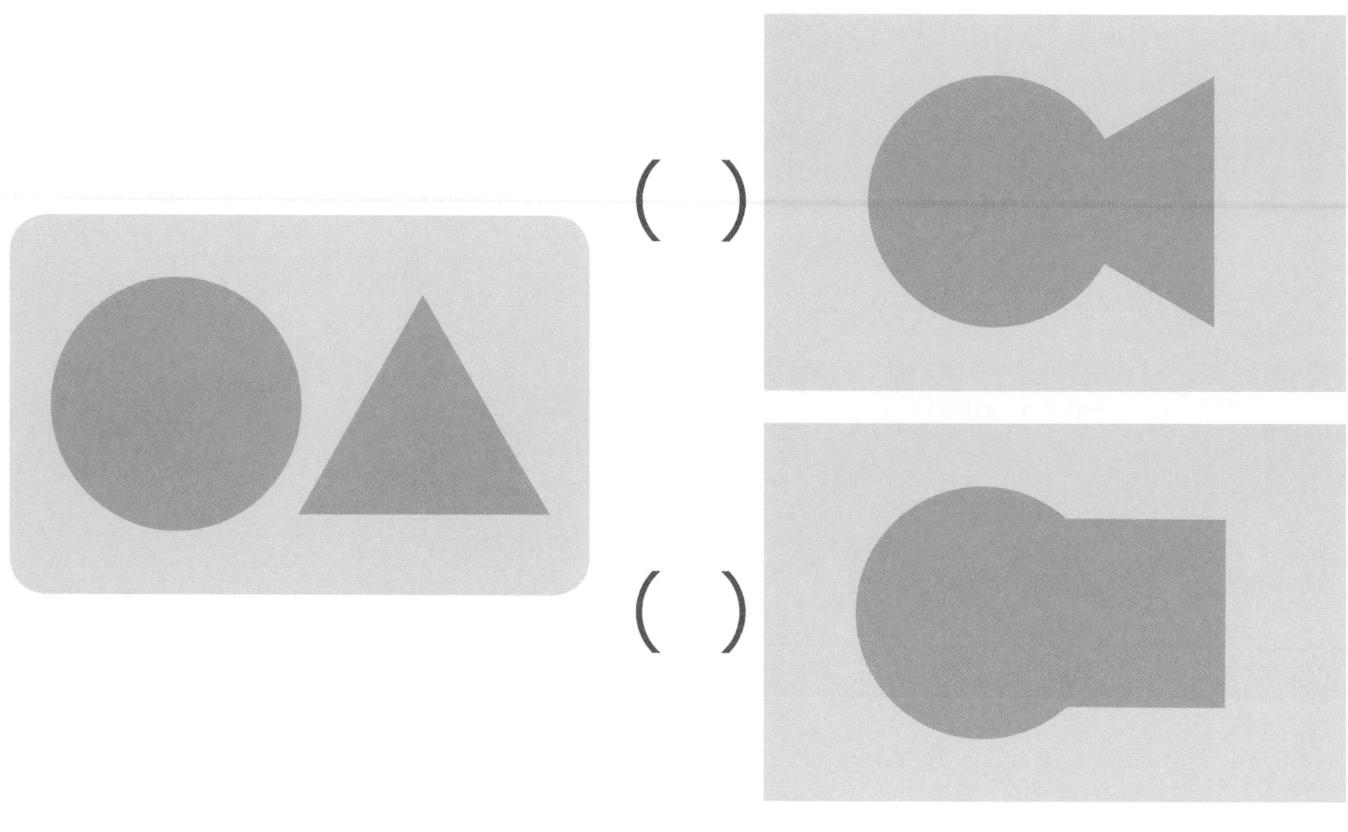

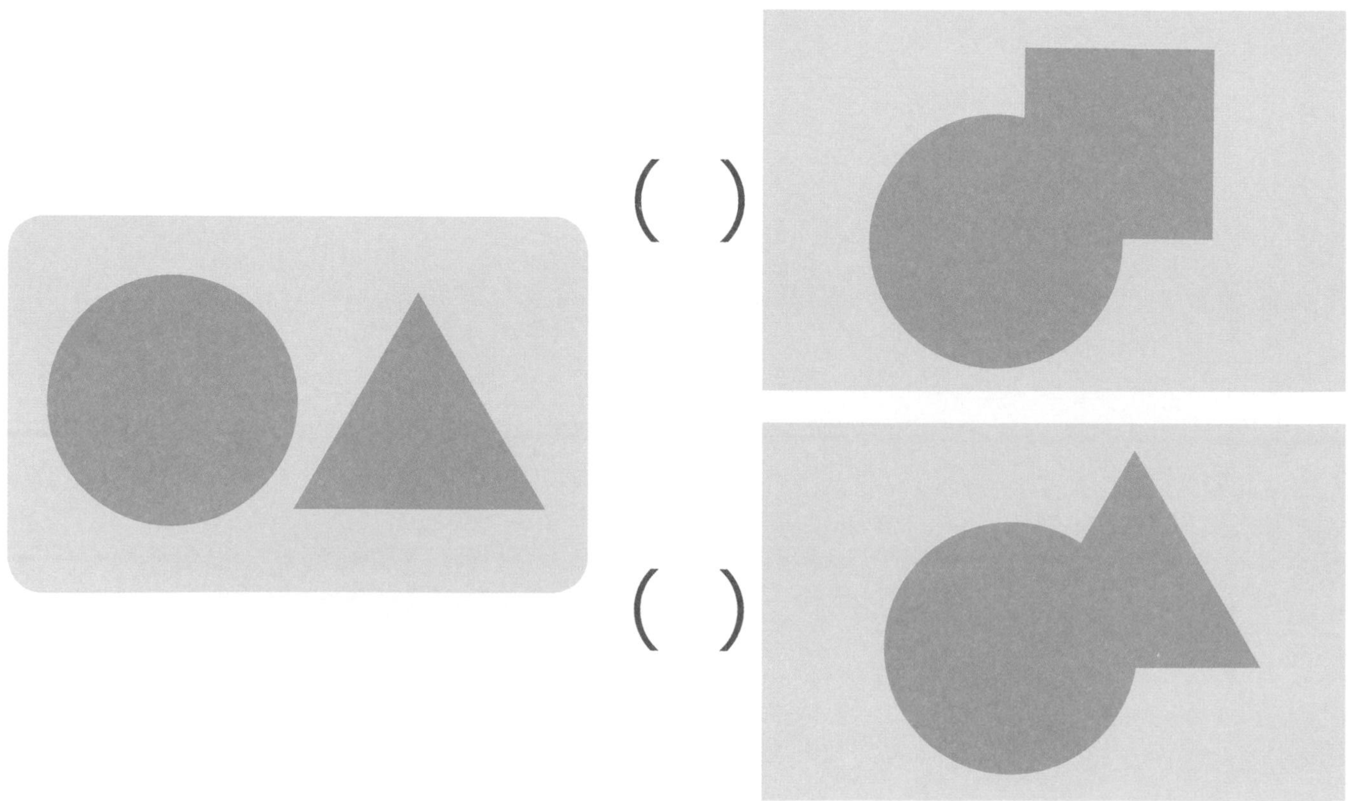

Reasoning with Shapes

Circle & Heart

Name

Date

To parents
Have your child look at the shape of the heart and check if the illustrations in the right column have a part of the heart.

■ Choose which picture shows the two shapes put together. Write a check mark (✓) beside the picture.

( ) 

( ) 

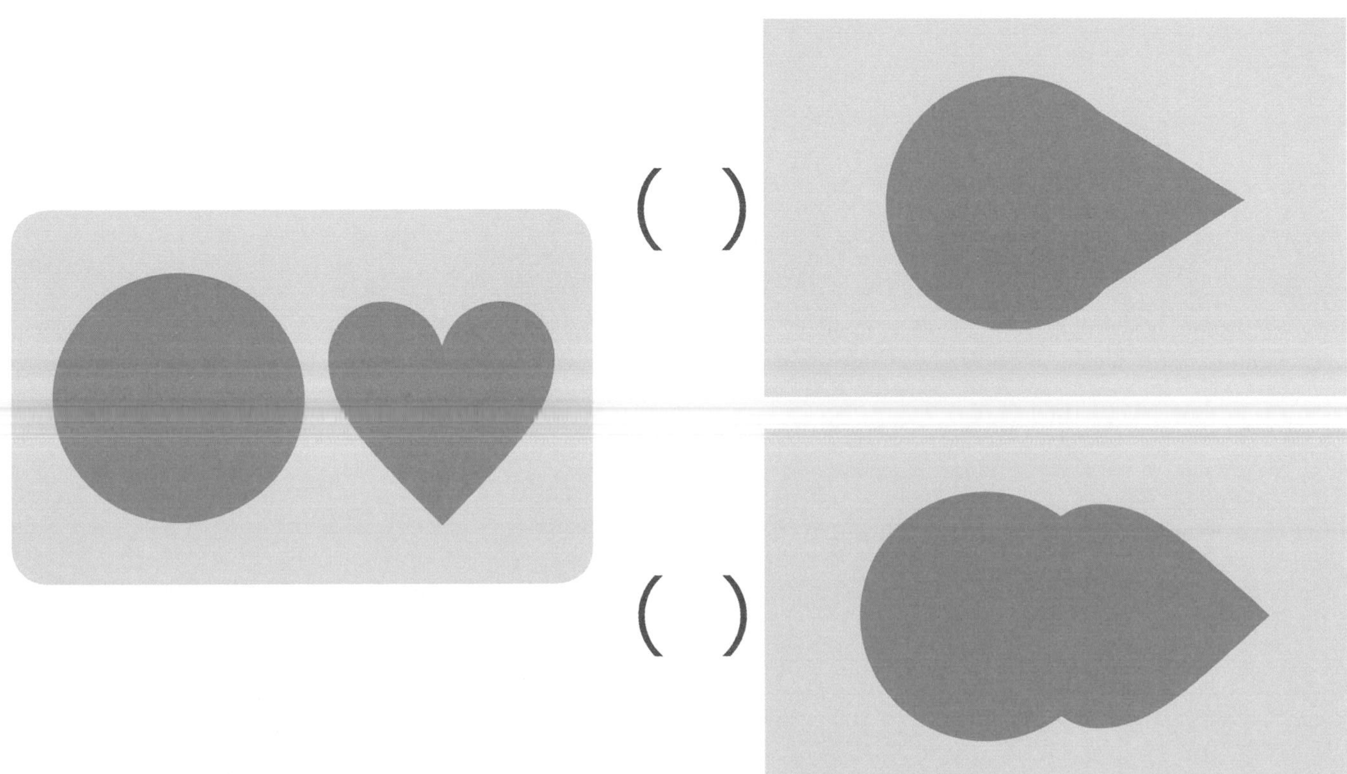

( )

( )

■ Choose which picture shows the two shapes put together. Write a check mark (✓) beside the picture.

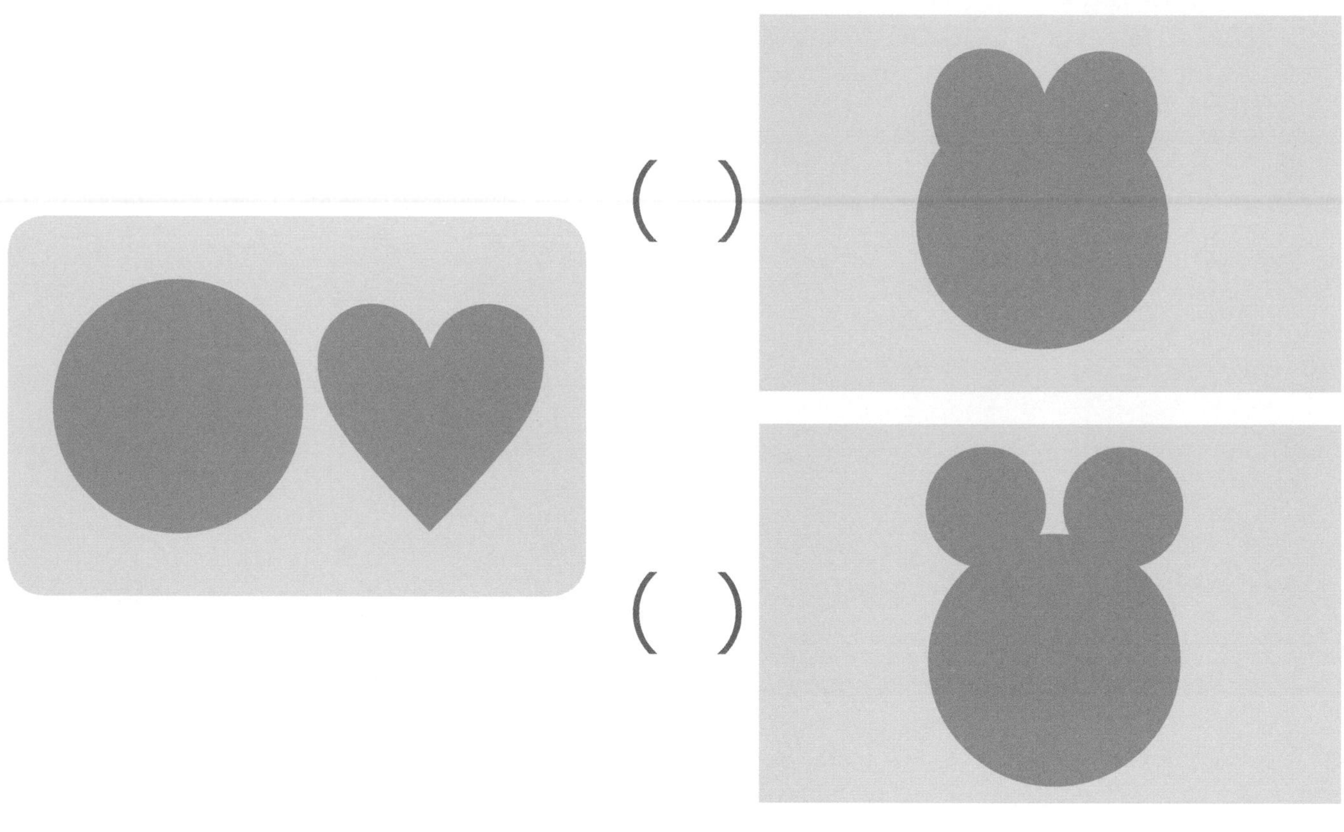

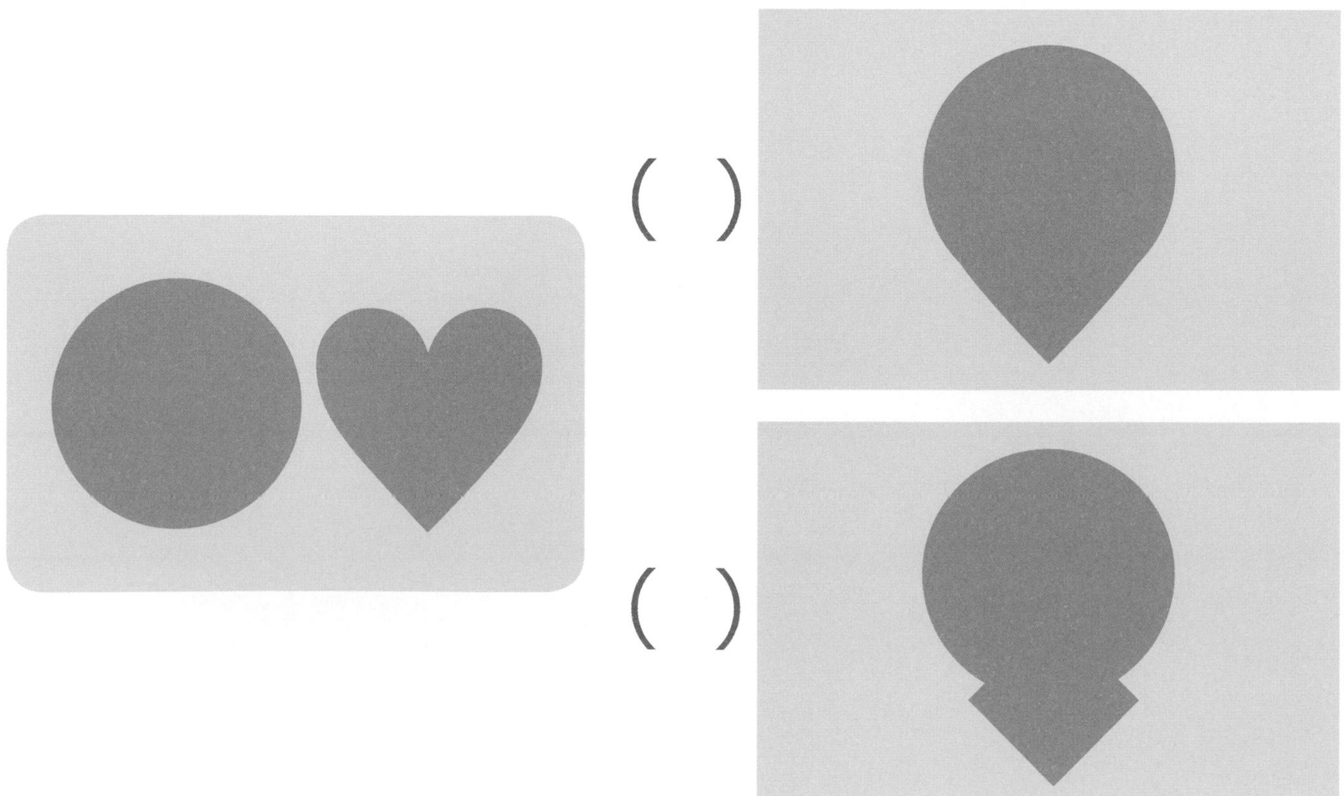

Reasoning with Shapes

Square & Clover

Name

Date

To parents
Encourage your child to look for the illustrations that correctly show the clover.

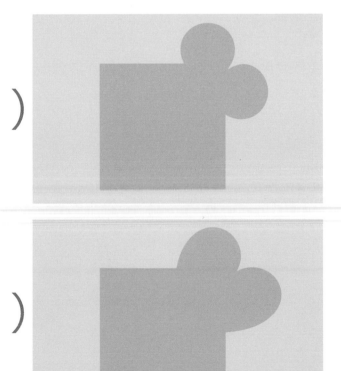

■ Choose which picture shows the two shapes put together. Write a check mark (✓) beside the picture.

( ) 

( ) 

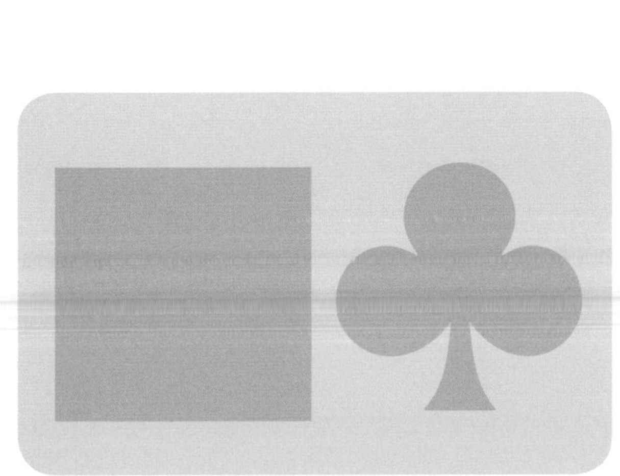

( ) 

( ) 

■ Choose which picture shows the two shapes put together. Write a check mark (✓) beside the picture.

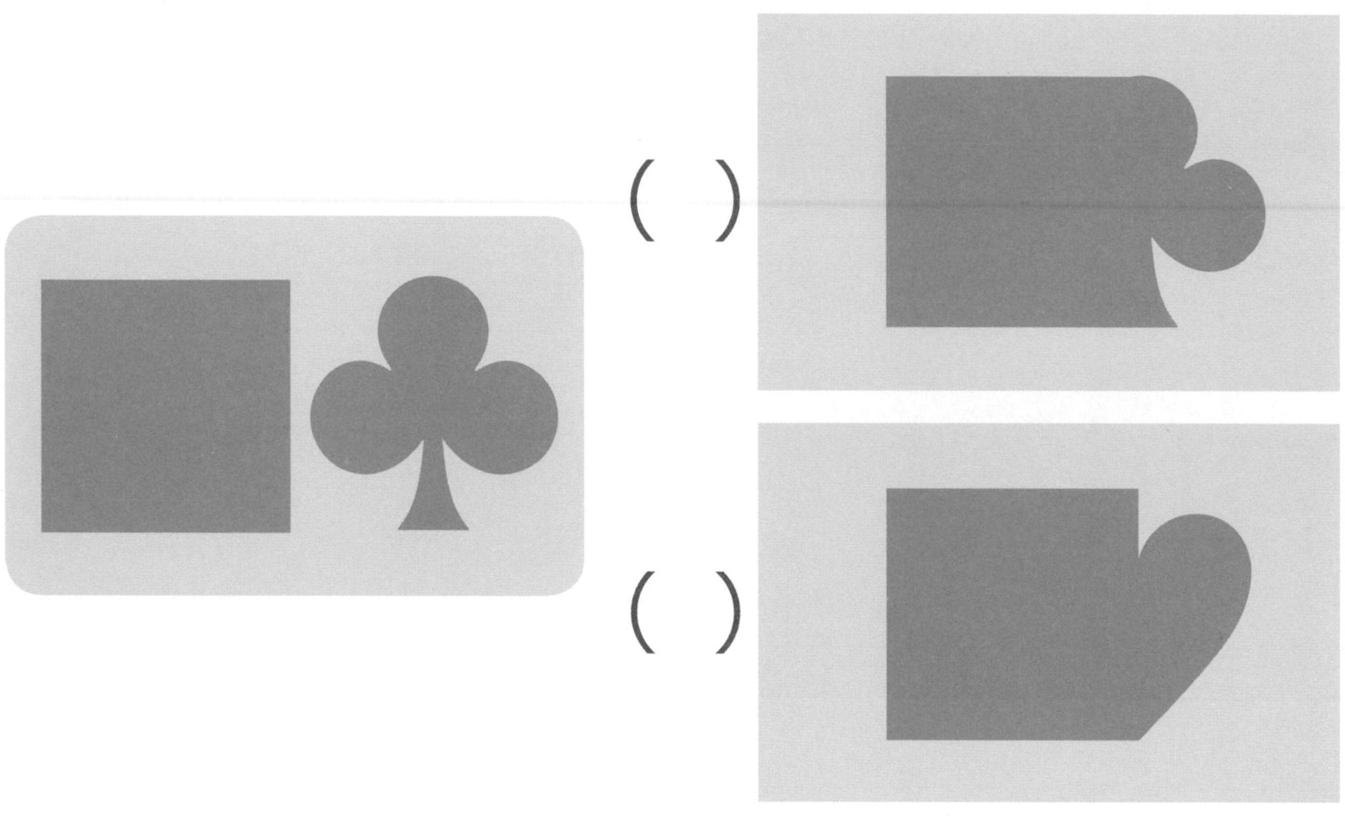

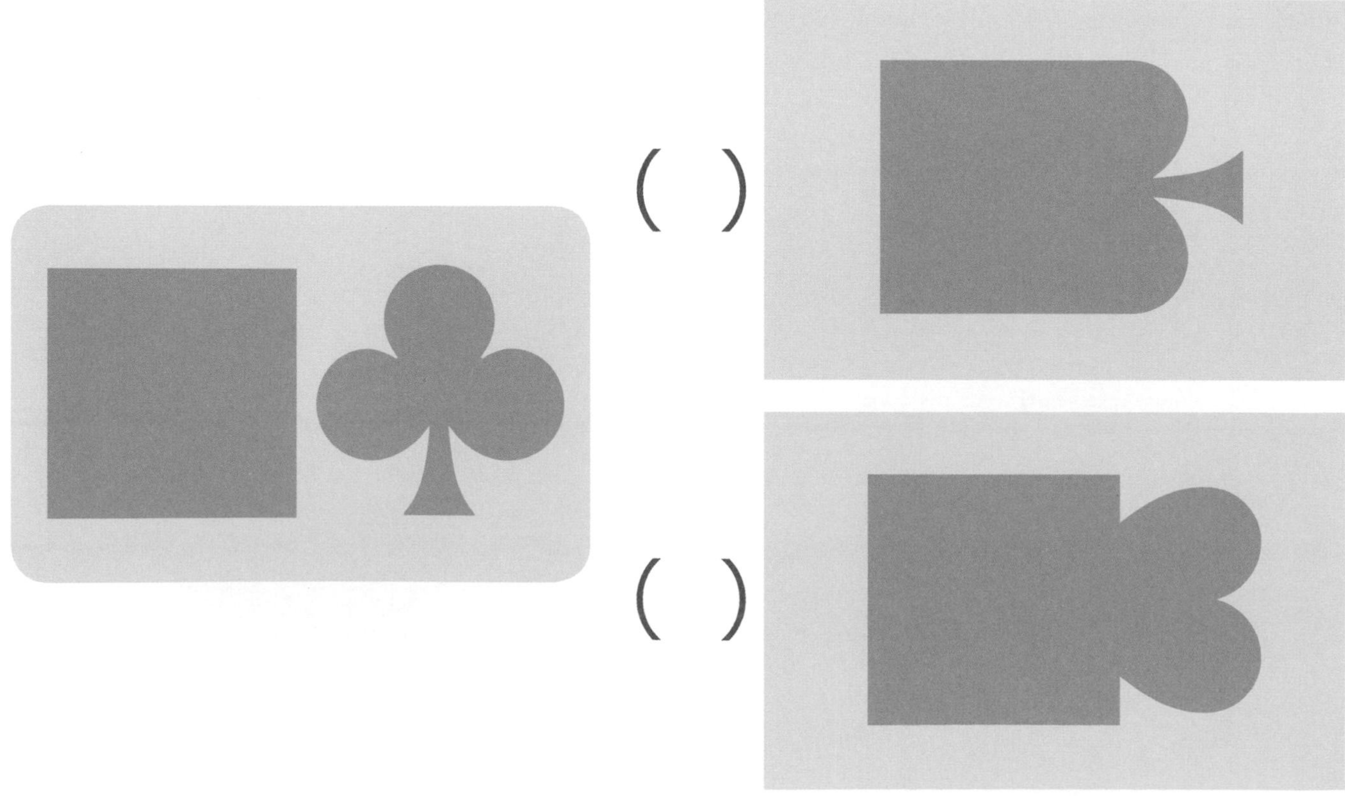

Reasoning with Shapes

Hexagon & Heart/Clover

Name

Date

To parents
The exercises now include three answer choices instead of two. It is okay for your child to take his or her time when working on these exercises.

■ Choose which picture shows the two shapes put together. Write a check mark (✓) above the picture.

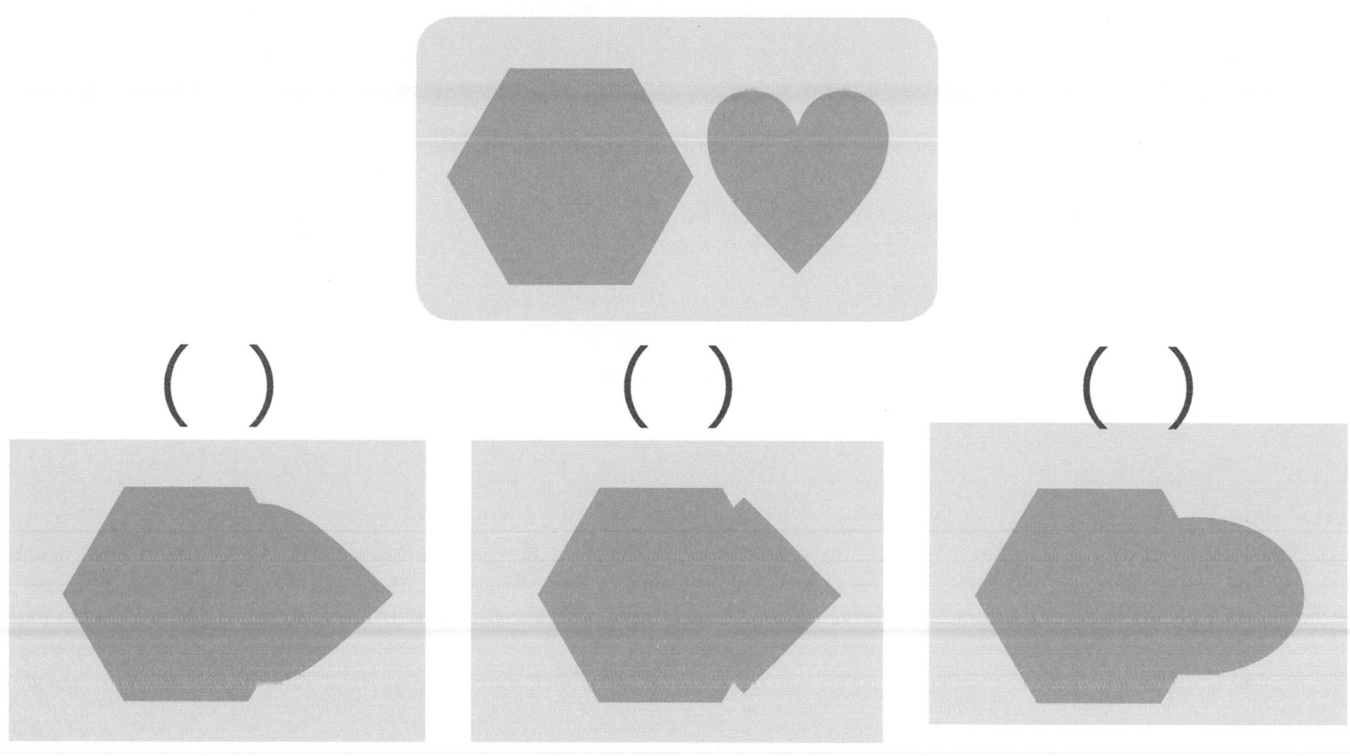

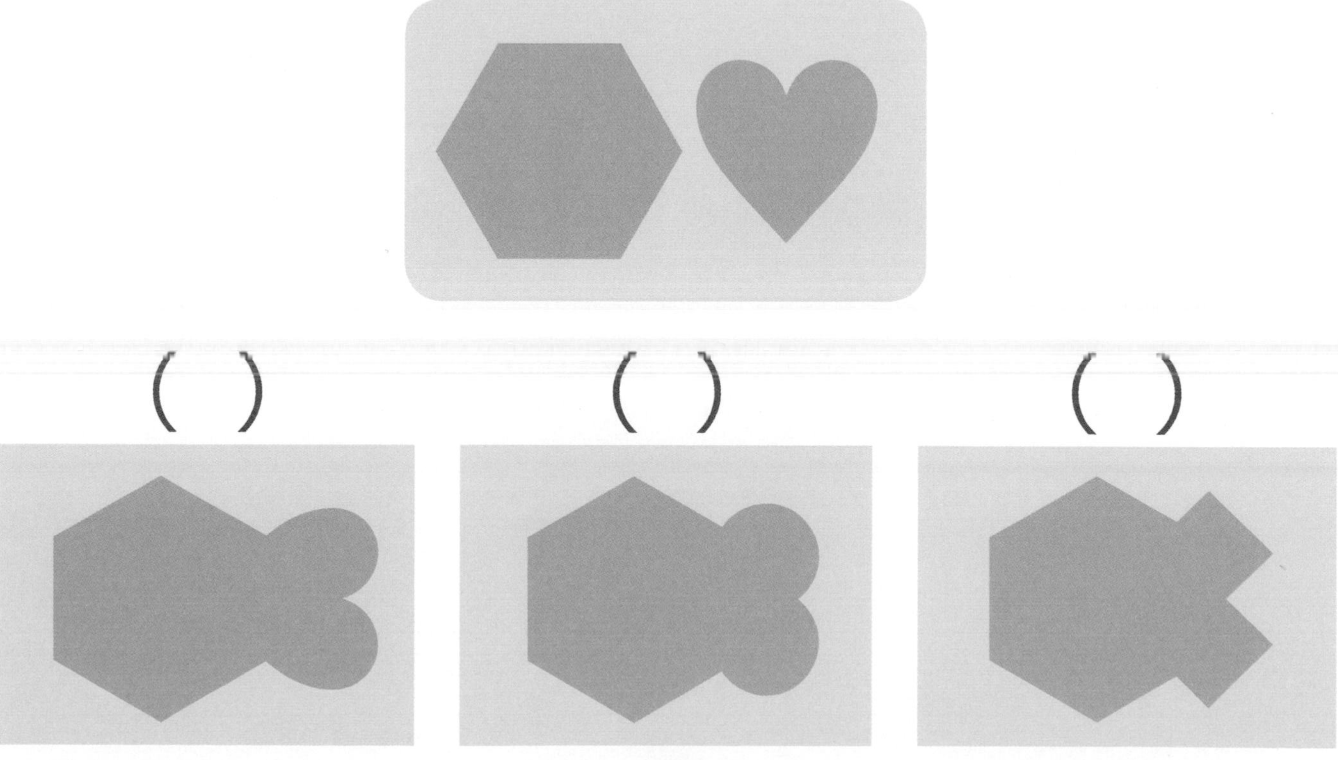

■ Choose which picture shows the two shapes put together.
Write a check mark (✓) above the picture.

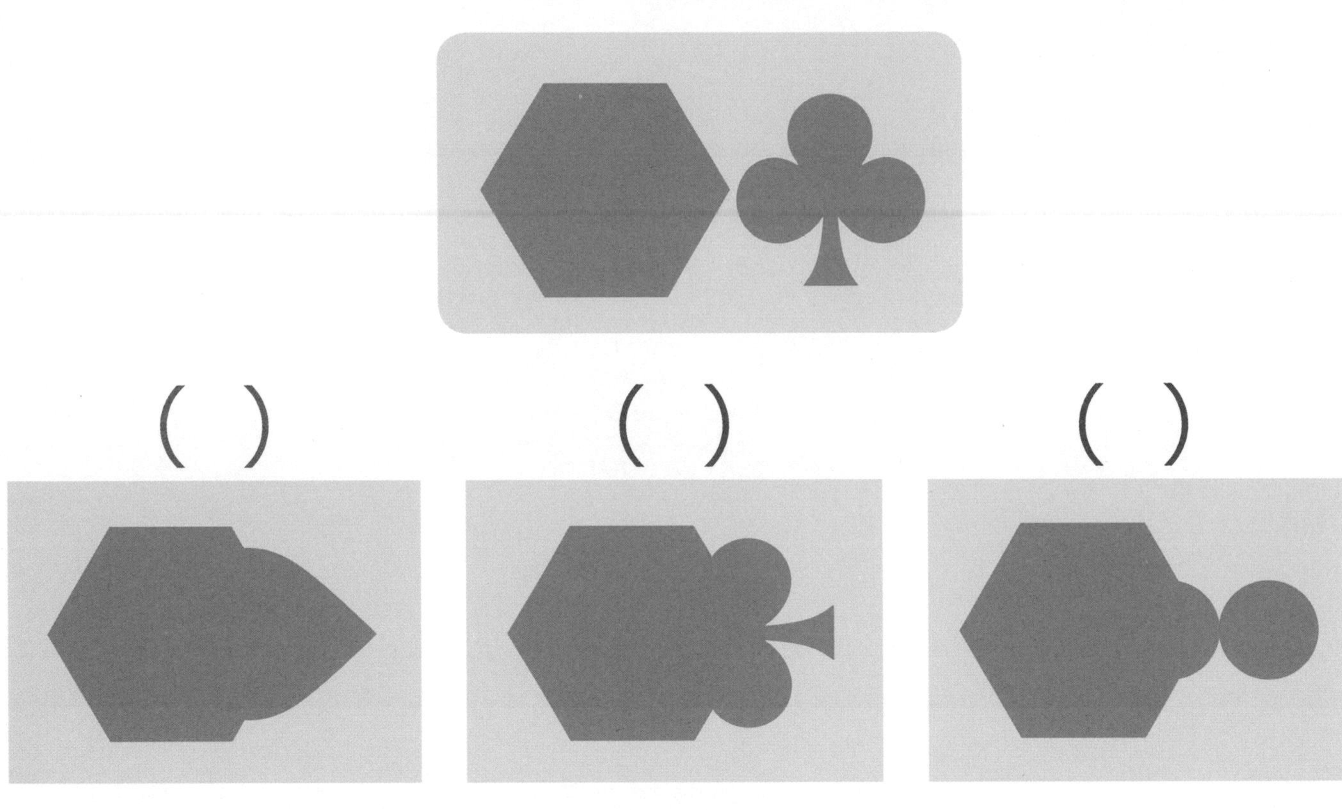

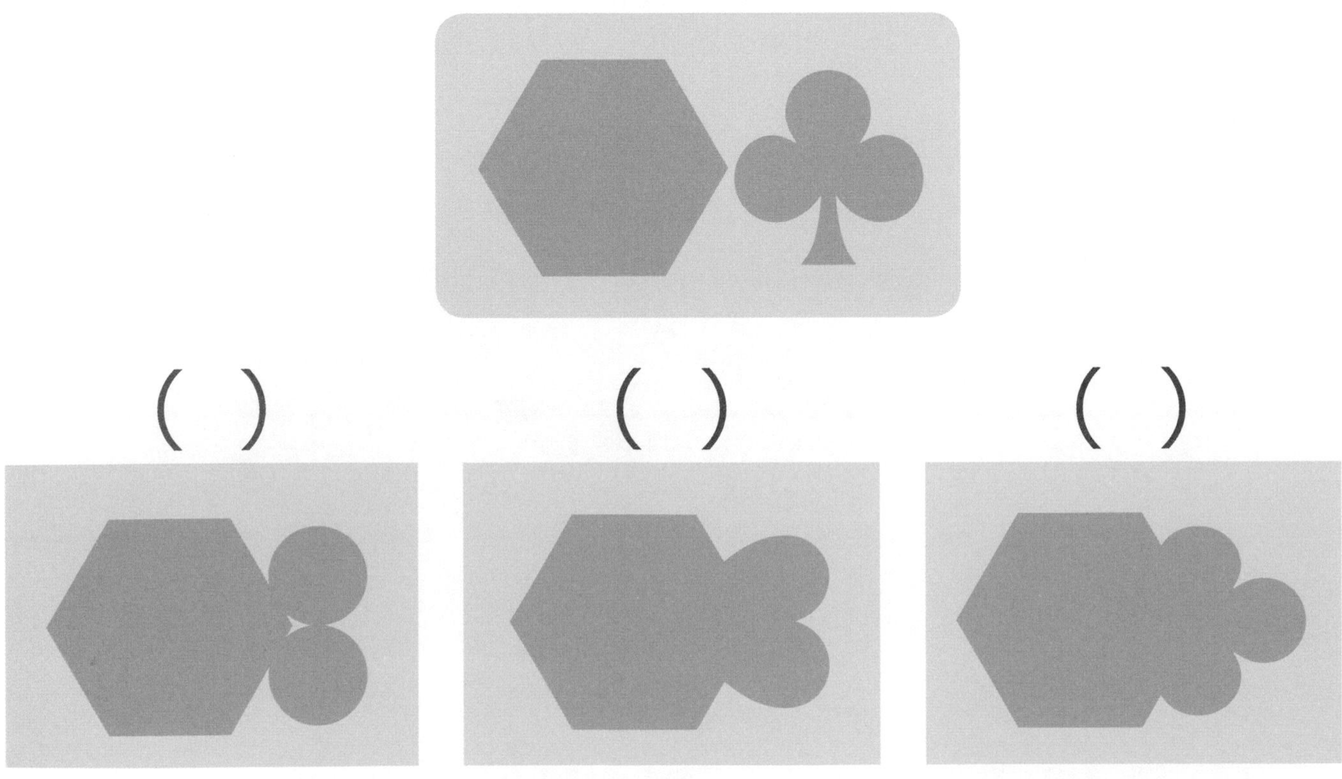

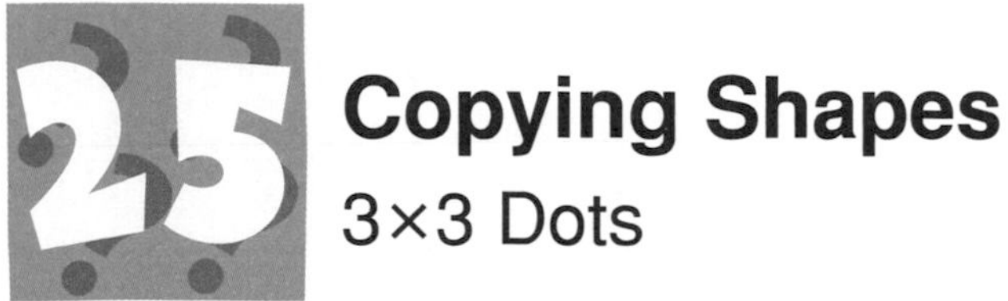

25 Copying Shapes
3×3 Dots

Name

Date

To parents
If your child draws any of the lines incorrectly, encourage him or her to erase only the incorrect lines and to try again.

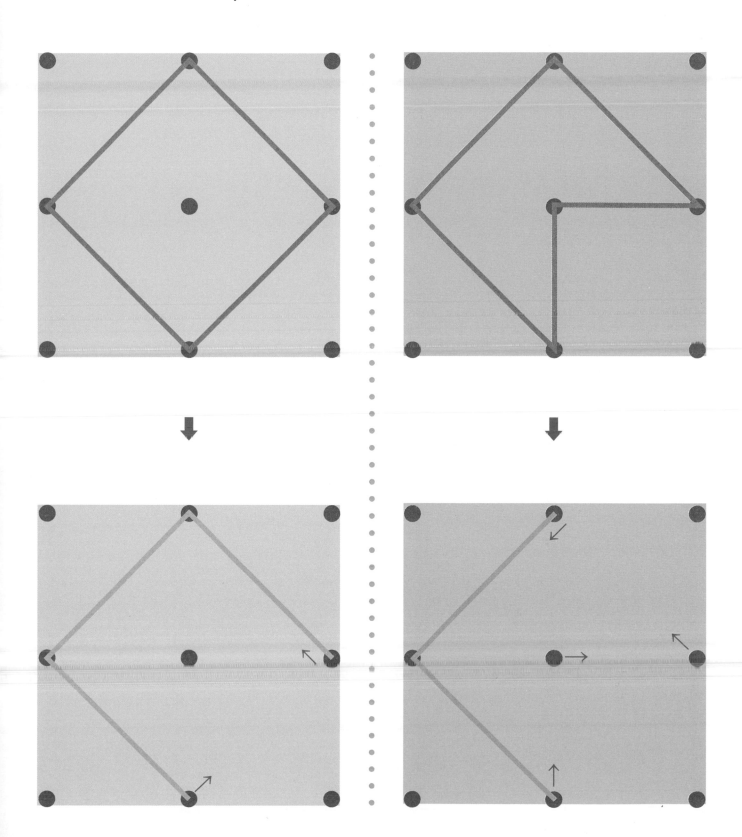

■ Draw the same shape.

To parents
Your child can start drawing from any dot he or she likes.

■ Draw the same shape.

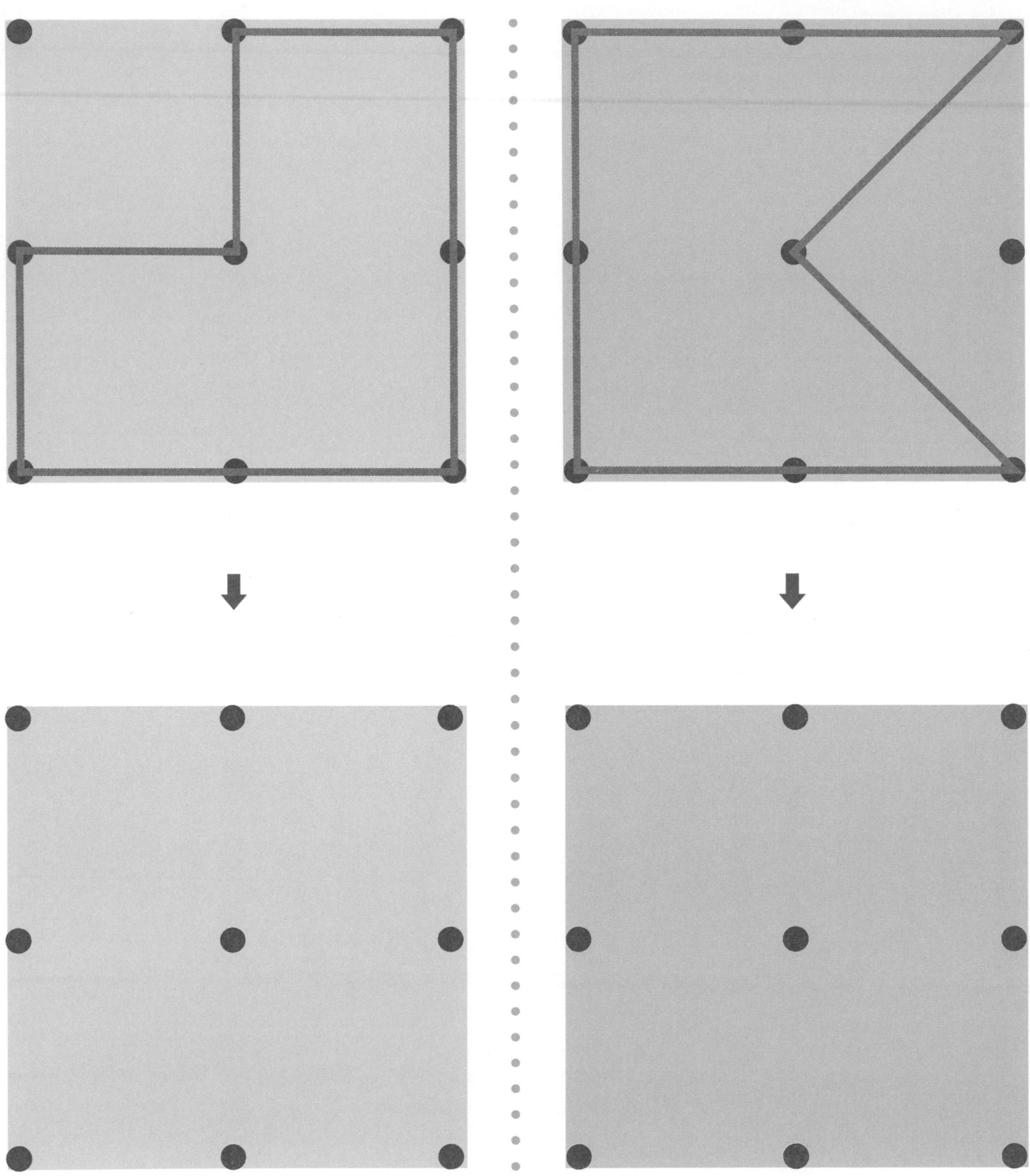

Copying Shapes
3×3 Dots

Name

Date

To parents
To make this exercise easier, encourage your child to draw a straight line from one dot to the next, and so on, instead of drawing a line through several dots in one motion.

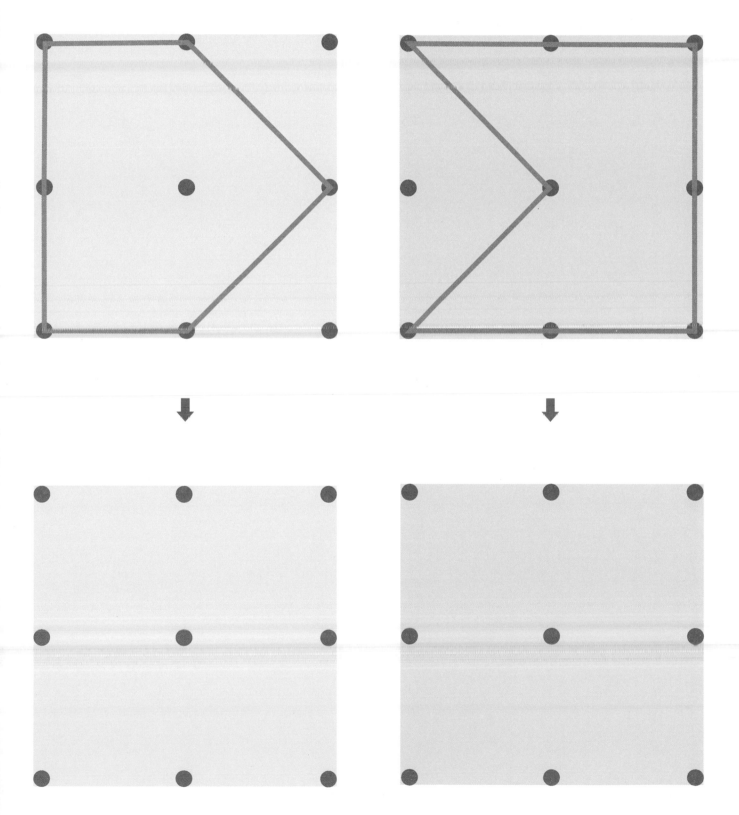

■ Draw the same shape.

■ Draw the same shape.

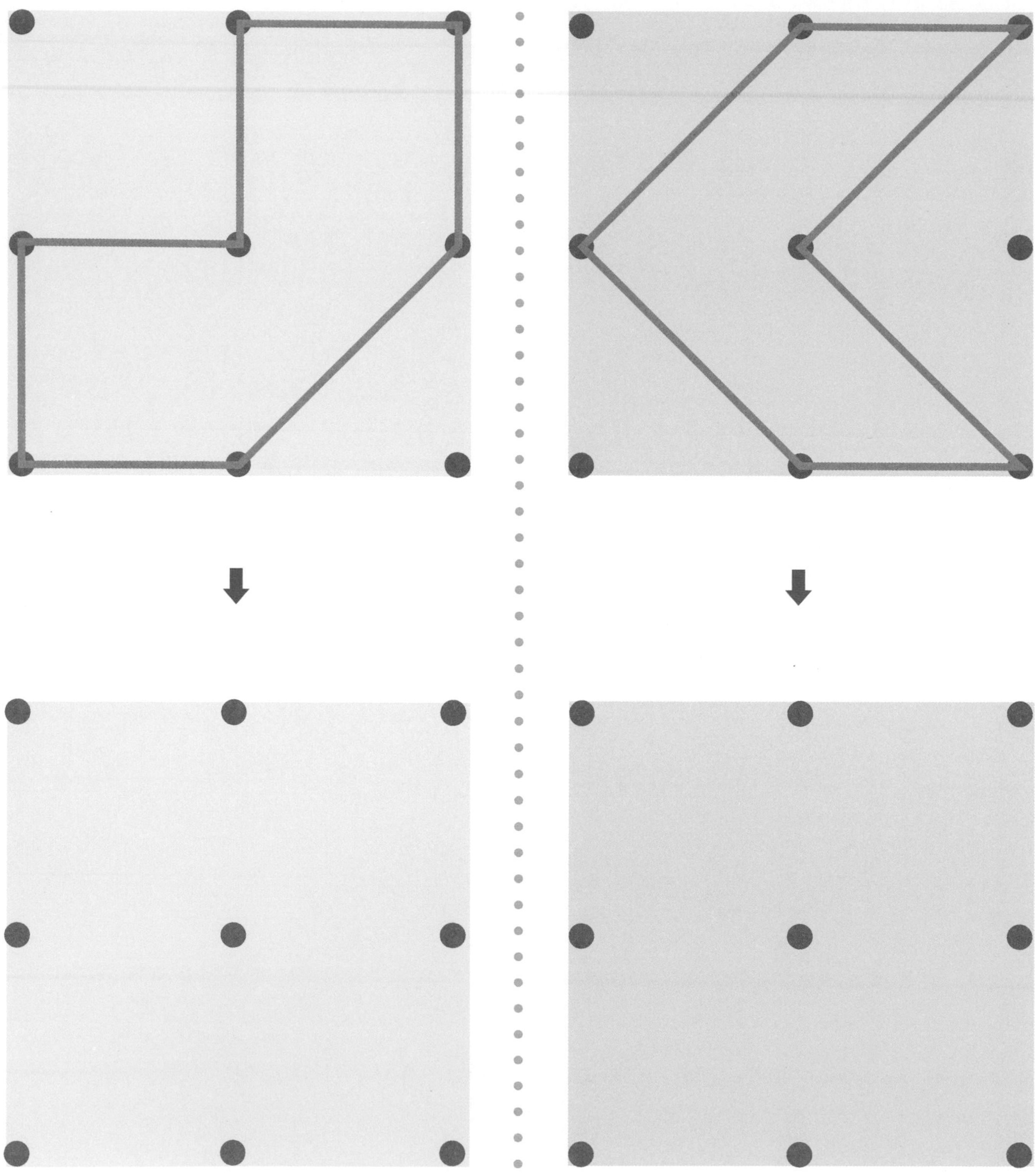

Copying Shapes

4×4 Dots

Name

Date

To parents
The number of dots in the grid has increased. Guide your child to look carefully at the shapes before starting to draw.

■ Draw the same shape.

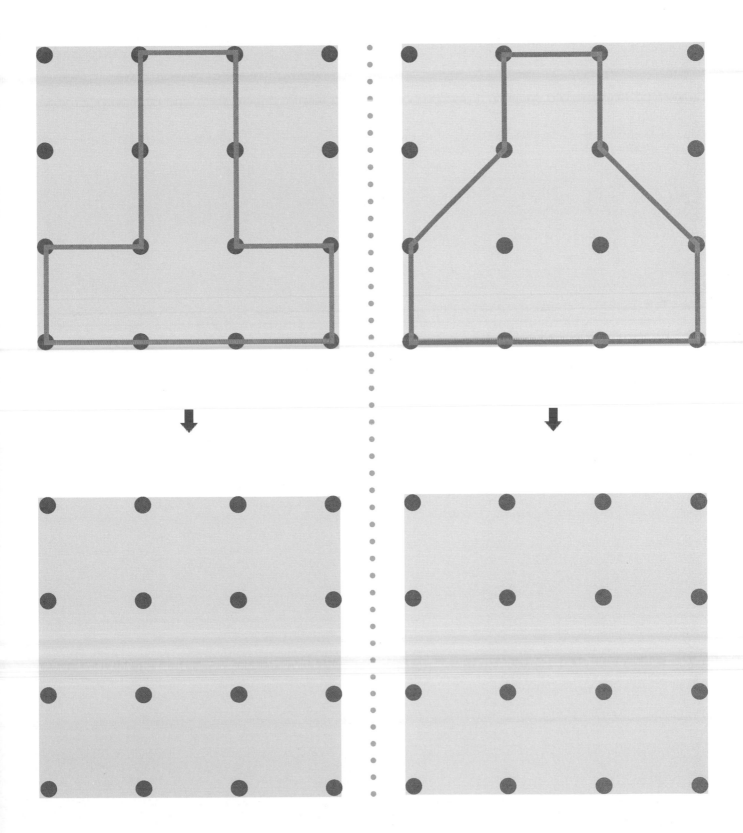

■ Draw the same shape.

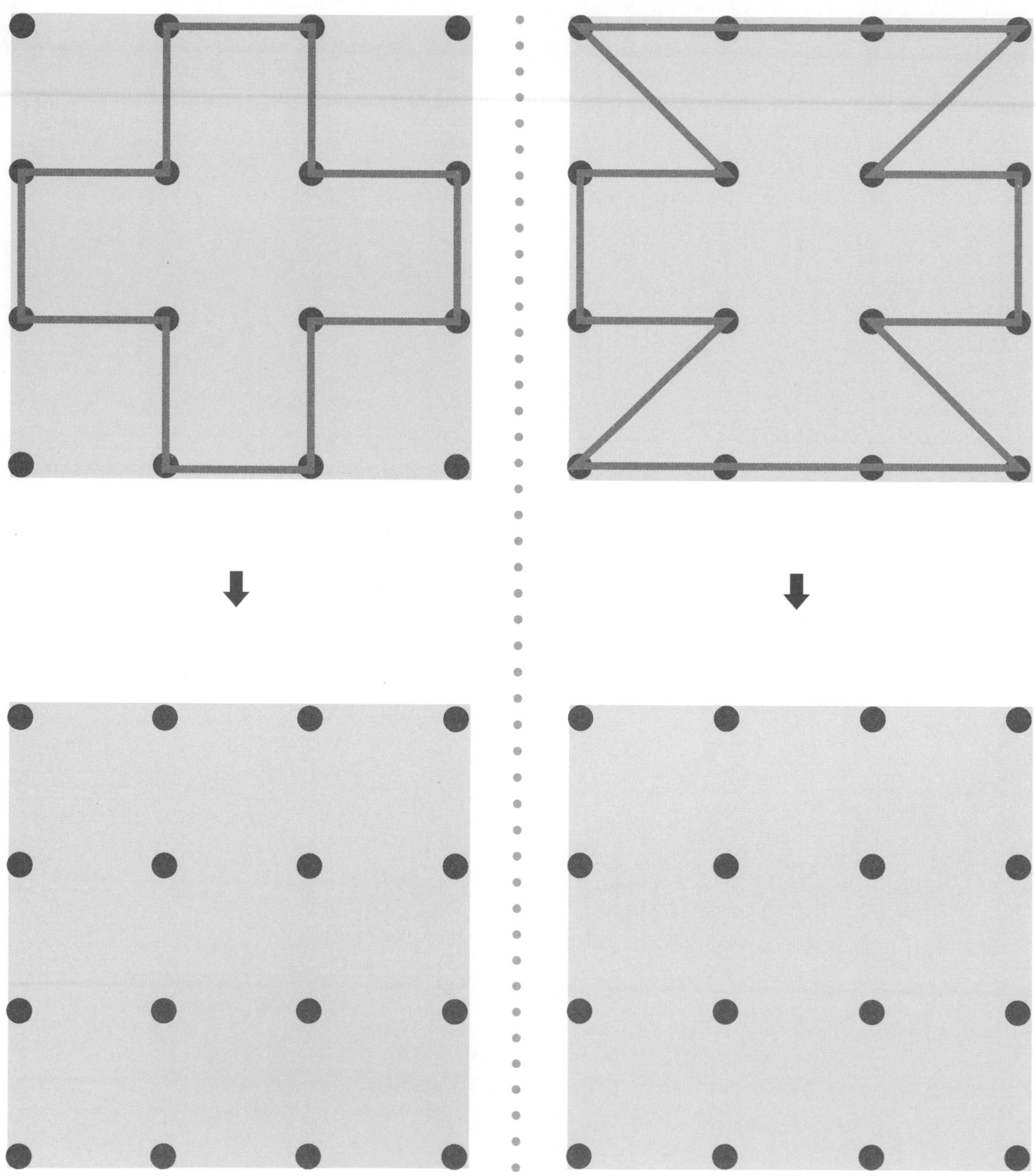

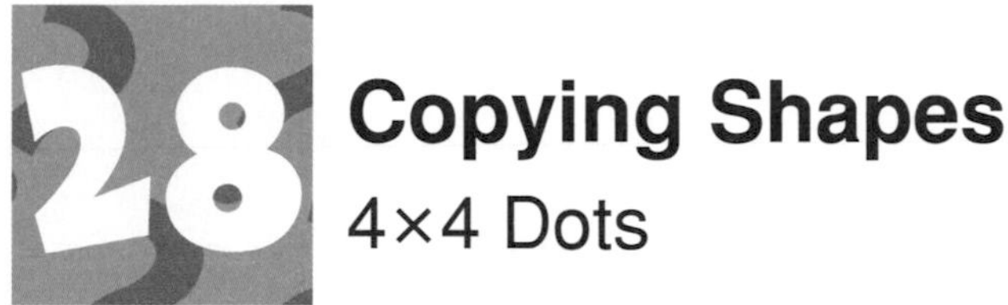

28 Copying Shapes

4×4 Dots

Name

Date

To parents
From this point on, the shapes become more complicated. Give your child a lot of praise for his or her effort when your child finishes drawing.

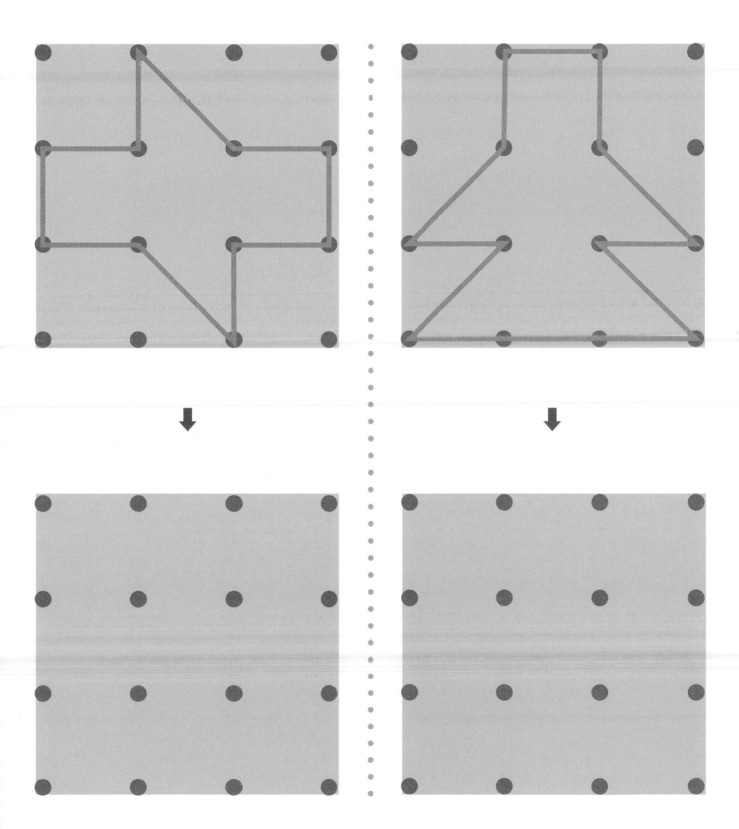

■ Draw the same shape.

■ Draw the same shape.

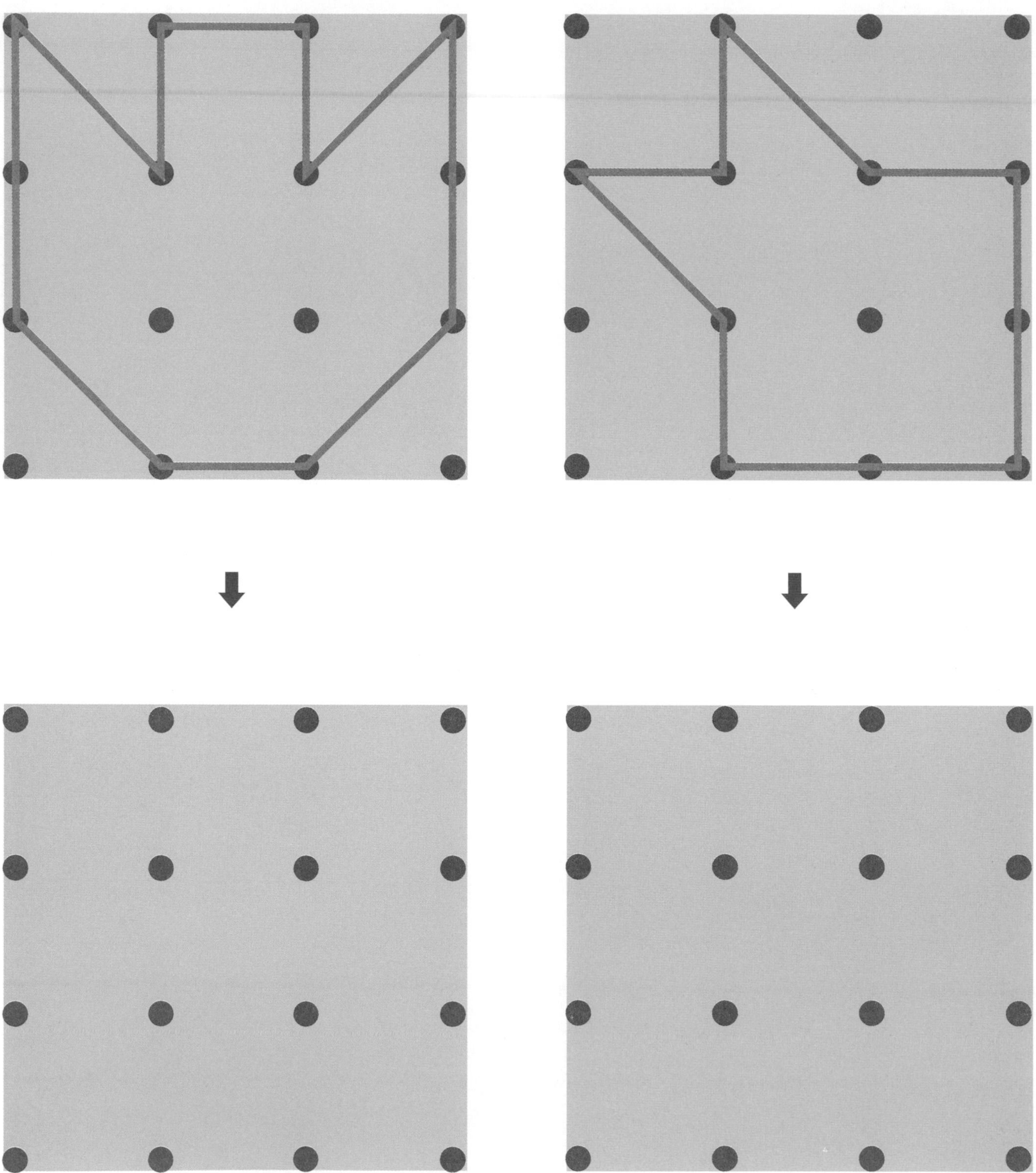

Comparing Height

Level One

Name
Date

To parents
Encourage your child to find the answer based on the illustrations instead of his or her knowledge.

■ Look at the picture of the animals. Then write a check mark (✓) beside the animal that is taller.

(✓) 

( ) 

( ) 

( ) 

■ Look at the picture of the animals. Then write a check mark (✓) beside the animal that is tallest.

( )

( )

( )

( )

( )

( )

Comparing Height
Level Two

Name

Date

To parents
The number of animals in each illustration has increased. Encourage your child to compare all of the animals.

■ Look at the picture of the animals. Then write a check mark (✓) beside the animal that is tallest.

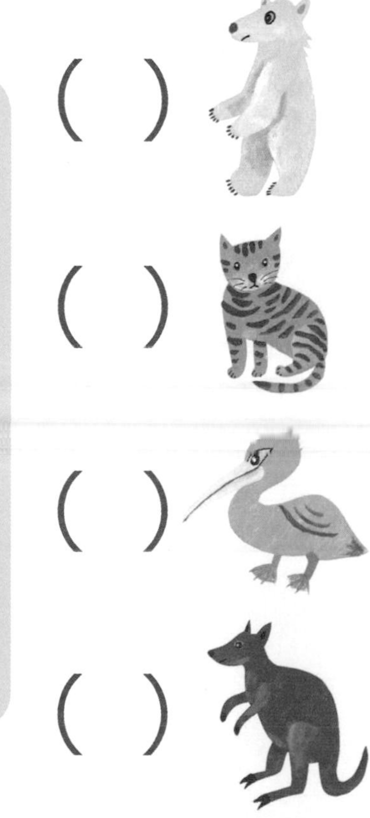

■ Look at the picture of the animals. Then write a check mark (✓) beside the animal that is tallest.

Comparing Height
Level Three

Name

Date

■ Look at the picture of the animals. Then write a check mark (✓) beside the animal that is taller.

To parents
Help your child compare the height of each animal in the illustration. Your child should not include the height of the stool.

( )

( )

( )

( )

■ Look at the picture of the animals. Then write a check mark (✓) beside the animal that is tallest.

( )

( )

( )

( )

( )

( )

Comparing Height
Level Four

Name

Date

To parents
Give your child a lot of praise when he or she finds the right answer.

■ Look at the picture of the animals. Then write a check mark (✓) beside the animal that is taller.

( )

( )

( )

( )

■ Look at the picture of the animals. Then write a check mark (✓) beside the animal that is tallest.

Coloring Patterns
Two Colors

Name

Date

To parents
From this page on, your child should use colored pencils. Give your child the colors listed in the instructions.

■ Color each white area with the correct color.

□ → red　□ → yellow

■ Color each white area with the correct color.

35 Coloring Patterns

Four Colors

Name

Date

■ Color each pattern with the correct color.

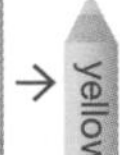

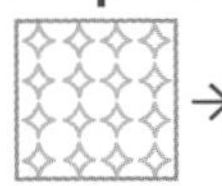

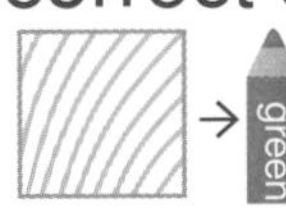

■ Color each pattern with the correct color.

Coloring Patterns
Five Colors

Name

Date

To parents
Help your child use the instructions to match up each pattern with the correct color.

■ Color each pattern with the correct color.

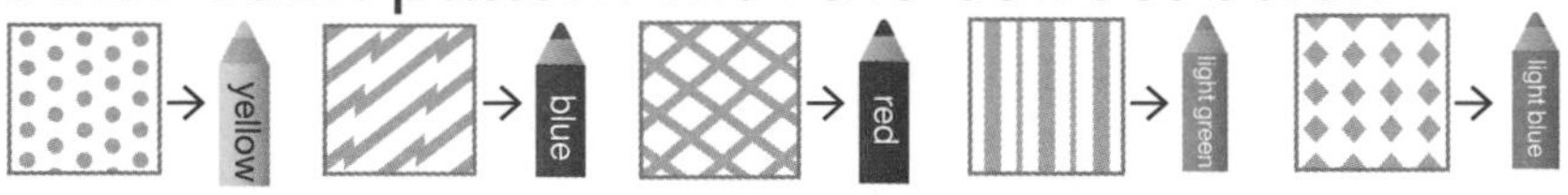

Coloring Patterns Five Colors

To parents
This is the last exercise of this section. Please praise your child for the effort it took to complete this workbook.

■ Color each pattern with the correct color.

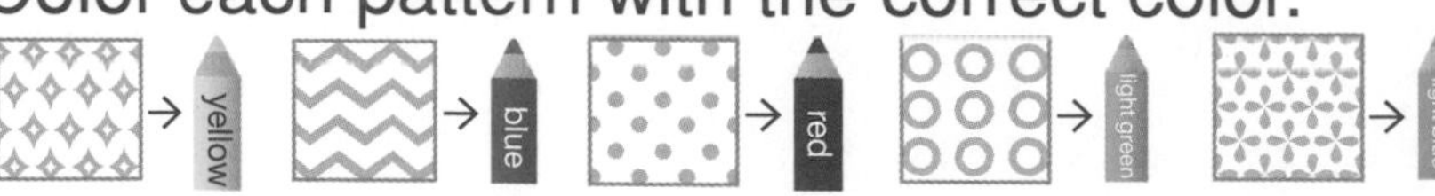

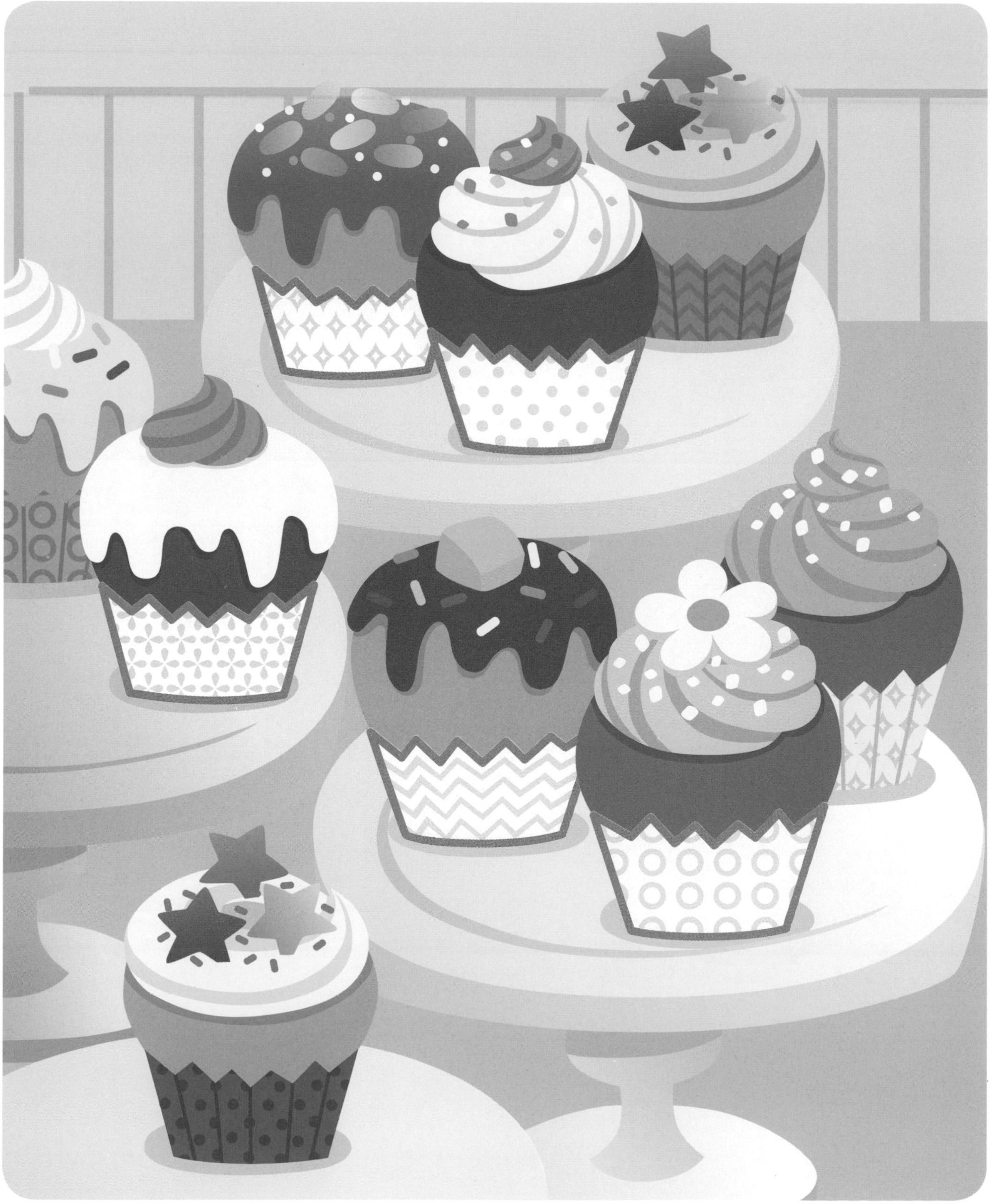

Thinking Skills Pre-K Spatial Reasoning Answer Key

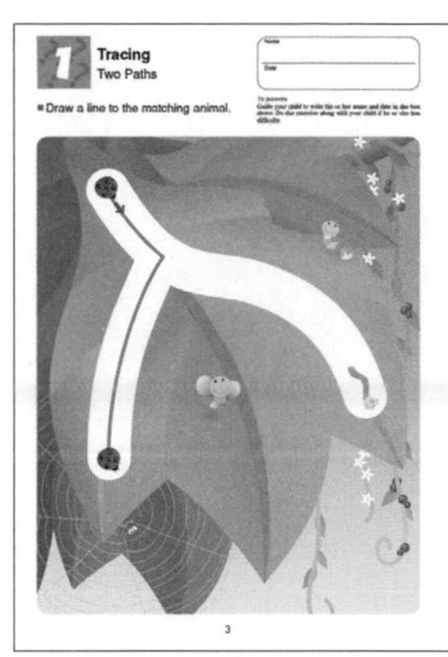

pages 3 and 4

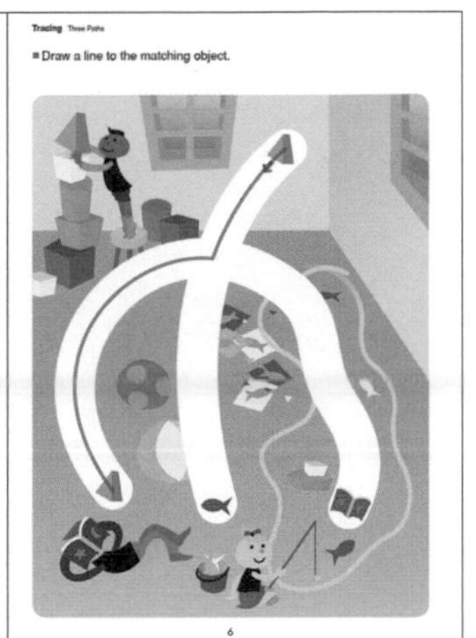

pages 5 and 6

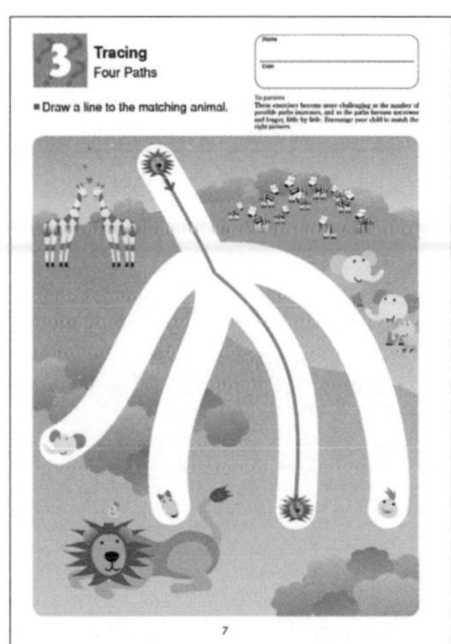

pages 7 and 8

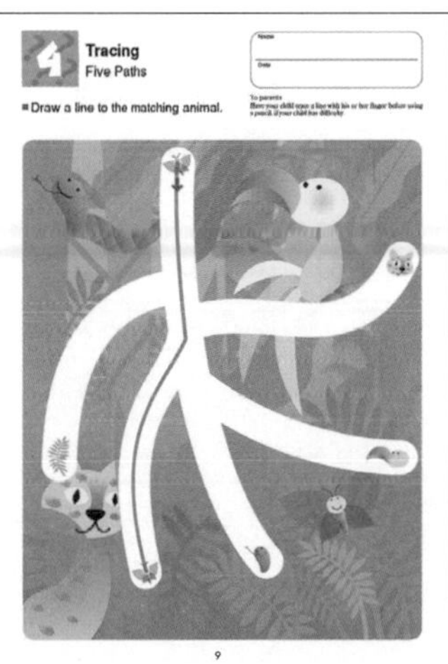

4
Tracing
Five Paths
Draw a line to the matching animal.

Draw a line to the matching object.

pages 9 and 10

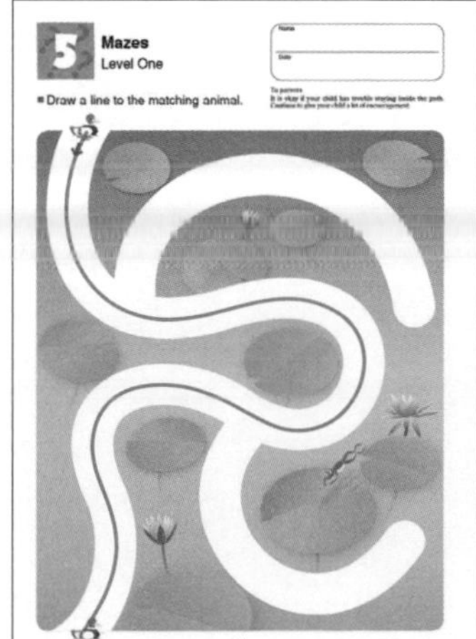

pages 11 and 12

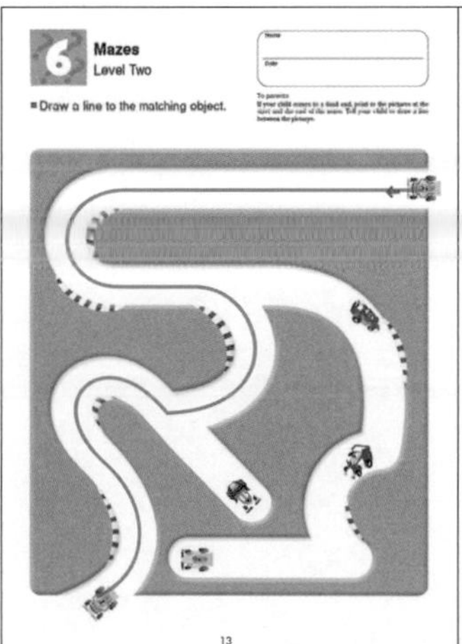

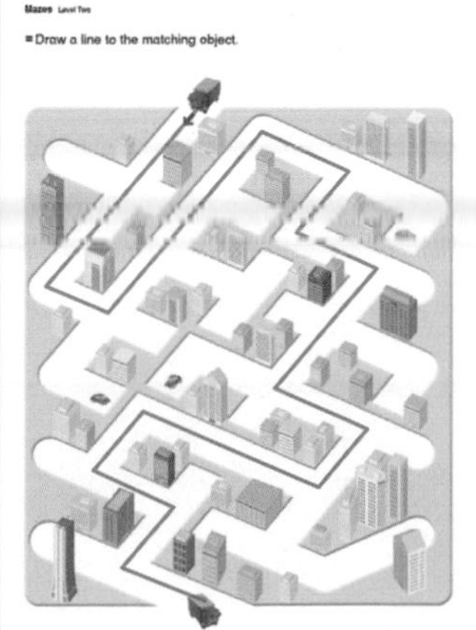

pages 13 and 14

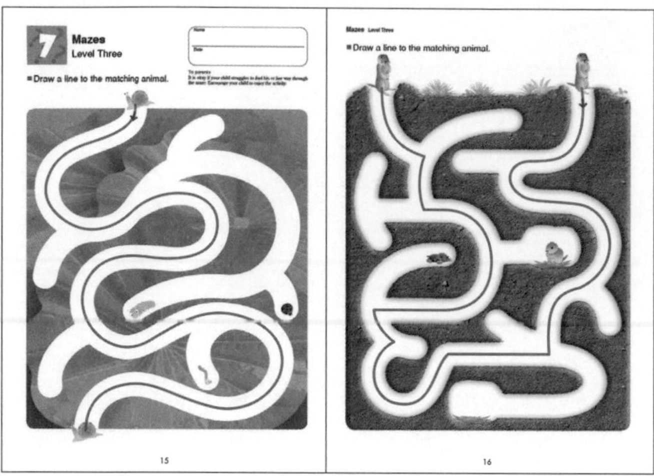

pages 15 and 16

8 Mazes Level Four

Draw a line to the matching animal.

pages 17 and 18

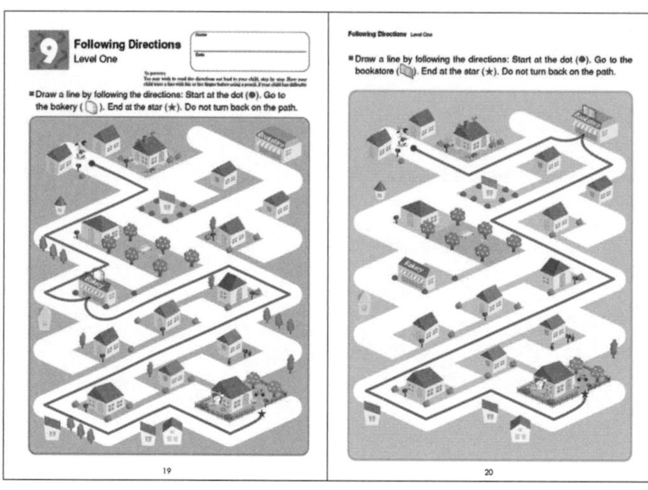

pages 19 and 20

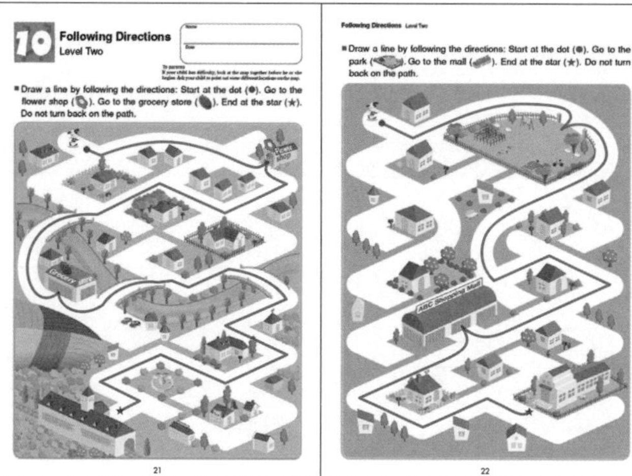

pages 21 and 22

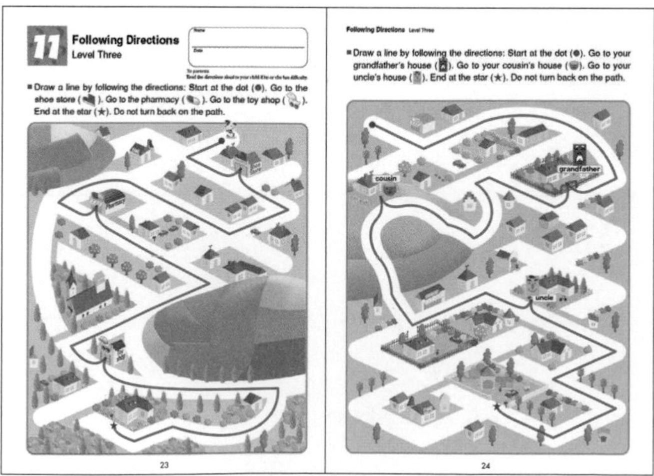

pages 23 and 24

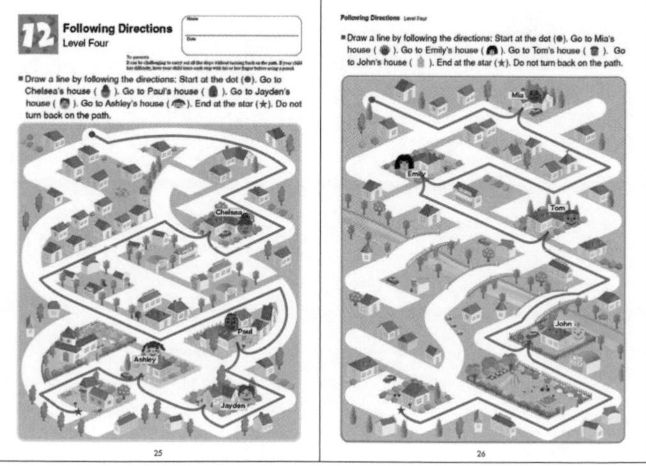

pages 25 and 26

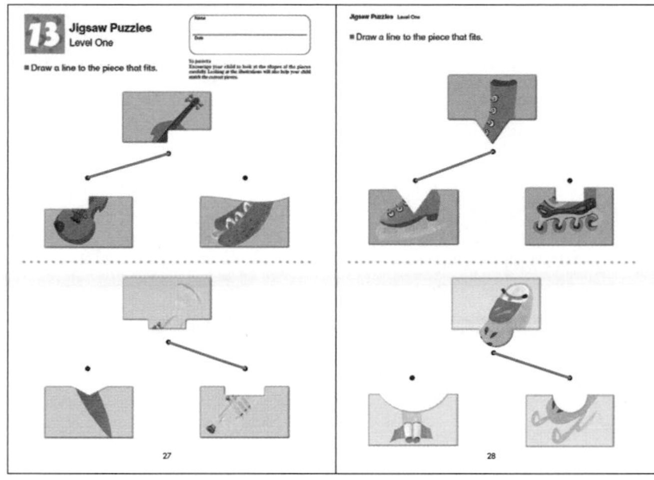
pages 27 and 28

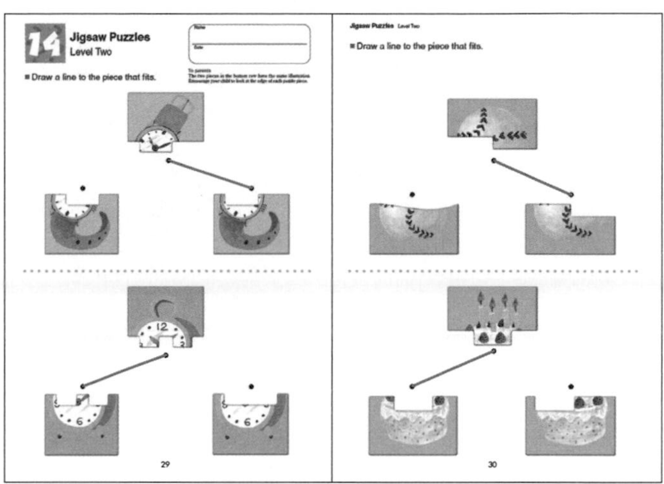
pages 29 and 30

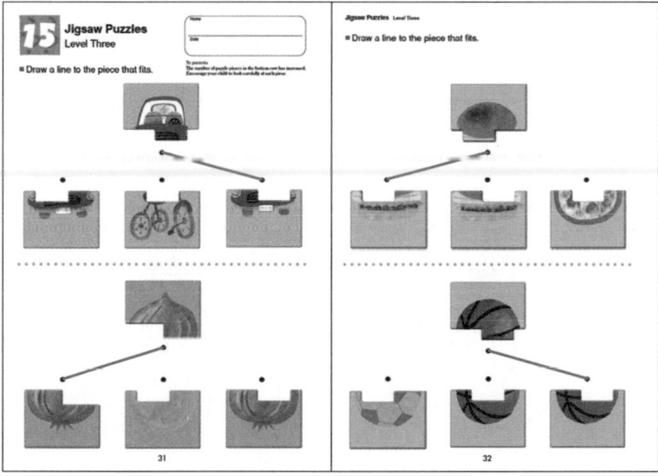
pages 31 and 32

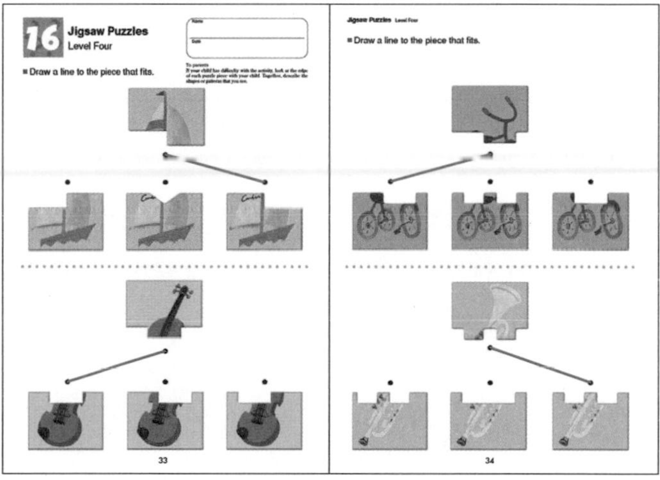
pages 33 and 34

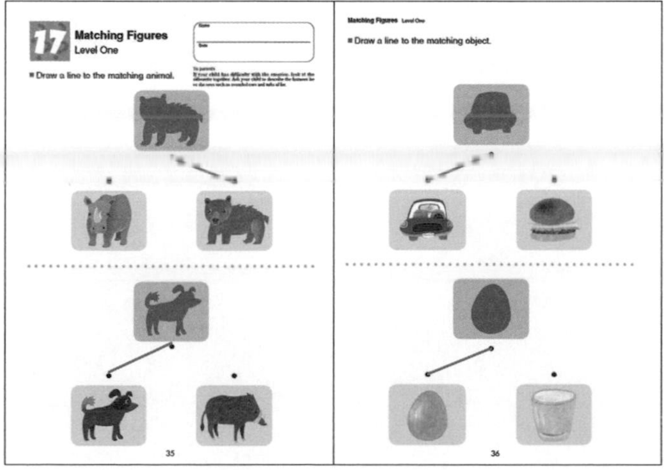
pages 35 and 36

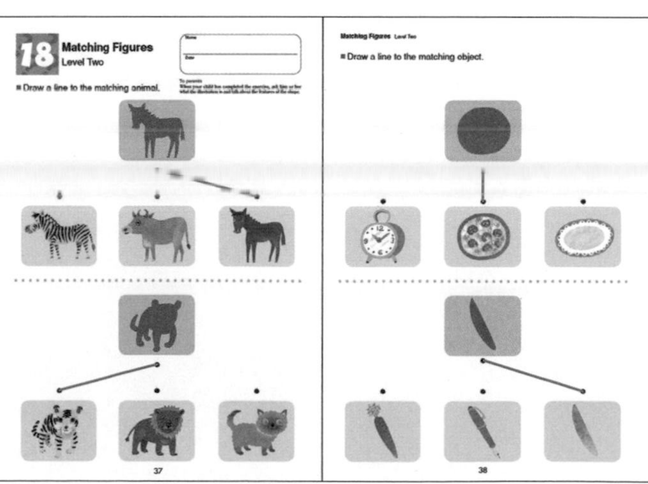
pages 37 and 38

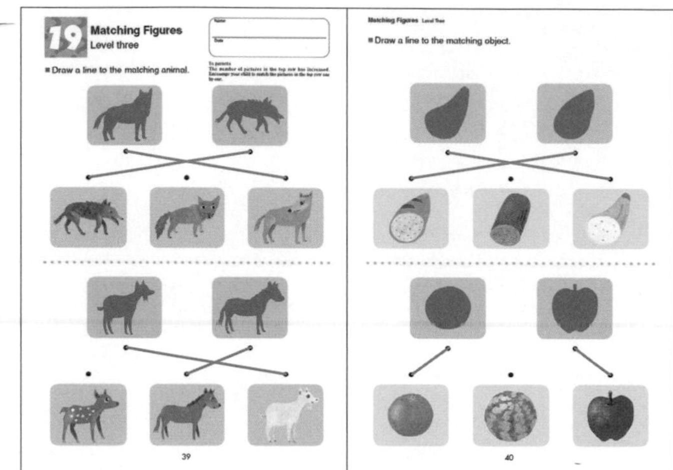

pages 39 and 40

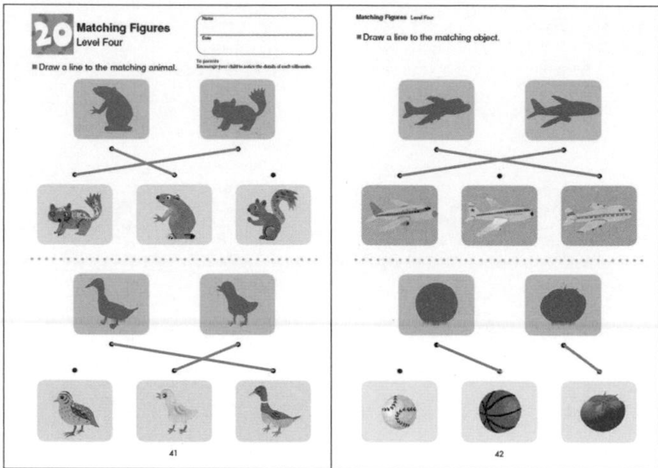

pages 41 and 42

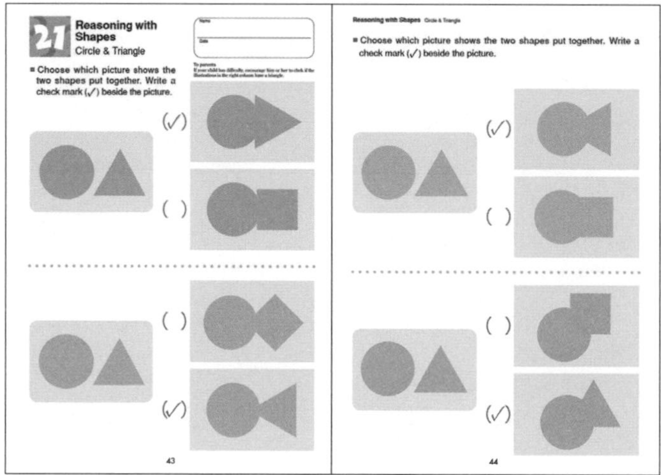

pages 43 and 44

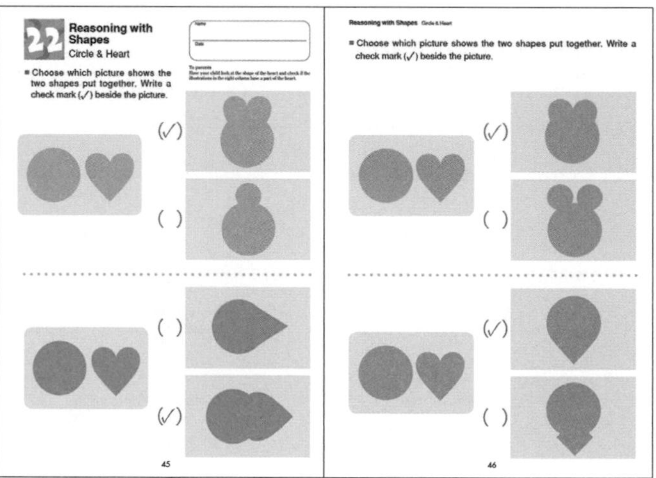

pages 45 and 46

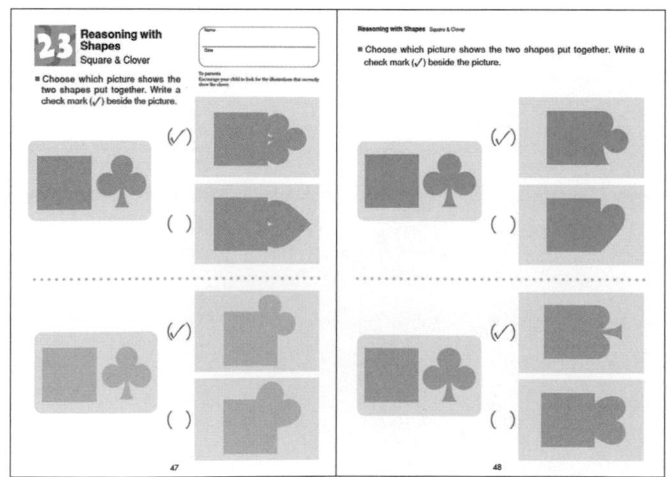

pages 47 and 48

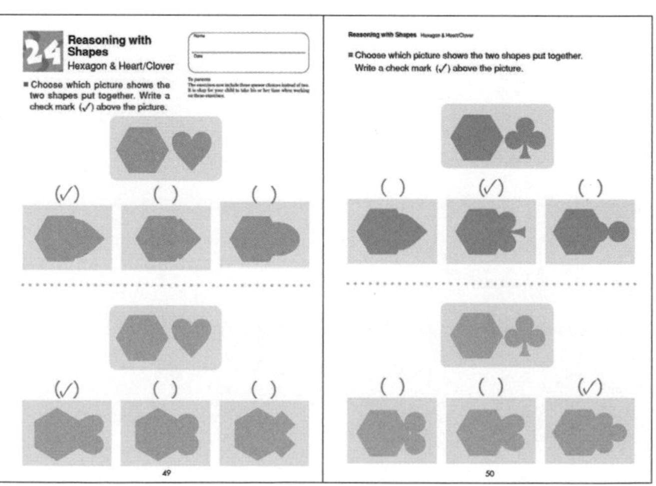

pages 49 and 50

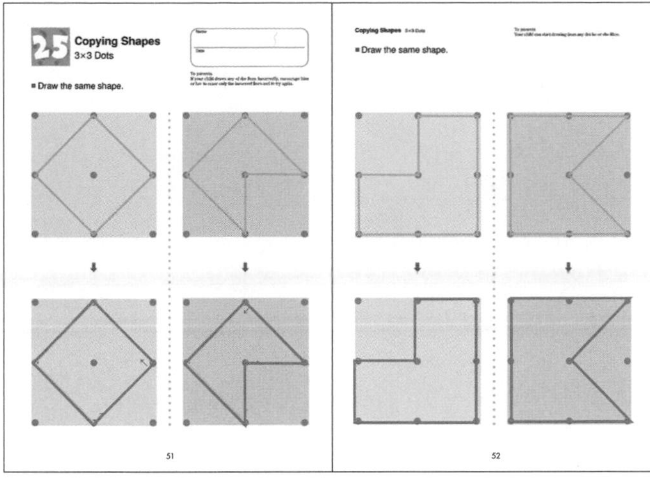

pages 51 and 52

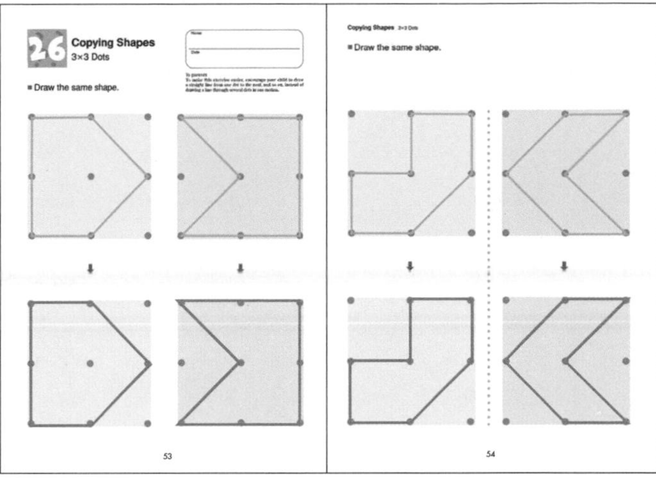

pages 53 and 54

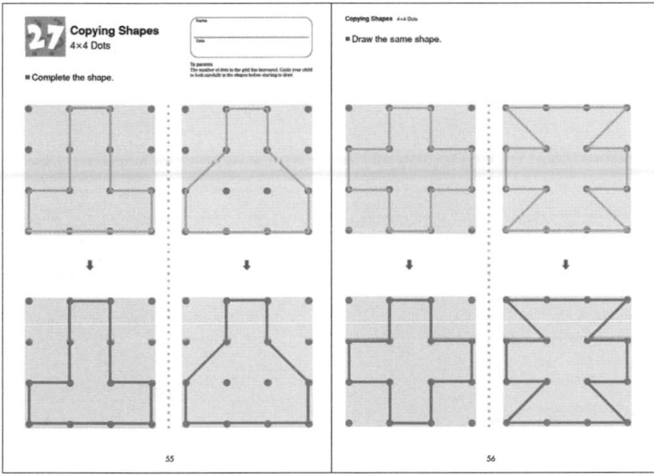

pages 55 and 56

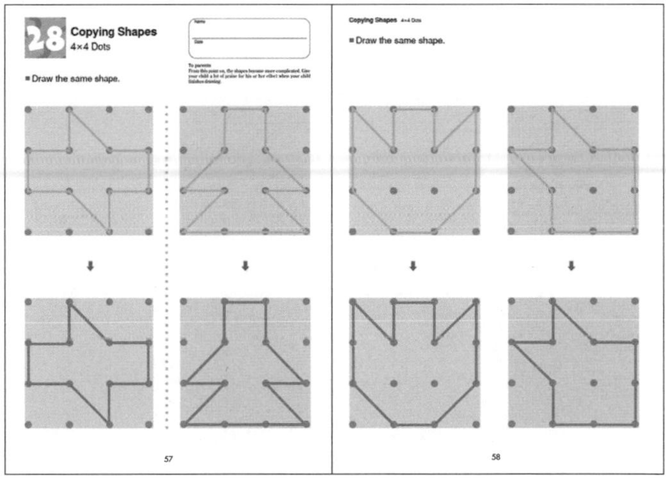

pages 57 and 58

pages 59 and 60

pages 61 and 62

pages 63 and 64

pages 65 and 66

pages 67 and 68

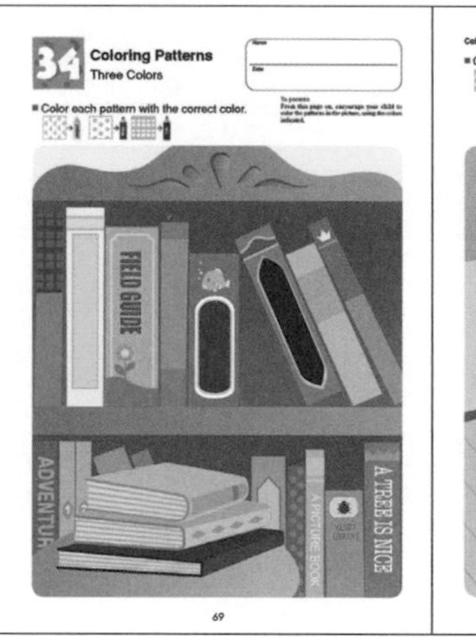

pages 69 and 70

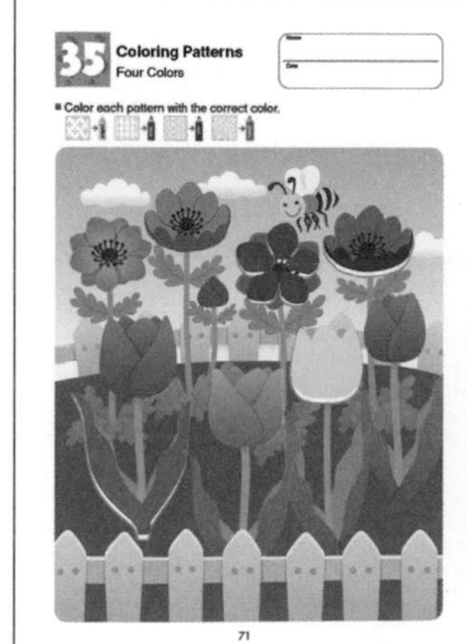

pages 71 and 72

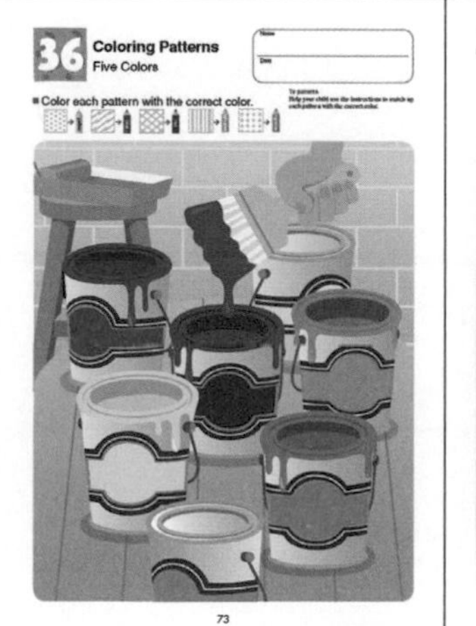

pages 73 and 74

Logic

Table of Contents

To parents:

Logic

In this section, your child will complete activities to develop his or her logical thinking skills. This section contains activities such as making comparisons, distinguishing real from pretend, and analyzing patterns. By completing this section your child will strengthen his or her ability to think logically about problems and questions.

Each skill is introduced in a step-by-step manner that allows your child to master it without frustration. Over the course of the section, the difficulty level of these activities increases as your child gains confidence in his or her ability to think logically.

Matching Features
Level One

Name

Date

To parents
Guide your child to write his or her name and date in the box above. Do the exercise along with your child if he or she has difficulty.

■ Draw a line to the matching animal.

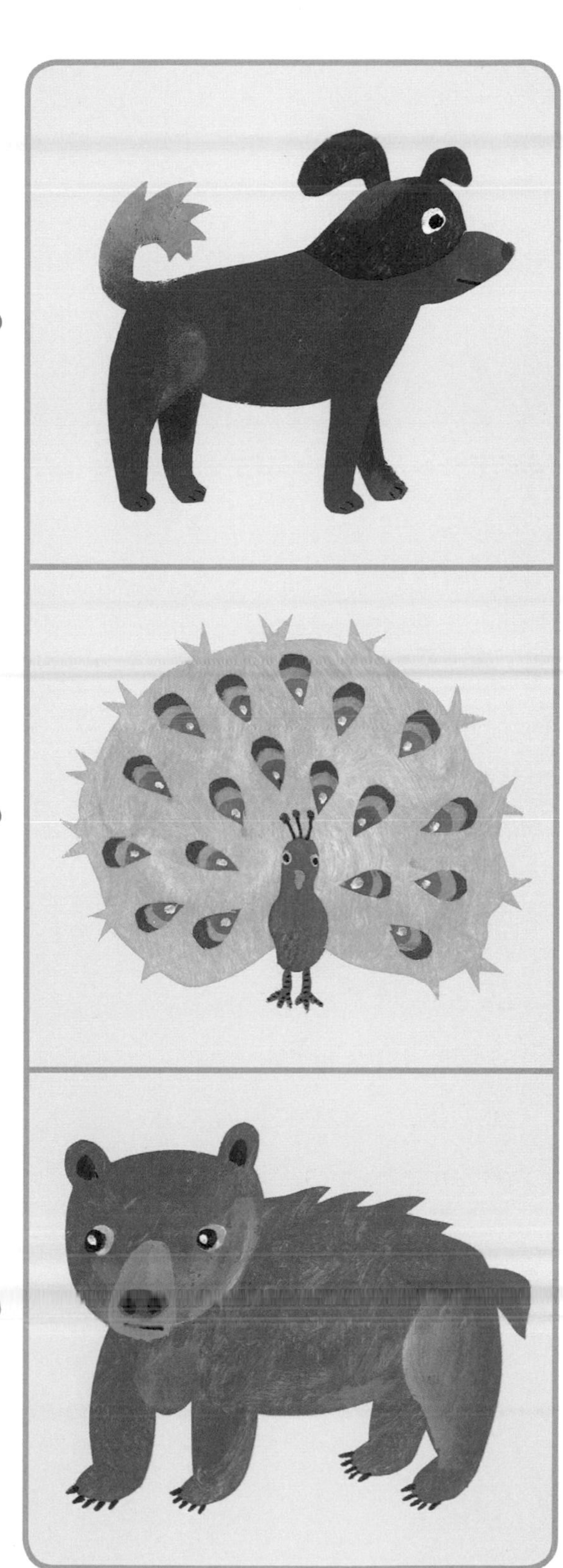

■ Draw a line to the matching fruit.

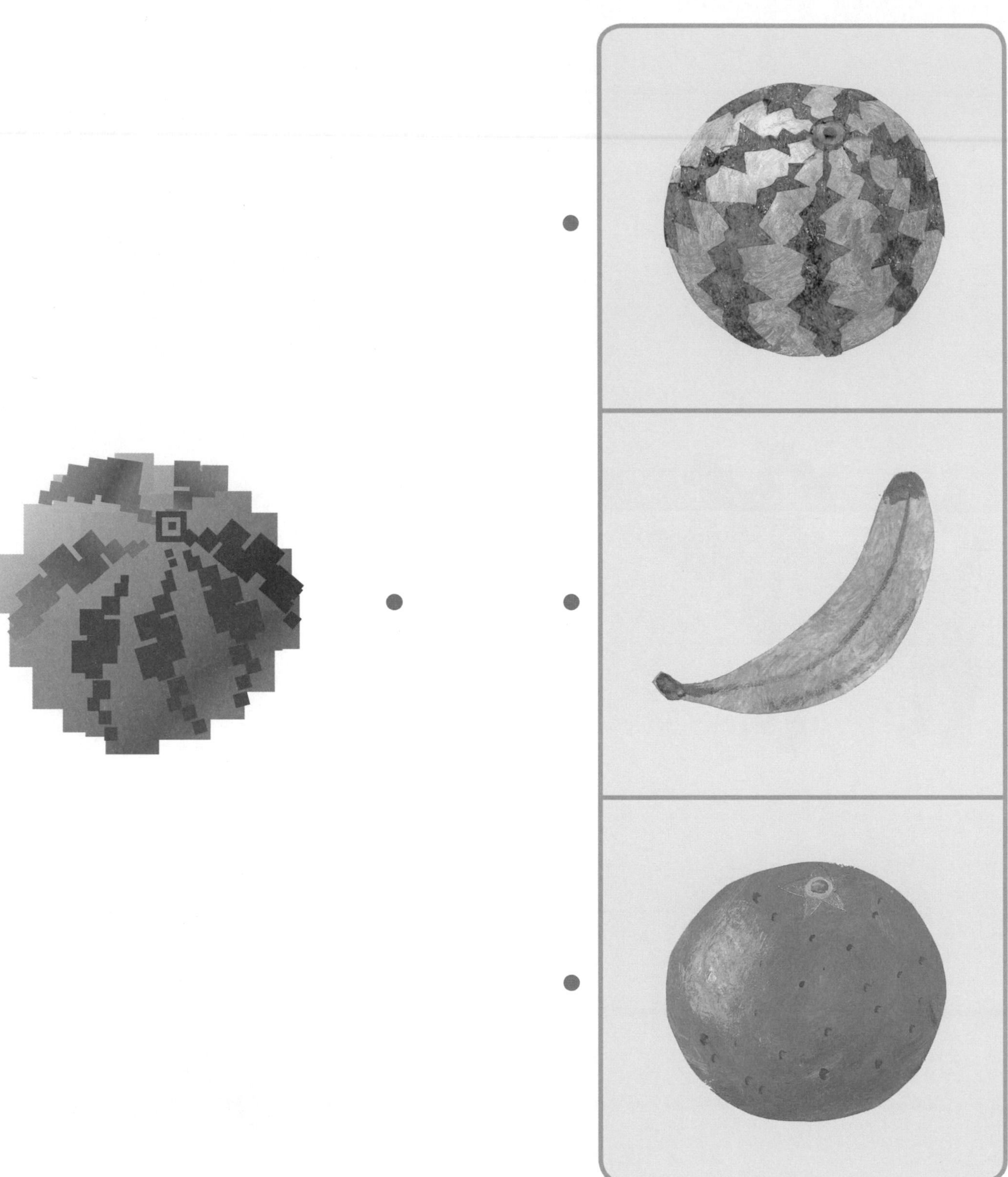

Matching Features
Level Two

Name

Date

To parents
If your child has difficulty, encourage him or her to compare the pixelated animal with each animal in the right column.

■ Draw a line to the matching animal.

■ Draw a line to the matching object.

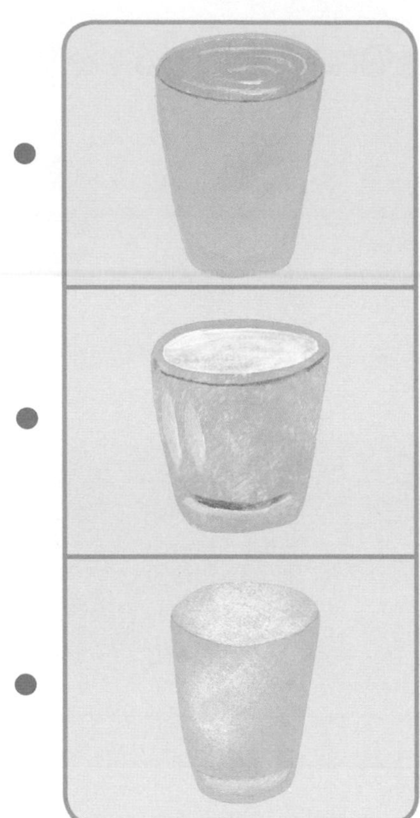

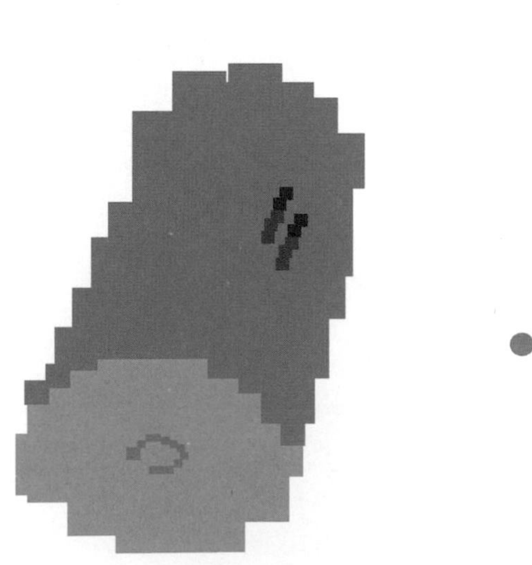

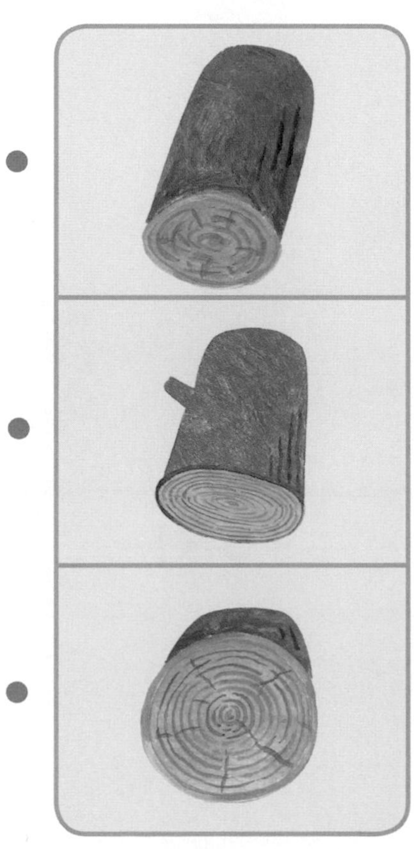

Matching Features

Level Three

Name

Date

To parents
Looking for pictures that have the same colors might help your child find the answers.

■ Draw a line to the matching animal.

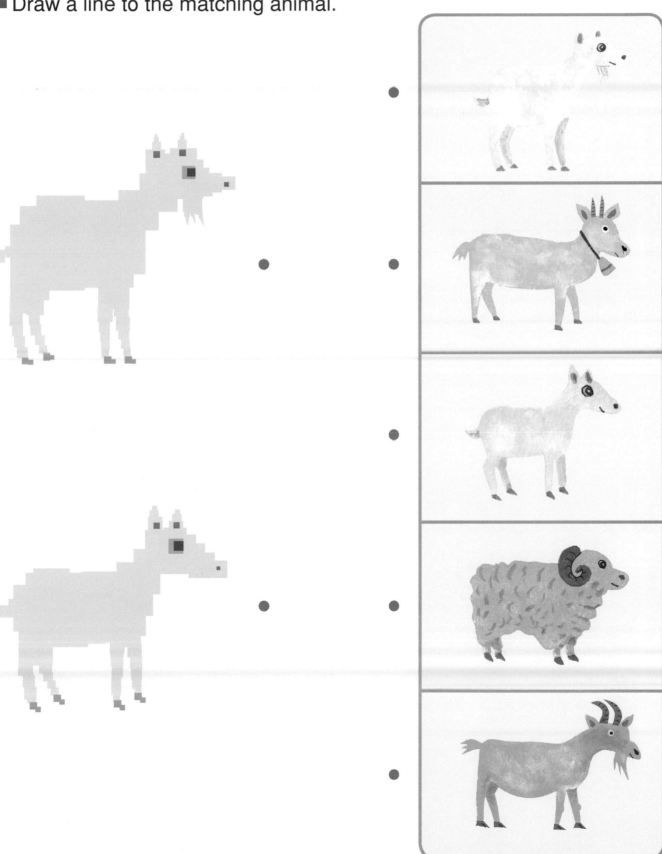

■ Draw a line to the matching object.

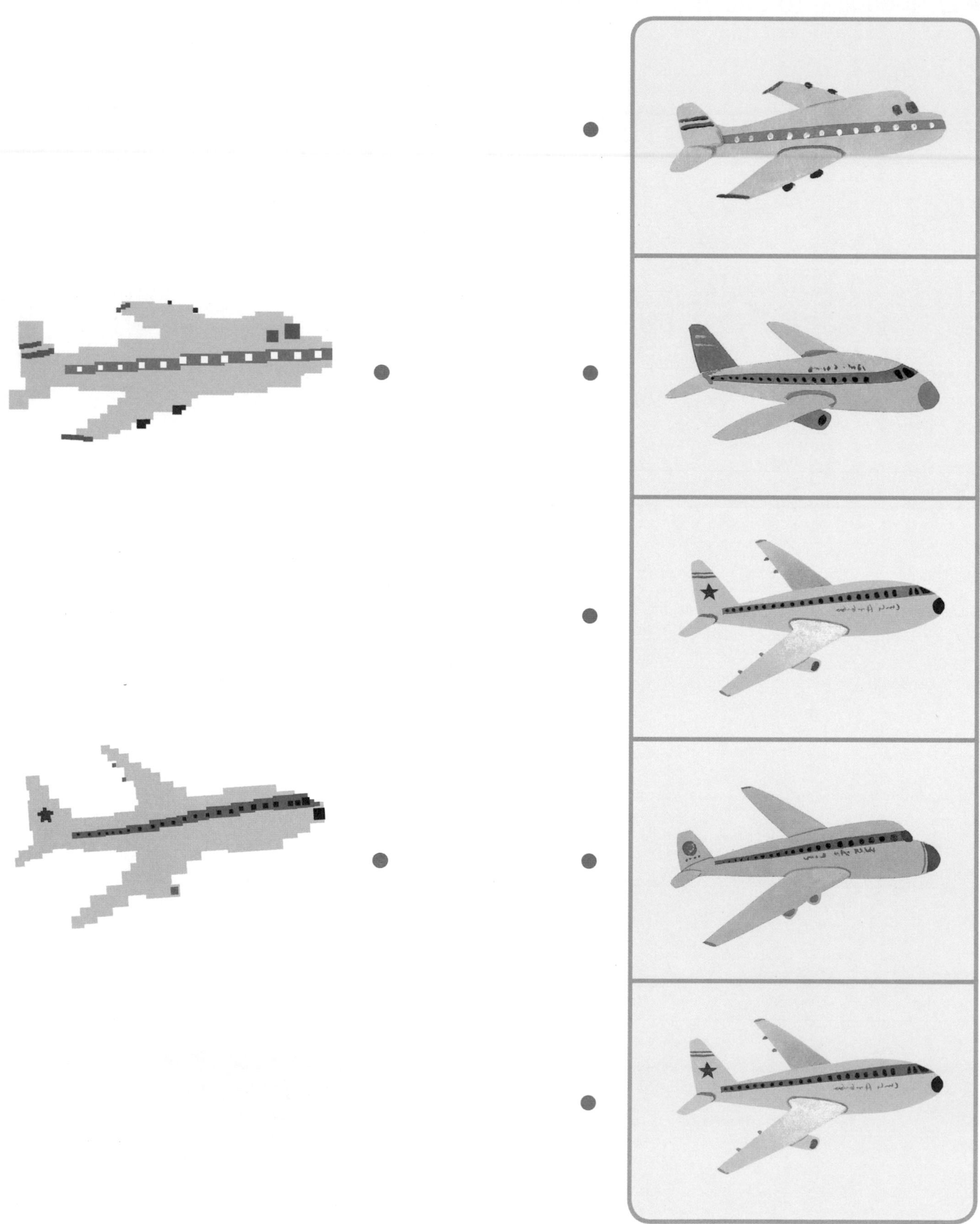

Matching Features

Level Four

Name

Date

To parents
Help your child pay close attention to details such as the shapes of the animals' tails and ears.

■ Draw a line to the matching animal.

■ Draw a line to the matching object.

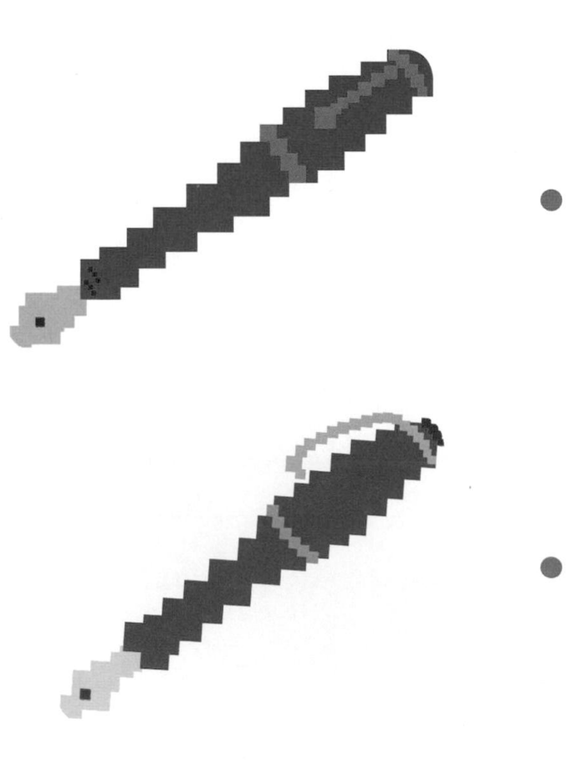

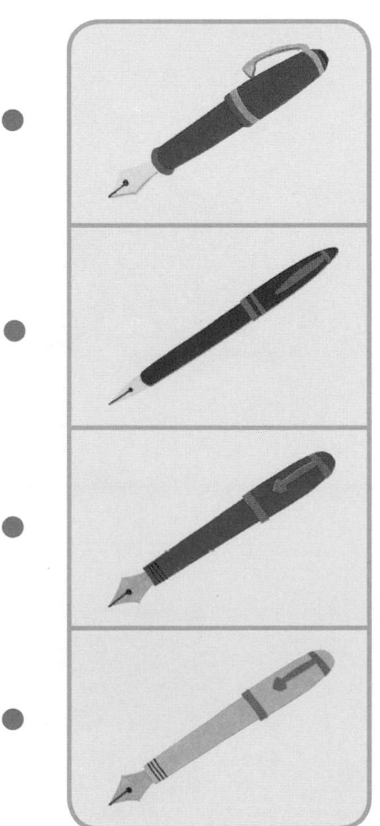

Drawing Conclusions

Level One

Name

Date

To parents
If your child has difficulty, explain that the picture on the left shows an object cut down the middle.

■ Draw a line to the picture that shows the whole object.

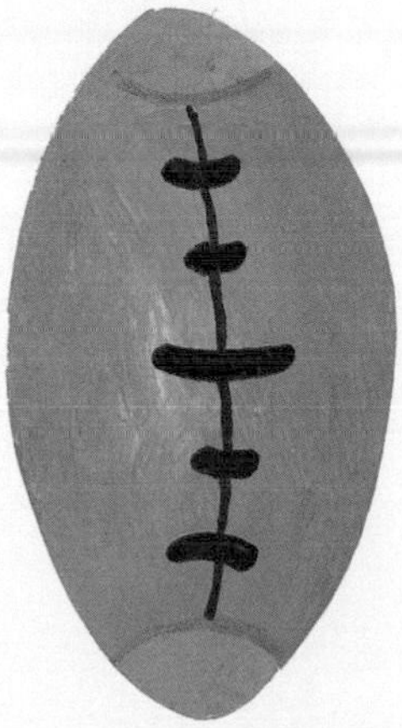

■ Draw a line to the picture that shows the whole object.

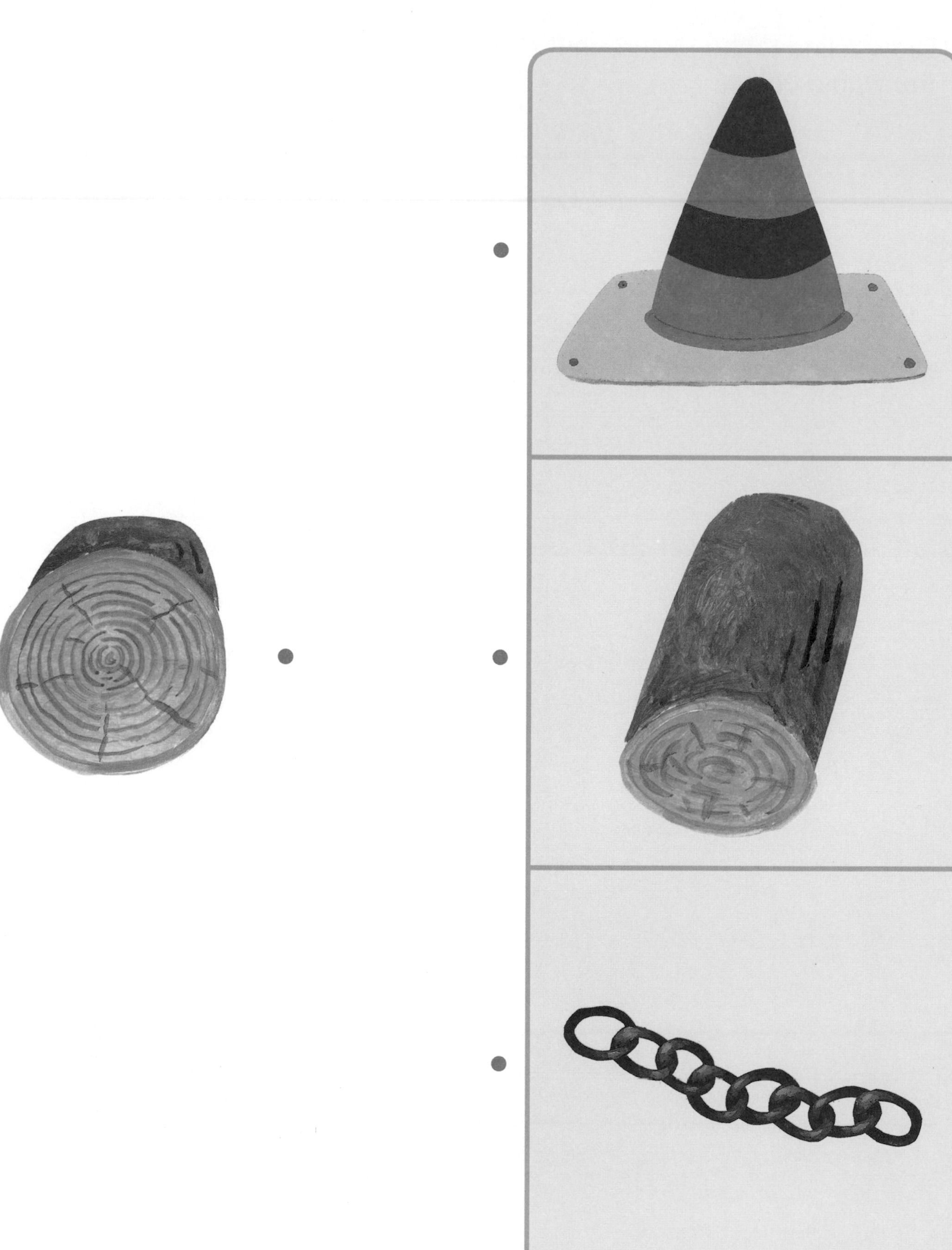

Drawing Conclusions
Level Two

Name

Date

To parents
If your child has difficulty, talk together about the shapes and colors that you see in the pictures.

■ Draw a line to the picture that shows the whole object.

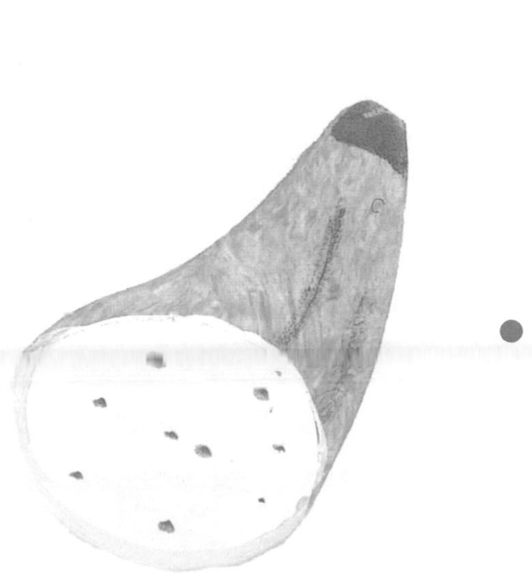

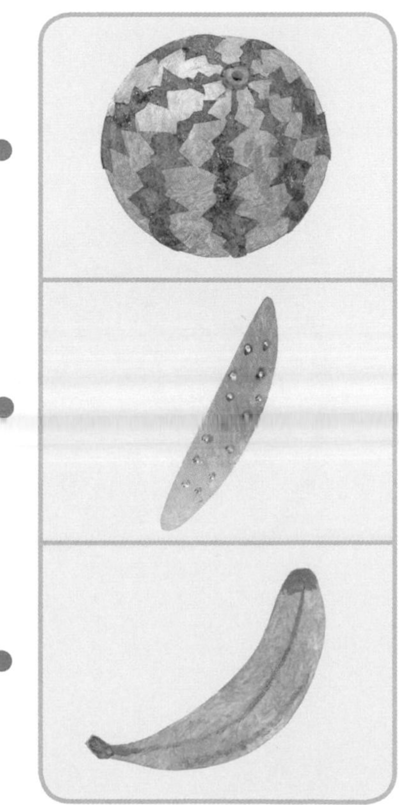

■ Draw a line to the picture that shows the whole object.

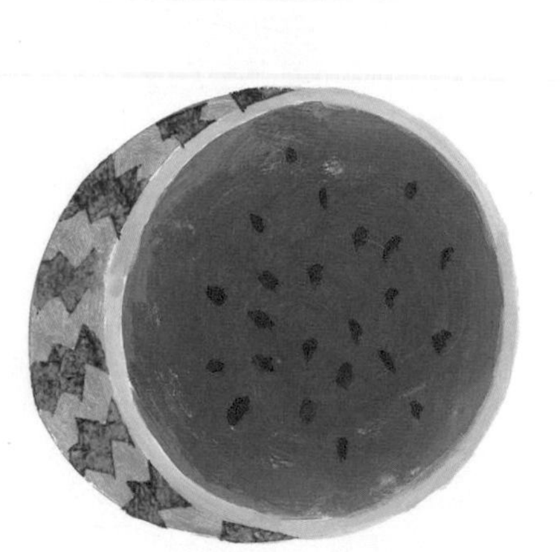

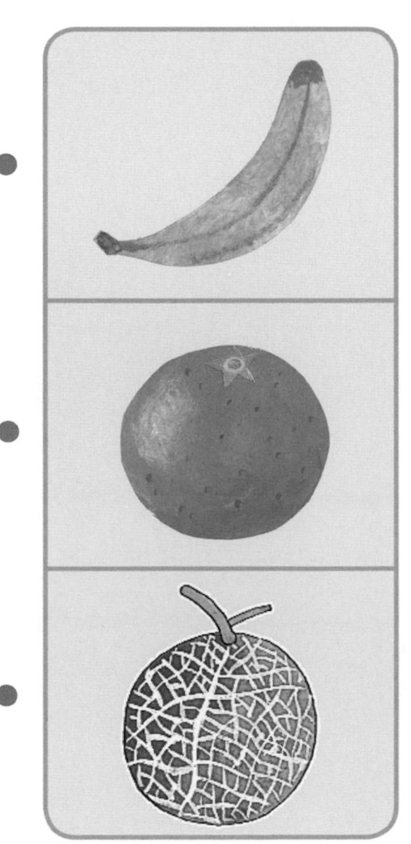

Drawing Conclusions

Level Three

Name

Date

To parents
Encourage your child to compare the general shape of each picture.

■ Draw a line to the picture that shows the whole object.

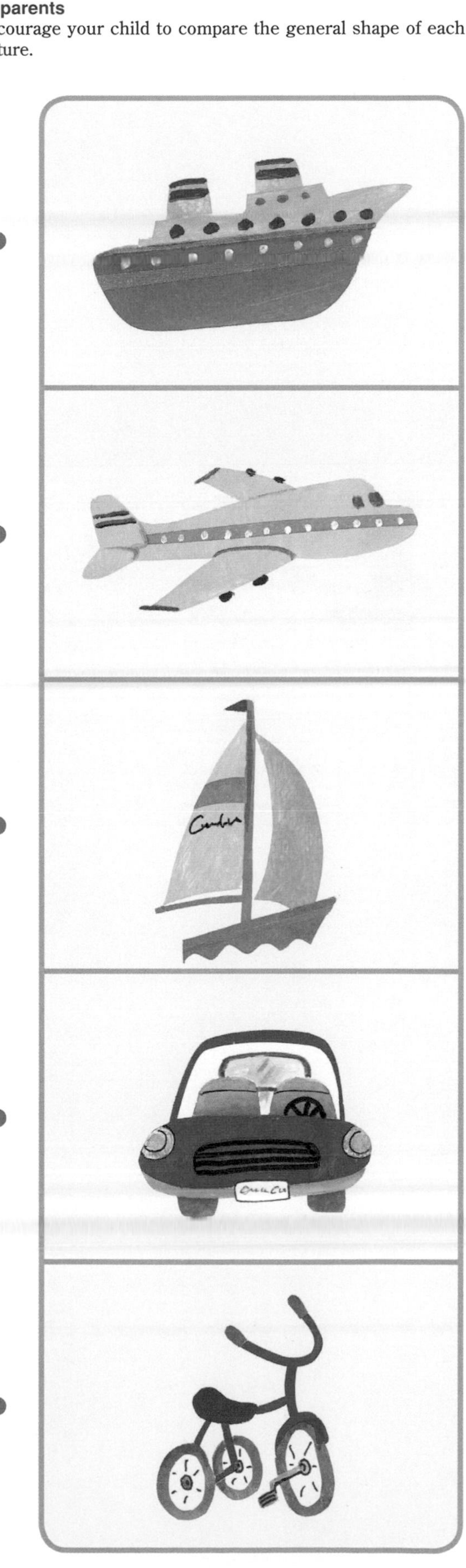

■ Draw a line to the picture that shows the whole object.

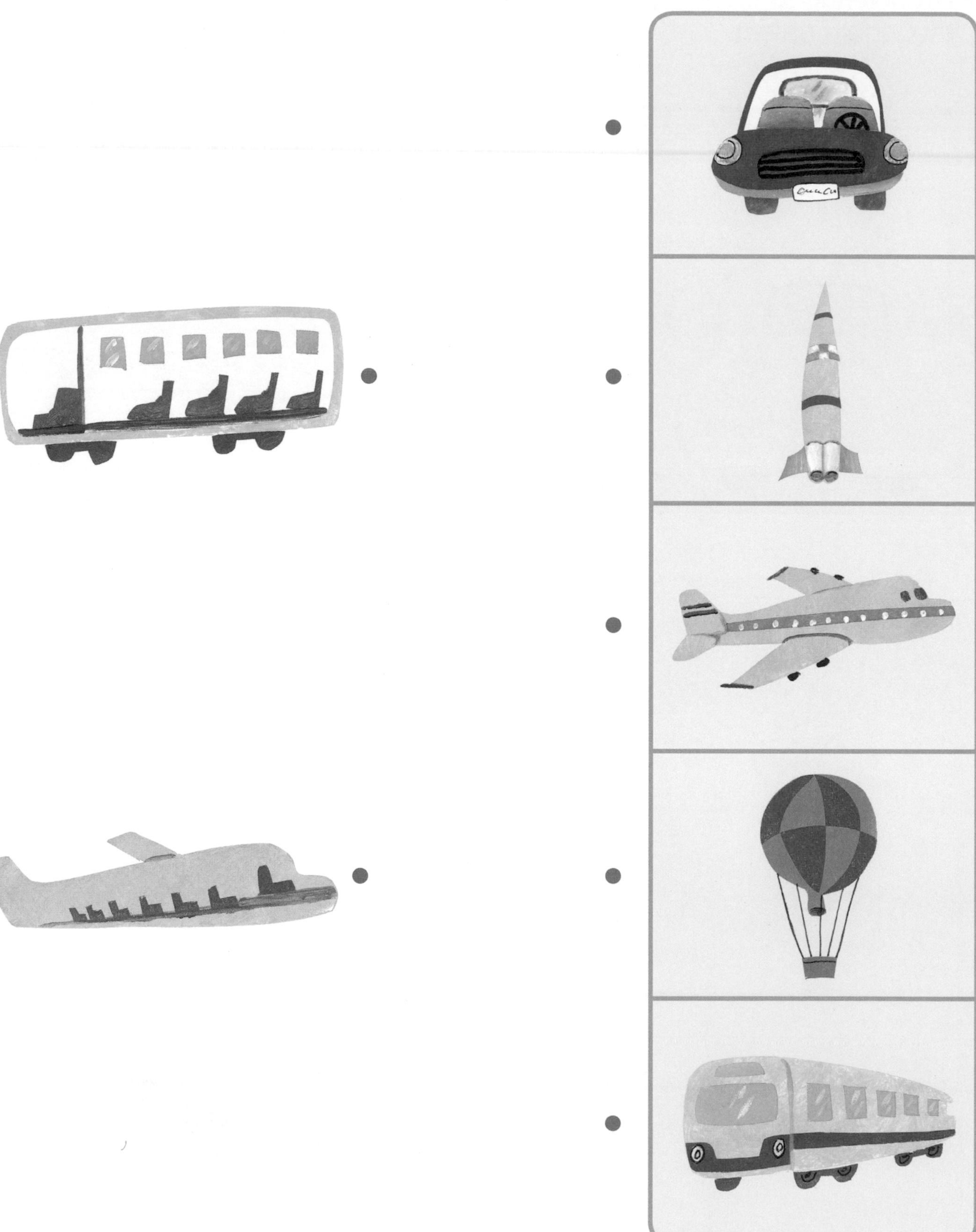

Drawing Conclusions

Level Four

Name

Date

To parents
Encourage your child to find the answer based on the illustrations instead of his or her knowledge.

■ Draw a line to the picture that shows the whole object.

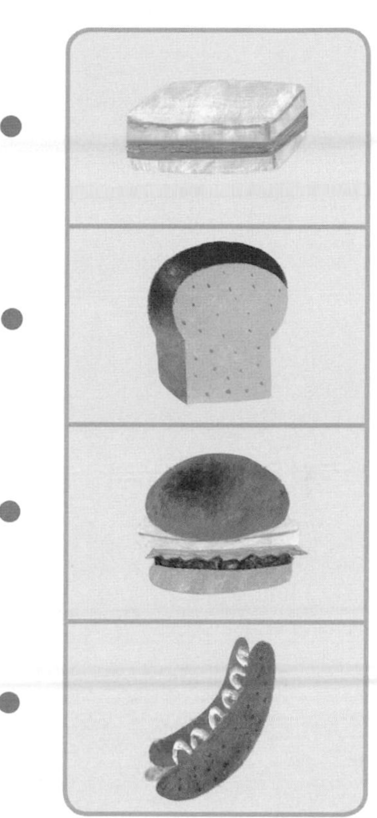

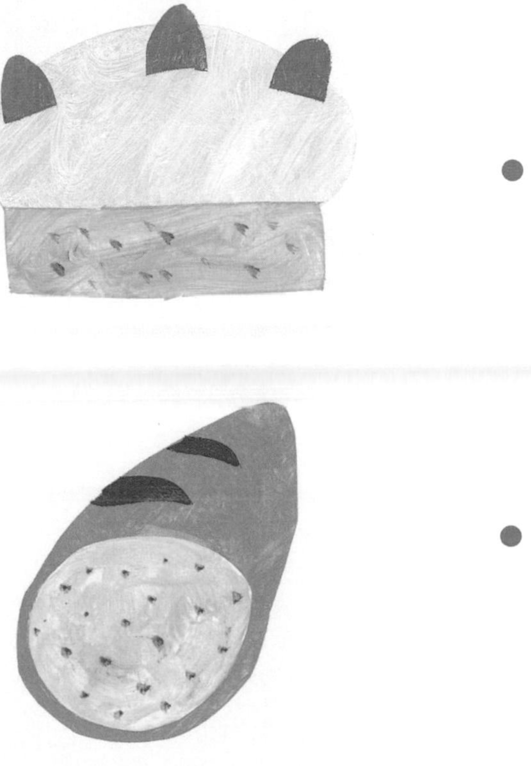

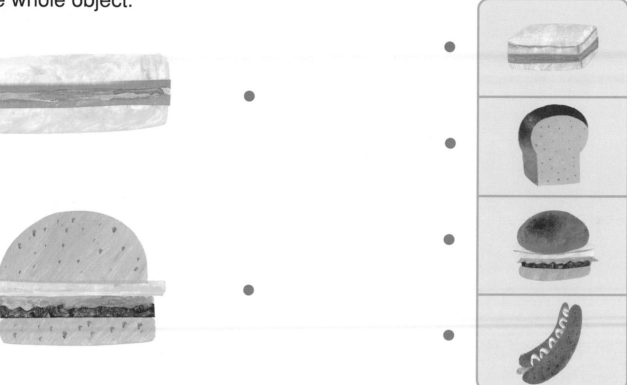

■ Draw a line to the picture that shows the whole object.

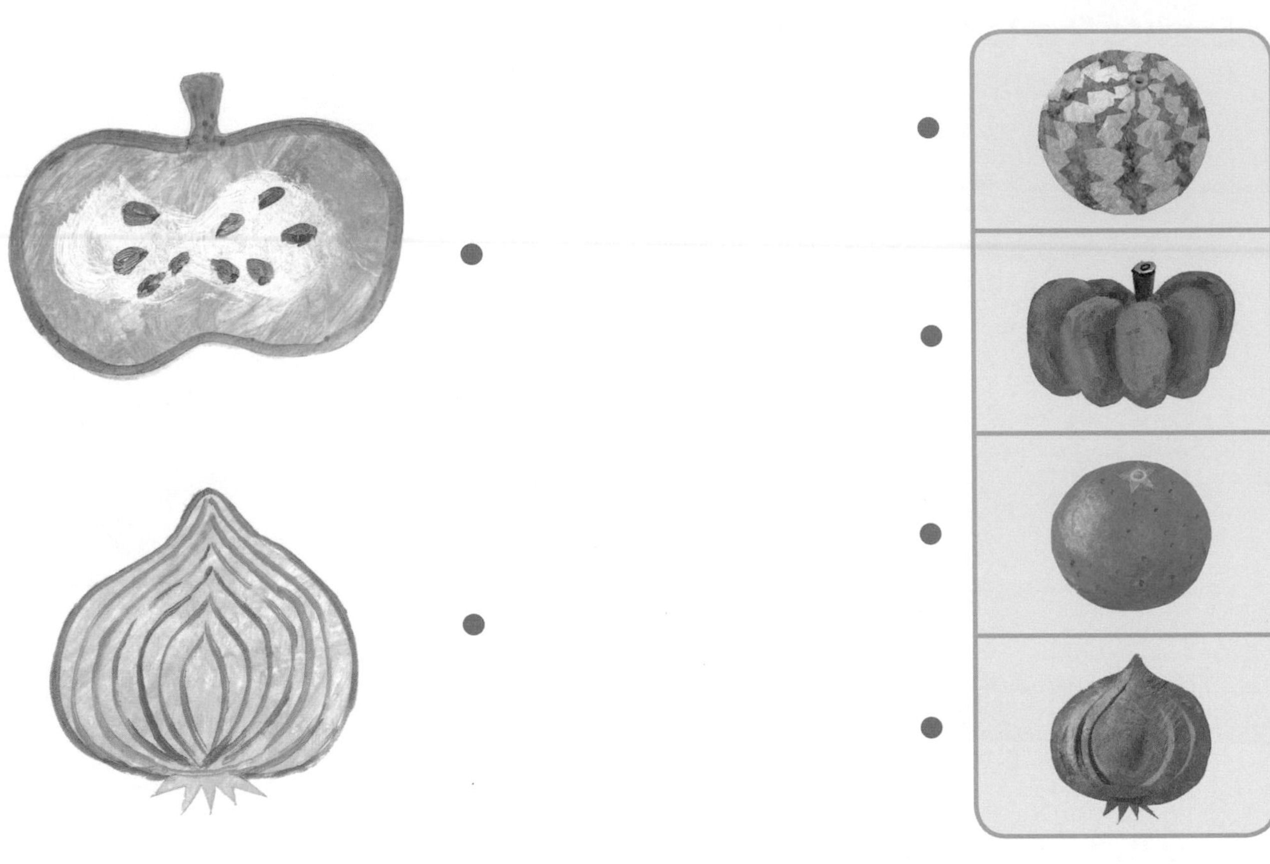

Relationships

Level One

Name

Date

To parents
If your child has difficulty, encourage him or her to compare the animal on the left with each animal in the right column.

■ Draw a line to the animal's parent.

■ Draw a line to the animal's parent.

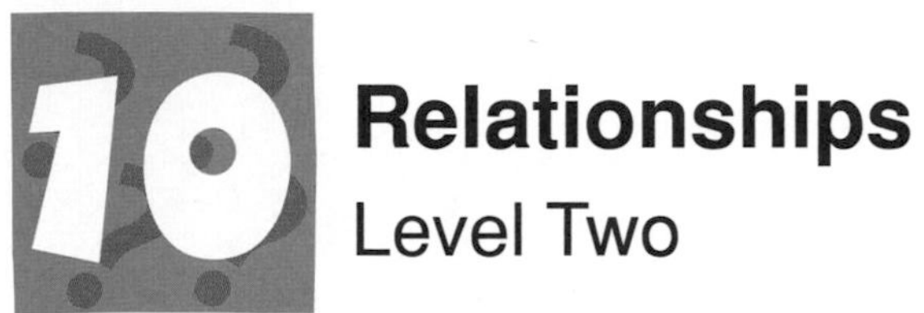

Relationships
Level Two

Name

Date

To parents
Looking for pictures that have the same colors might help your child find the answers.

■ Draw a line to the animal's parent.

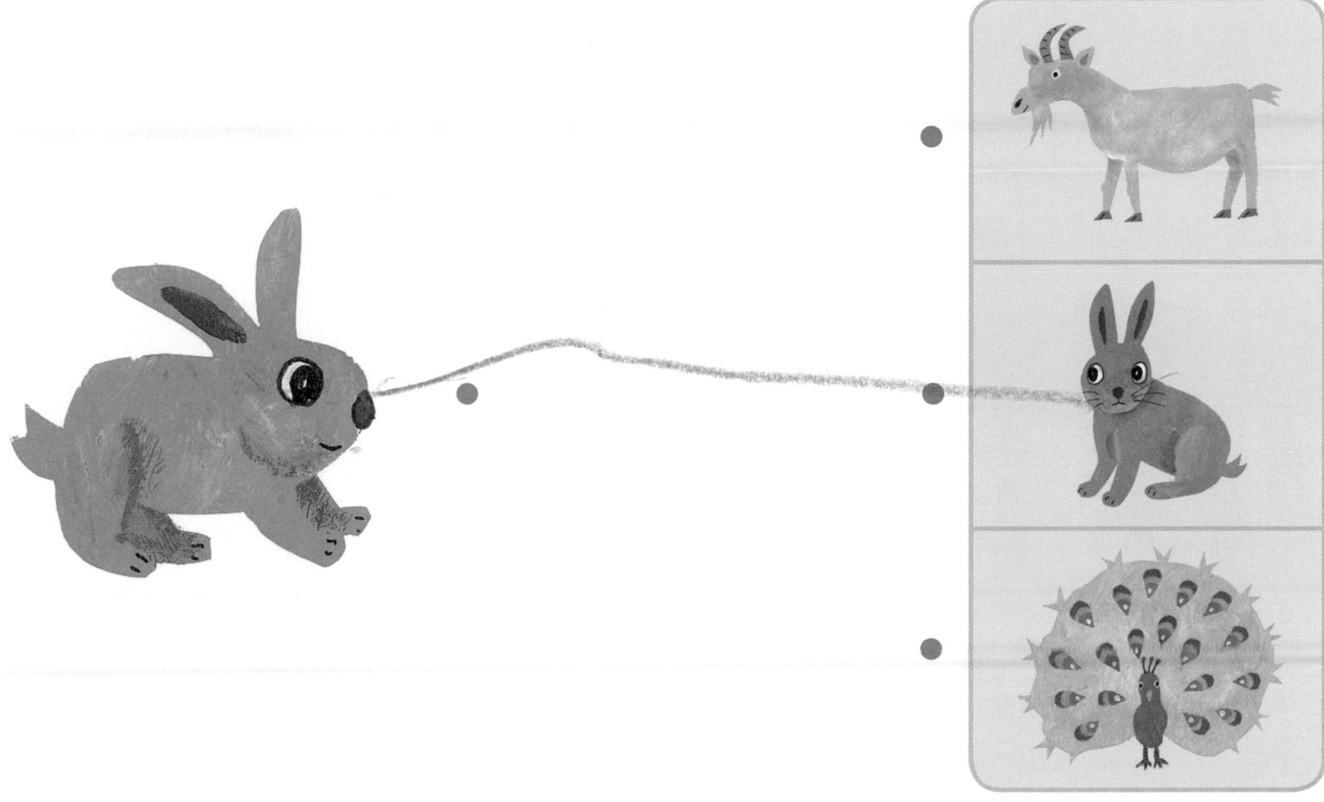

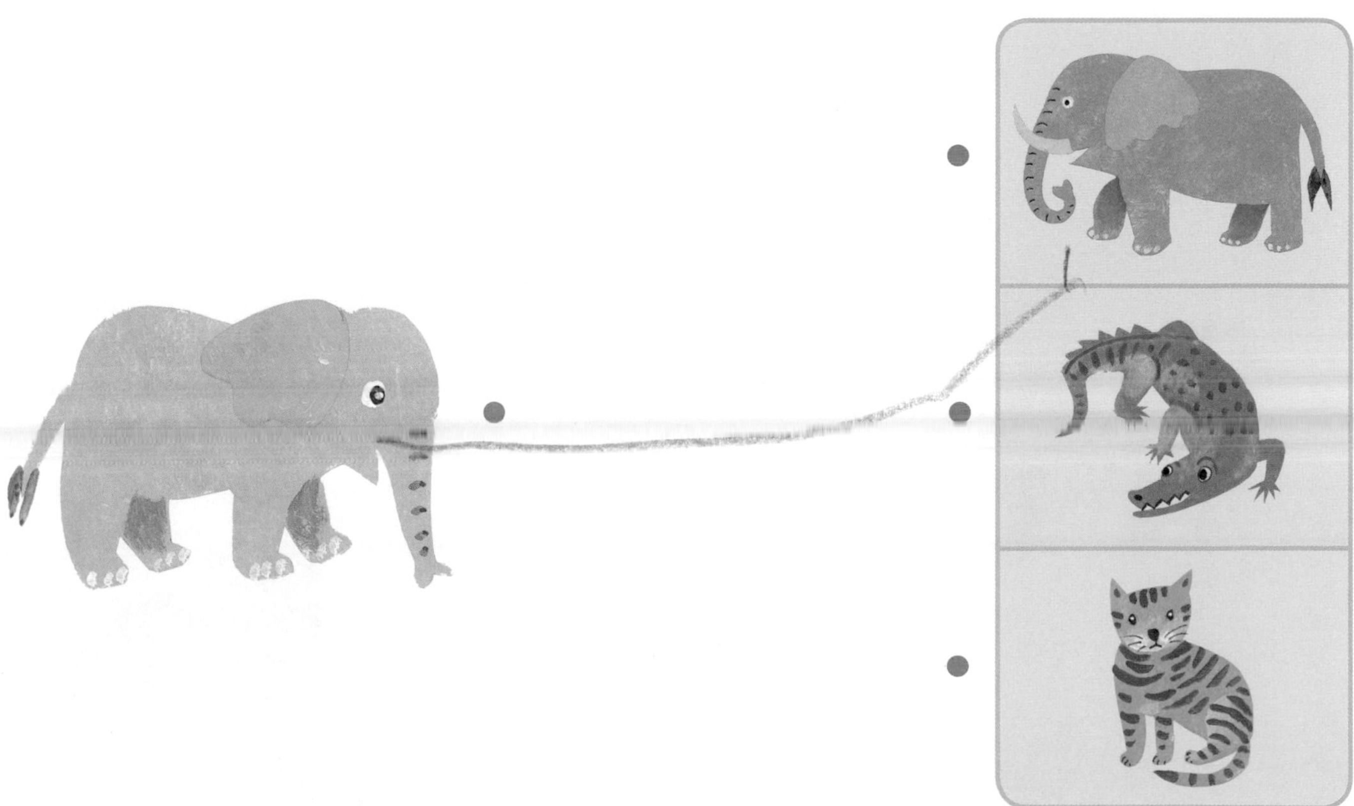

■ Draw a line to the animal's parent.

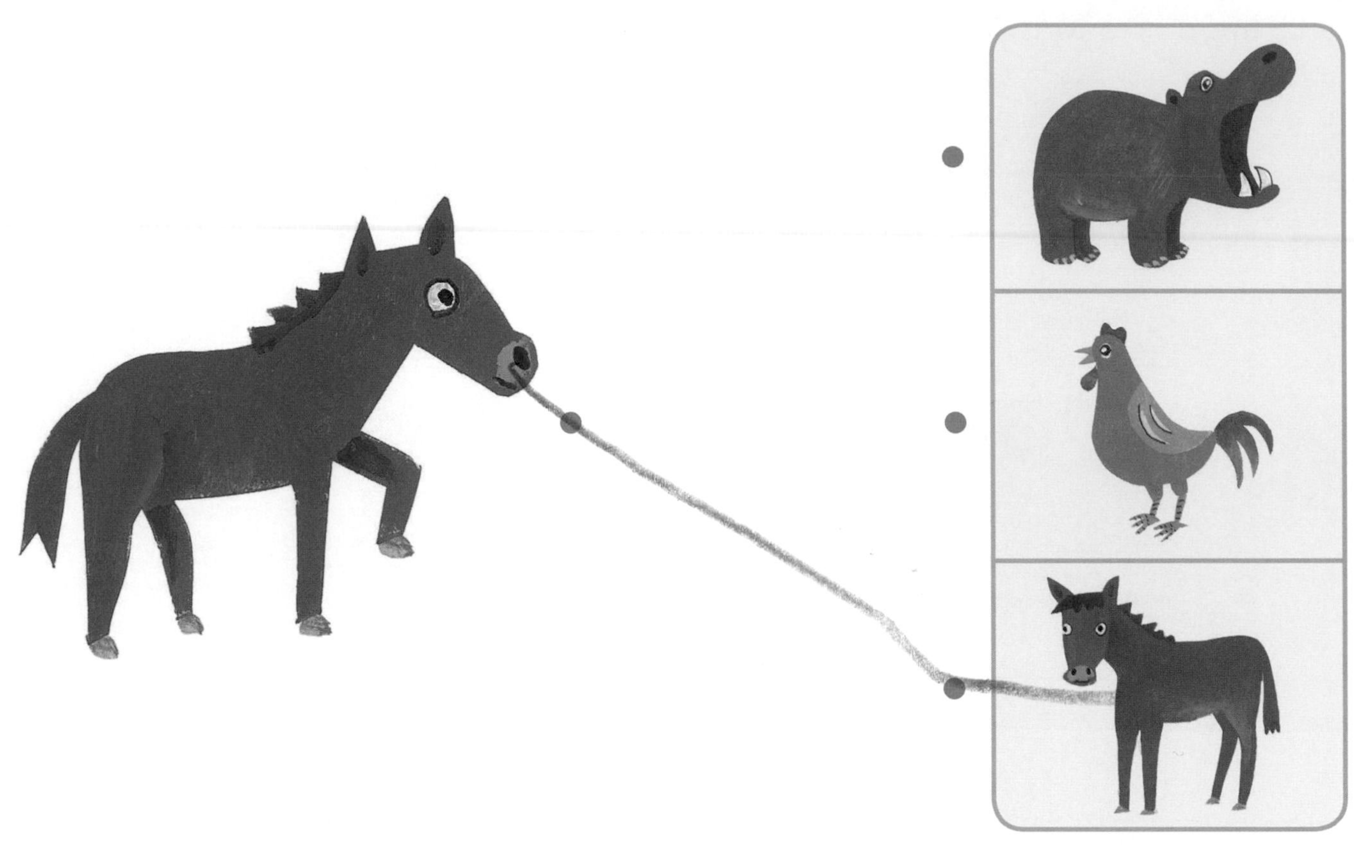

Relationships

Level Three

Name

Date

To parents
Encourage your child to notice the details of each animal's features.

■ Draw a line to the animal's parent.

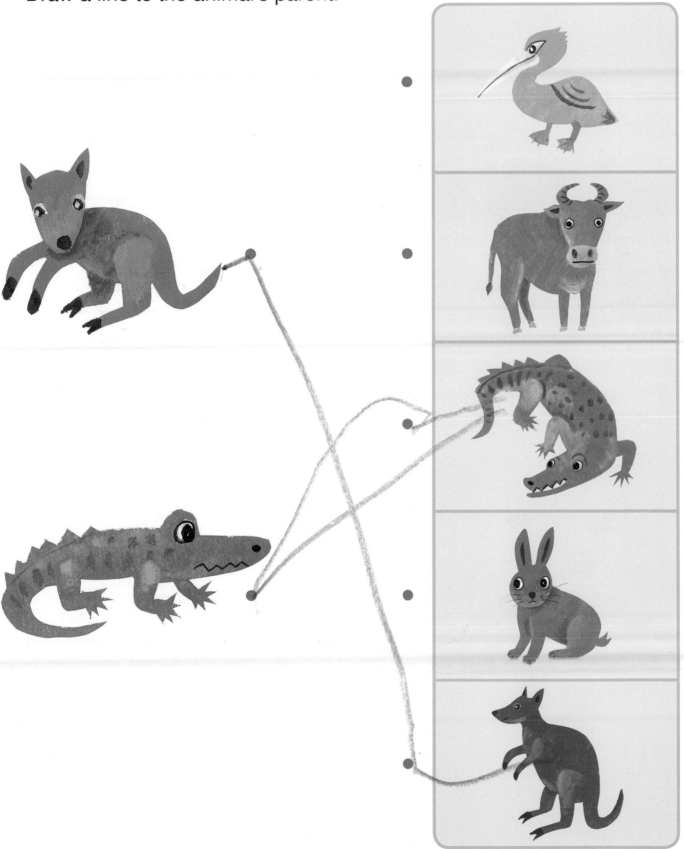

■ Draw a line to the animal's parent.

Relationships
Level Four

Name

Date

■ Draw a line to the animal's parent.

To parents
If your child has difficulty, explain that some animals develop new features or change color when they are older.

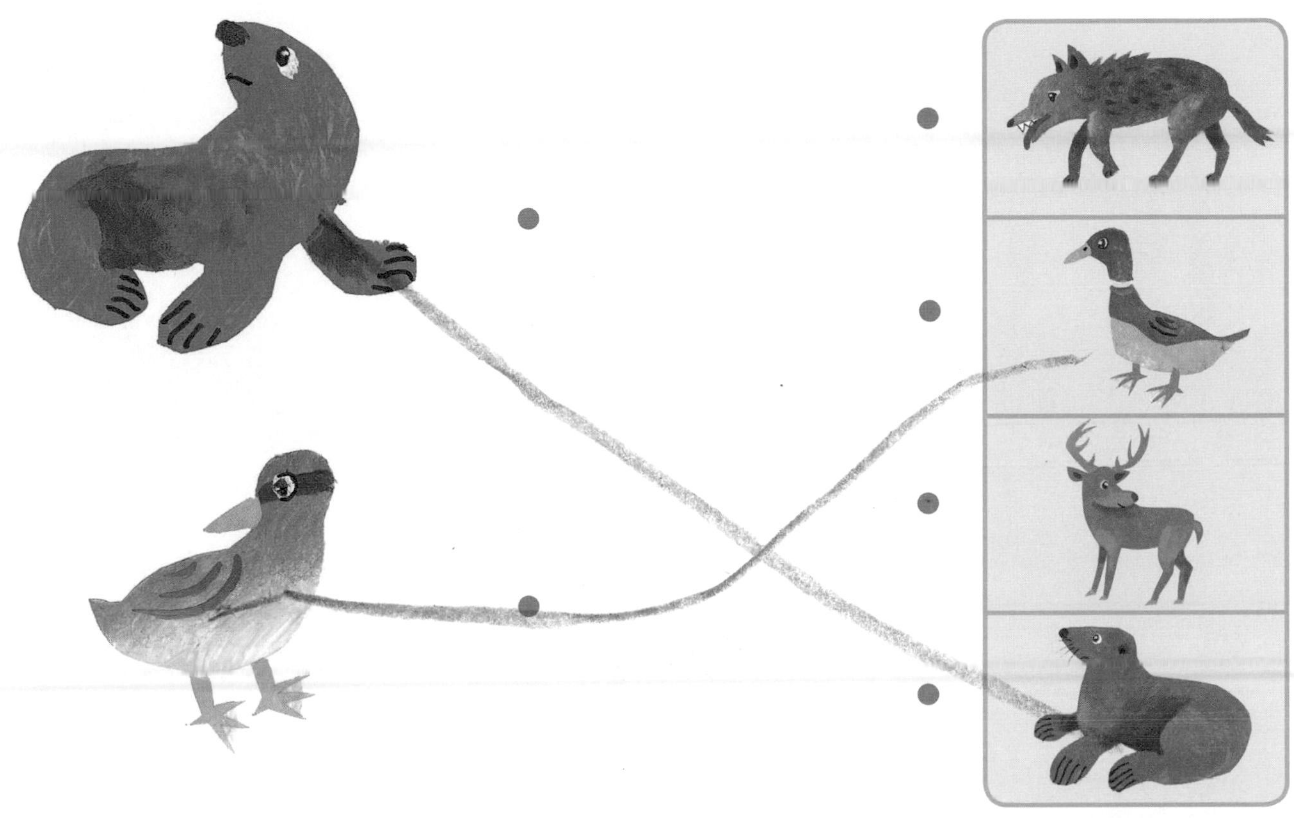

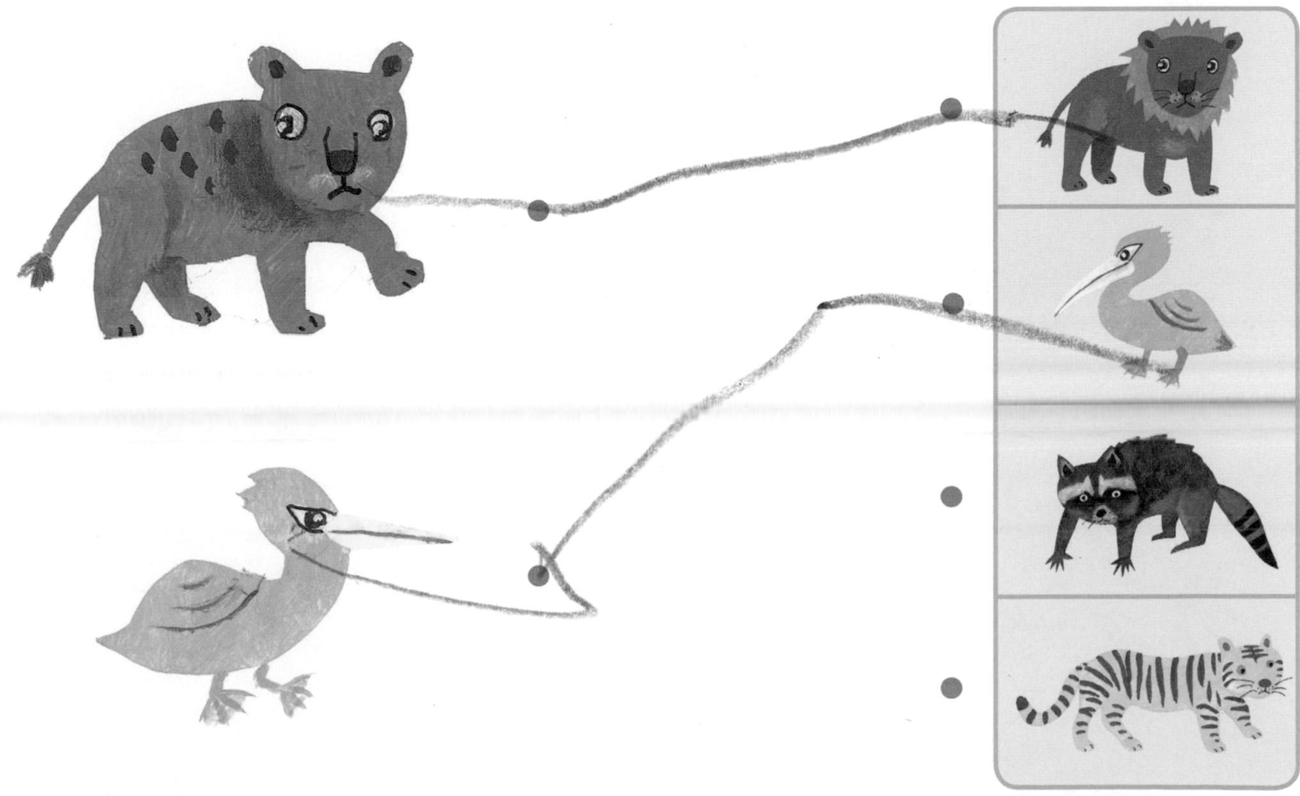

■ Draw a line to the animal's parent.

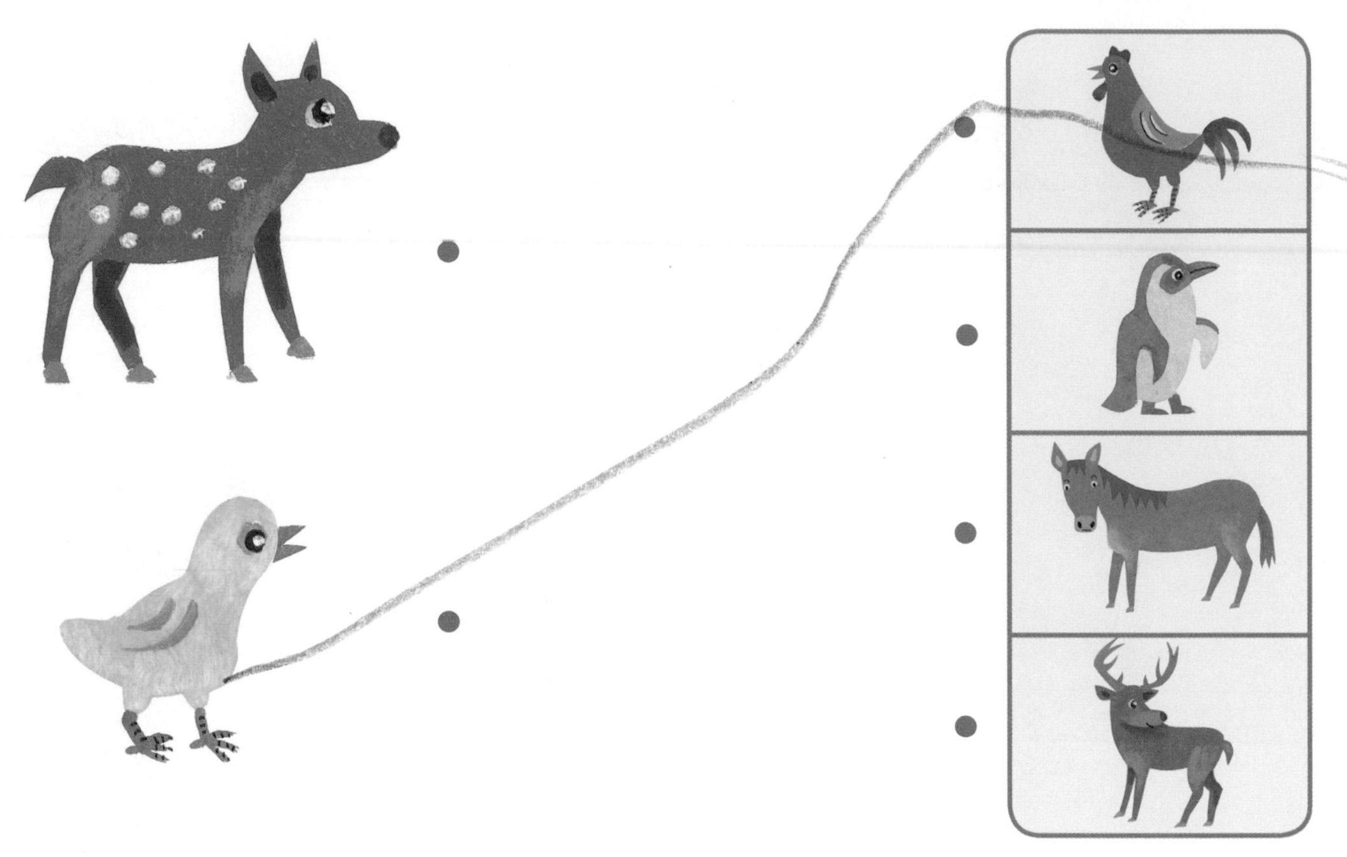

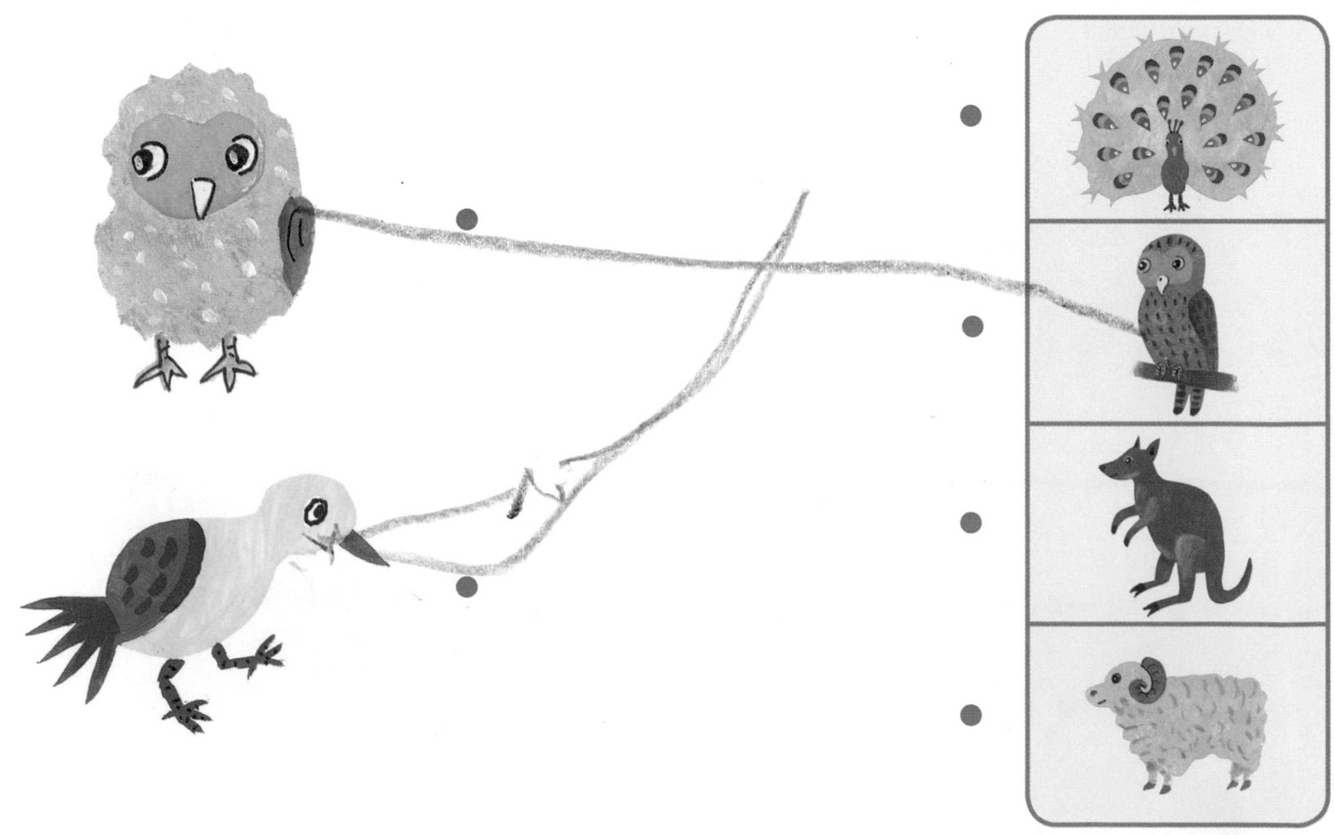

Comparing Weight

Level One

Name

Date

To parents
For a hands-on example of this concept, have your child hold a small book and then a large book. Ask which is heavier.

■ Write a check mark (✓) above the picture that shows the correct difference in weight.

(✓)

( )

( )

■ Write a check mark (✓) above the picture that shows the correct difference in weight.

Comparing Weight

Level Two

Name

Date

To parents
If your child has difficulty, ask your child which animal is likely to be heavier.

■ Write a check mark (✓) beside the picture that shows the correct difference in weight.

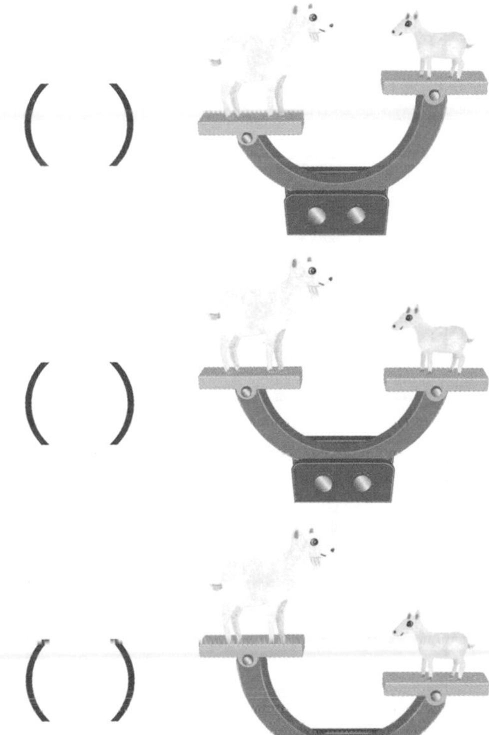

( )

( )

( )

( )

( )

( )

■ Write a check mark (✓) beside the picture that shows the correct difference in weight.

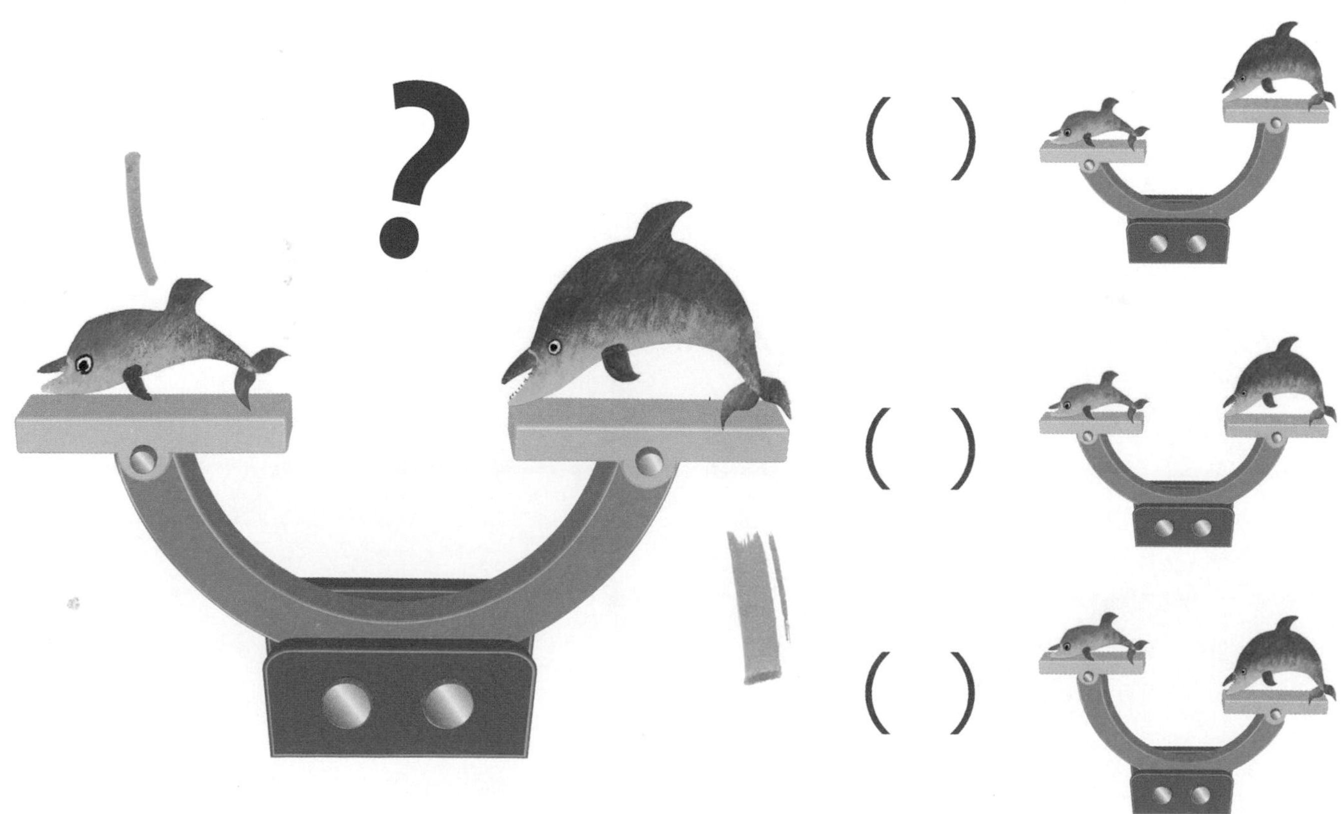

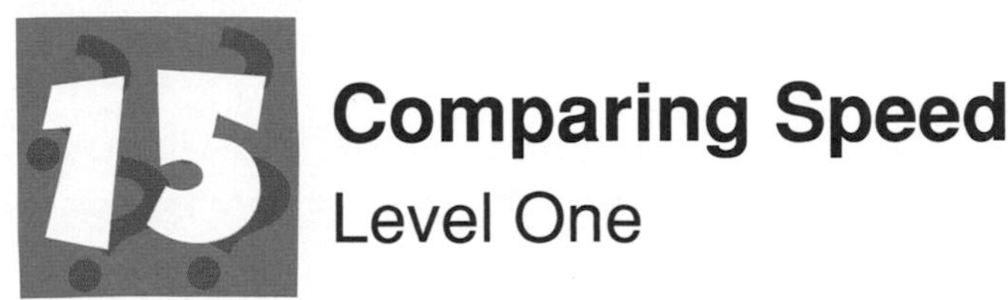

15 Comparing Speed

Level One

Name

Date

To parents
If your child has difficulty, ask him or her which object can travel faster.

■ Write a check mark (✓) beside the picture that shows the correct difference in speed.

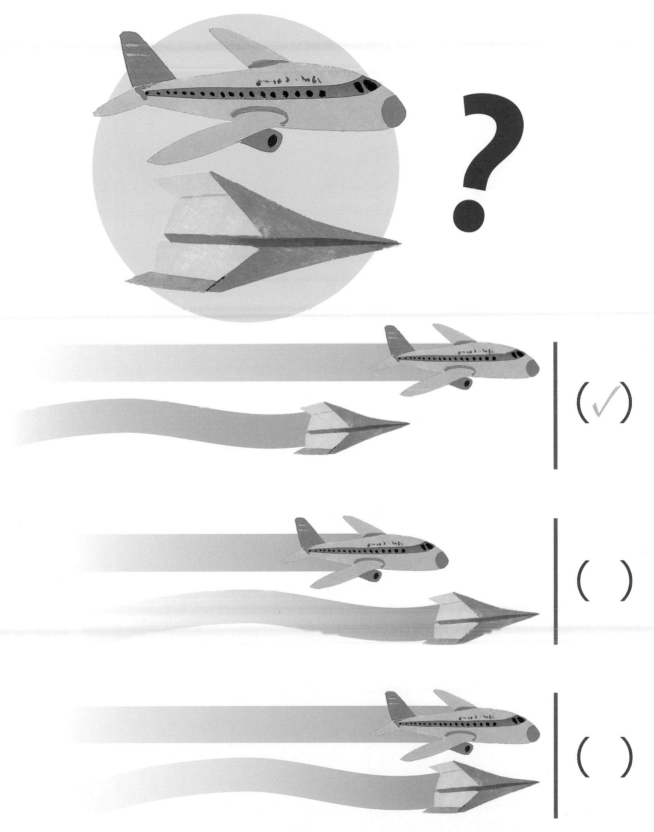

?

(✓)

( )

( )

■ Write a check mark (✓) beside the picture that shows the correct difference in speed.

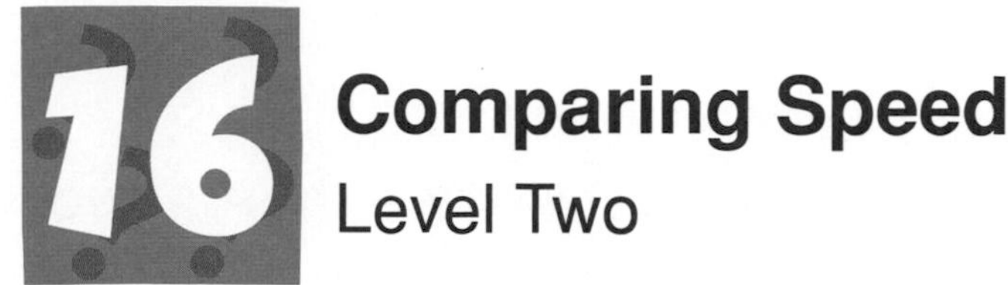

Comparing Speed
Level Two

Name

Date

To parents
If your child has difficulty, say that the red line is the finish line in a race. Ask which animal will get there first.

■ Write a check mark (✓) beside the picture that shows the correct difference in speed.

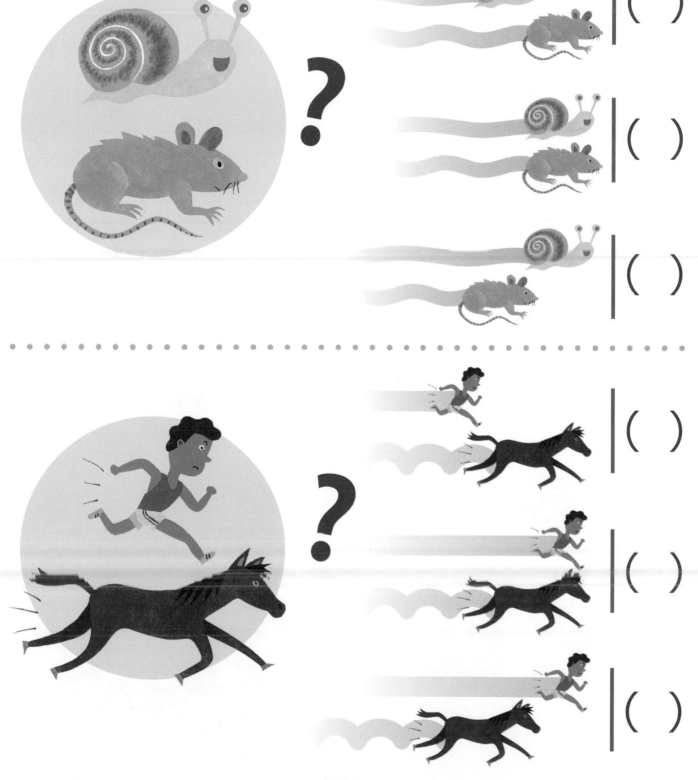

( )

( )

( )

( )

( )

( )

■ Write a check mark (✓) beside the picture that shows the correct difference in speed.

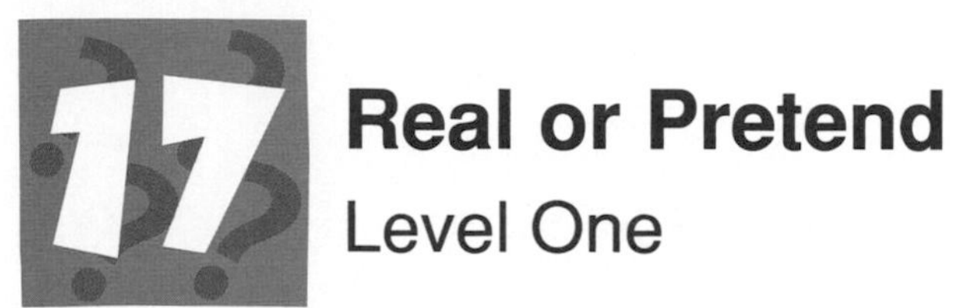

Real or Pretend
Level One

Name

Date

To parents
Encourage your child to find the picture that cannot happen in real life.

■ Write a check mark (✓) above the picture that is pretend.

( )

( )

( )

(✓)

■ Write a check mark (✓) above the picture that is pretend.

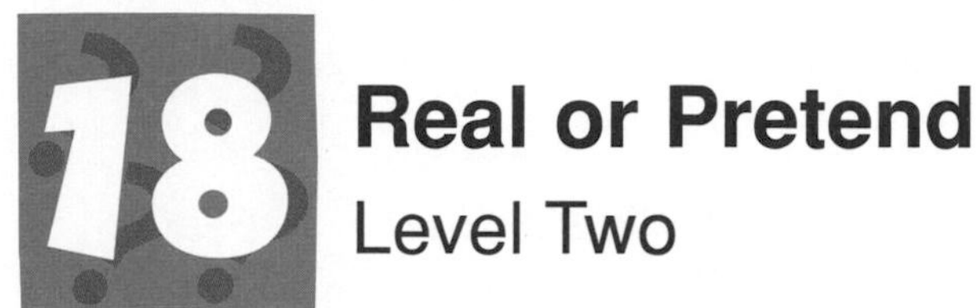

18 Real or Pretend

Level Two

Name

Date

To parents
If your child has difficulty, ask him or her to describe the pictures.

■ Write a check mark (✓) beside the picture that is pretend.

( ) ( )

( ) ( )

( ) ( )

( ) ( )

■ Write a check mark (✓) beside the picture that is pretend.

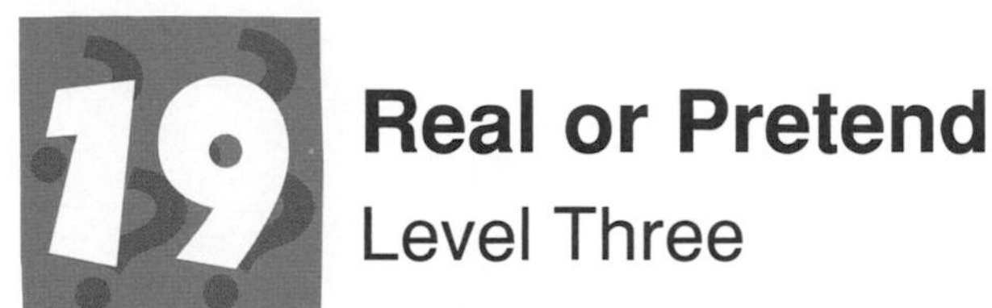

Real or Pretend

Level Three

Name

Date

To parents
From this page on, the events that are pretend are shown as parts of a larger picture.

■ Circle the two parts of the picture that are pretend.

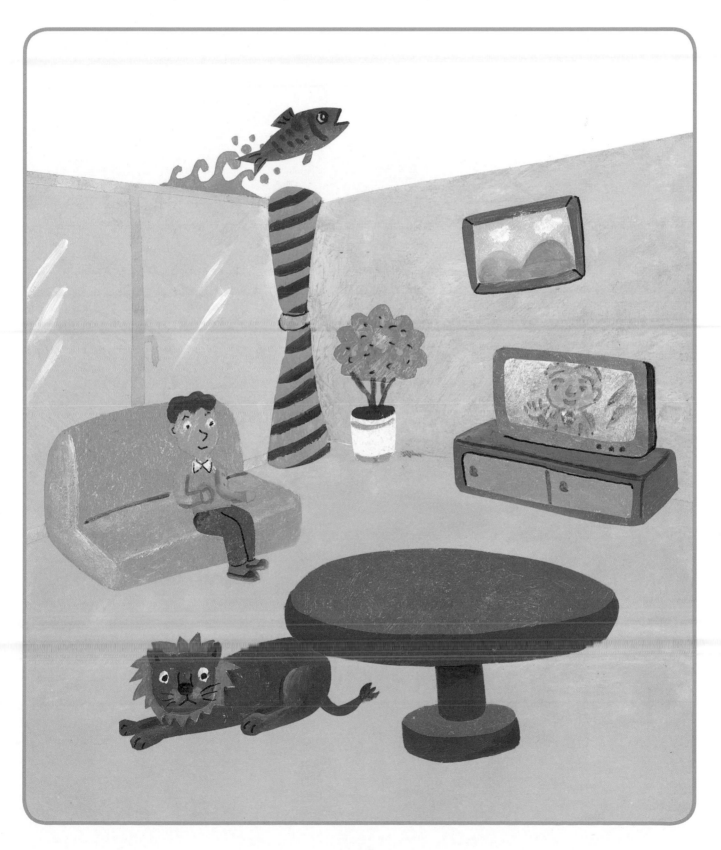

■ Circle the three parts of the picture that are pretend.

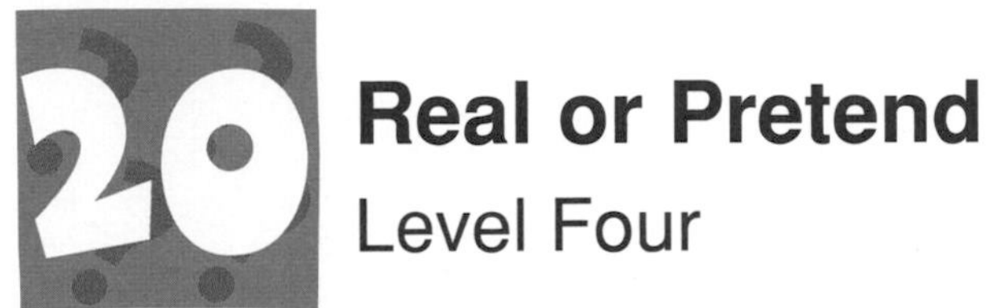

Real or Pretend

Level Four

Name

Date

To parents
The number of pretend events has increased. Help your child find all of the pretend events.

■ Circle the four parts of the picture that are pretend.

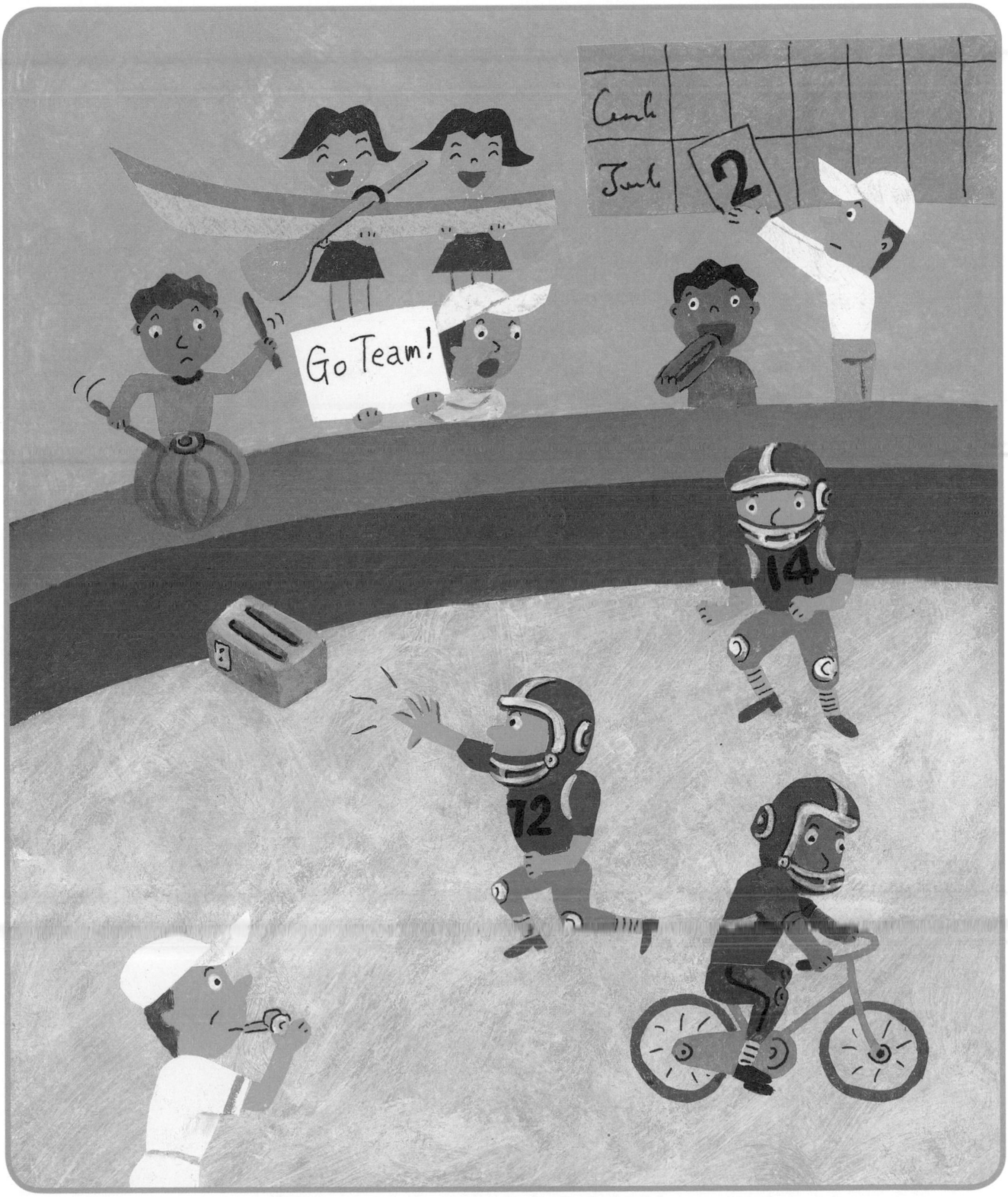

■ Circle the five parts of the picture that are pretend.

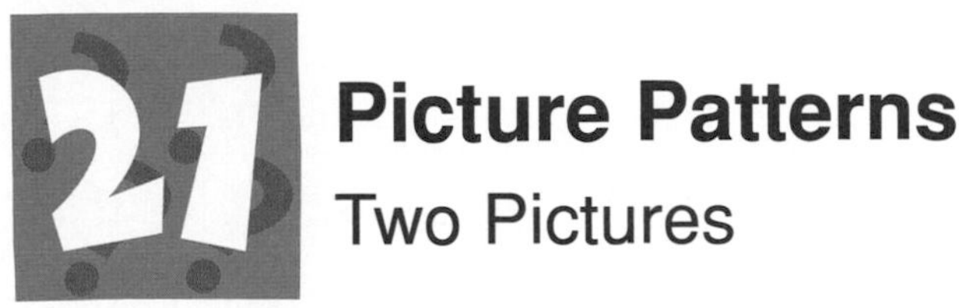

Picture Patterns

Two Pictures

Name

Date

To parents
If your child has difficulty, encourage him or her to say the sequence of pictures out loud.

■ Write a check mark (✓) above the picture that comes next in the pattern.

■ Write a check mark (✓) above the picture that comes next in the pattern.

Picture Patterns

Three Pictures

Name

Date

To parents
The patterns are now arranged vertically. Guide your child to start with the top picture.

■ Write a check mark (✓) above the picture that comes next in the pattern.

( )

( )

( )

?

■ Write a check mark (✓) above the picture that comes next in the pattern.

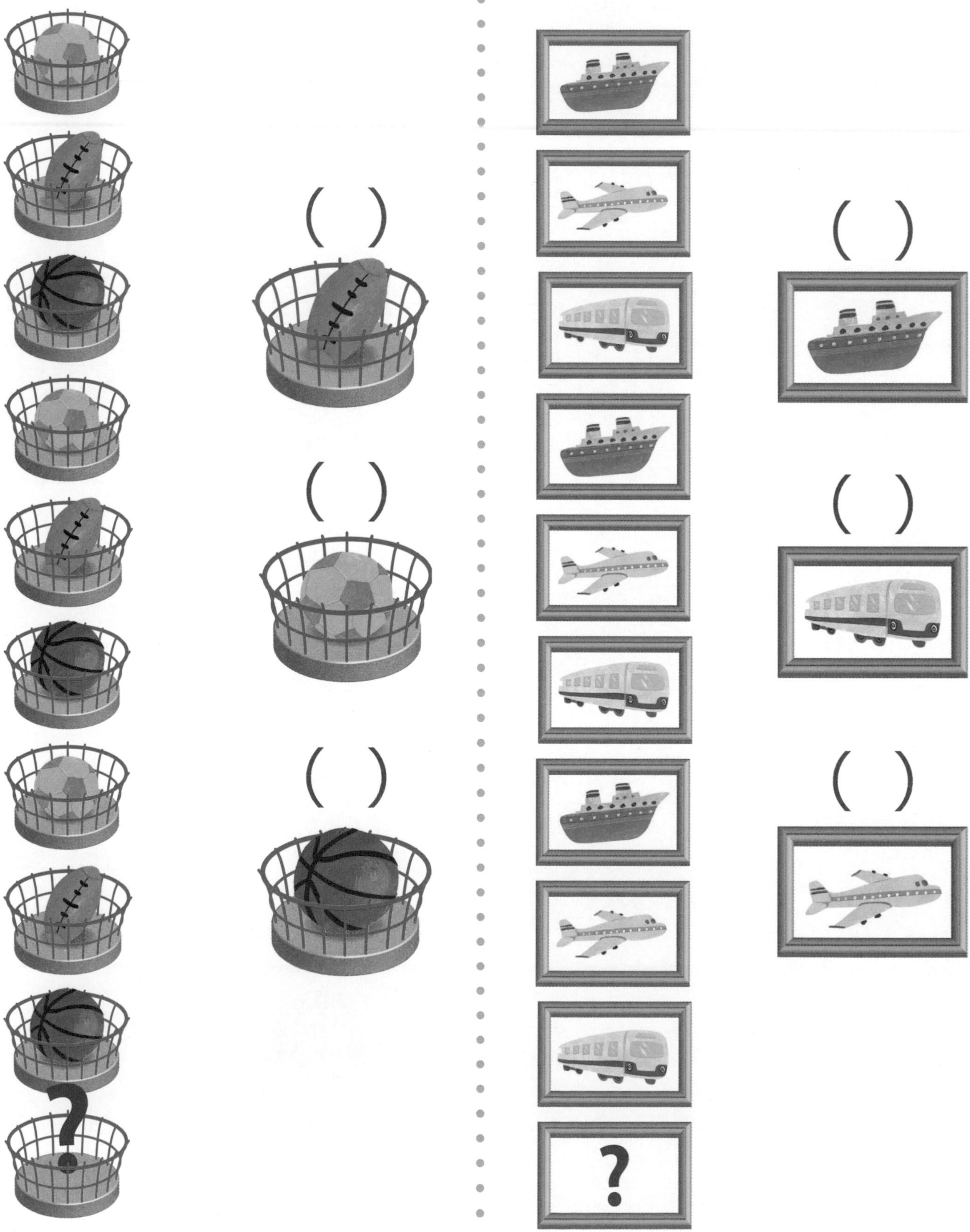

Picture Patterns

Two Shapes

Name

Date

To parents
The patterns are now made up of geometric shapes. Encourage your child to differentiate between the shapes.

■ Write a check mark (✓) above the picture that comes next in the pattern.

?

( )

( )

?

( )

( )

■ Write a check mark (✓) above the picture that comes next in the pattern.

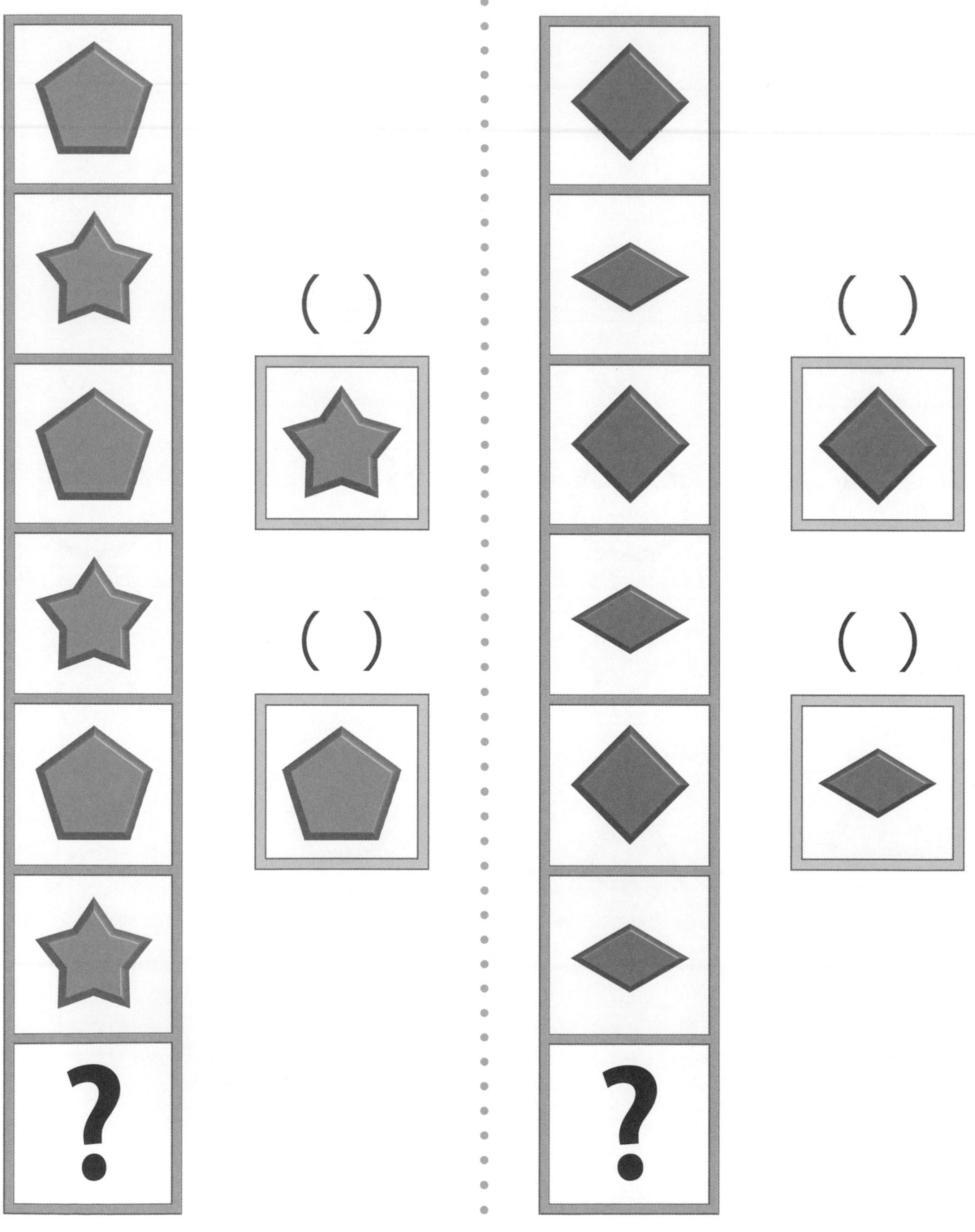

Picture Patterns

Three Shapes

Name

Date

To parents
If your child has difficulty, ask him or her to describe the three different shapes in the sequence.

■ Write a check mark (✓) above the picture that comes next in the pattern.

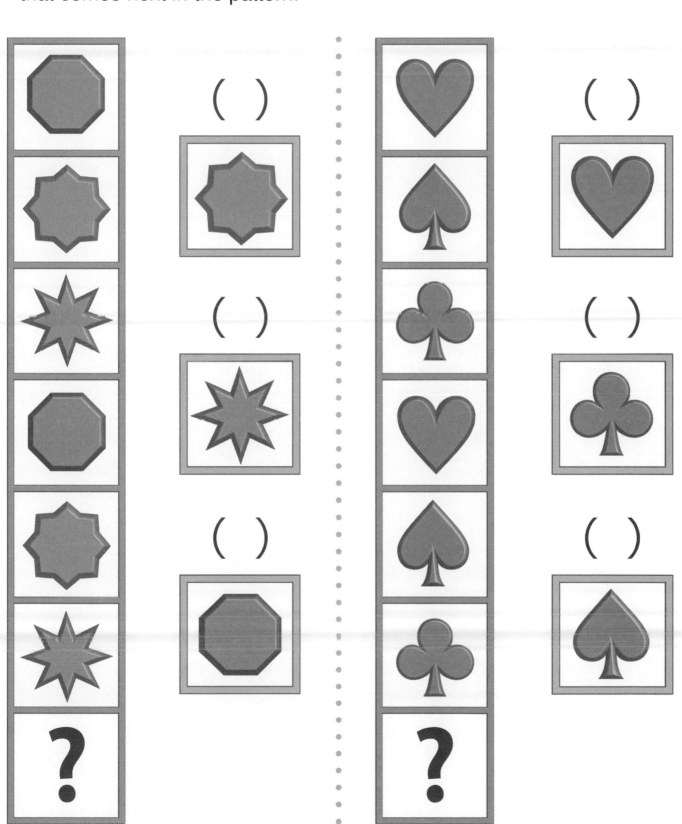

( )

( )

( )

?

( )

( )

( )

?

■ Write a check mark (✓) above the picture that comes next in the pattern.

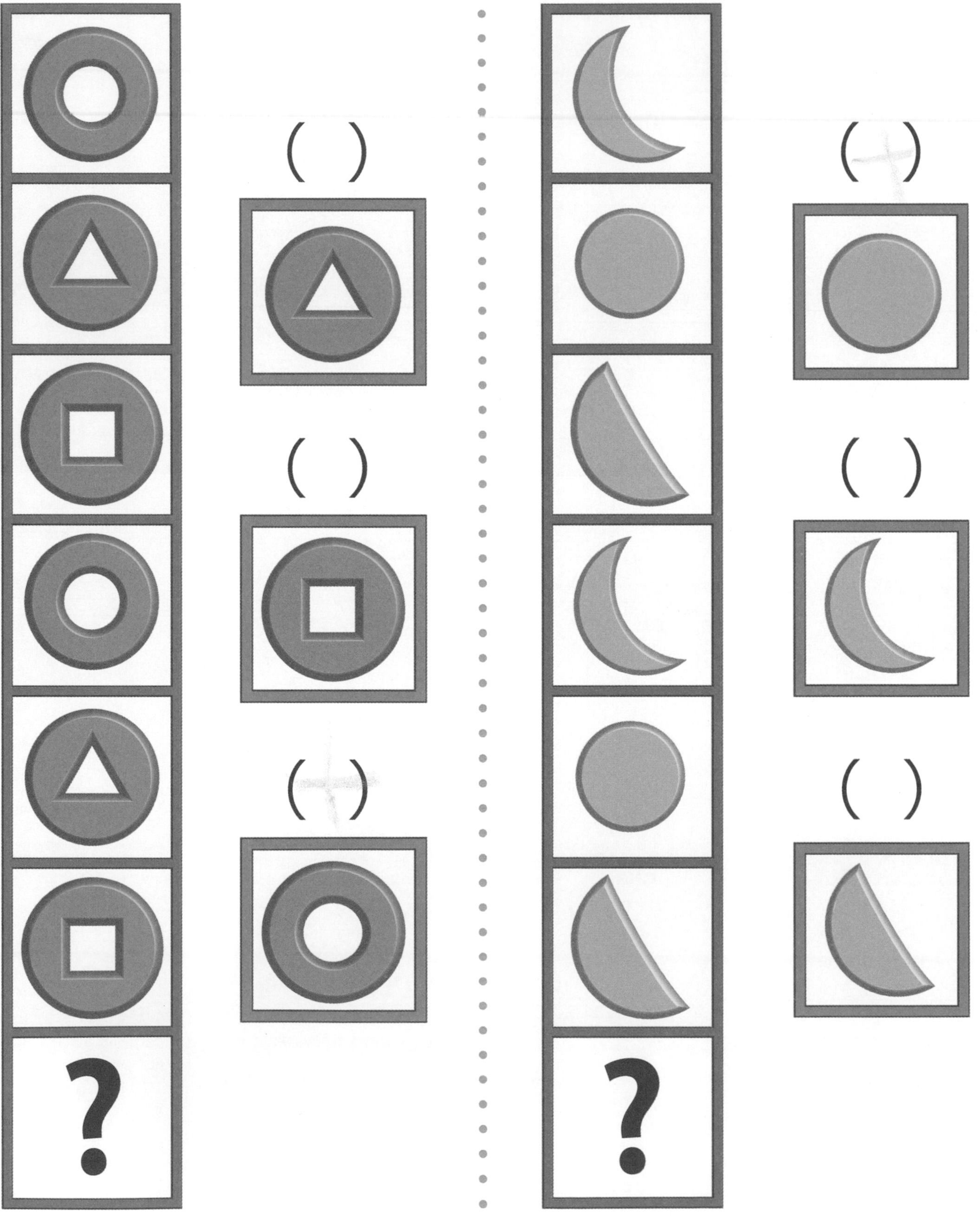

25 Patterns with Rotating Blocks

One Quarter Turn

Name

Date

To parents
The cube has been rotated 90 degrees. If your child has difficulty, it may help to rotate this workbook 90 degrees.

■ Write a check mark (✓) above the picture that comes next in the pattern.

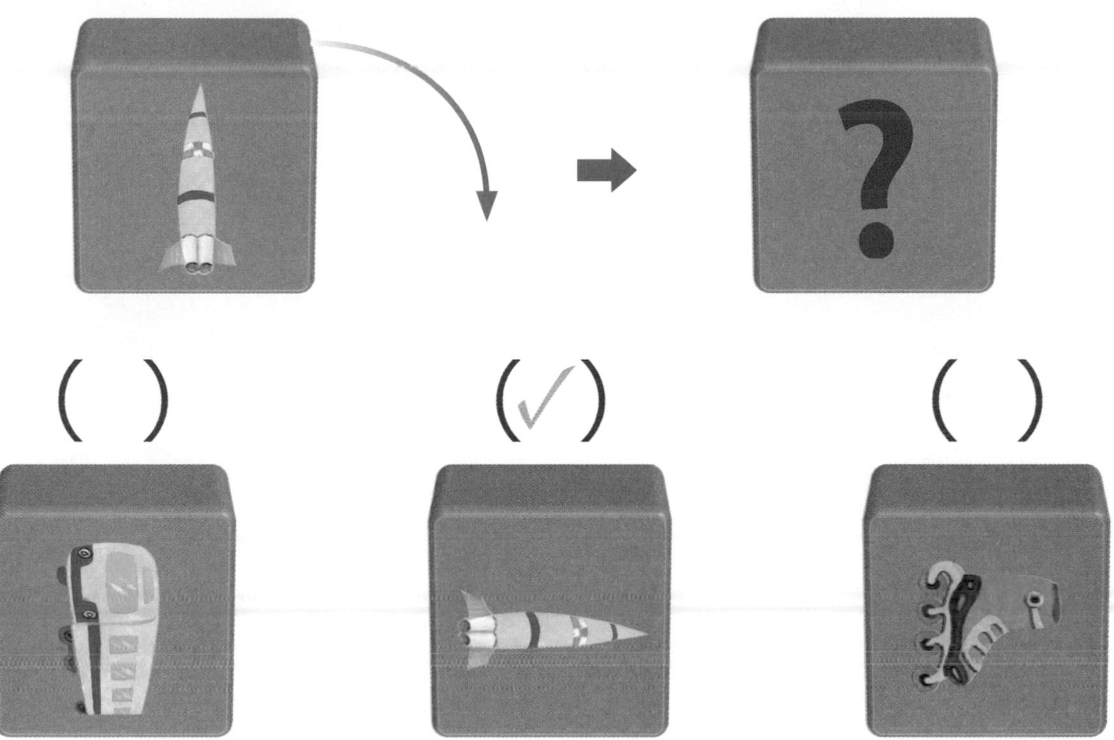

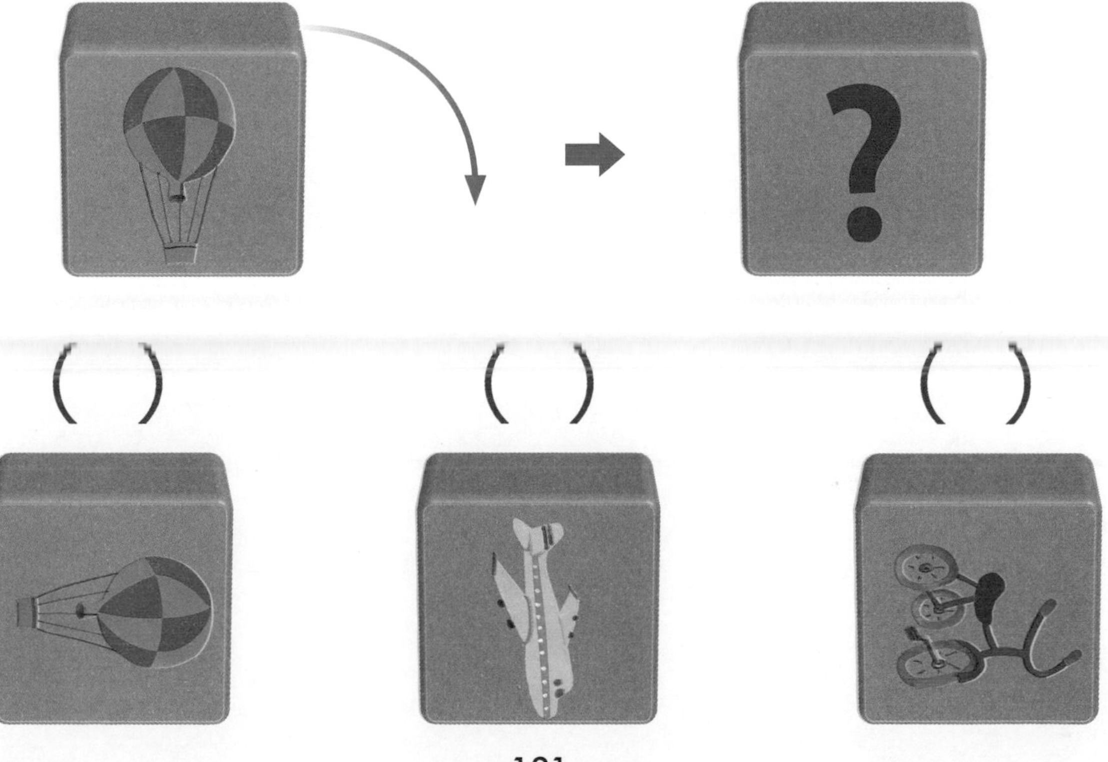

■ Write a check mark (✓) above the picture that comes next in the pattern.

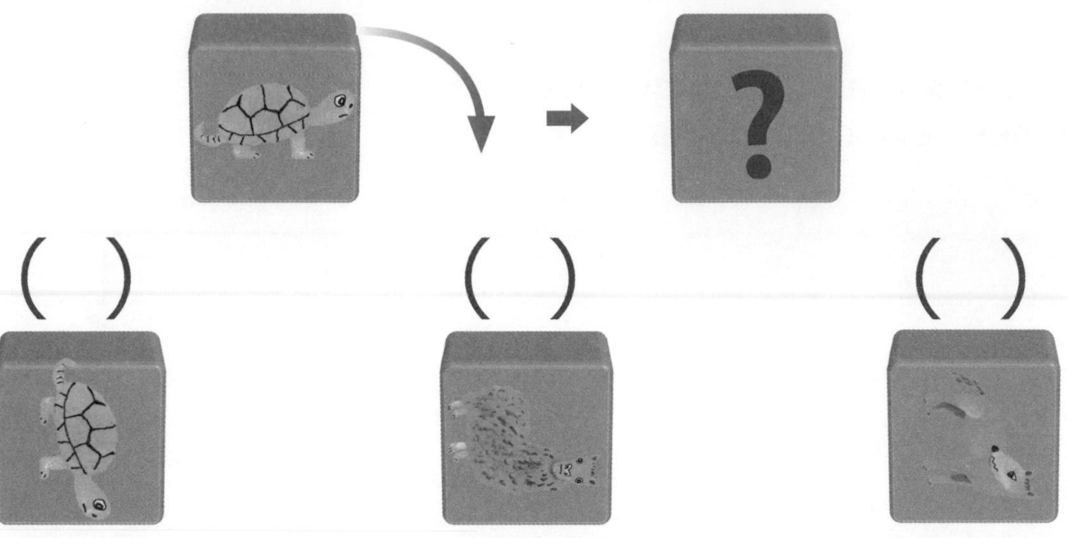

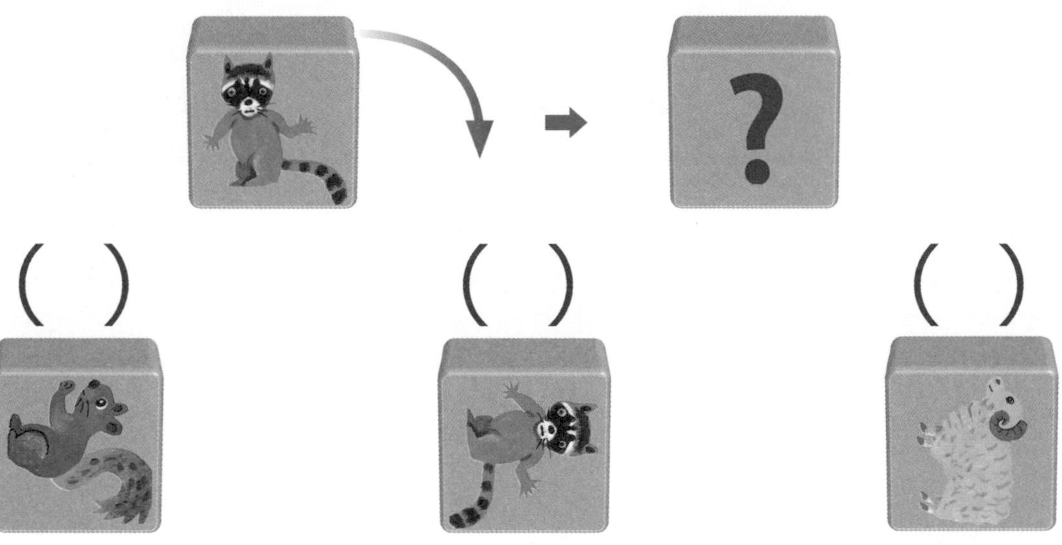

Patterns with Rotating Blocks

One Quarter Turn

Name

Date

To parents
Two pictures in the bottom row have the same illustration. Encourage your child to look carefully at each picture.

■ Write a check mark (✓) above the picture that comes next in the pattern.

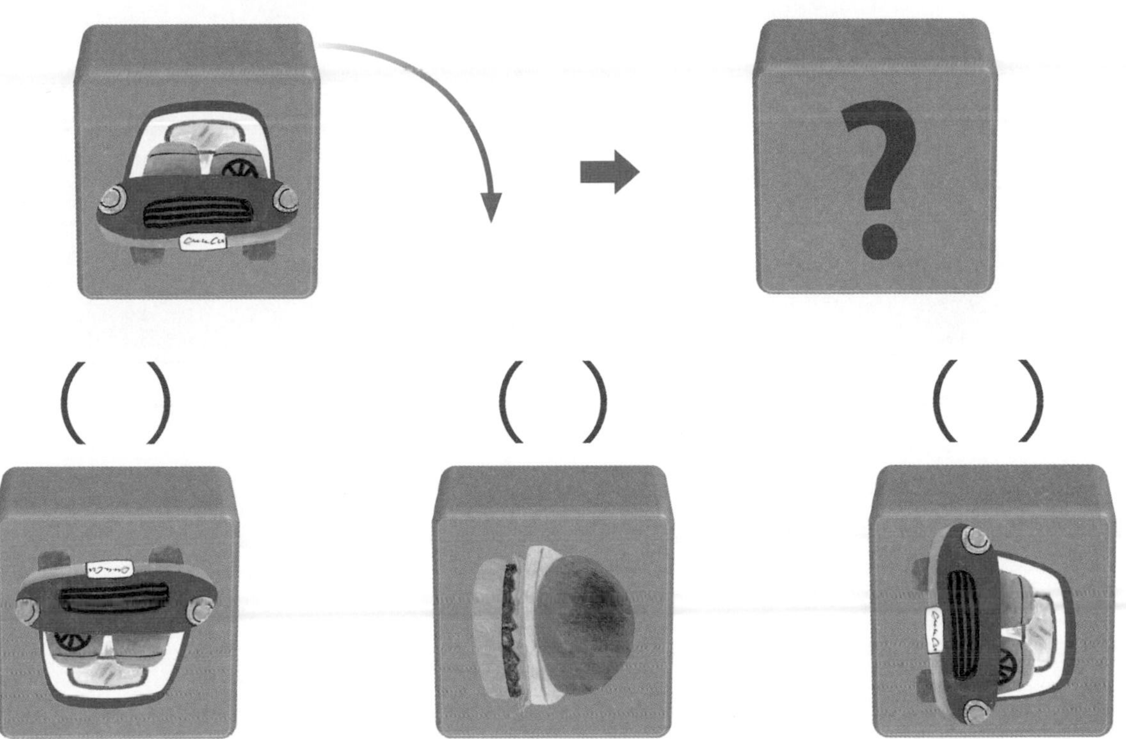

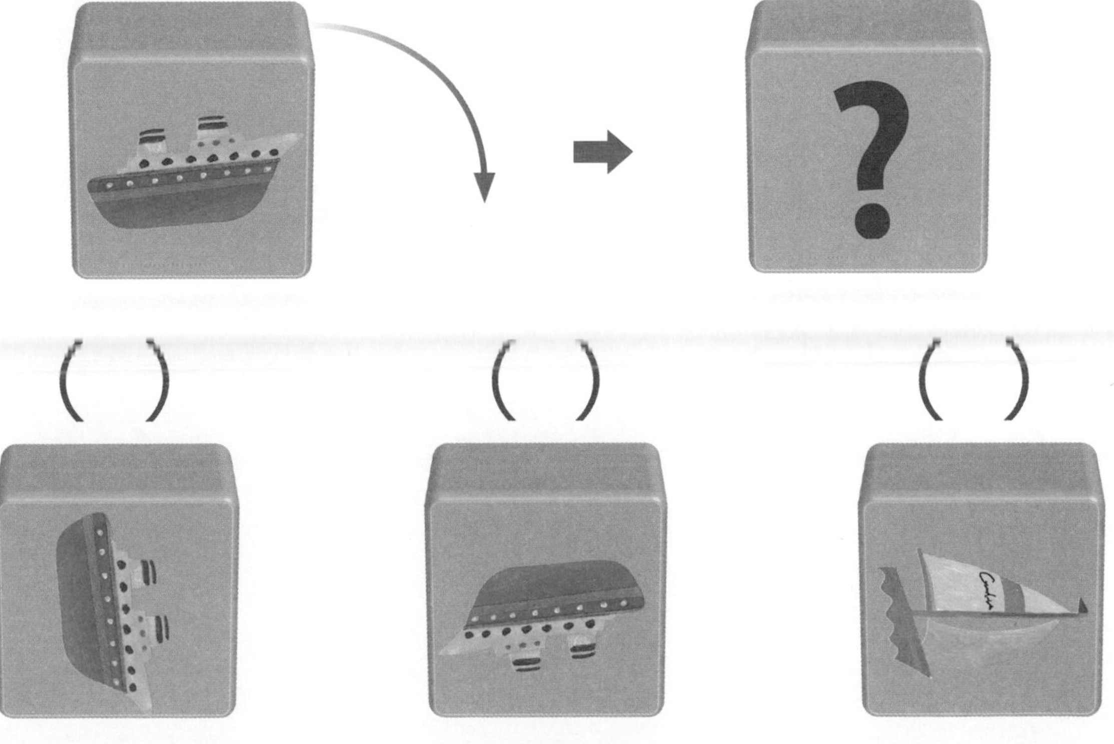

■ Write a check mark (✓) above the picture that comes next in the pattern.

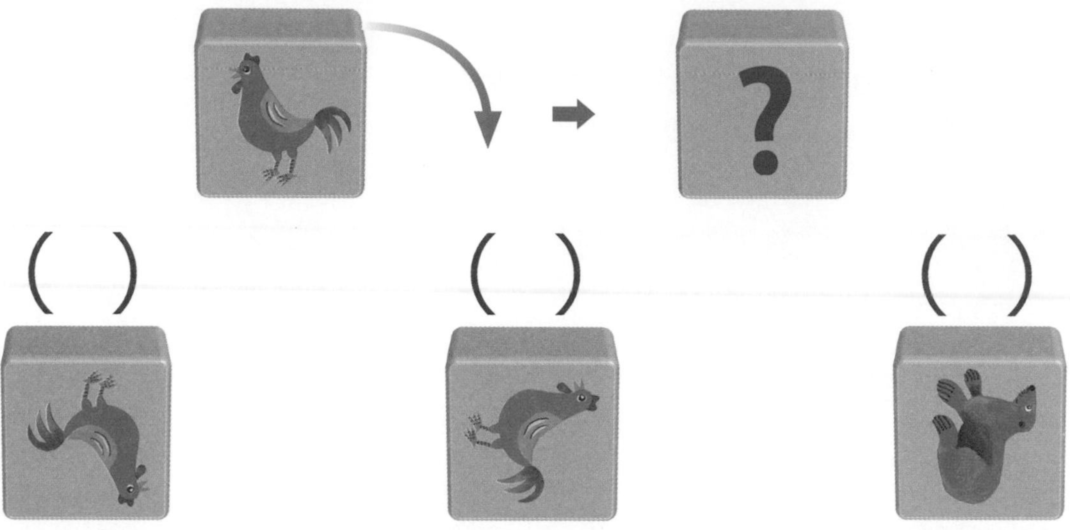

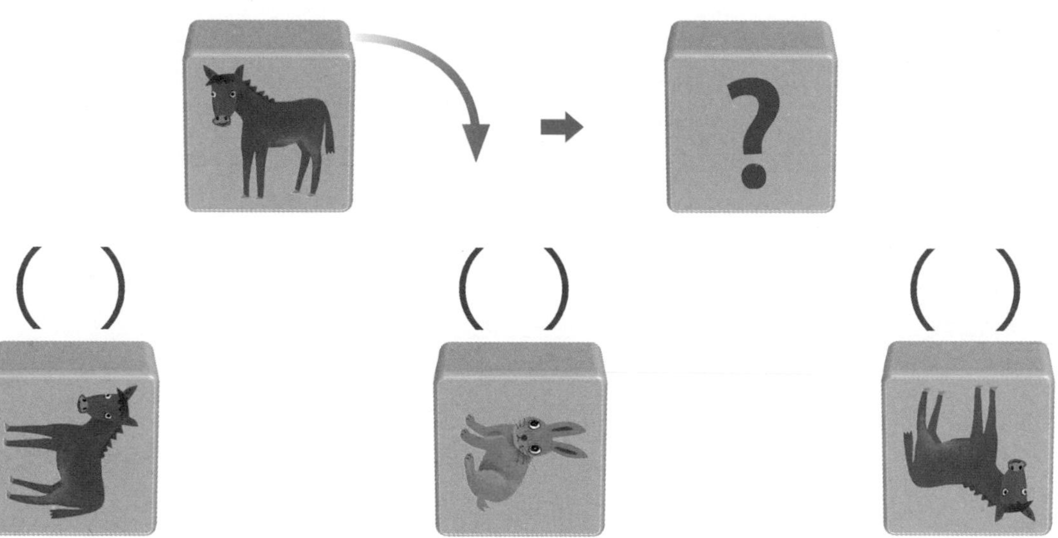

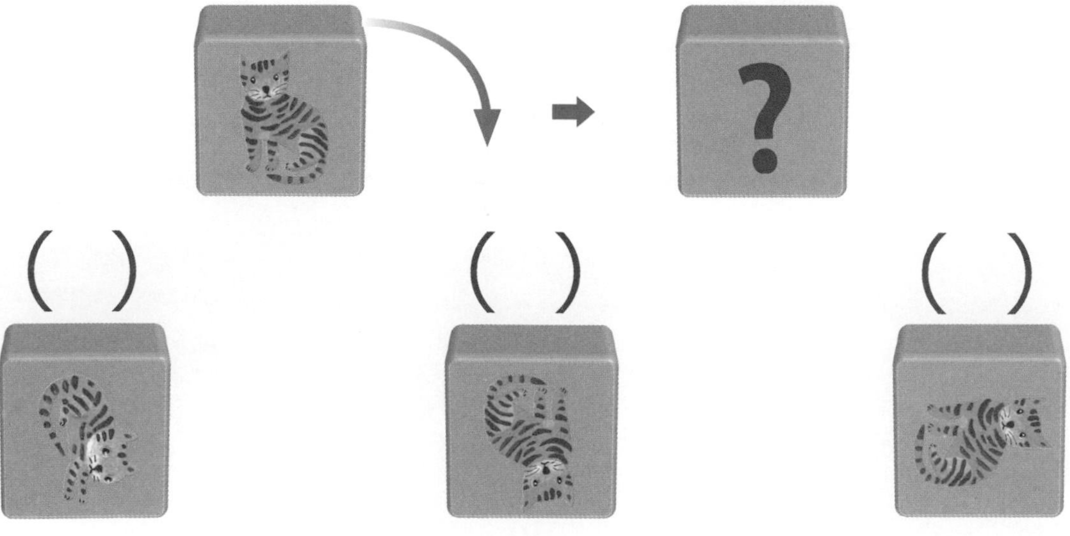

27 Patterns with Rotating Blocks

Two Quarter Turns

Name

Date

To parents
Help your child understand that the cube is upside down after a rotation of 180 degrees.

■ Write a check mark (✓) above the picture that comes next in the pattern.

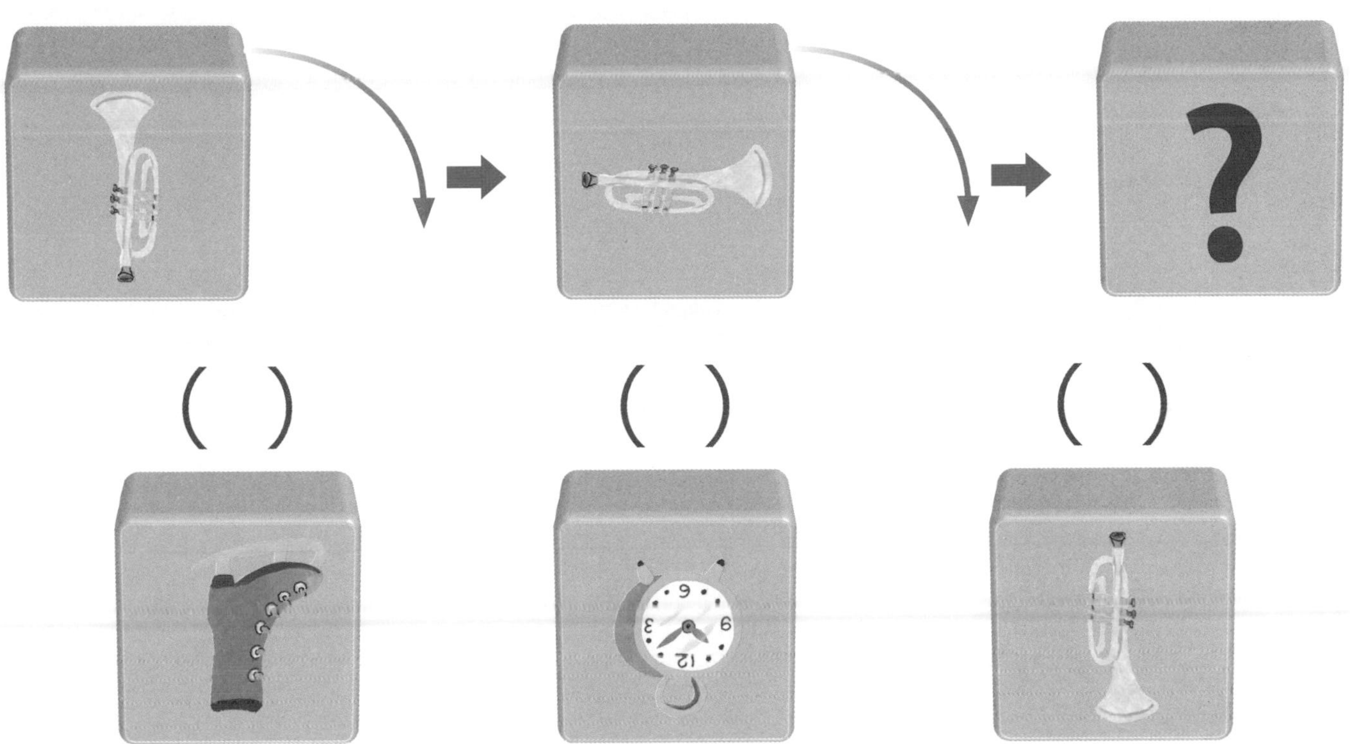

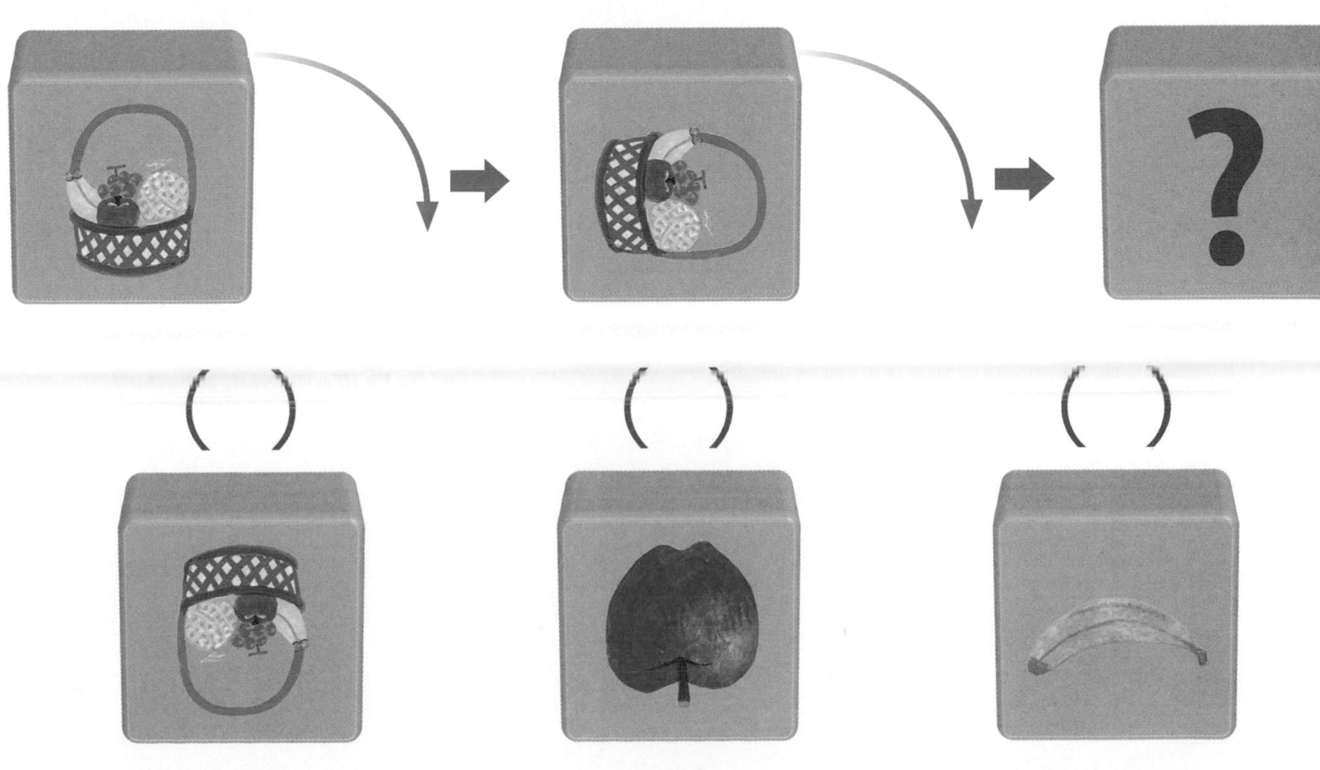

■ Write a check mark (✓) above the picture that comes next in the pattern.

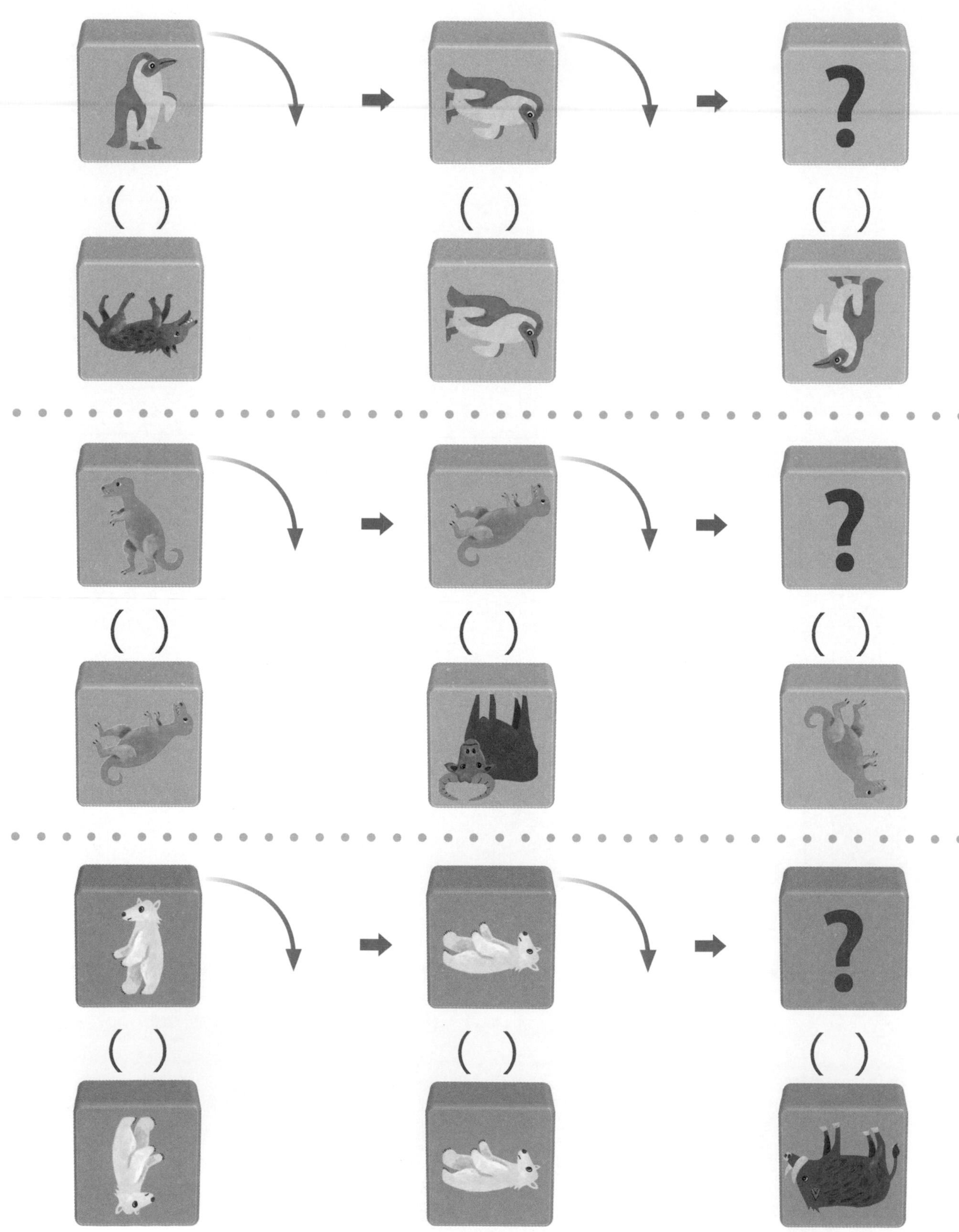

28 Patterns with Rotating Blocks

Two Quarter Turns

Name

Date

To parents
After this activity, you may ask your child what the correct answer would look like if a cube were rotated 360 degrees.

■ Write a check mark (✓) above the picture that comes next in the pattern.

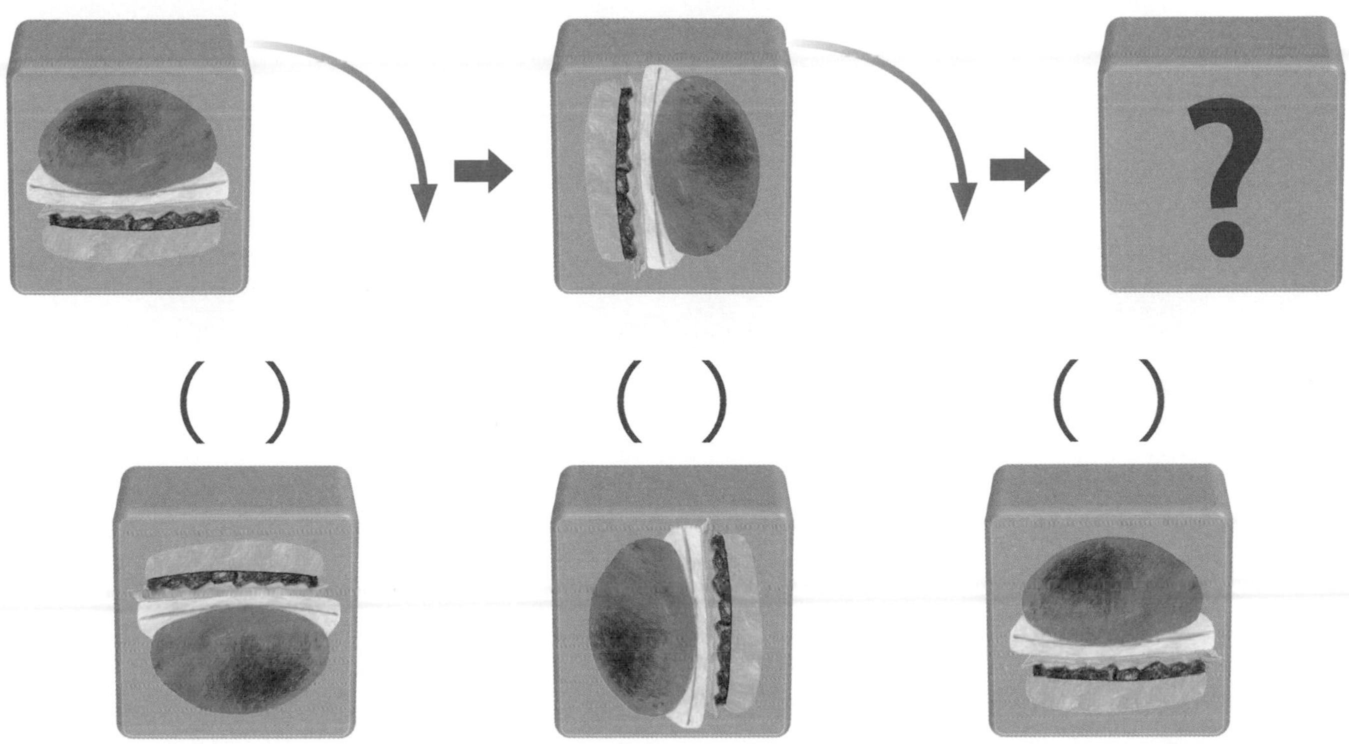

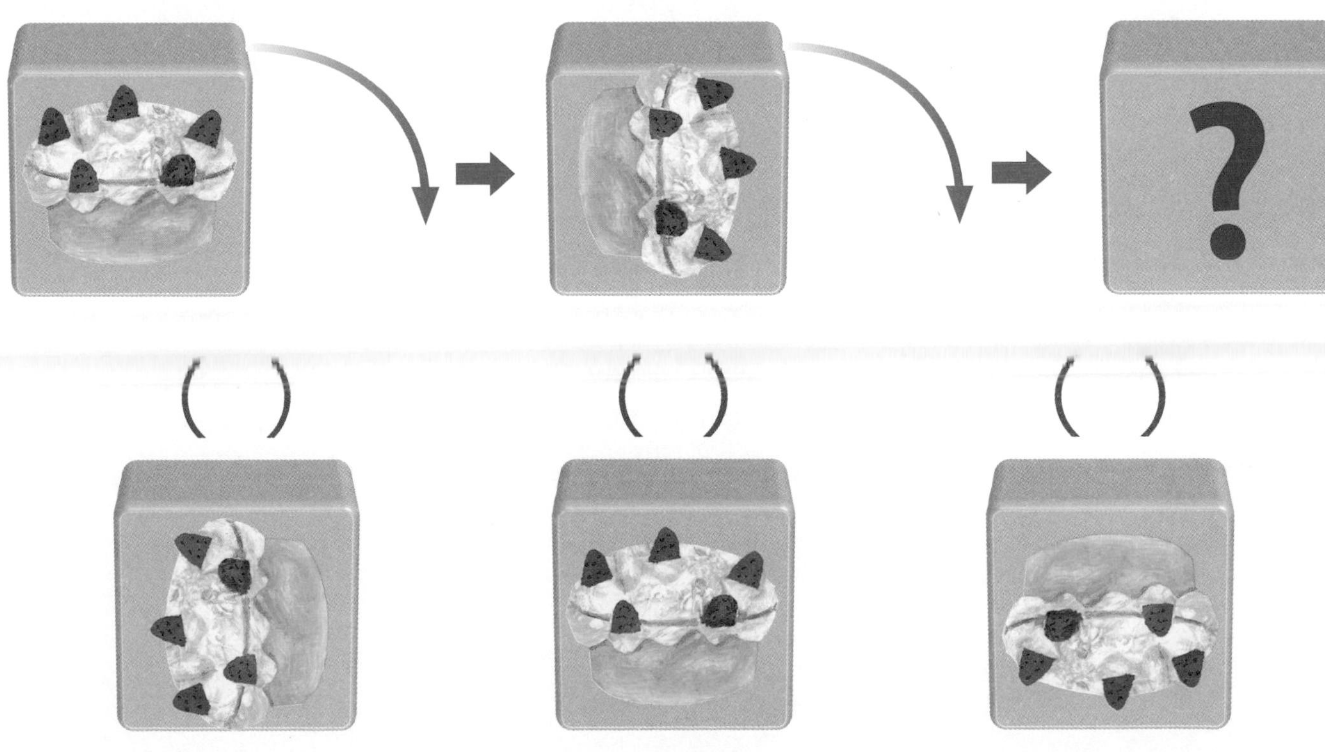

■ Write a check mark (✓) above the picture that comes next in the pattern.

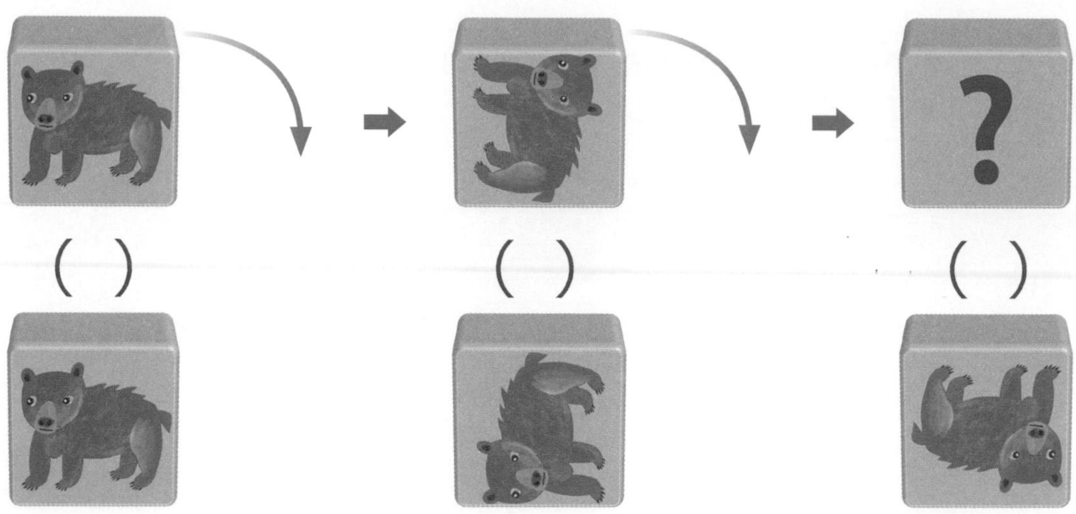

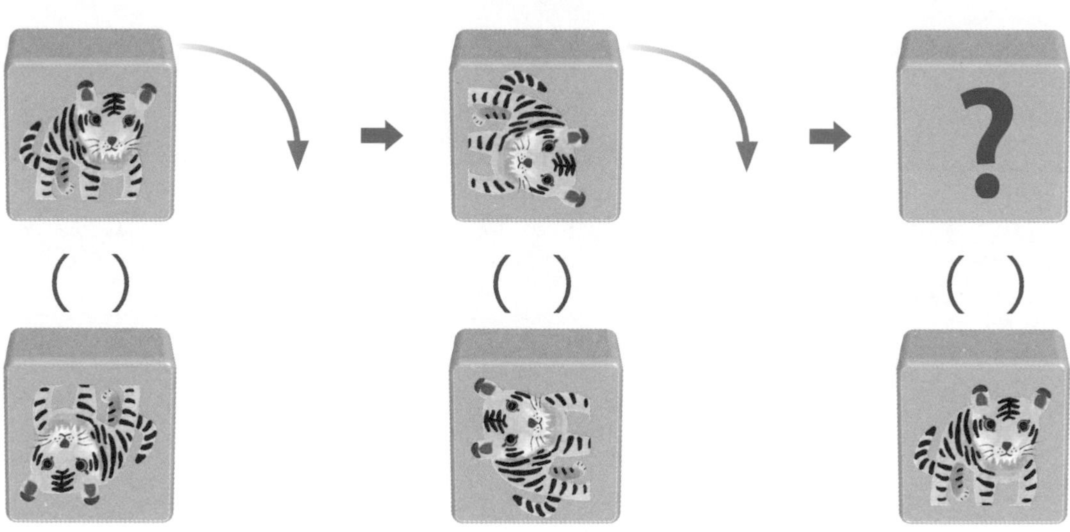

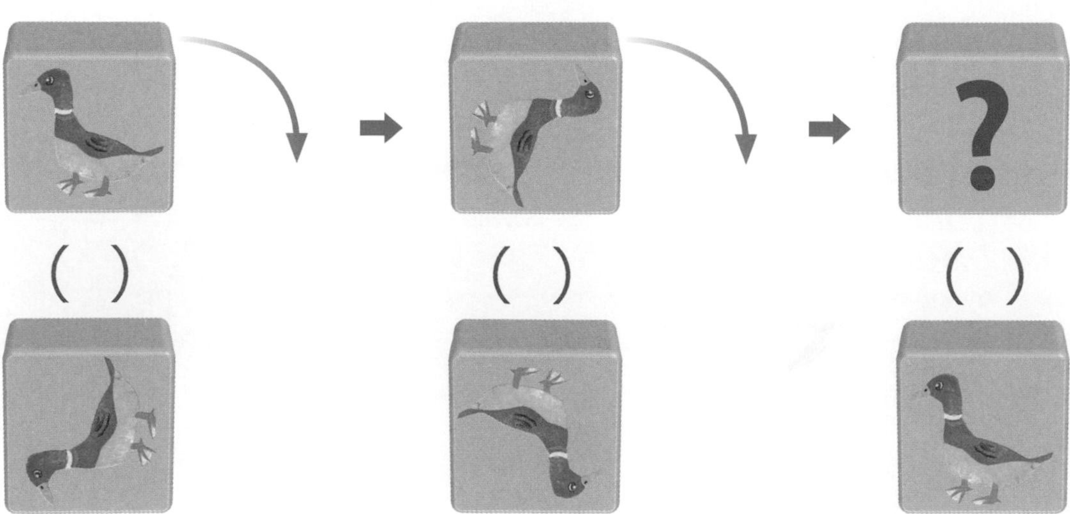

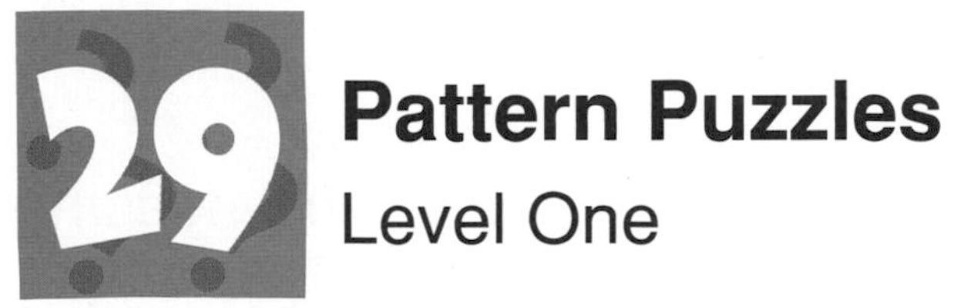

Pattern Puzzles
Level One

Name

Date

To parents
Encourage your child to notice which animals are next to one another.

■ Write a check mark (✓) above the picture that shows the missing animal.

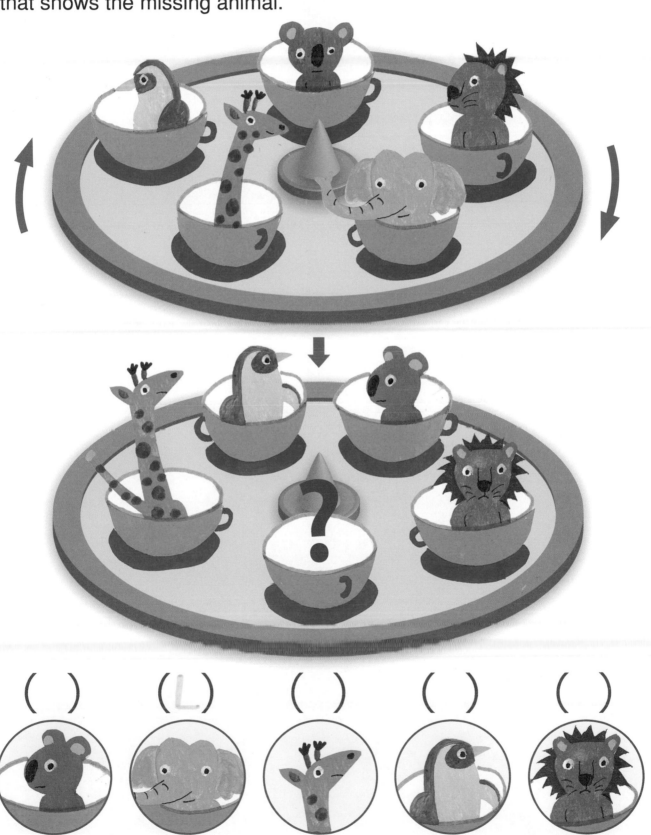

( ) ( ) ( ) ( ) ( )

■ Write a check mark (✓) above the picture that shows the missing animal.

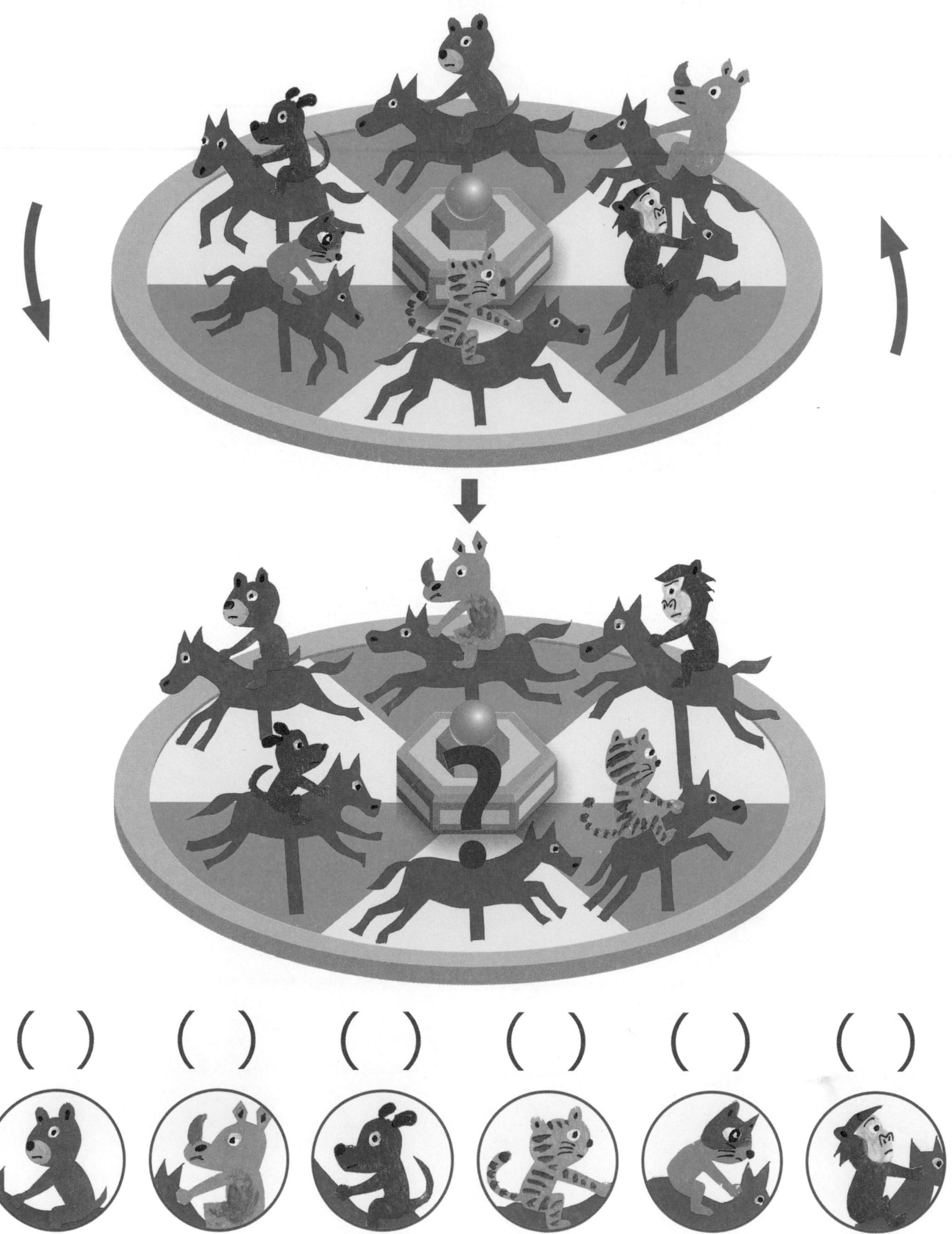

30 Pattern Puzzles
Level Two

Name

Date

To parents
If your child has difficulty, ask him or her how many positions an animal has moved.

■ Write a check mark (✓) above the picture that shows the missing animal.

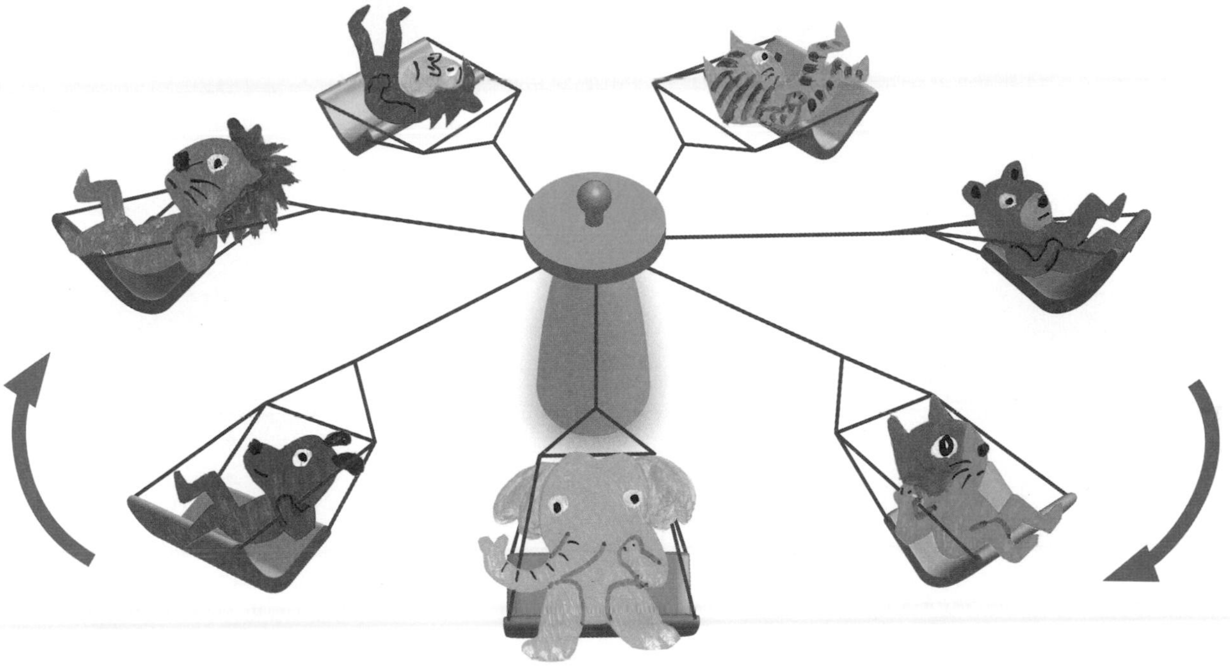

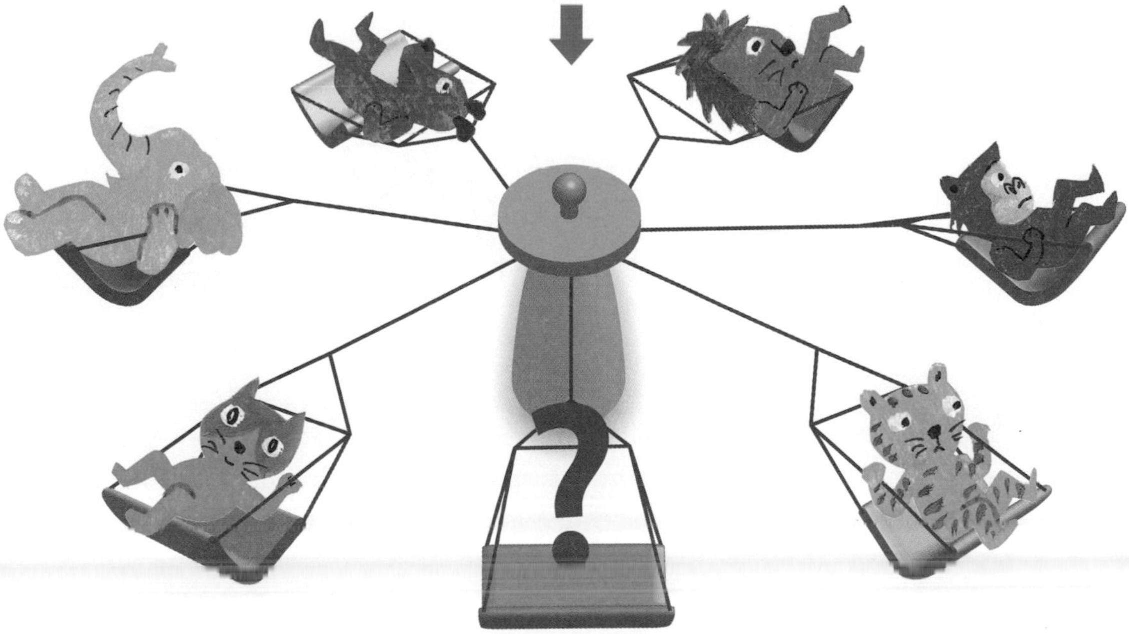

( ) ( ) ( ) ( ) ( ) ( ) ( )

■ Write a check mark (✓) above the picture that shows the missing sail.

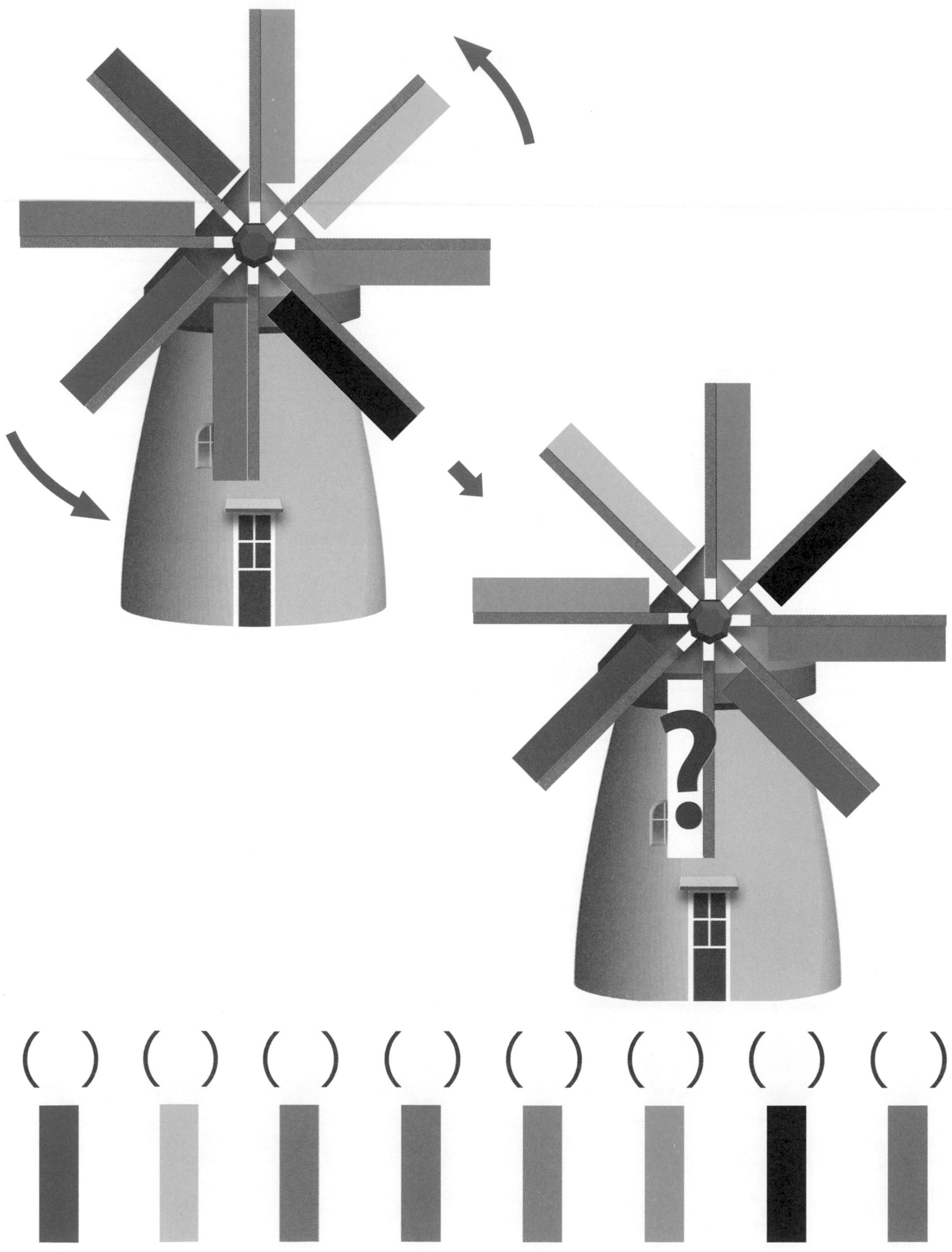

( ) ( ) ( ) ( ) ( ) ( ) ( ) ( )

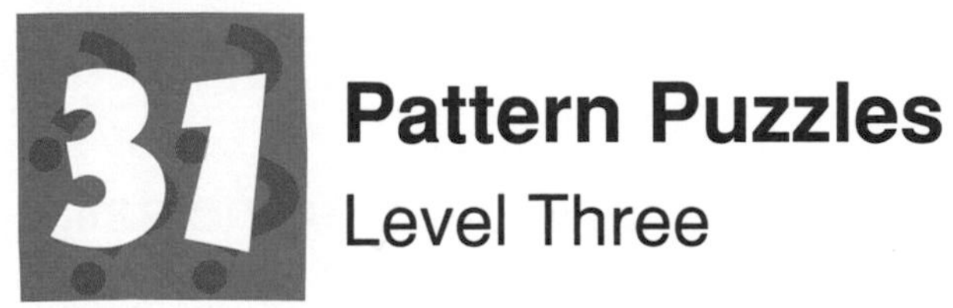

Pattern Puzzles
Level Three

Name

Date

To parents
The activities are now more difficult because part of the sequence is hidden. Encourage your child to find a pattern.

■ Write a check mark (✓) above the picture that shows the missing animal.

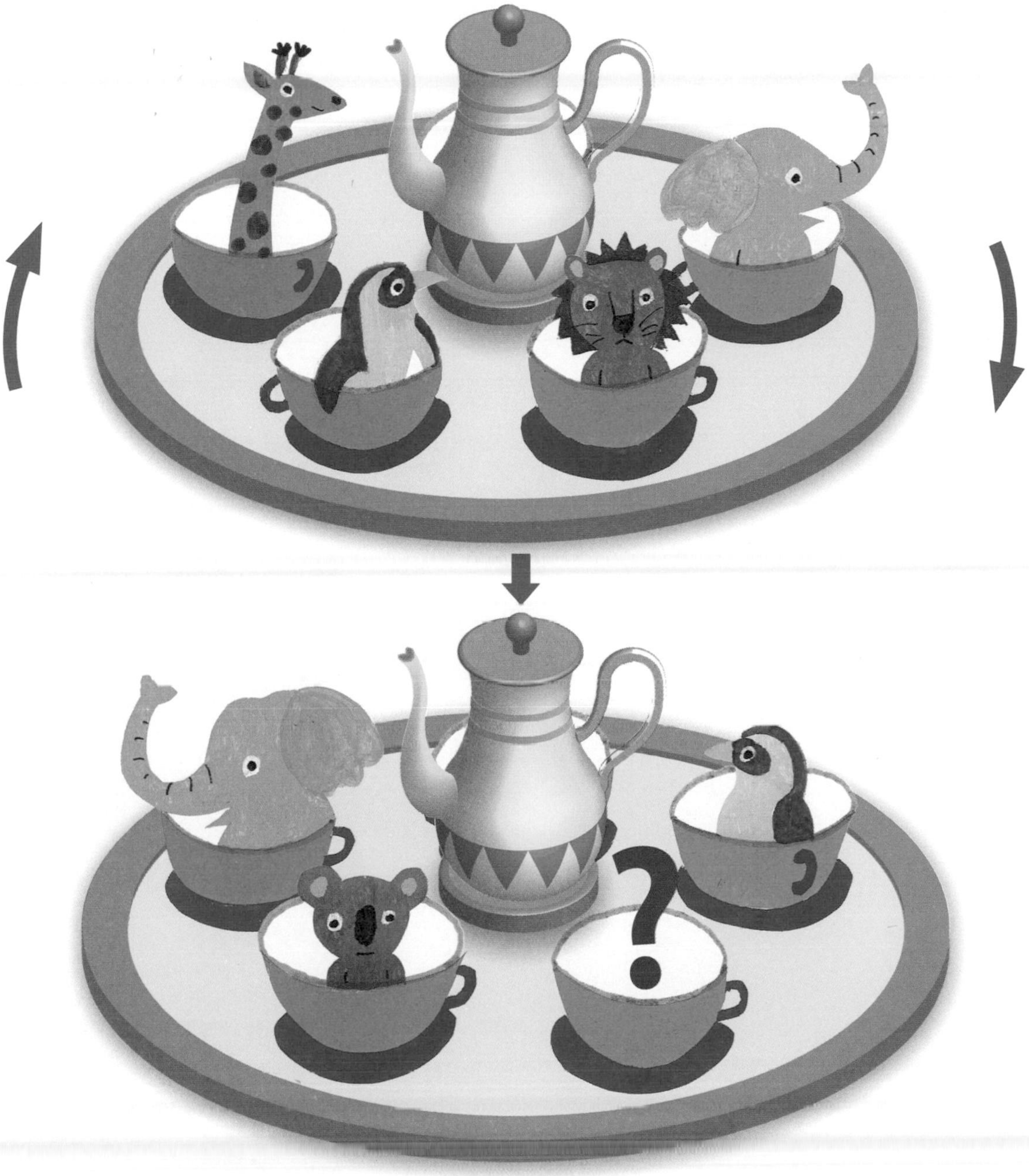

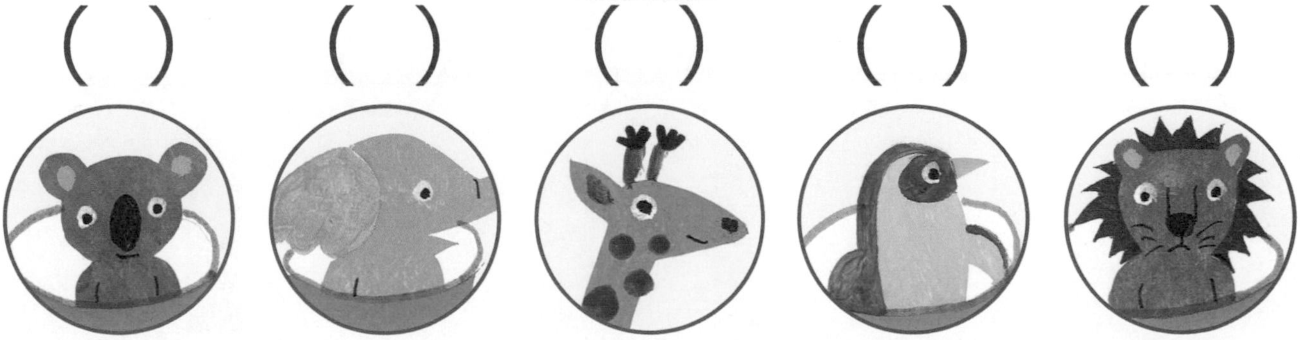

( ) ( ) ( ) ( ) ( )

■ Write a check mark (✓) above the picture that shows the missing sail.

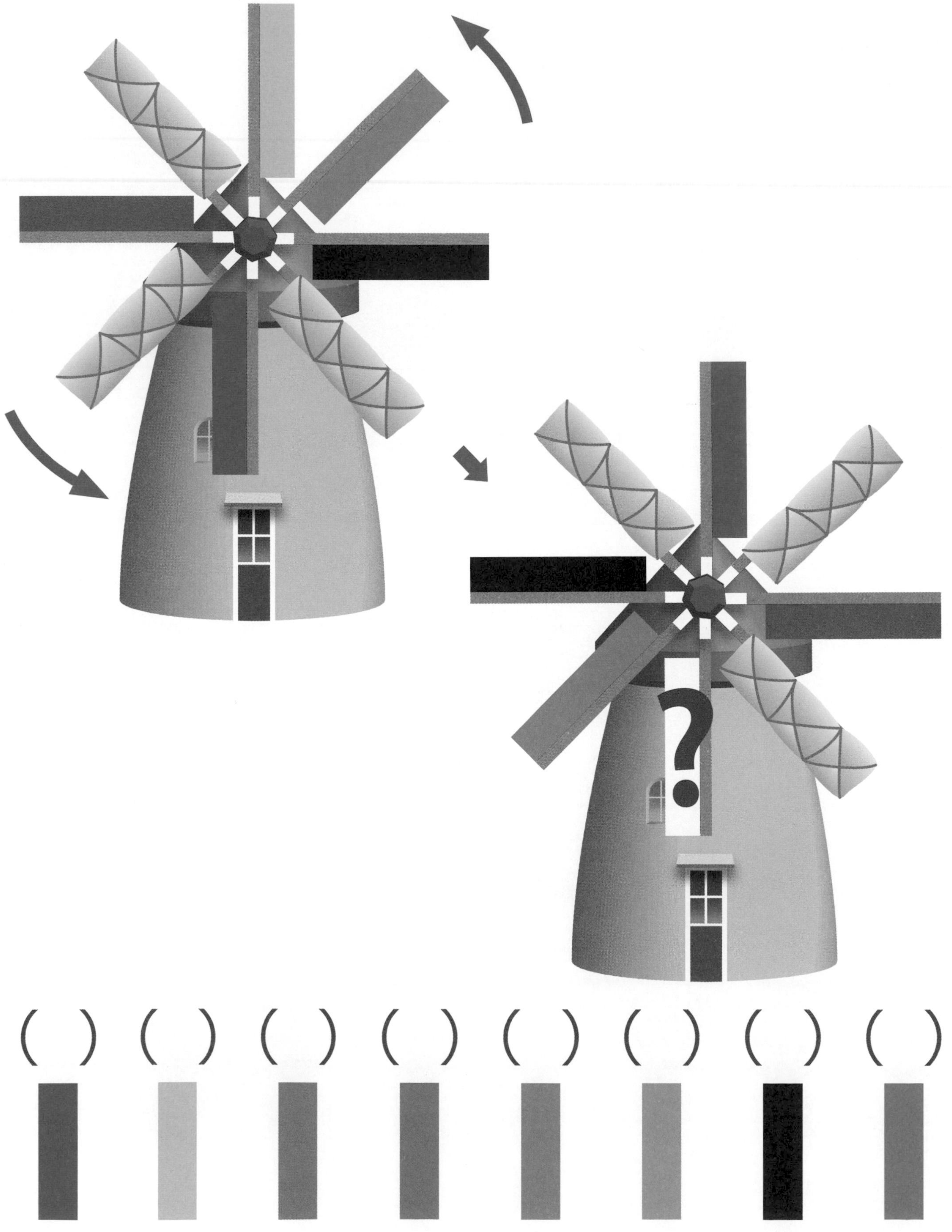

( ) ( ) ( ) ( ) ( ) ( ) ( ) ( )

Pattern Puzzles

Level Four

Name

Date

To parents
To identify the missing animal, it may help to identify which animals are hidden.

■ Write a check mark (✓) above the picture that shows the missing animal.

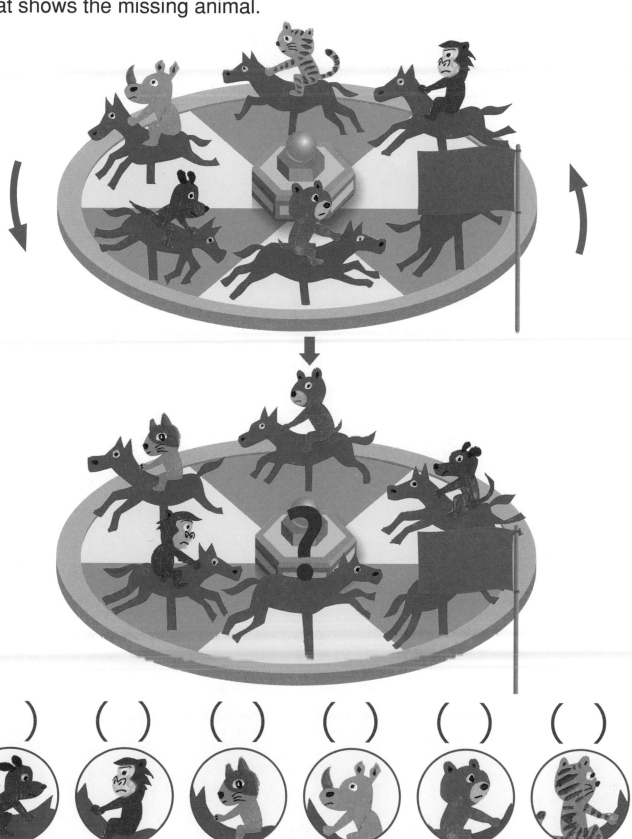

( ) ( ) ( ) ( ) ( ) ( )

■ Write a check mark (✓) above the picture that shows the missing animal.

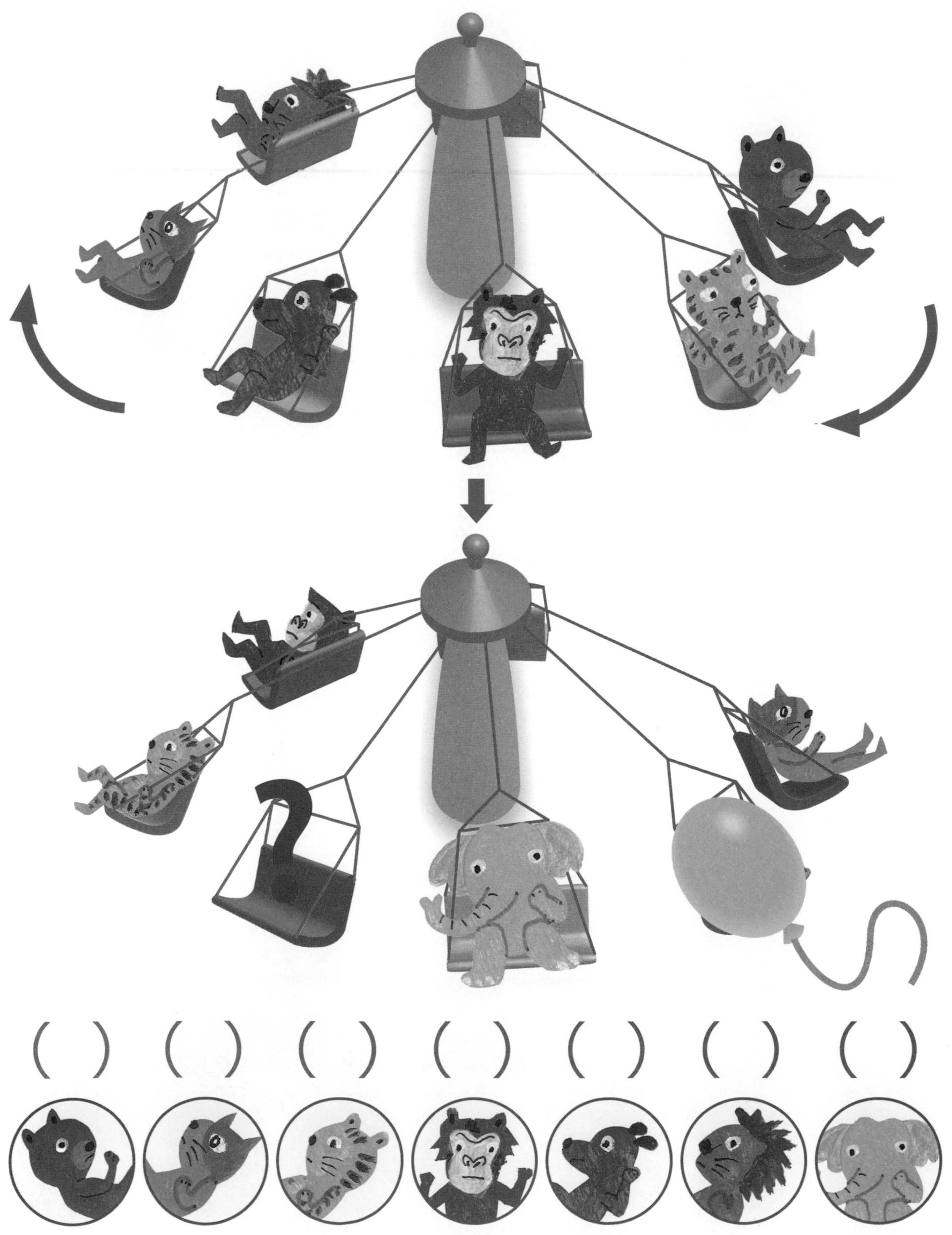

( ) ( ) ( ) ( ) ( ) ( ) ( )

33 Color and Shape Patterns
Level One

Name

Date

To parents
Colored pencils work best for these activities because the shape will remain visible after coloring.

■ Follow the pattern to color the picture in the margin.

■ Follow the pattern to color the picture in the margin.

34 Color and Shape Patterns

Level Two

Name

Date

To parents
If your child has difficulty with this exercise, guide him or her to select the shape first and then the color.

■ Follow the pattern to color the correct picture in the margin.

■ Follow the pattern to color the correct picture in the margin.

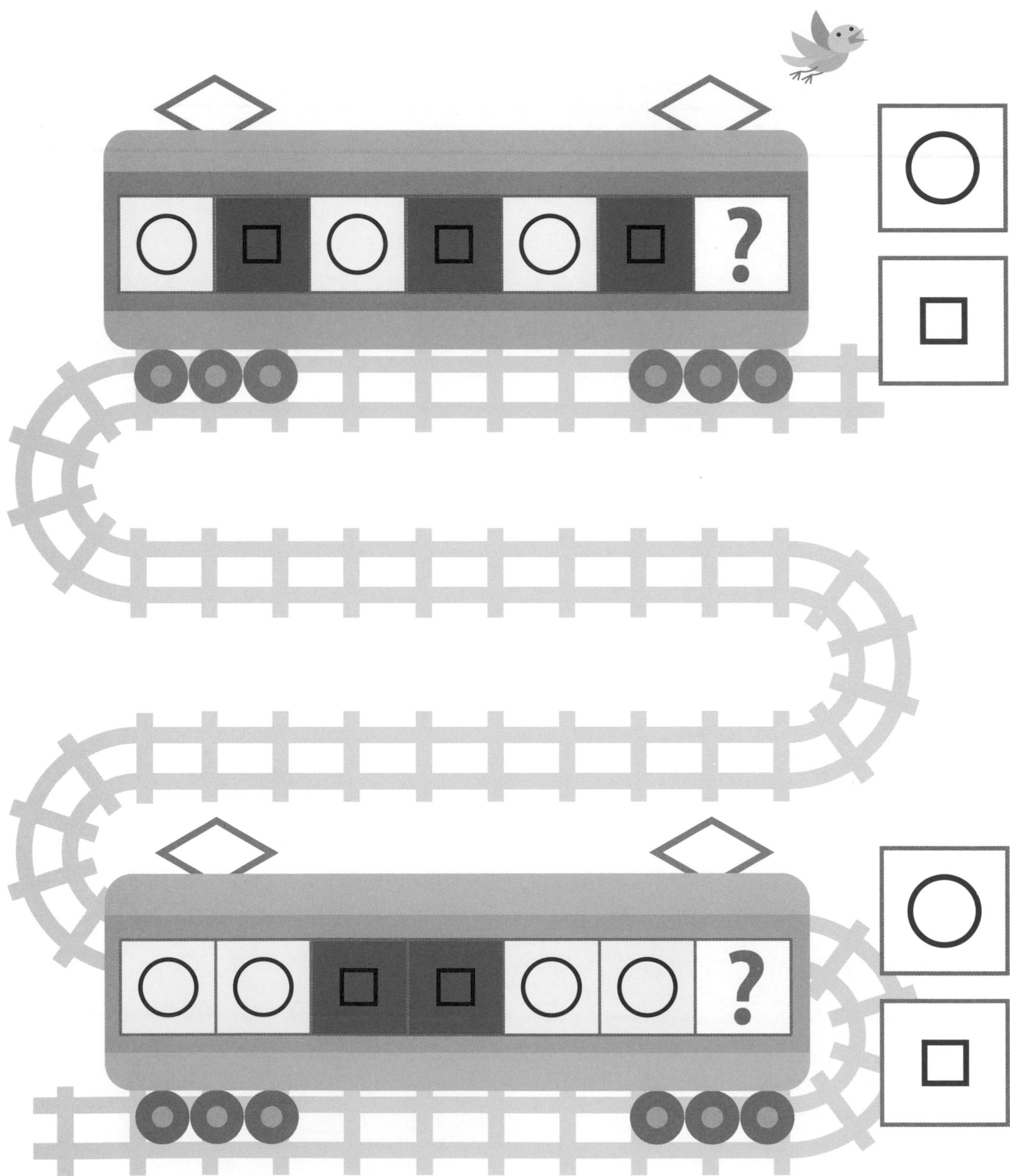

35 Color and Shape Patterns

Level Three

Name

Date

To parents
For each pattern, the complete sequence is shown at least once.

■ Follow the pattern to color the correct picture in the margin.

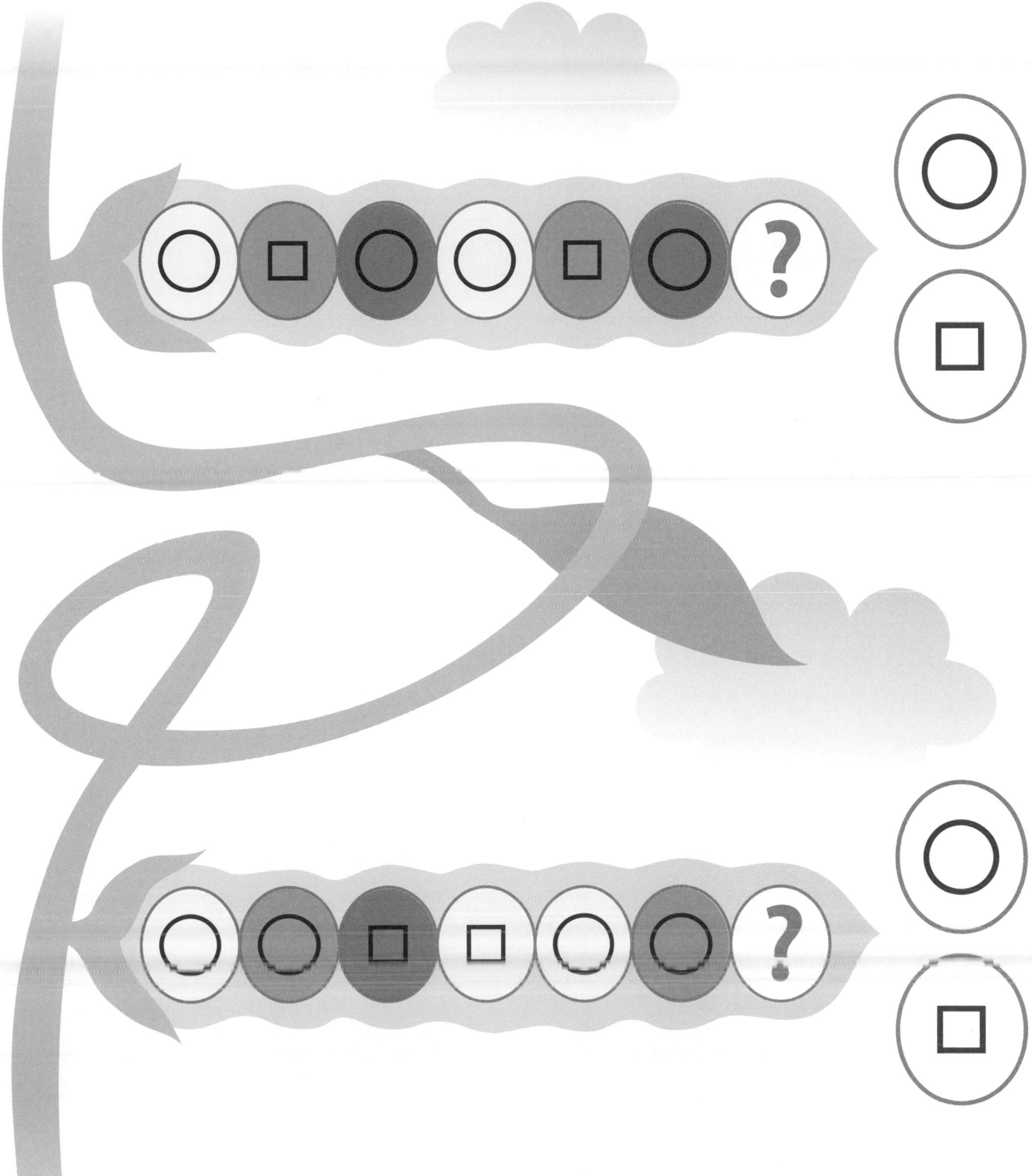

?

?

■ Follow the pattern to color the correct picture in the margin.

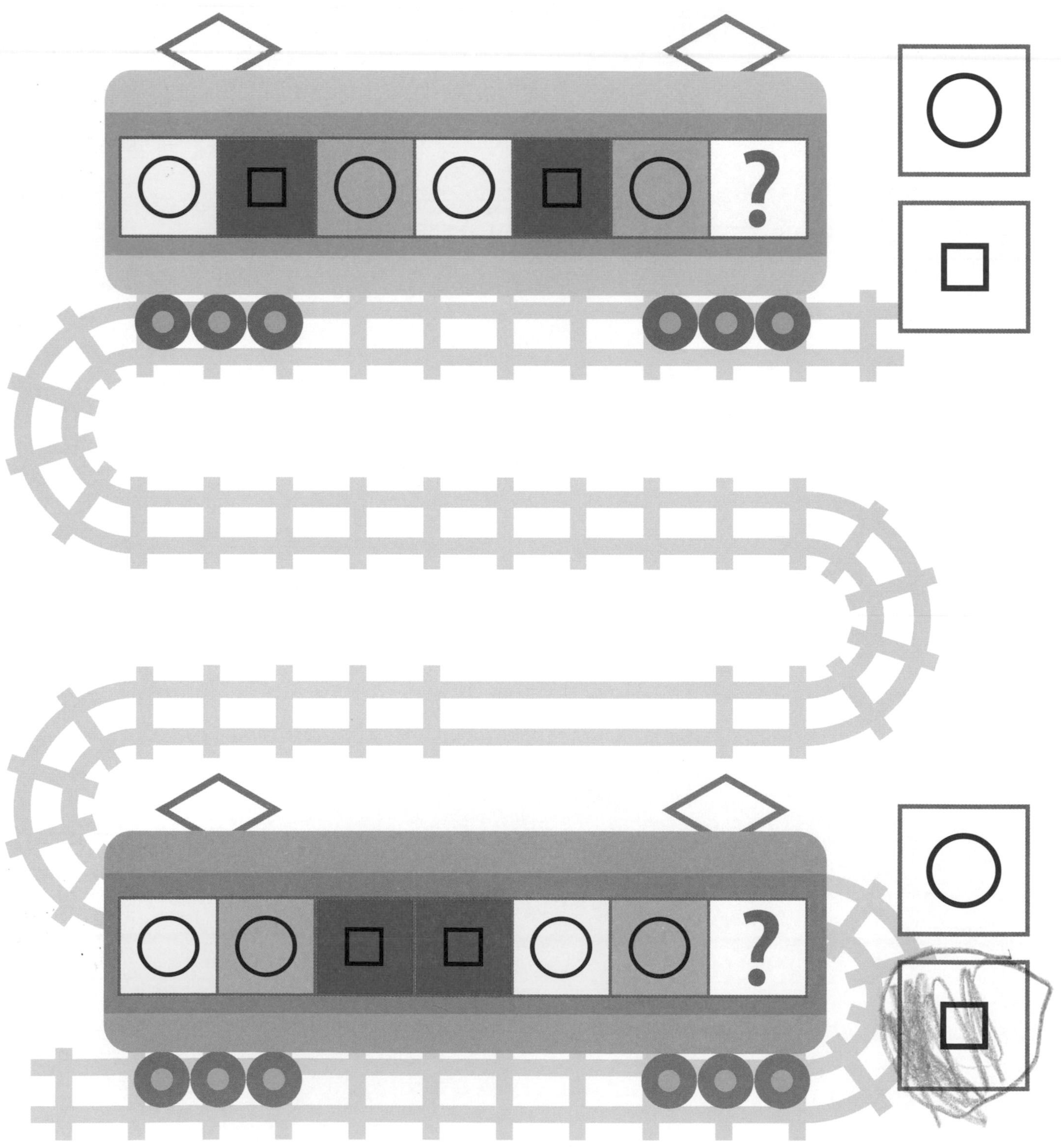

Color and Shape Patterns

Level Four

Name

Date

■ Follow the pattern to color the correct picture in the margin.

?

?

To parents
This is the last exercise of this section. Please praise your child for the effort it took to complete this workbook.

■ Follow the pattern to color the correct picture in the margin.

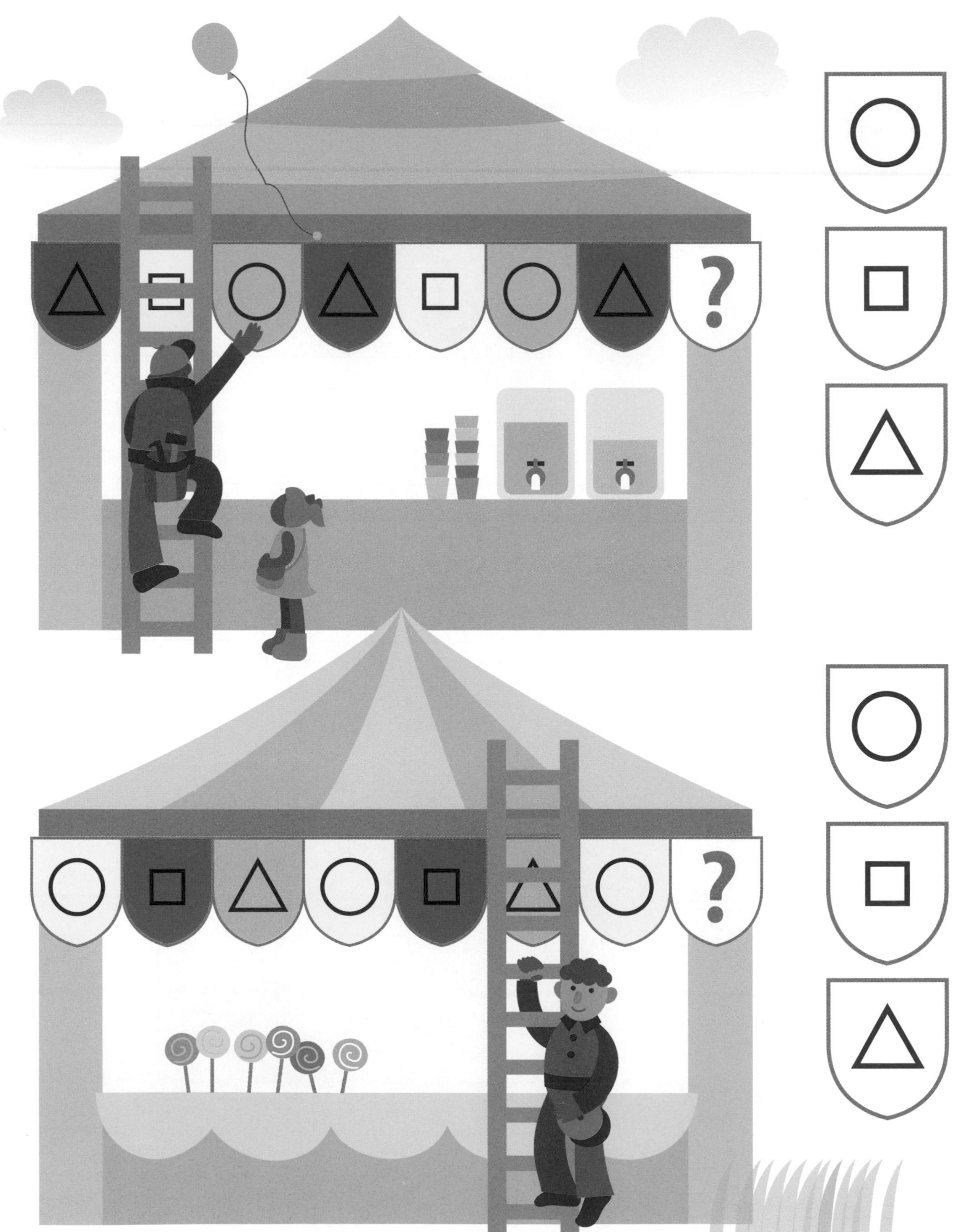

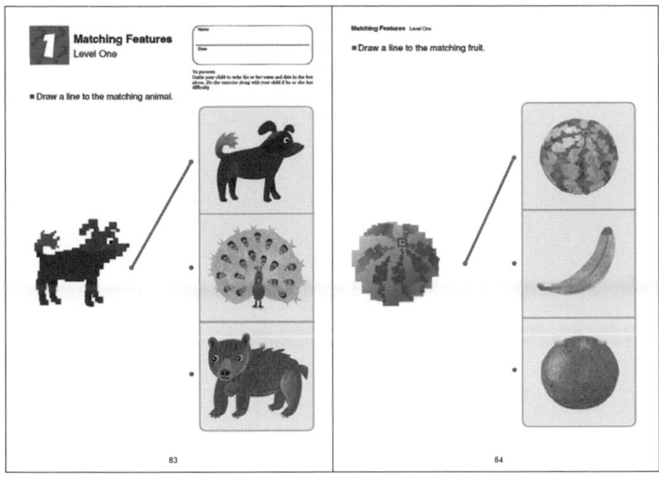

pages 83 and 84

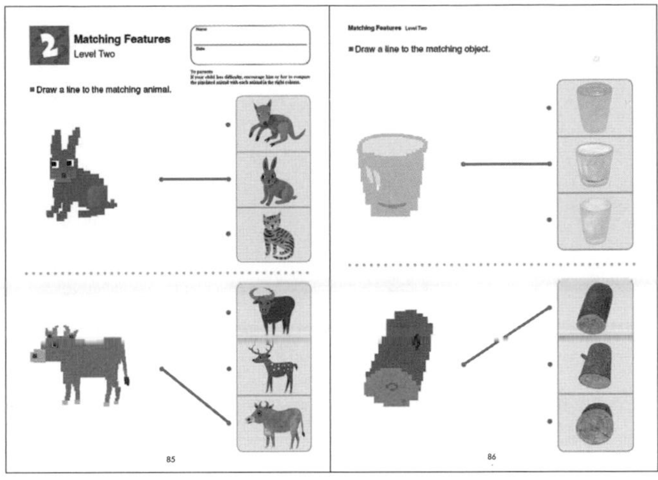

pages 85 and 86

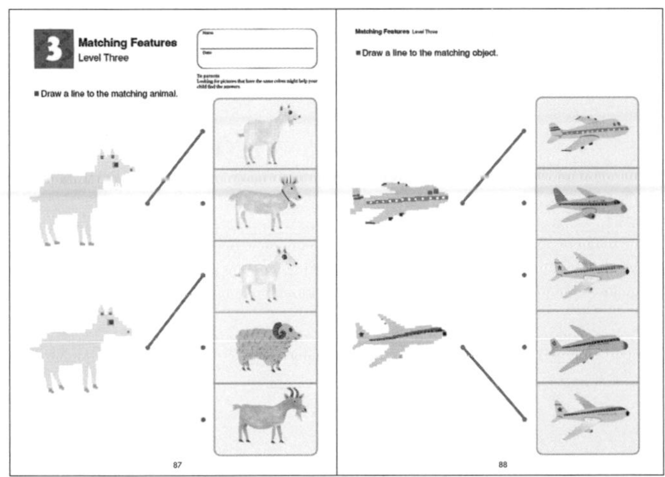

pages 87 and 88

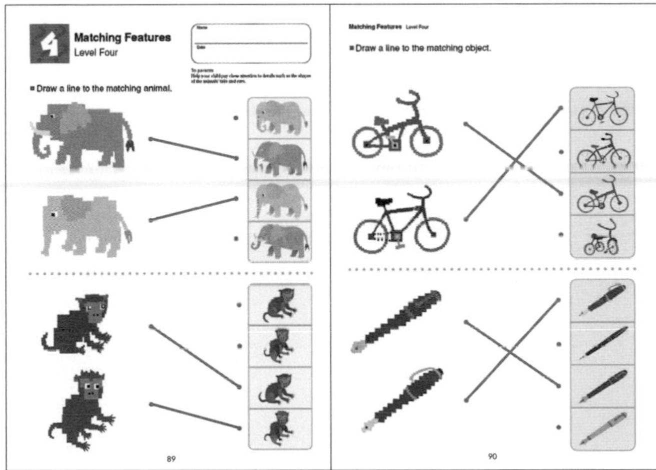

pages 89 and 90

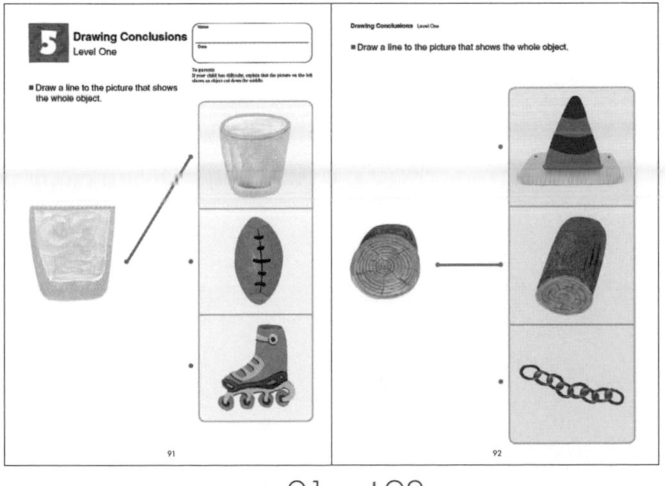

pages 91 and 92

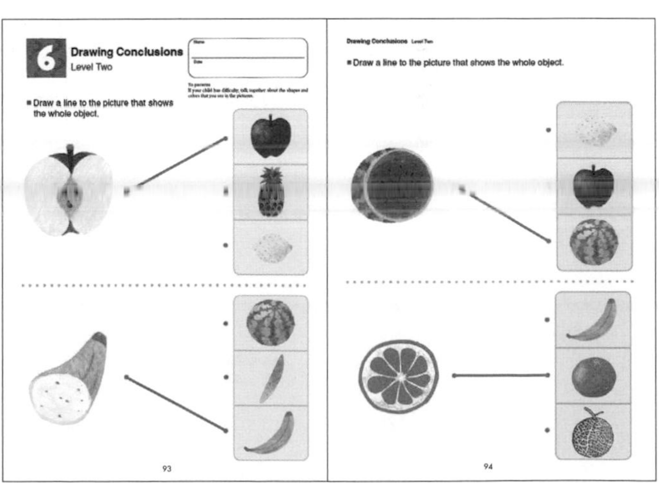

pages 93 and 94

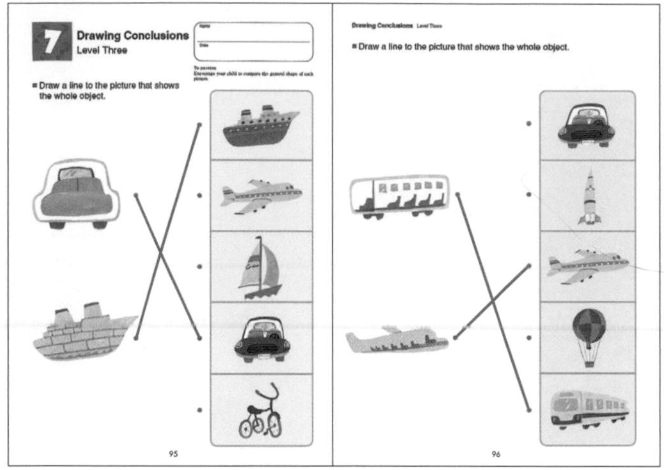
7 Drawing Conclusions
Level Three

■ Draw a line to the picture that shows the whole object.

95

Drawing Conclusions Level Three

■ Draw a line to the picture that shows the whole object.

96

pages 95 and 96

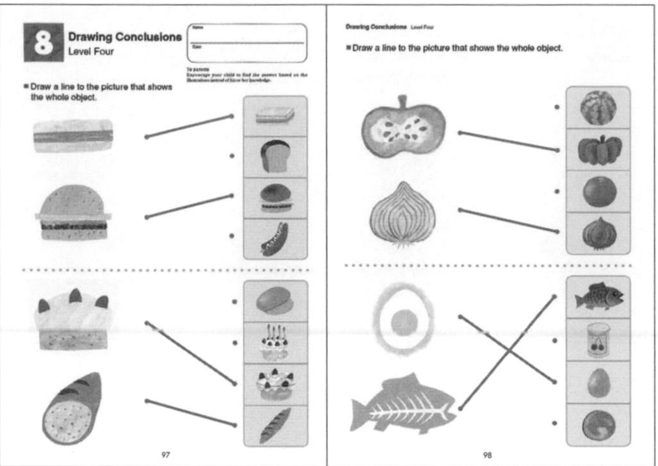
8 Drawing Conclusions
Level Four

■ Draw a line to the picture that shows the whole object.

97

Drawing Conclusions Level Four

■ Draw a line to the picture that shows the whole object.

98

pages 97 and 98

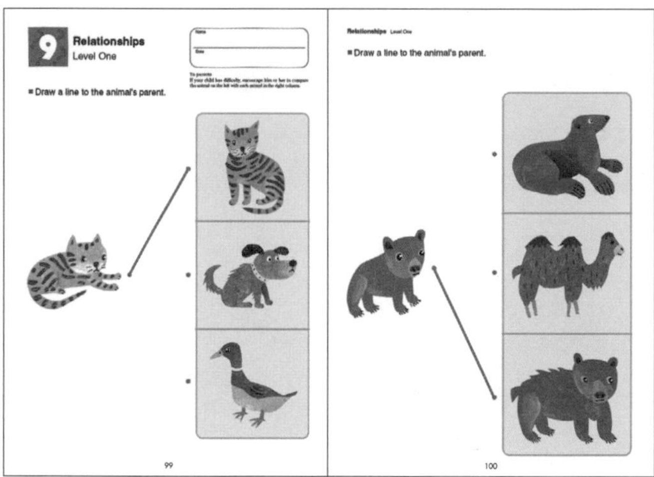
9 Relationships
Level One

■ Draw a line to the animal's parent.

99

Relationships Level One

■ Draw a line to the animal's parent.

100

pages 99 and 100

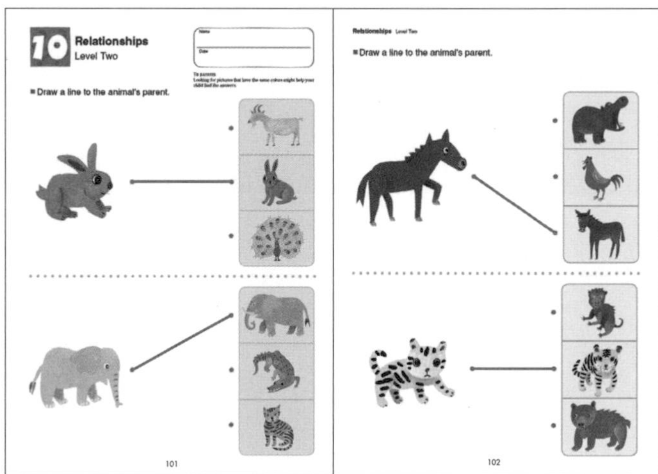
10 Relationships
Level Two

■ Draw a line to the animal's parent.

101

Relationships Level Two

■ Draw a line to the animal's parent.

102

pages 101 and 102

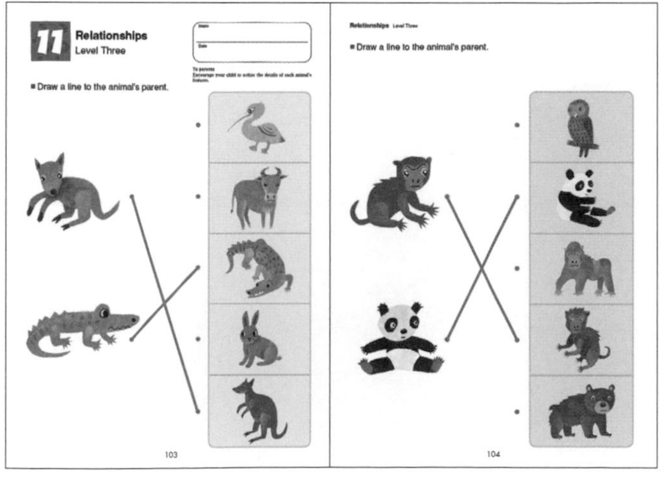
11 Relationships
Level Three

■ Draw a line to the animal's parent.

103

Relationships Level Three

■ Draw a line to the animal's parent.

104

pages 103 and 104

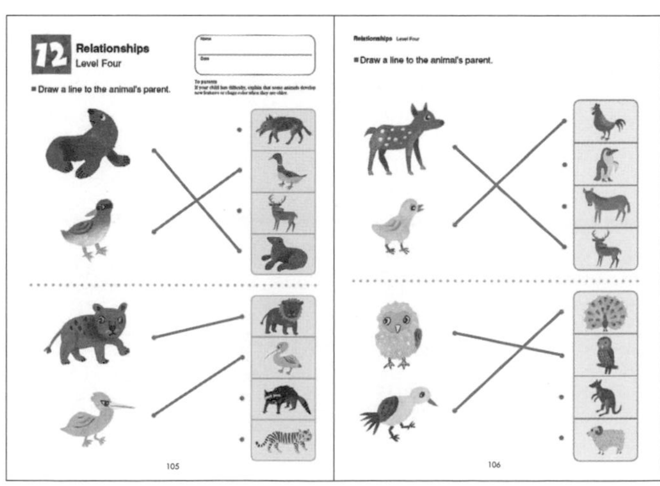
12 Relationships
Level Four

■ Draw a line to the animal's parent.

105

Relationships Level Four

■ Draw a line to the animal's parent.

106

pages 105 and 106

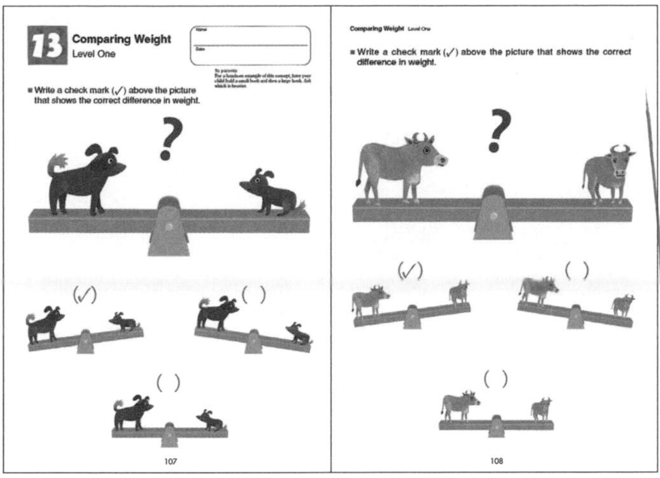
pages 107 and 108

pages 109 and 110

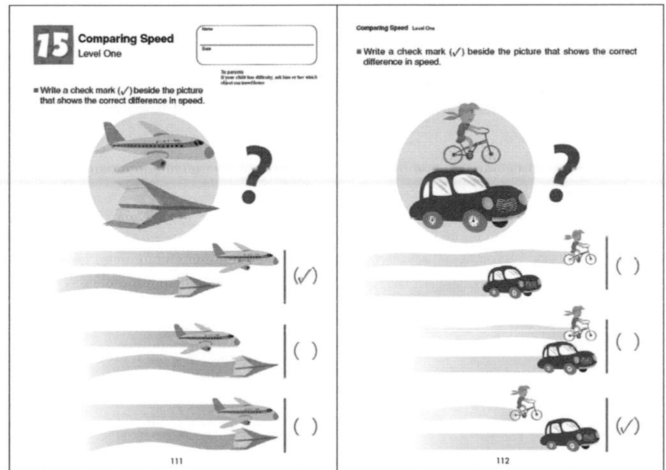
pages 111 and 112

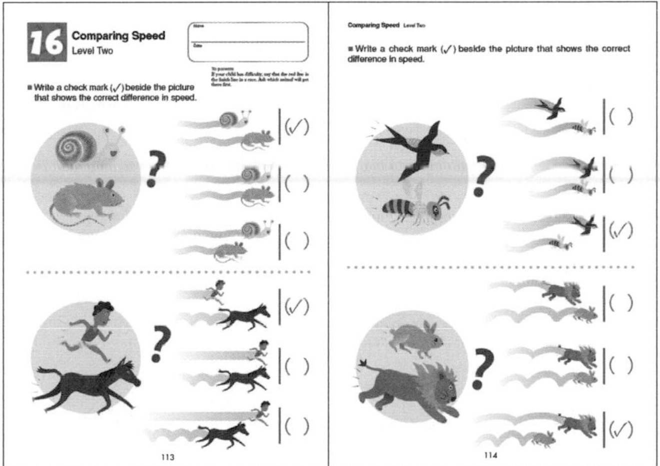
pages 113 and 114

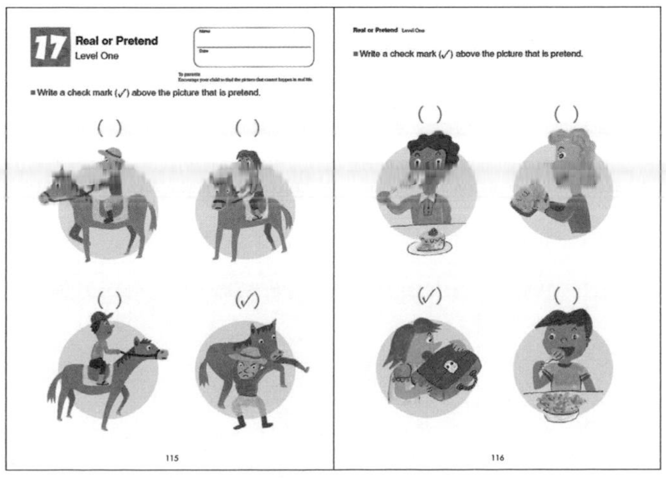
pages 115 and 116

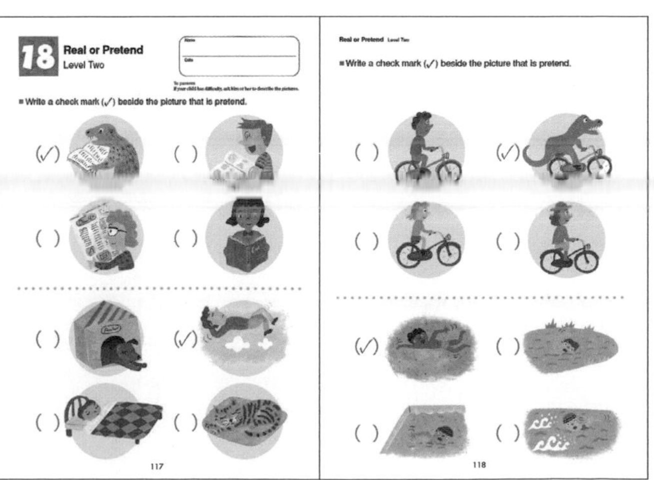
pages 117 and 118

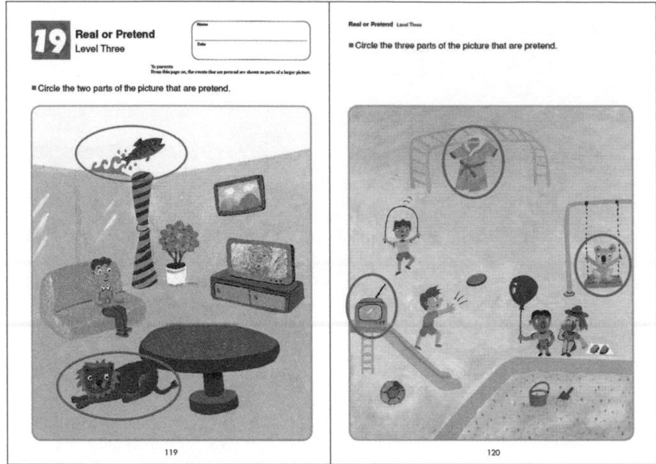

pages 119 and 120

pages 121 and 122

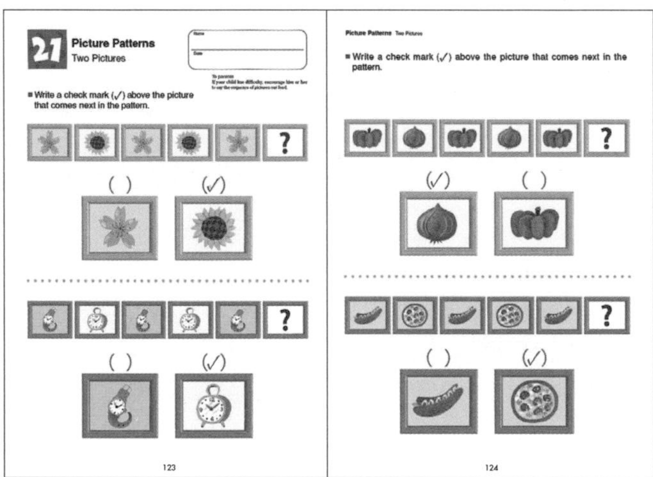

pages 123 and 124

pages 125 and 126

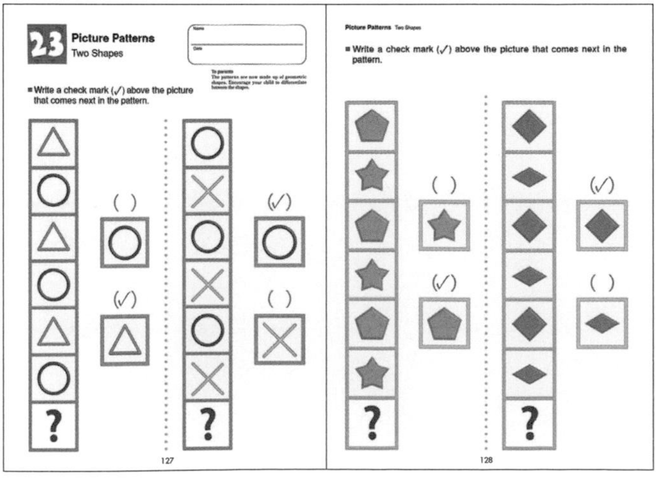

pages 127 and 128

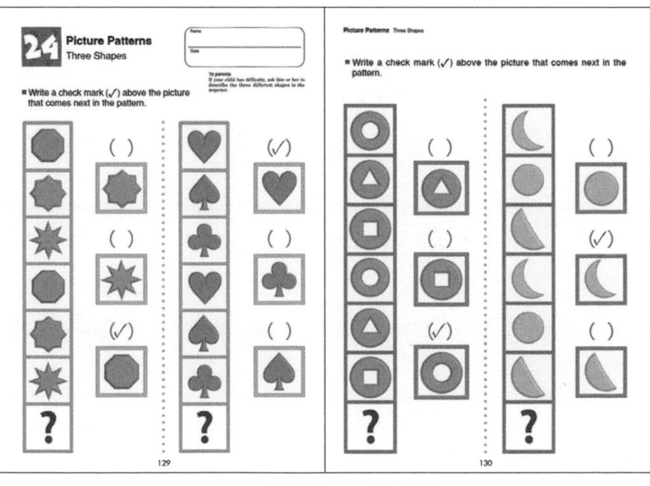

pages 129 and 130

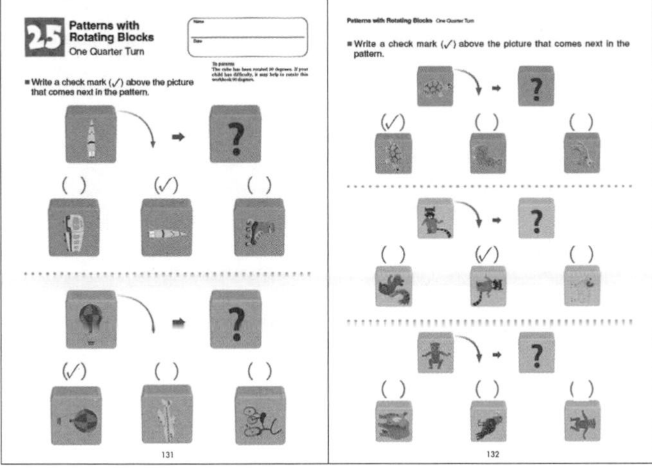
pages 131 and 132

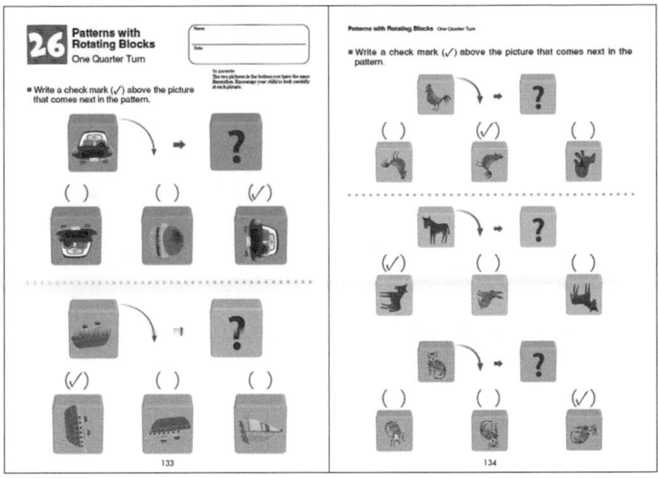
pages 133 and 134

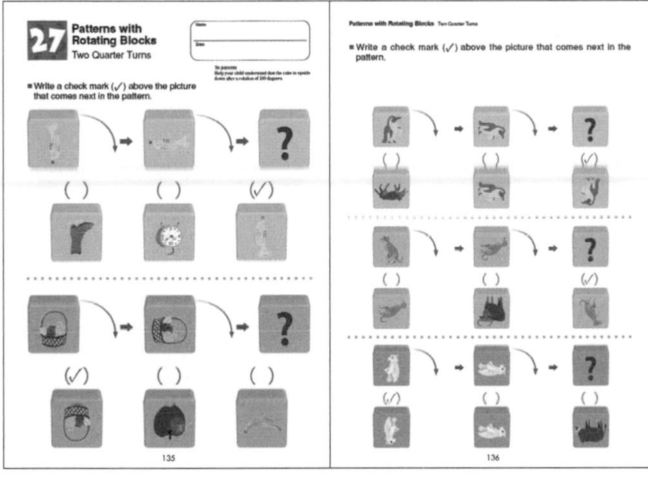
pages 135 and 136

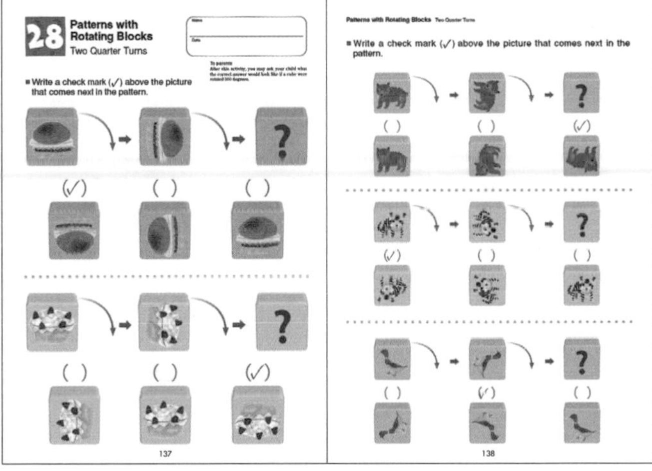
pages 137 and 138

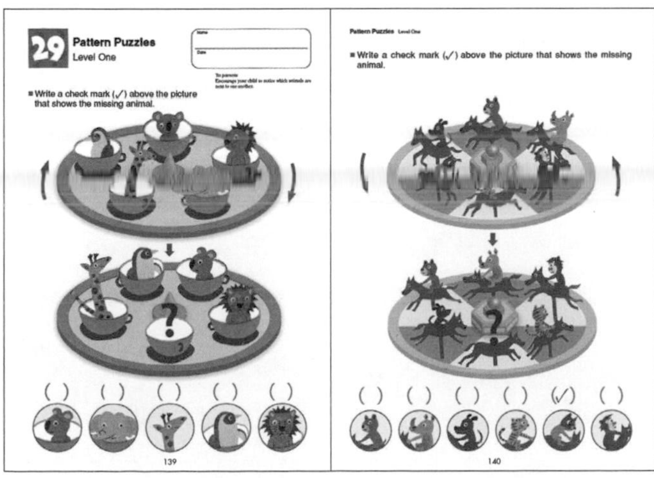
pages 139 and 140

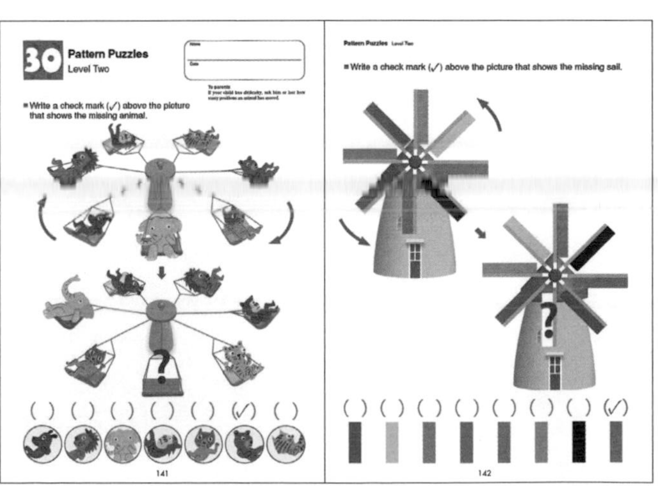
pages 141 and 142

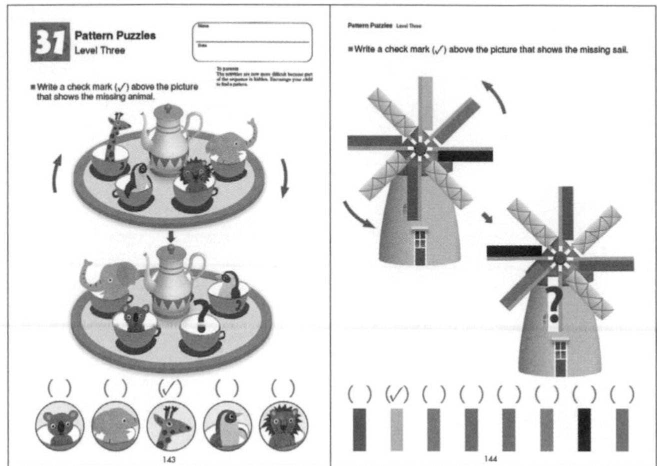

pages 143 and 144

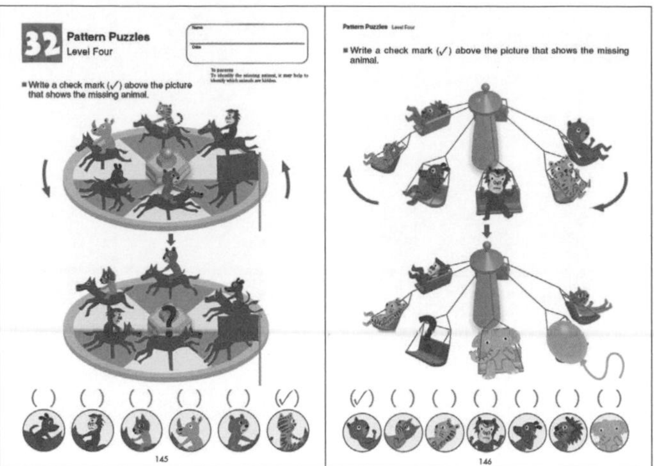

pages 145 and 146

pages 147 and 148

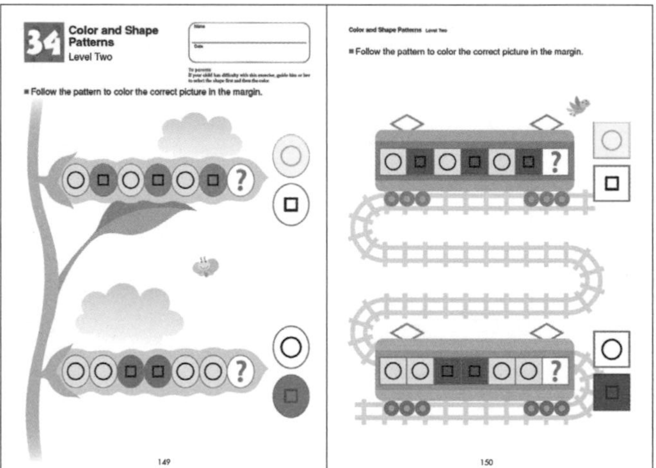

pages 149 and 150

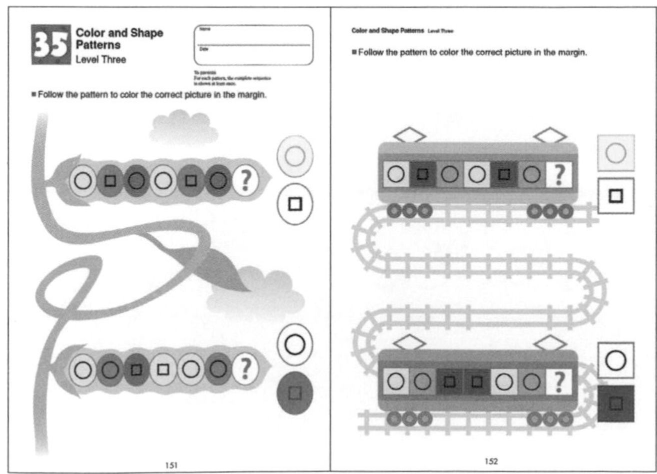

pages 151 and 152

pages 153 and 154

Same and Different

Table of Contents

To parents:

Same and Different

In this section, your child will complete activities to develop his or her differentiation skills. This section contains activities such as categorization and recognizing similarities and differences. By completing this section your child will strengthen his or her ability to find the similarities or differences between objects. Development of this skill will strengthen your child's critical thinking ability.

Each skill is introduced in a step-by-step manner that allows your child to master it without frustration. Over the course of the section, the difficulty level of these activities increases as your child gains confidence in his or her differentiation abilities.

Matching
Level One

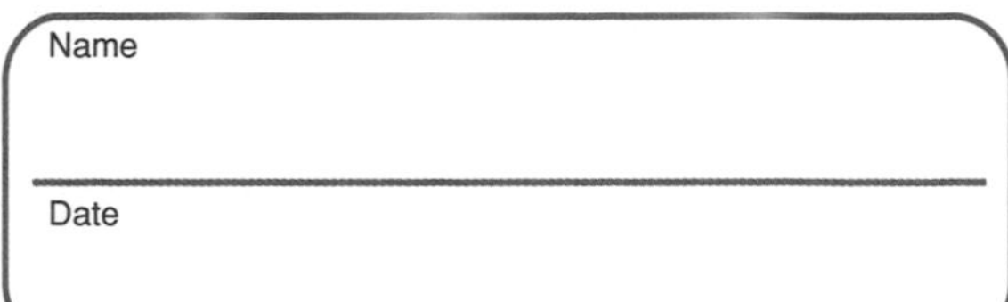

To parents
Guide your child to write his or her name and date in the box above. Do the exercise along with your child if he or she has difficulty.

■ Draw a line to the matching animal.

■ Draw a line to the matching object.

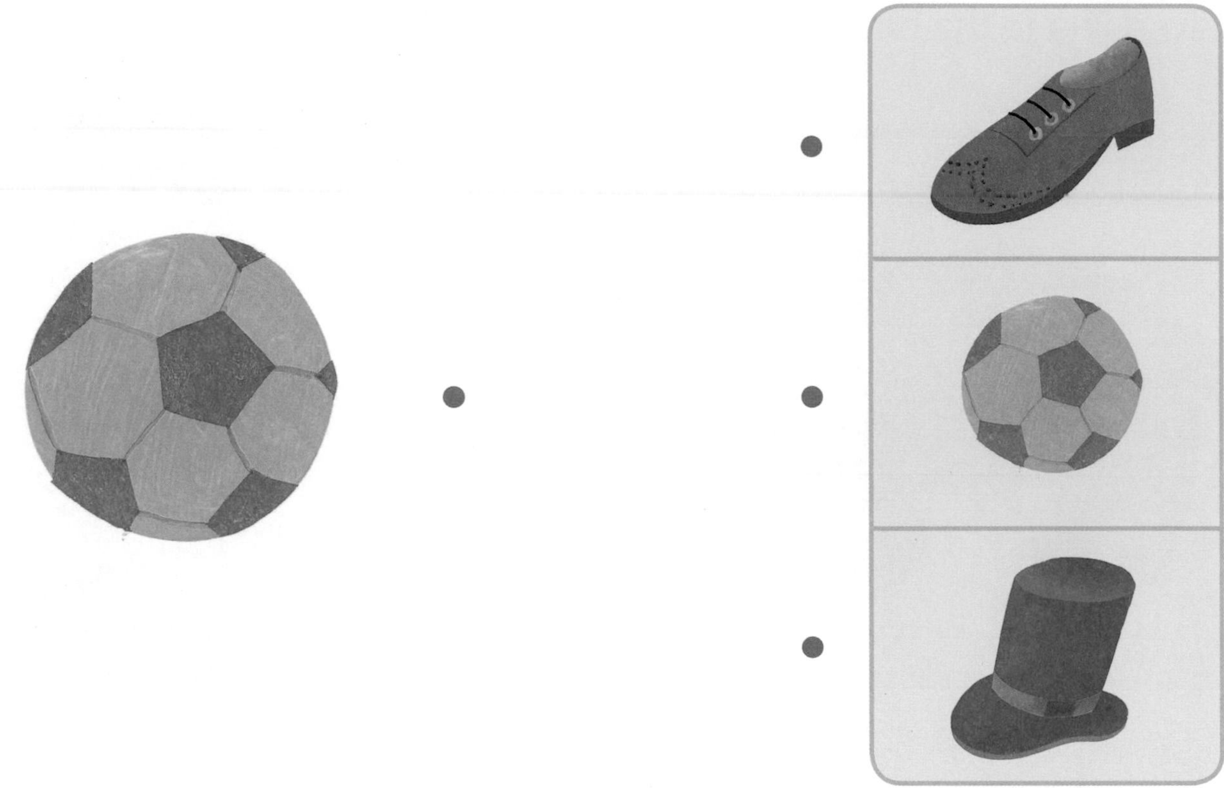

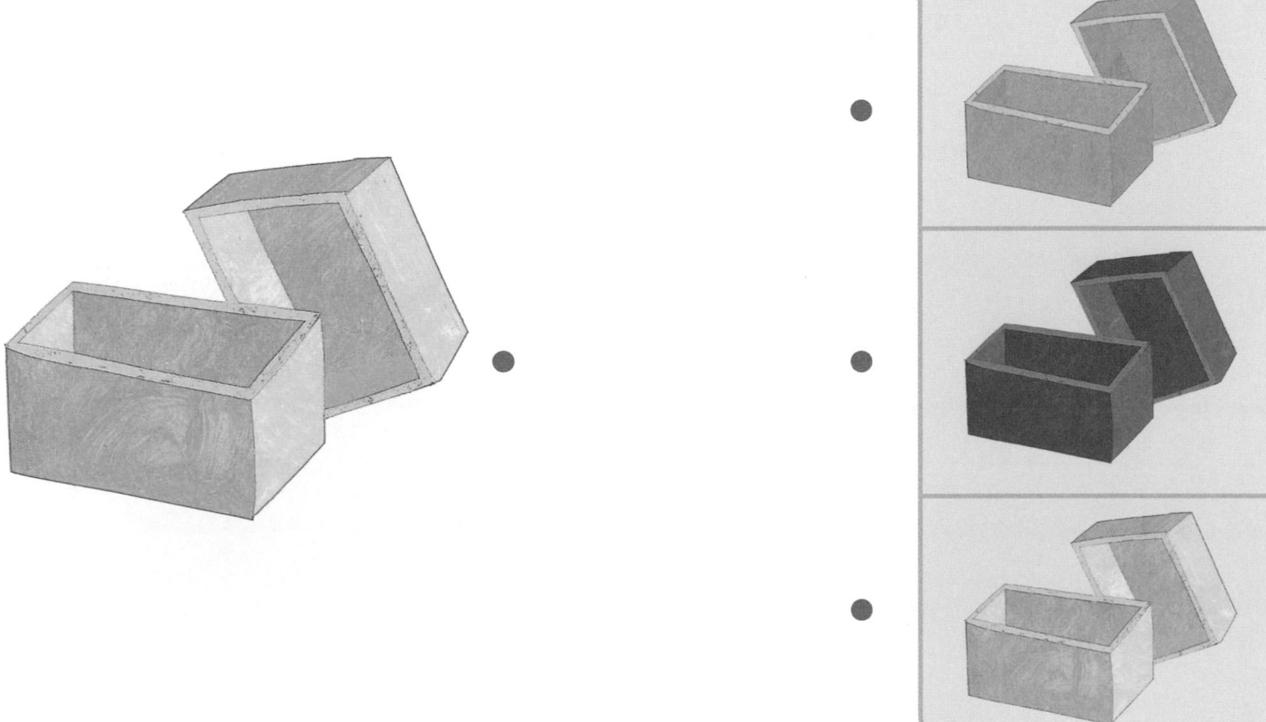

Matching

Level Two

Name

Date

■ Draw a line to the matching animal.

To parents

The number of answer choices in the right column has increased. Encourage your child to look carefully at each one.

■ Draw a line to the matching object.

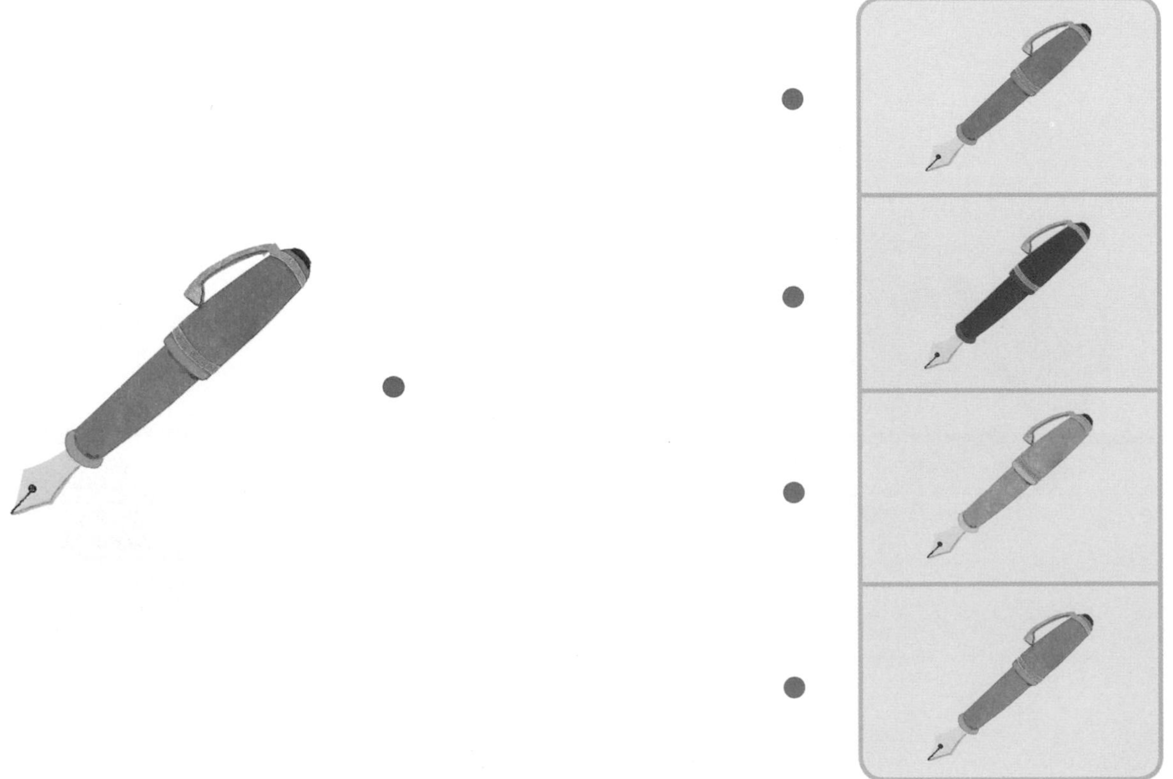

Matching
Level Three

Name

Date

To parents
If your child has difficulty, try reviewing the answer choices together, one by one. Cross off those that are incorrect.

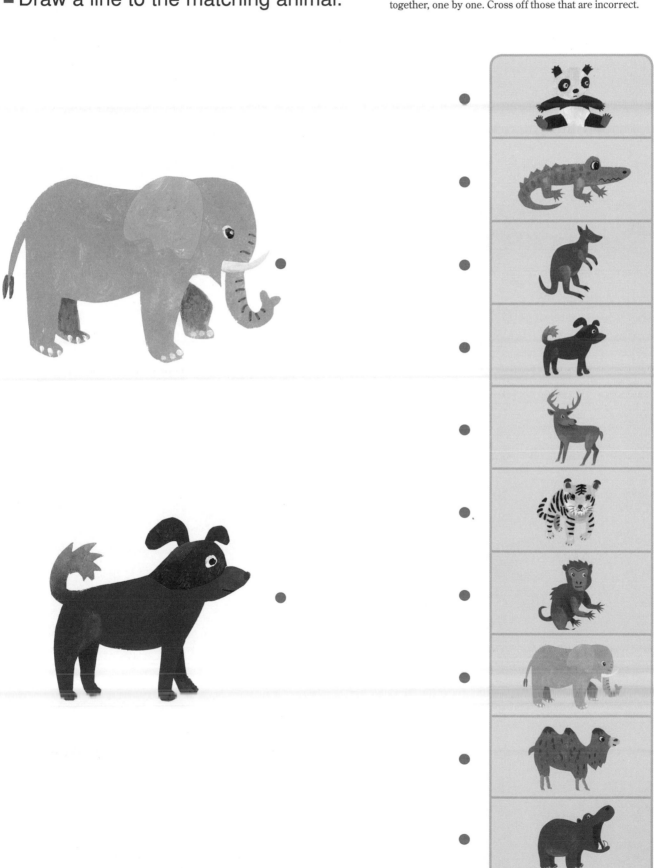

■ Draw a line to the matching animal.

■ Draw a line to the matching object.

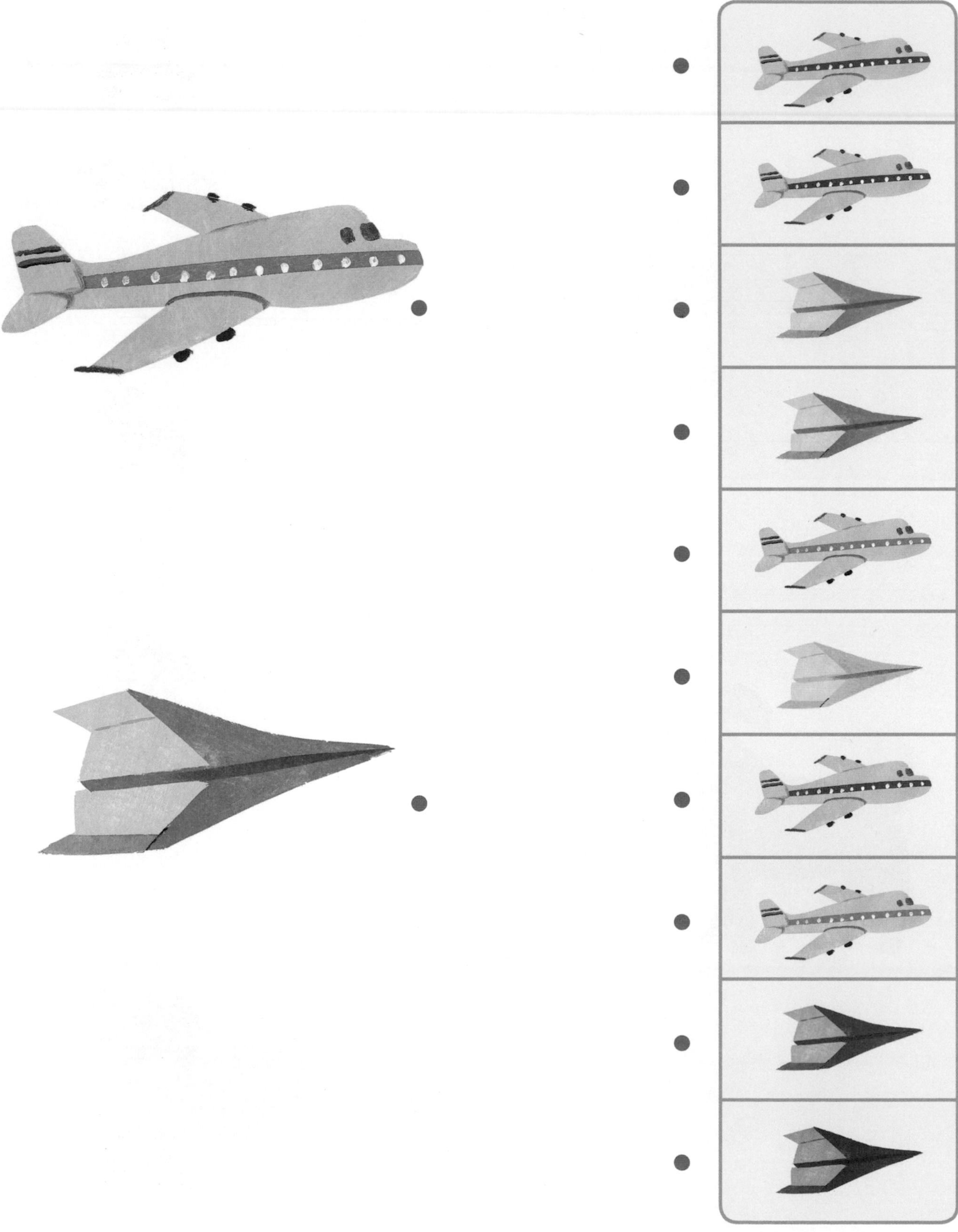

Matching
Level Four

■ Draw a line to the matching animal.

To parents

The activity is now more difficult because the animal is partly hidden. Guide your child to look at the features that are visible.

Name

Date

■ Draw a line to the matching object.

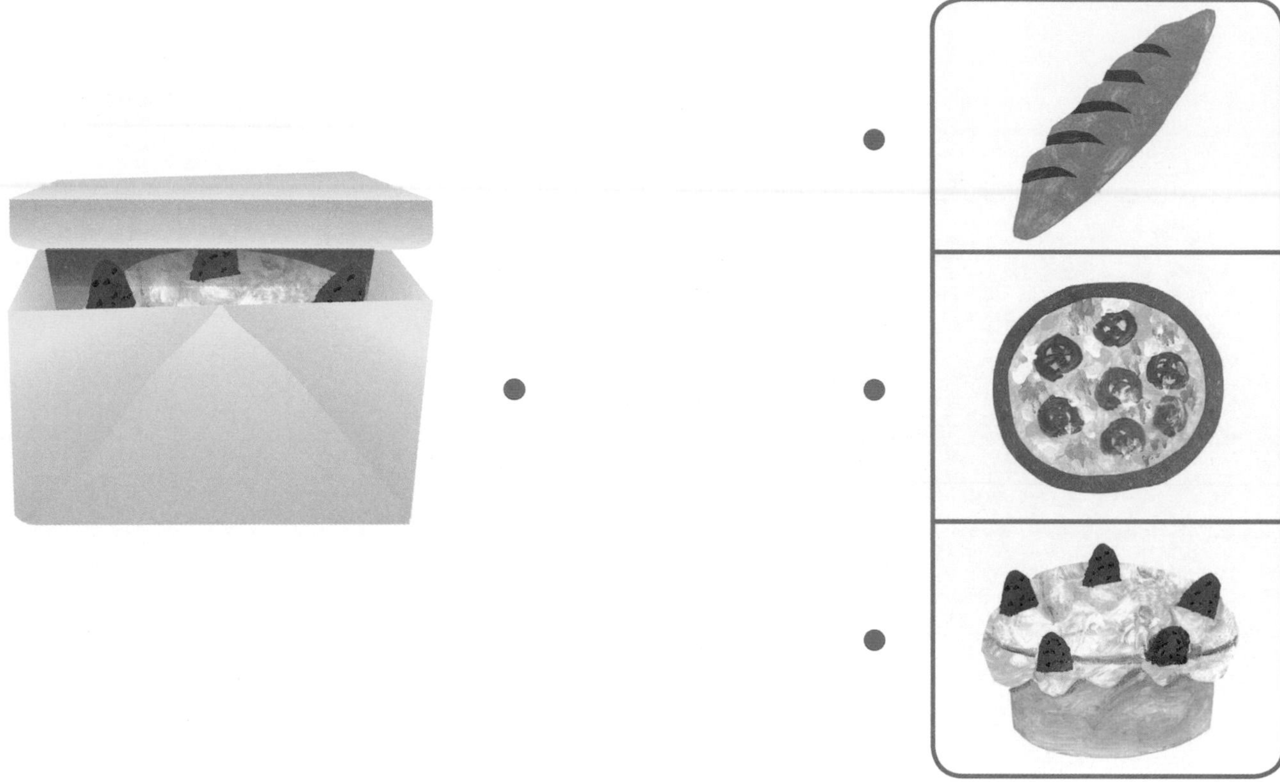

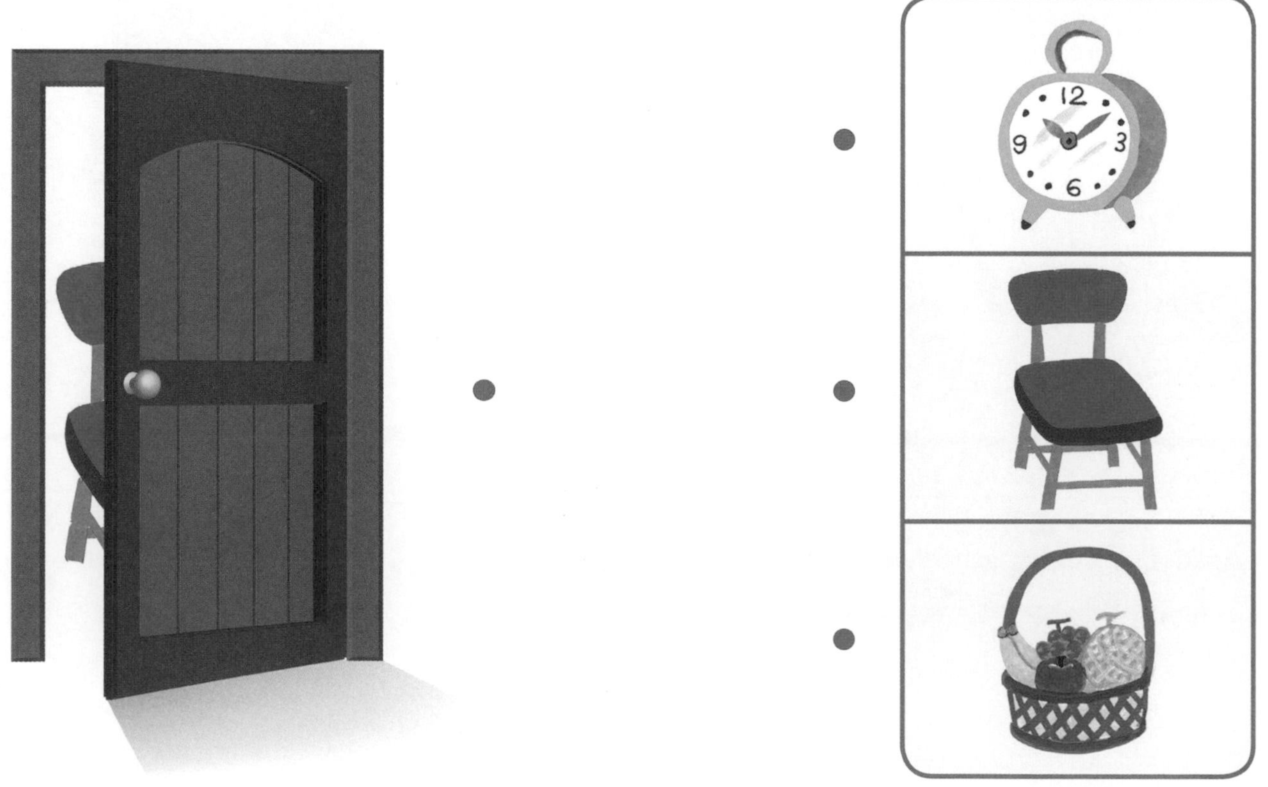

Matching
Level Five

Name

Date

To parents
If your child has difficulty, ask him or her to try to identify the animal hidden behind the plant.

■ Draw a line to the matching animal.

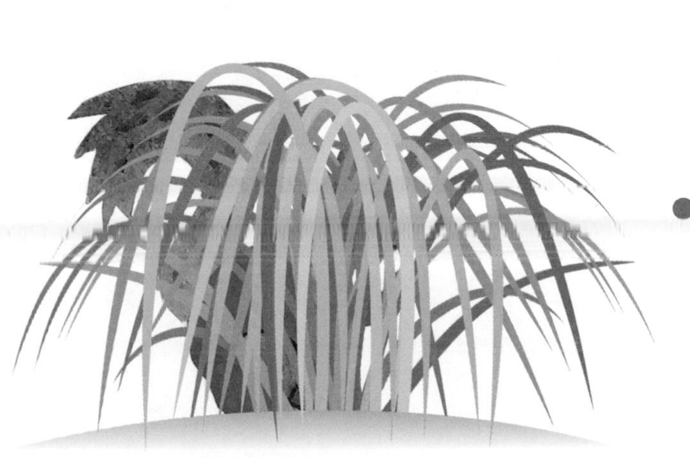

■ Draw a line to the matching object.

Matching

Level Six

Name

Date

To parents

The number of answer choices has increased. If your child has difficulty, help him or her eliminate answer choices one by one.

■ Draw a line to the matching animal.

■ Draw a line to the matching object.

Matching
Level One

Name

Date

To parents
If your child has difficulty, ask which two pictures show the front and back part of the same animal.

■ Draw a line to complete the picture.

■ Draw a line to complete the picture.

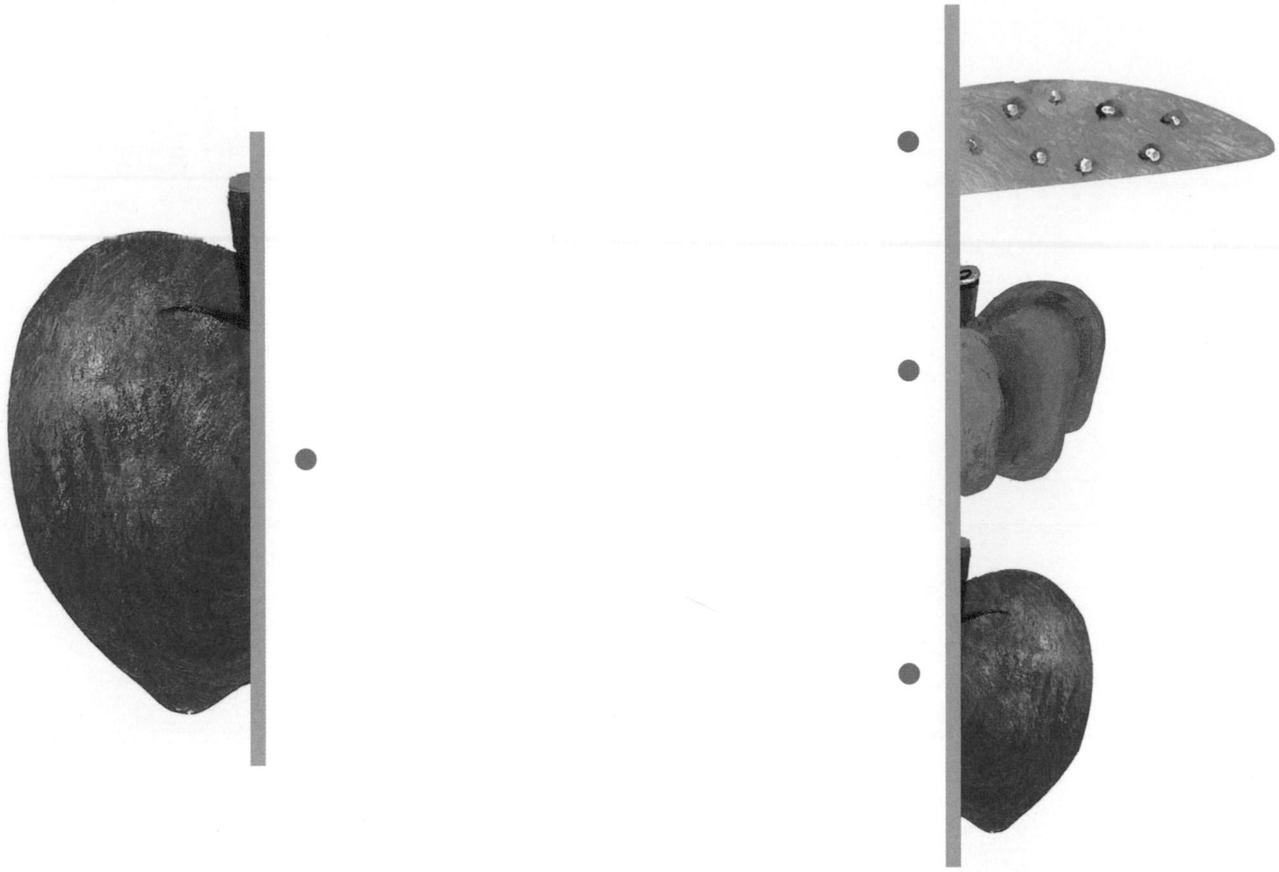

Matching
Level Two

Name

Date

To parents
If your child has difficulty, ask him or her to identify the animal shown on the left first, before looking for the matching picture.

■ Draw a line to complete the picture.

■ Draw a line to complete the picture.

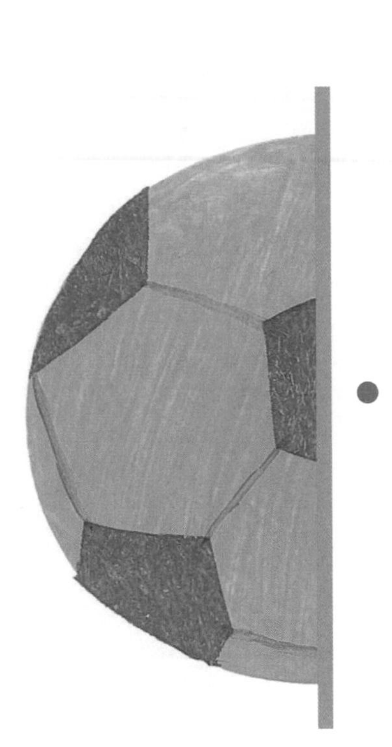

Matching
Level Three

Name

Date

To parents
The number of answer choices has increased. Encourage your child to look carefully at each one.

■ Draw a line to complete the picture.

■ Draw a line to complete the picture.

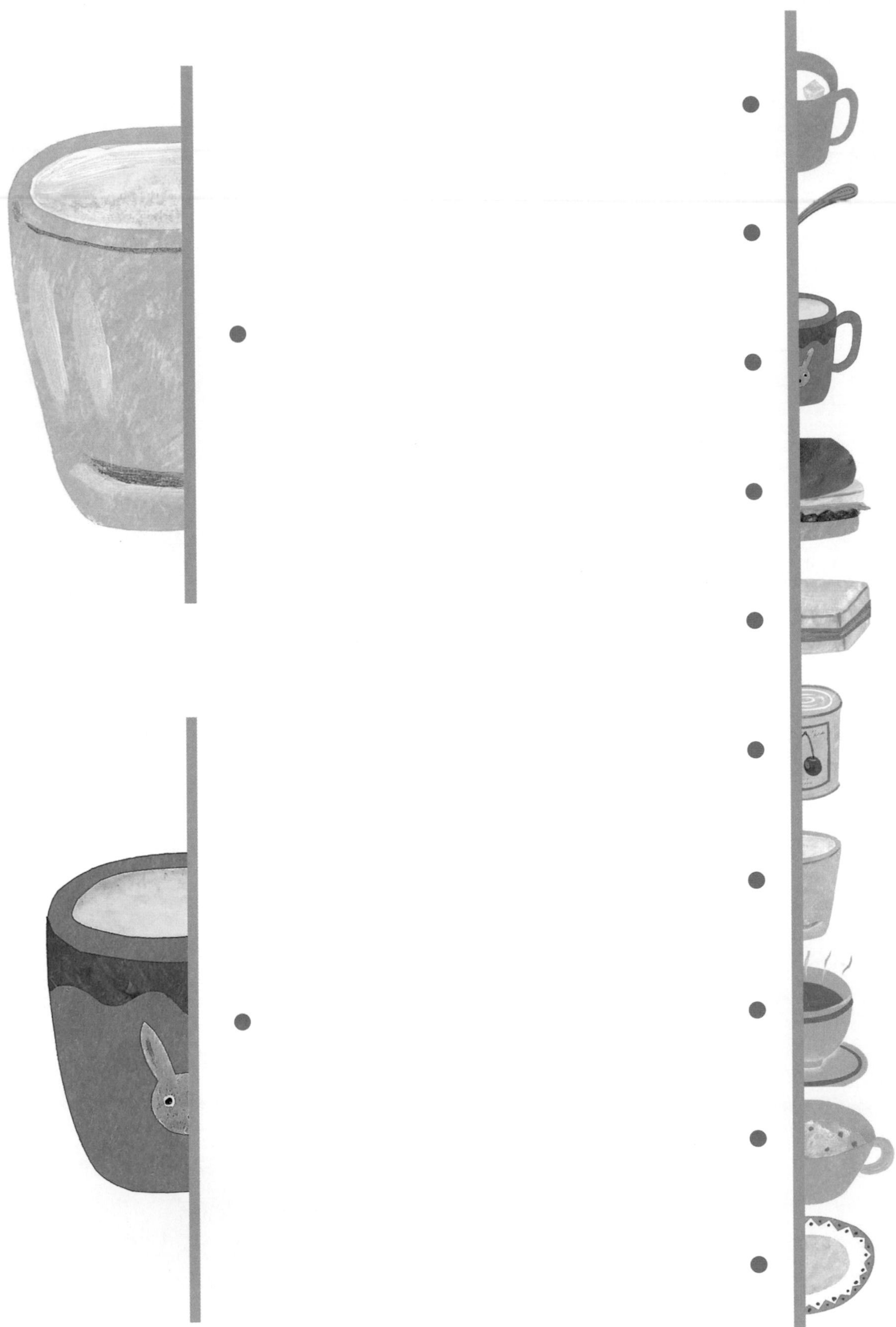

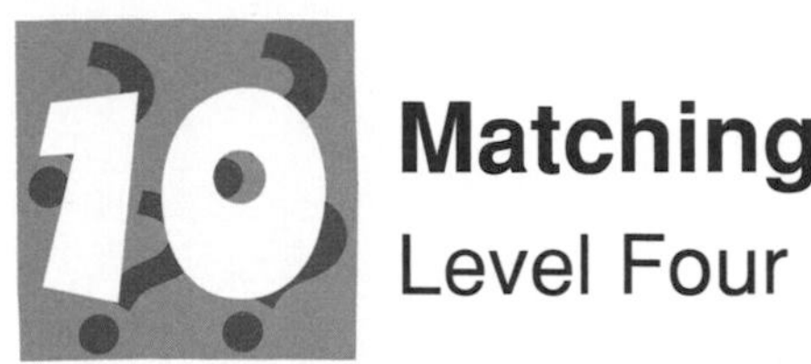

Matching
Level Four

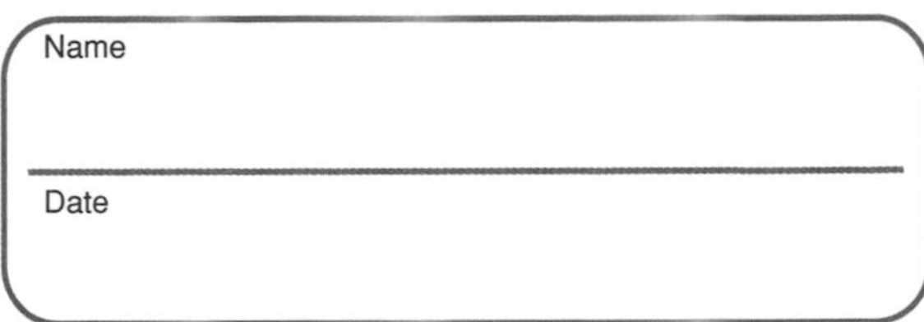

To parents

The activity is now more difficult because the pictures are partly hidden. Allow your child to take his or her time to complete this exercise.

■ Draw a line to complete the picture.

■ Draw a line to complete the picture.

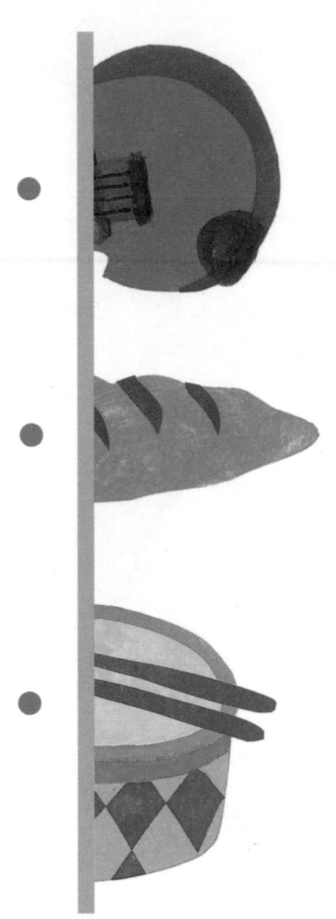

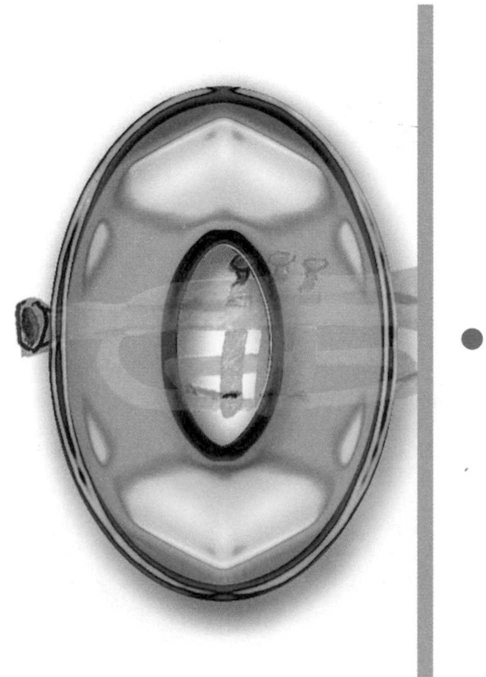

Matching
Level Five

Name

Date

To parents
It is okay if your child does not recognize all of the animals. Encourage your child to look carefully at the pictures.

■ Draw a line to complete the picture.

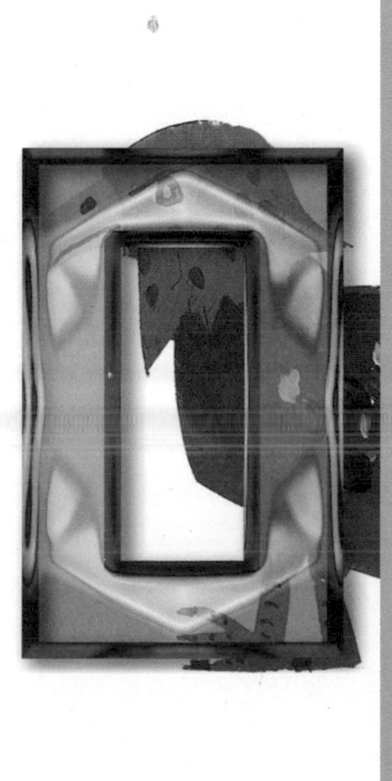

■ Draw a line to complete the picture.

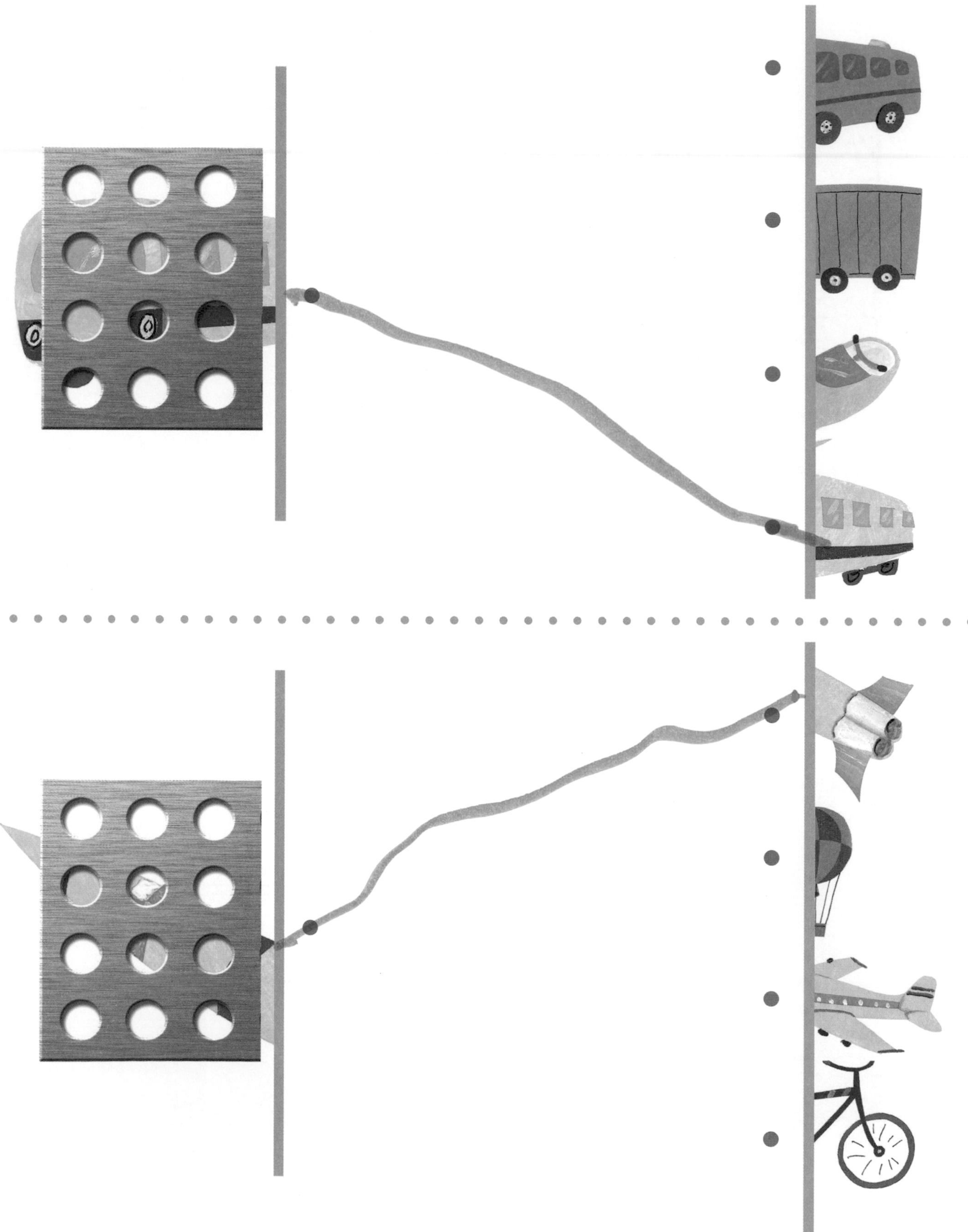

Matching
Level Six

Name

Date

To parents
If your child has difficulty, work together to point out small details in the pictures such as patterns on an animal's fur.

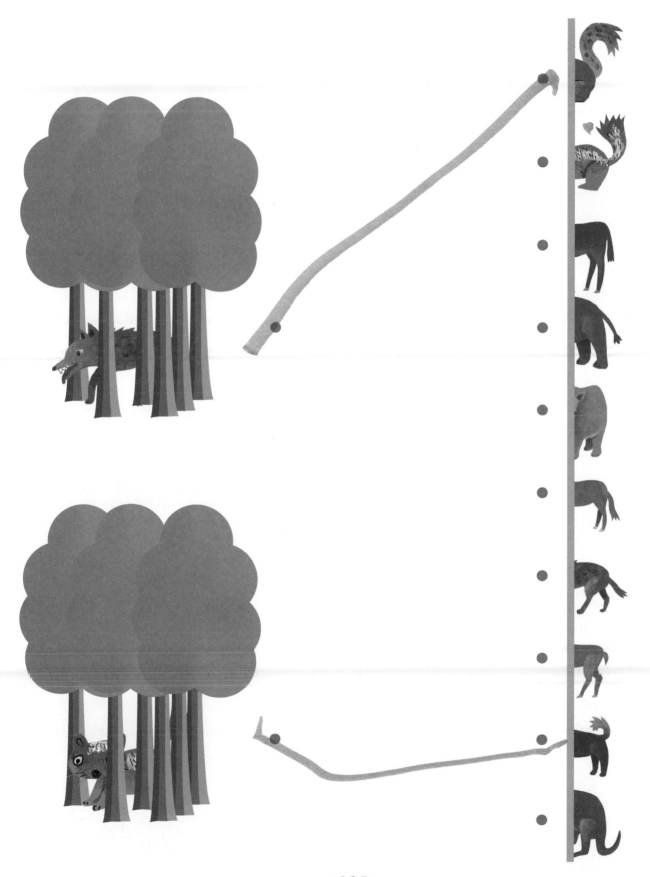

■ Draw a line to complete the picture.

■ Draw a line to complete the picture.

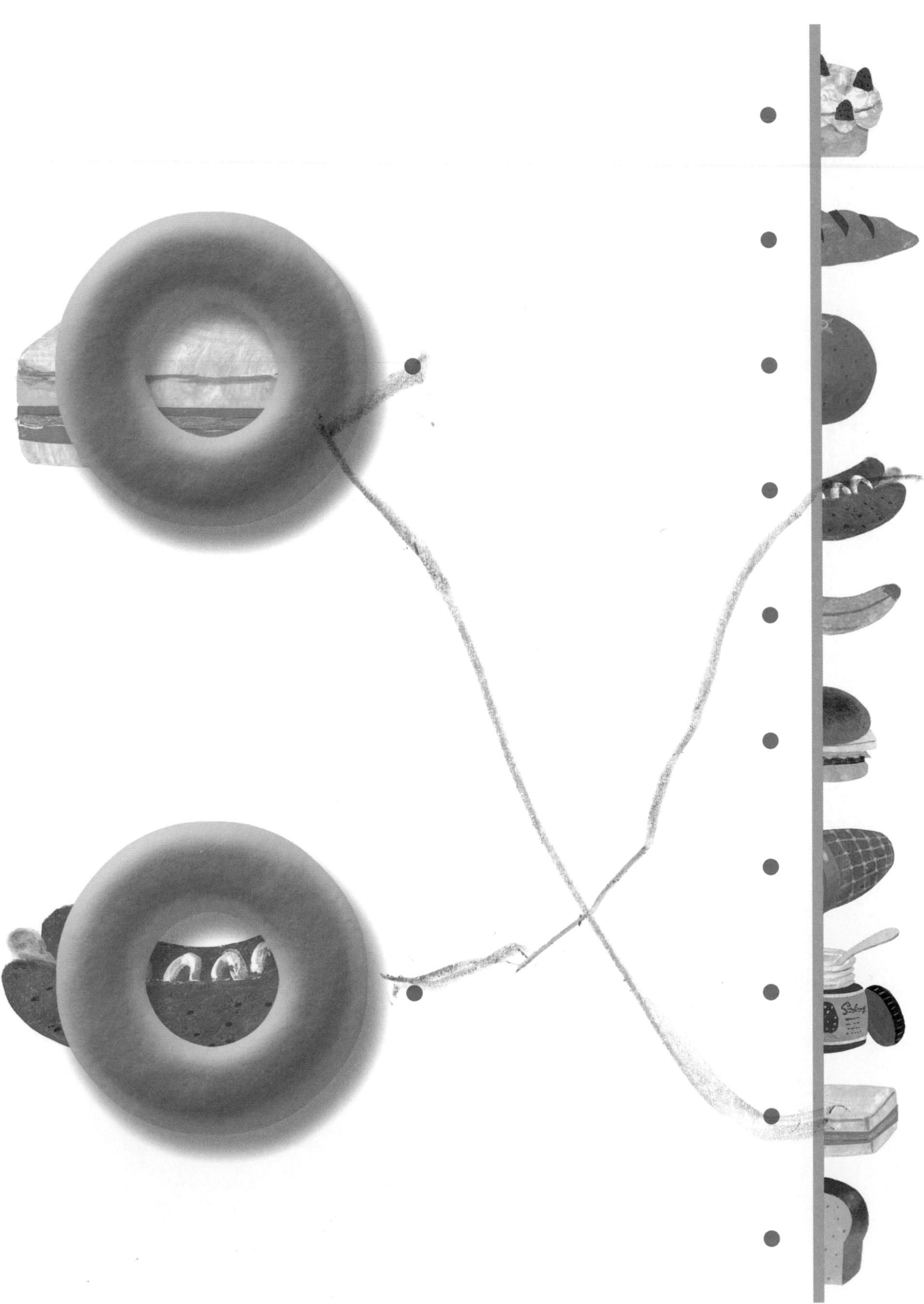

Matching
Level One

Name

Date

To parents
Help your child look carefully at the position or pose shown in each picture.

■ Draw a line to the matching picture.

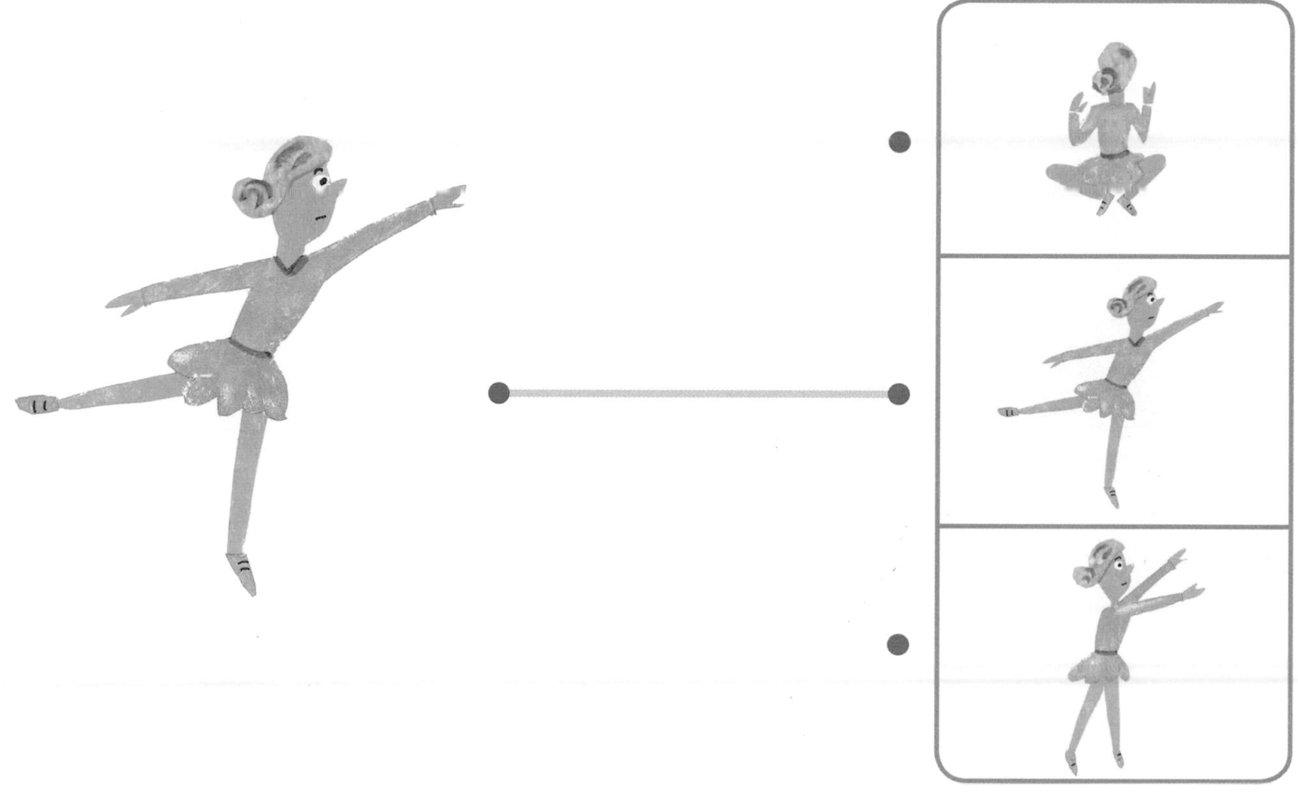

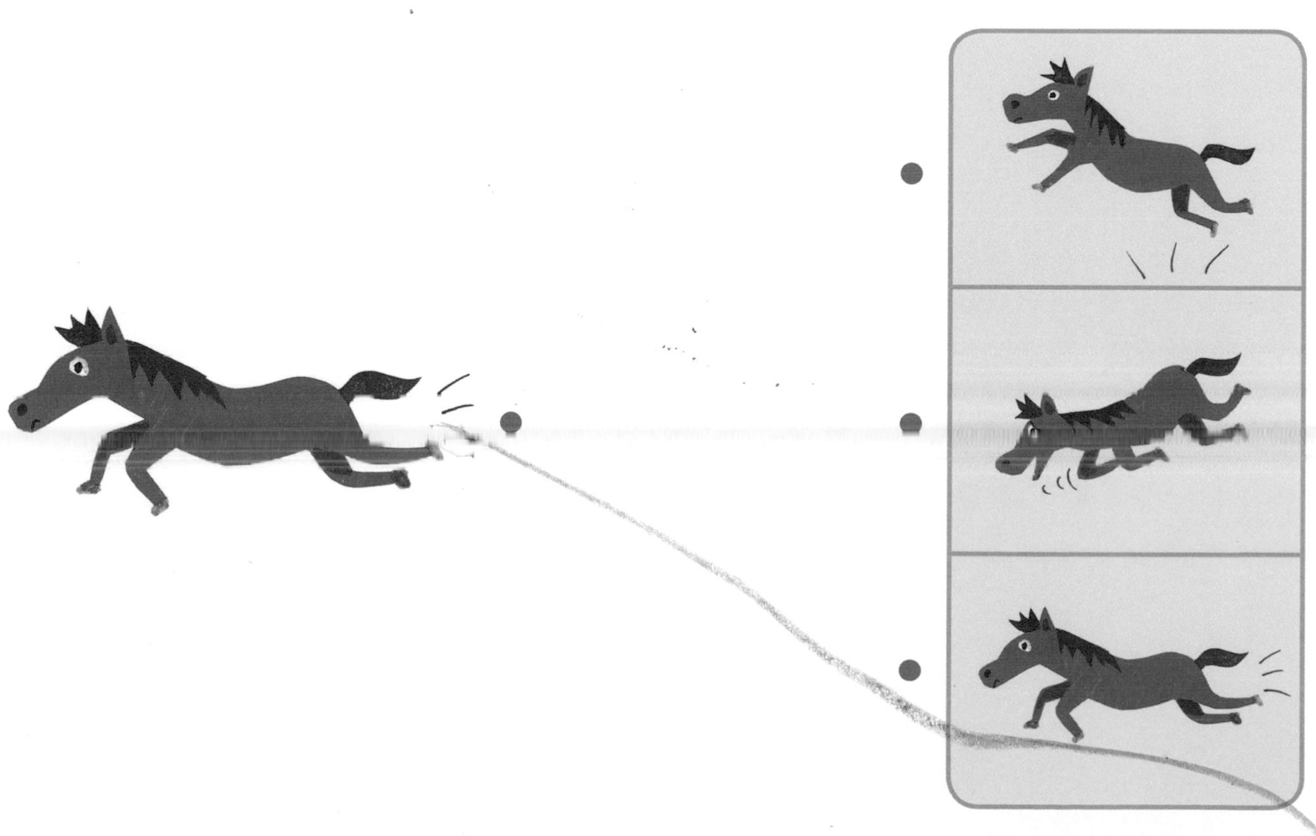

■ Draw a line to the matching picture.

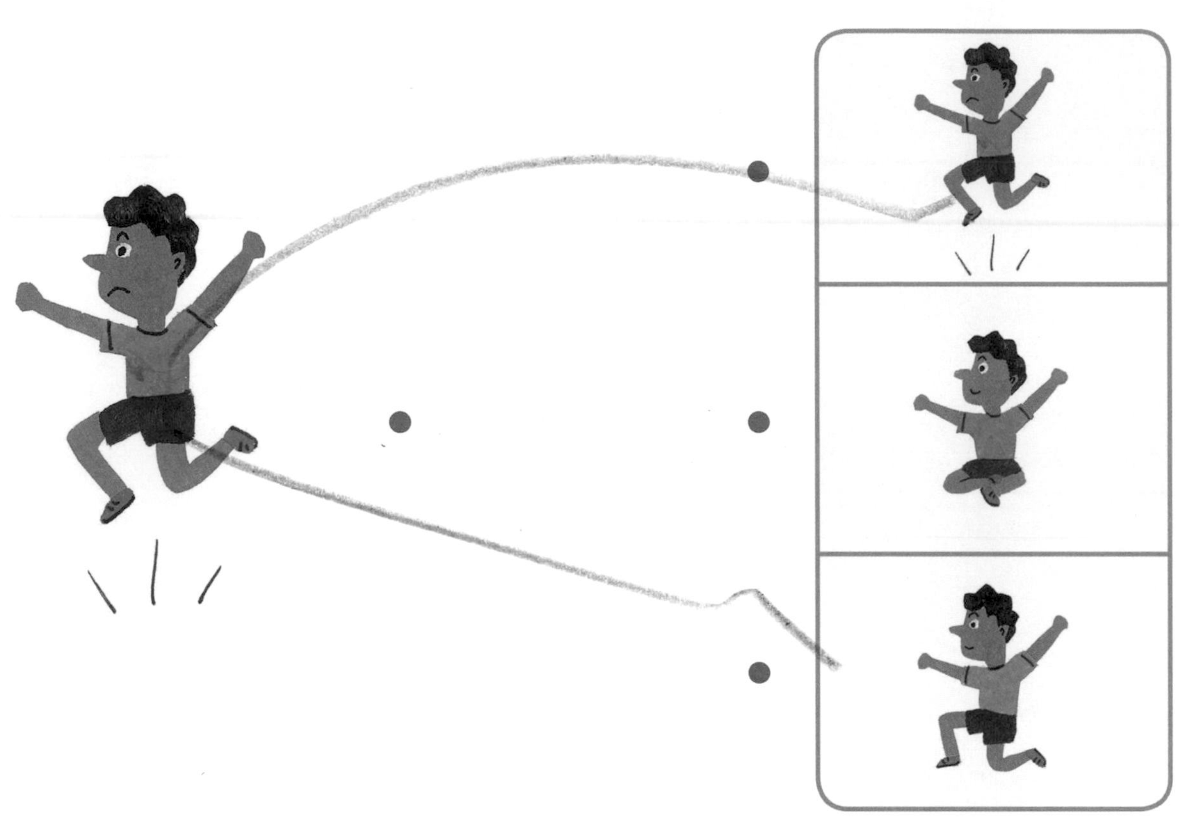

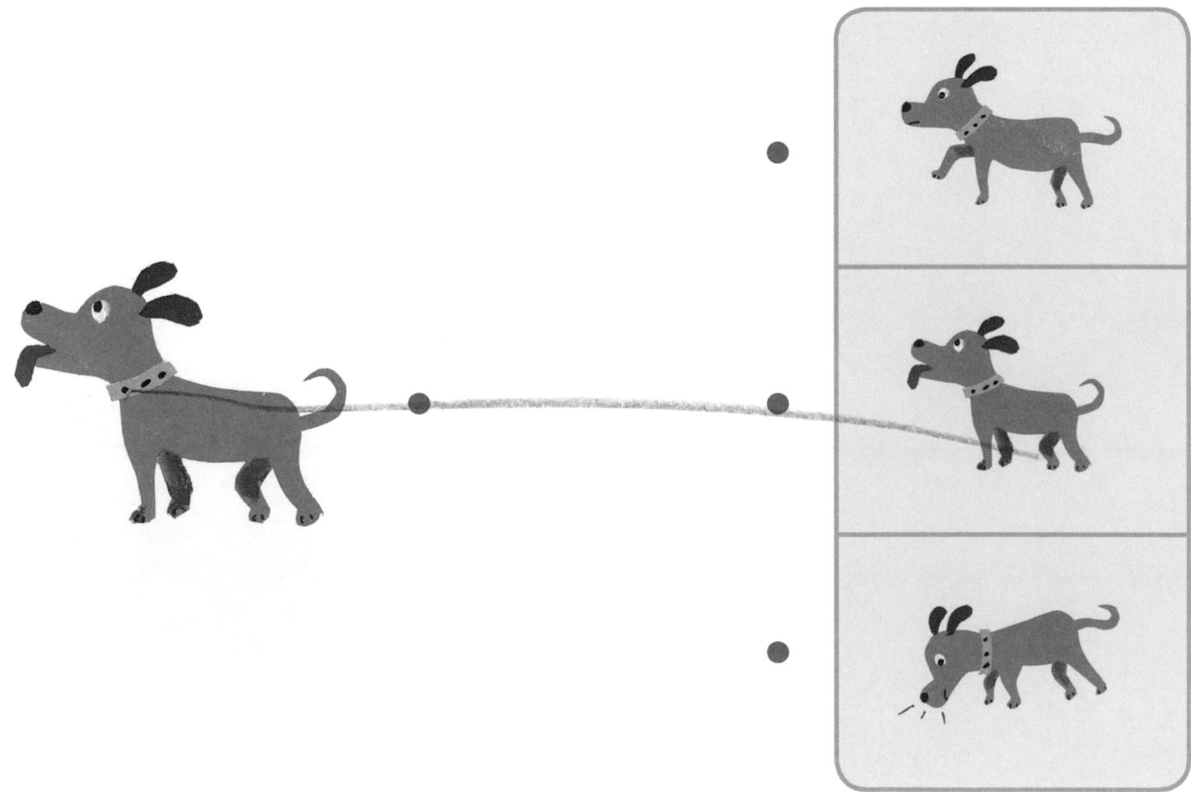

Matching
Level Two

Name

Date

To parents
If your child has difficulty, point to the picture on the left. Ask which picture on the right shows the same position.

■ Draw a line to the matching picture.

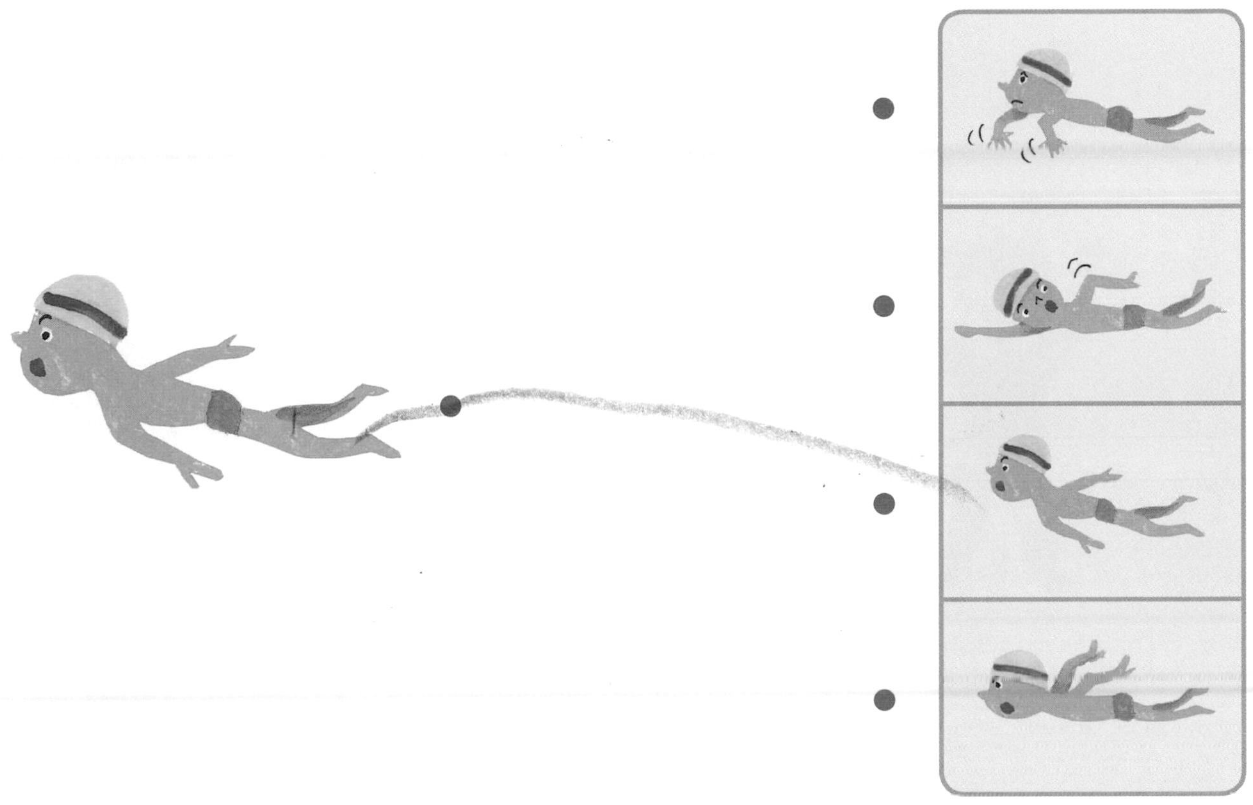

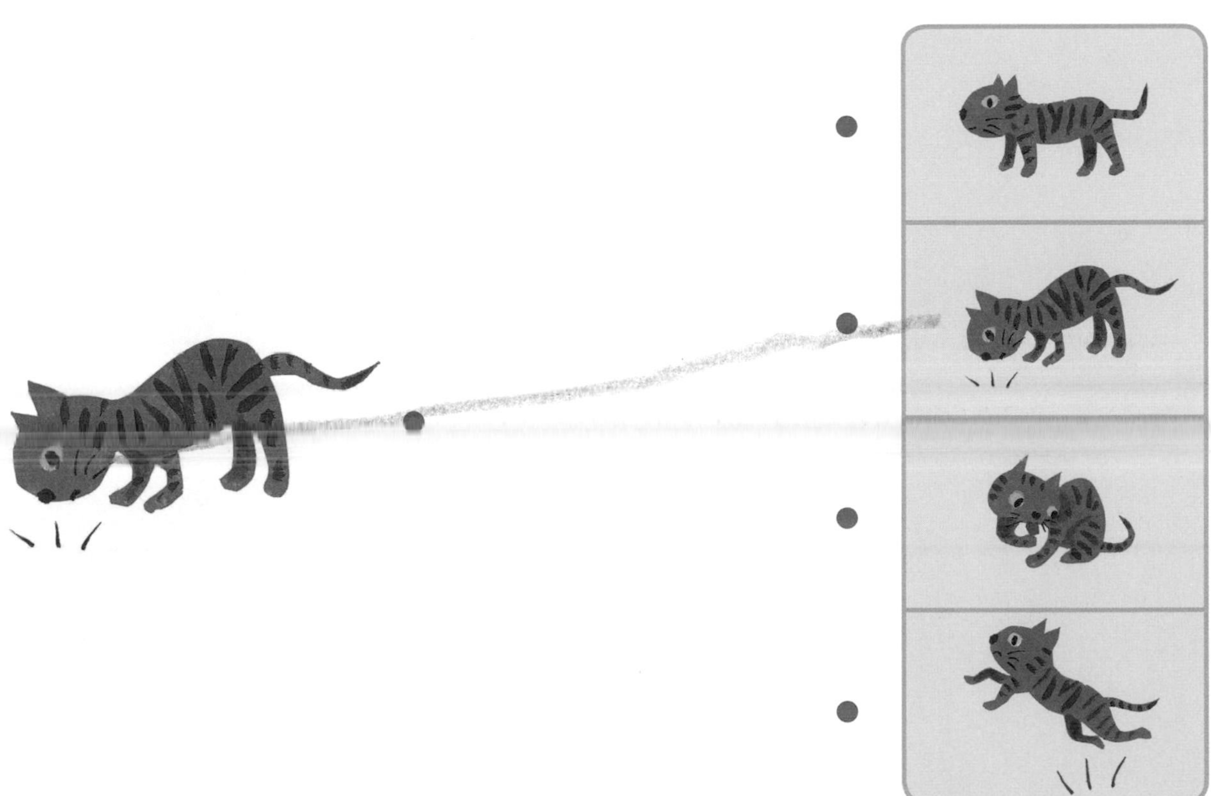

■ Draw a line to the matching picture.

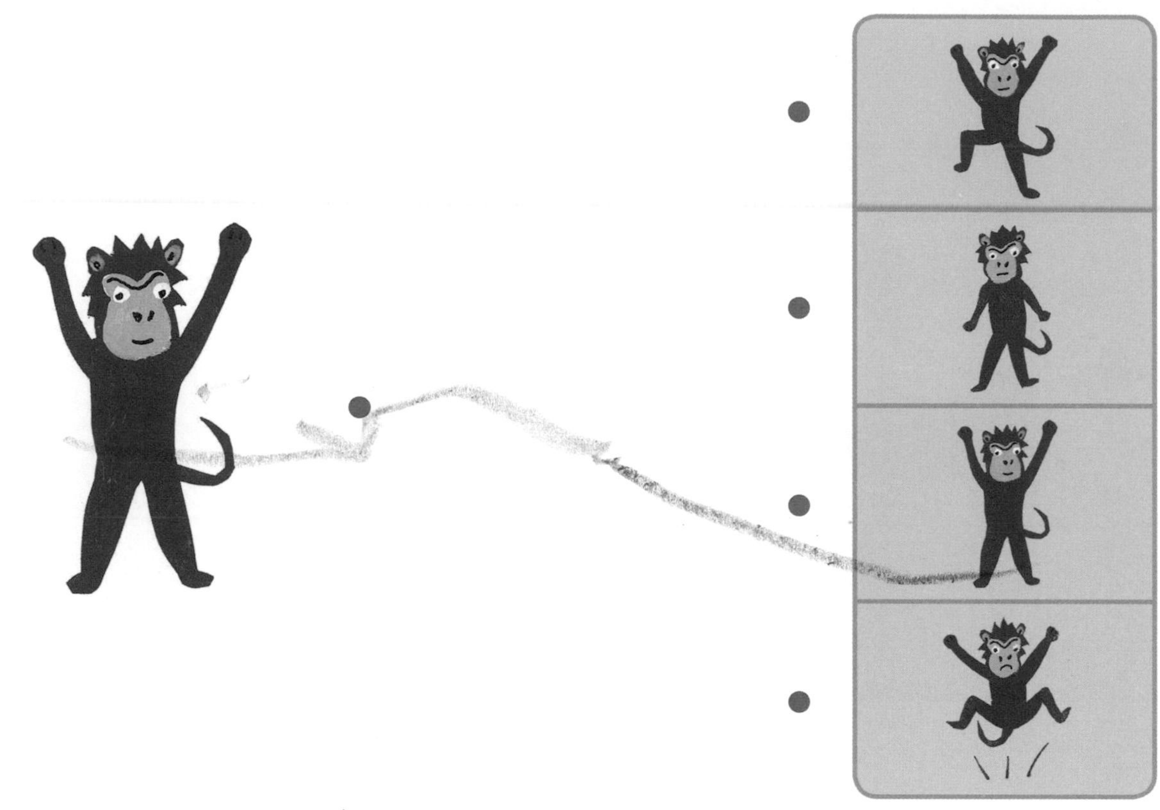

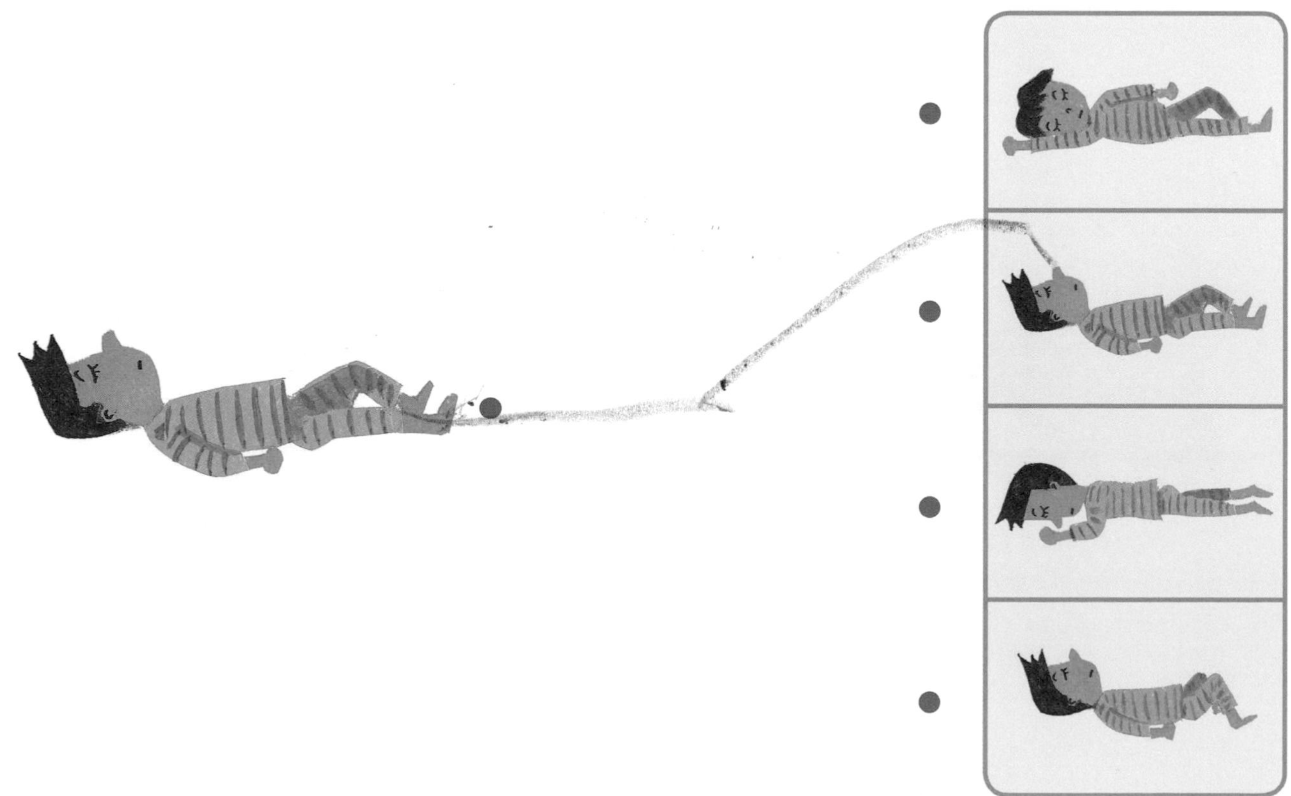

Matching
Level Three

Name

Date

To parents
This exercise has many answer choices. Guide your child to look for the matching animal first and then to check if the position matches.

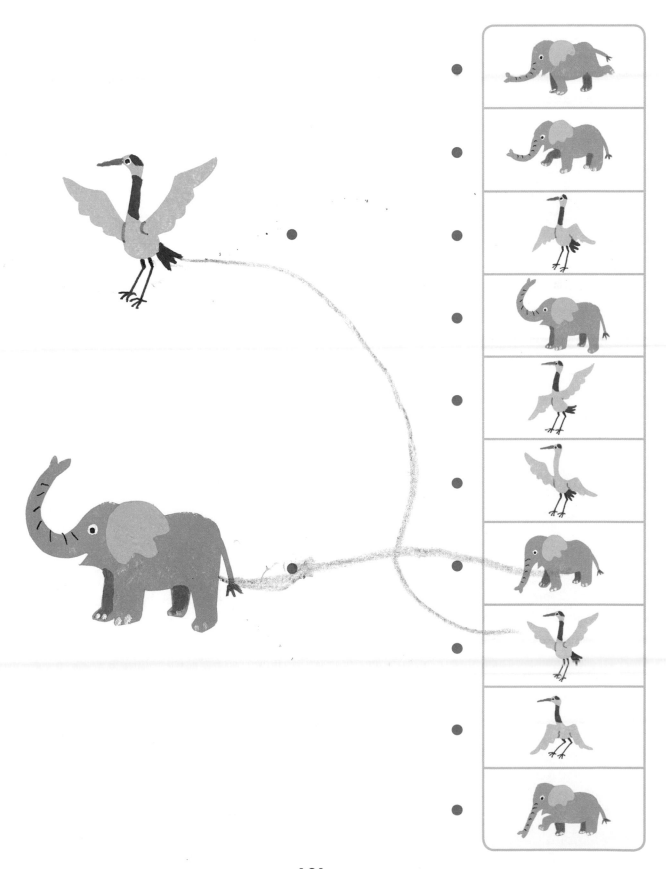

■ Draw a line to the matching picture.

■ Draw a line to the matching picture.

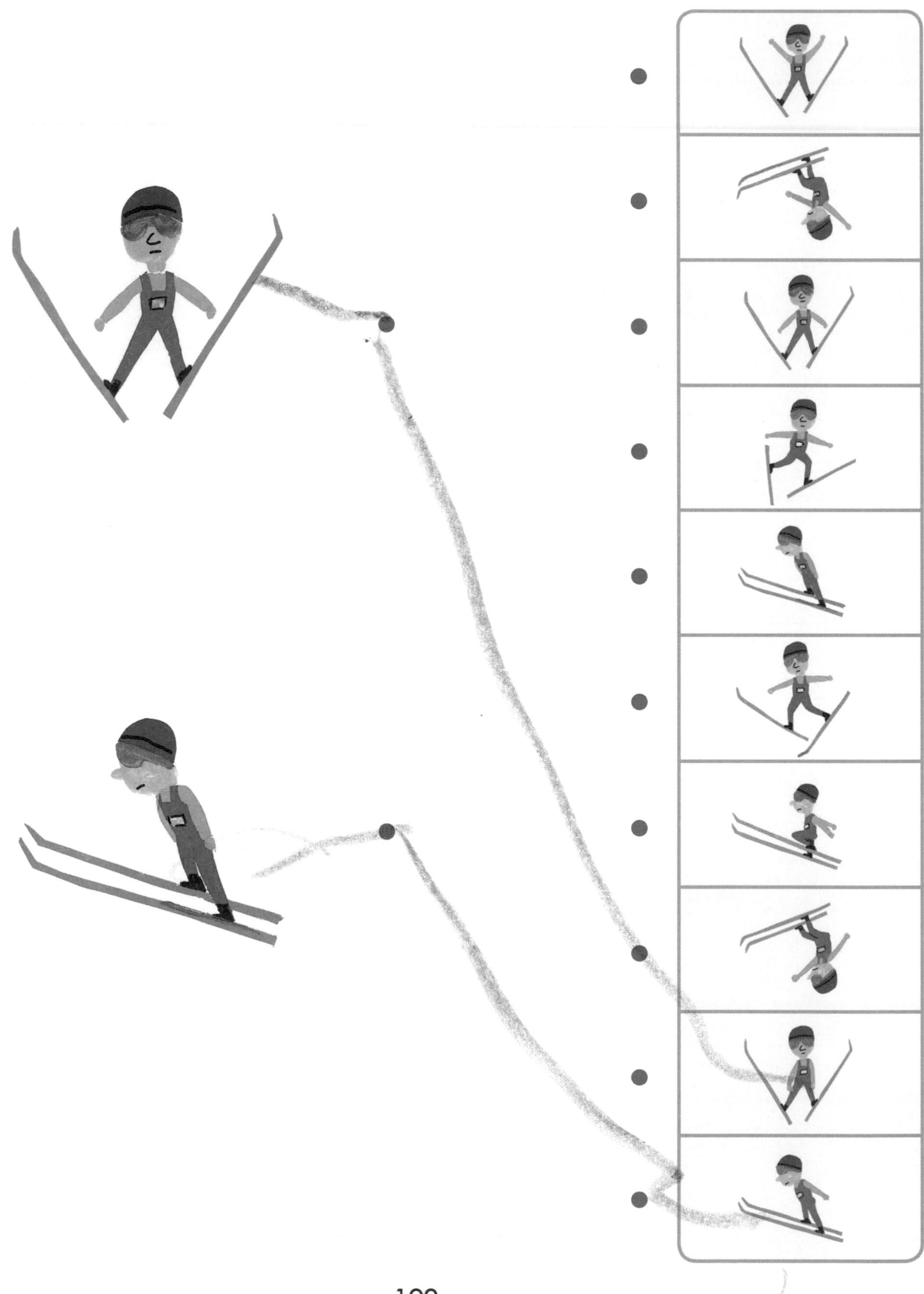

Matching Mirror Images

Level One

To parents

For a hands-on example, place a small mirror at a right angle with one of the pictures on this page. Have your child compare the picture with the mirror image.

■ Draw a line to the mirror image.

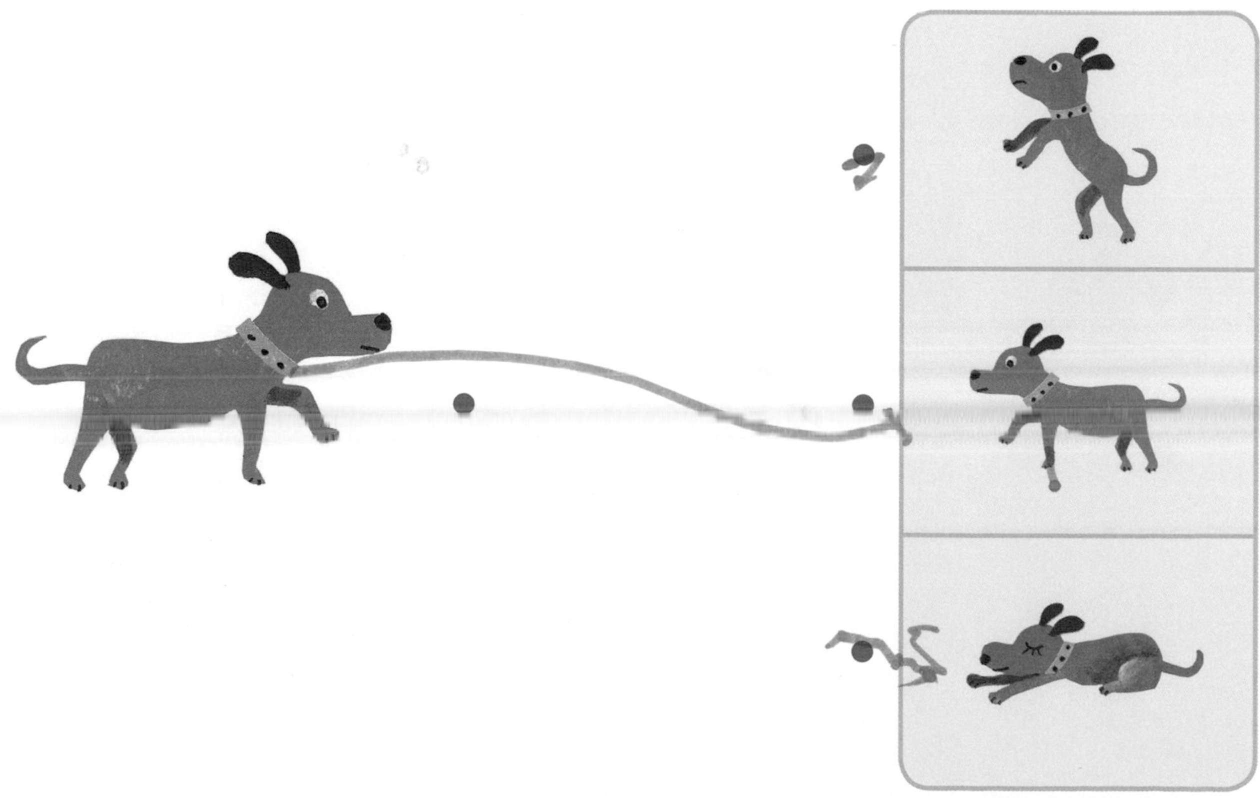

■ Draw a line to the mirror image.

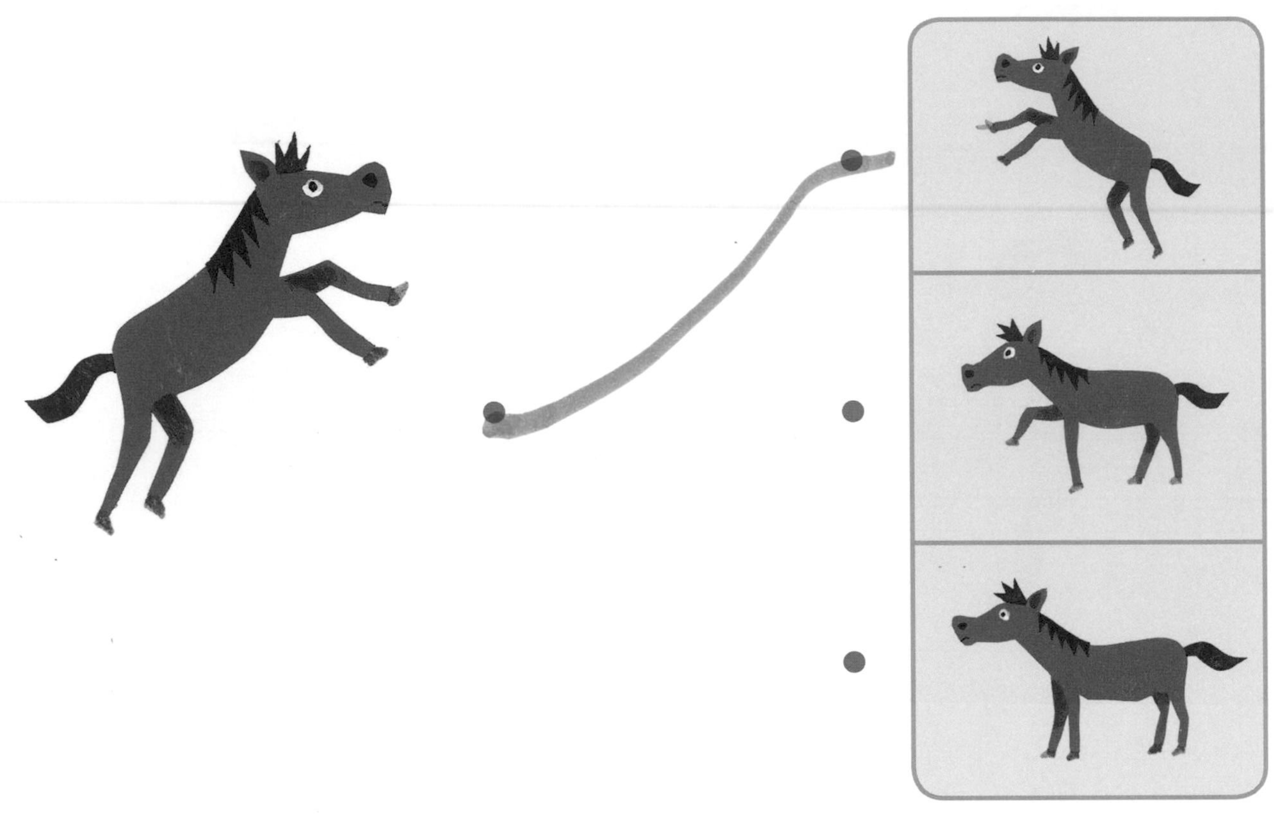

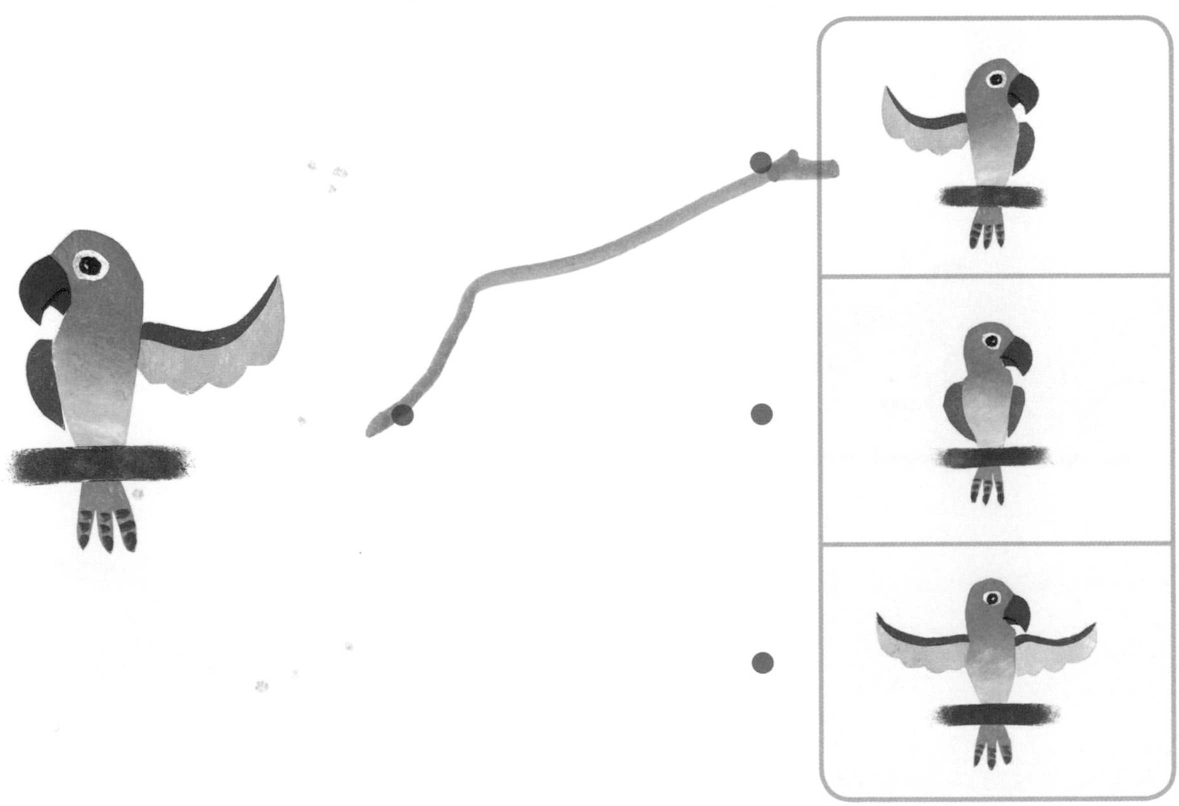

Matching Mirror Images

Level Two

Name

Date

To parents

The number of answer choices has increased. Encourage your child to look carefully at each one.

■ Draw a line to the mirror image.

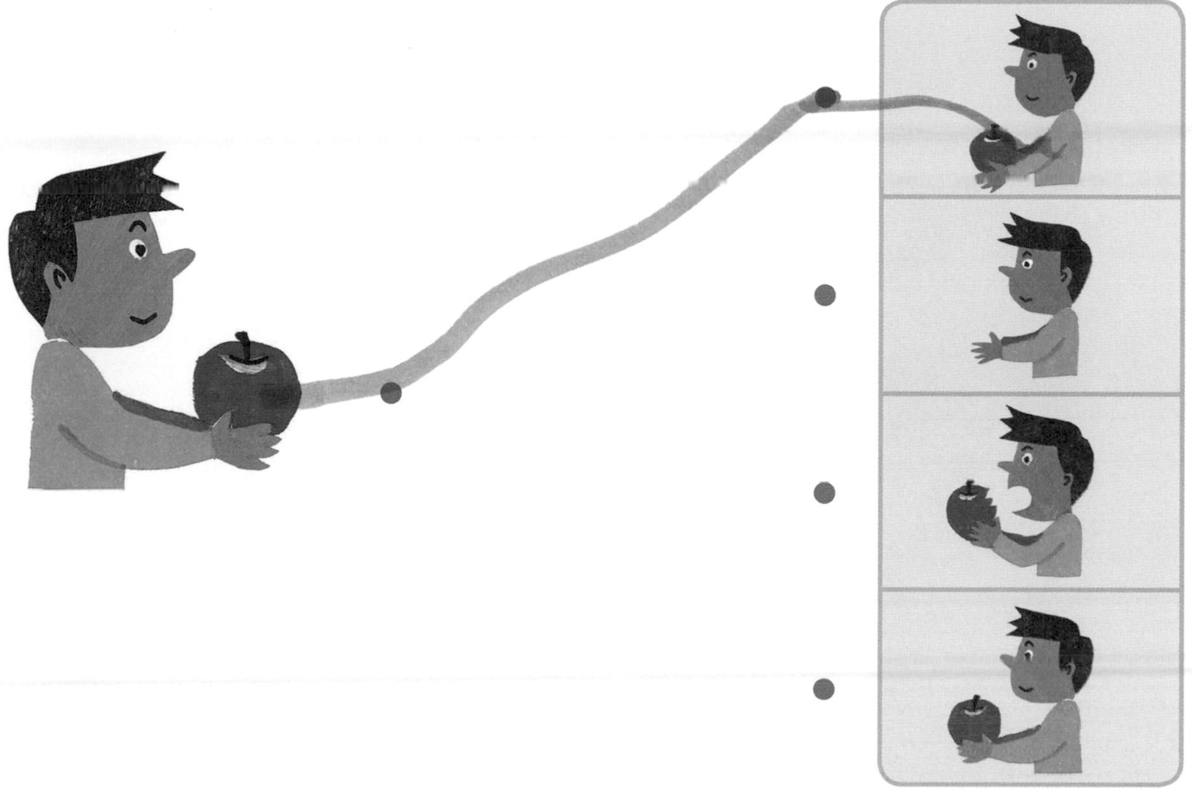

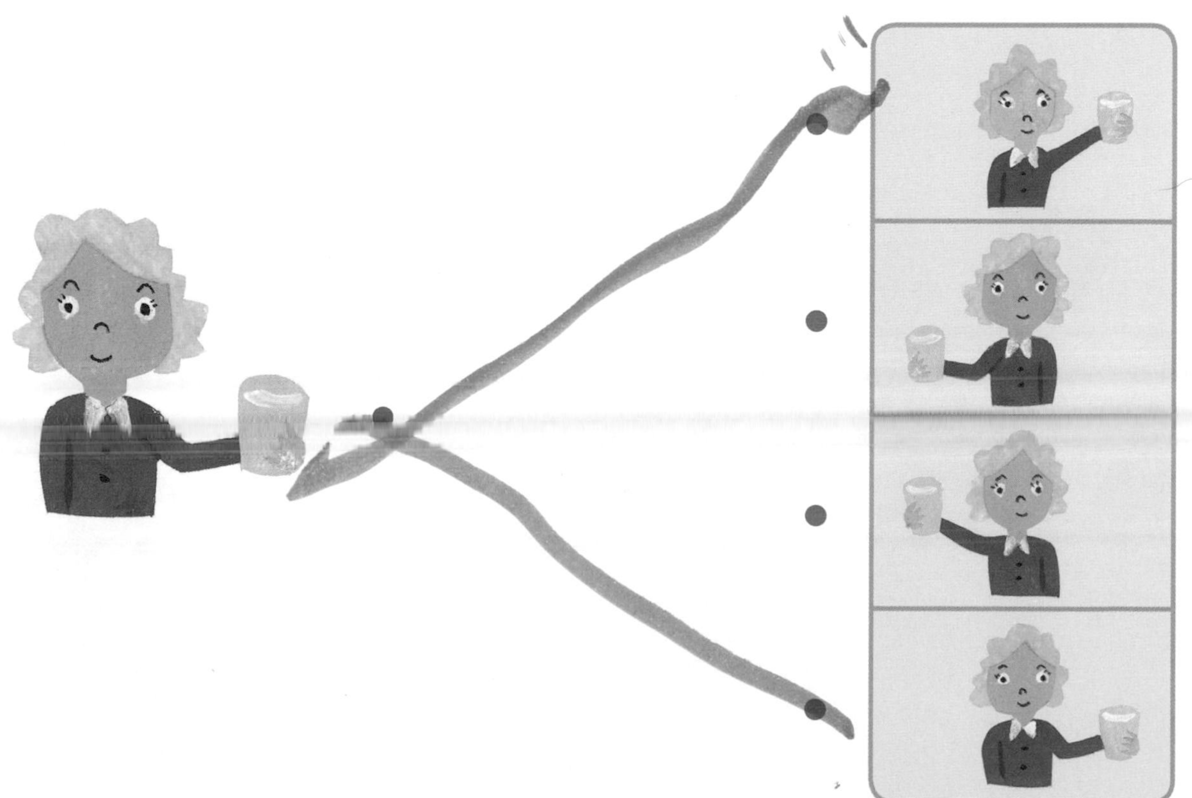

■ Draw a line to the mirror image.

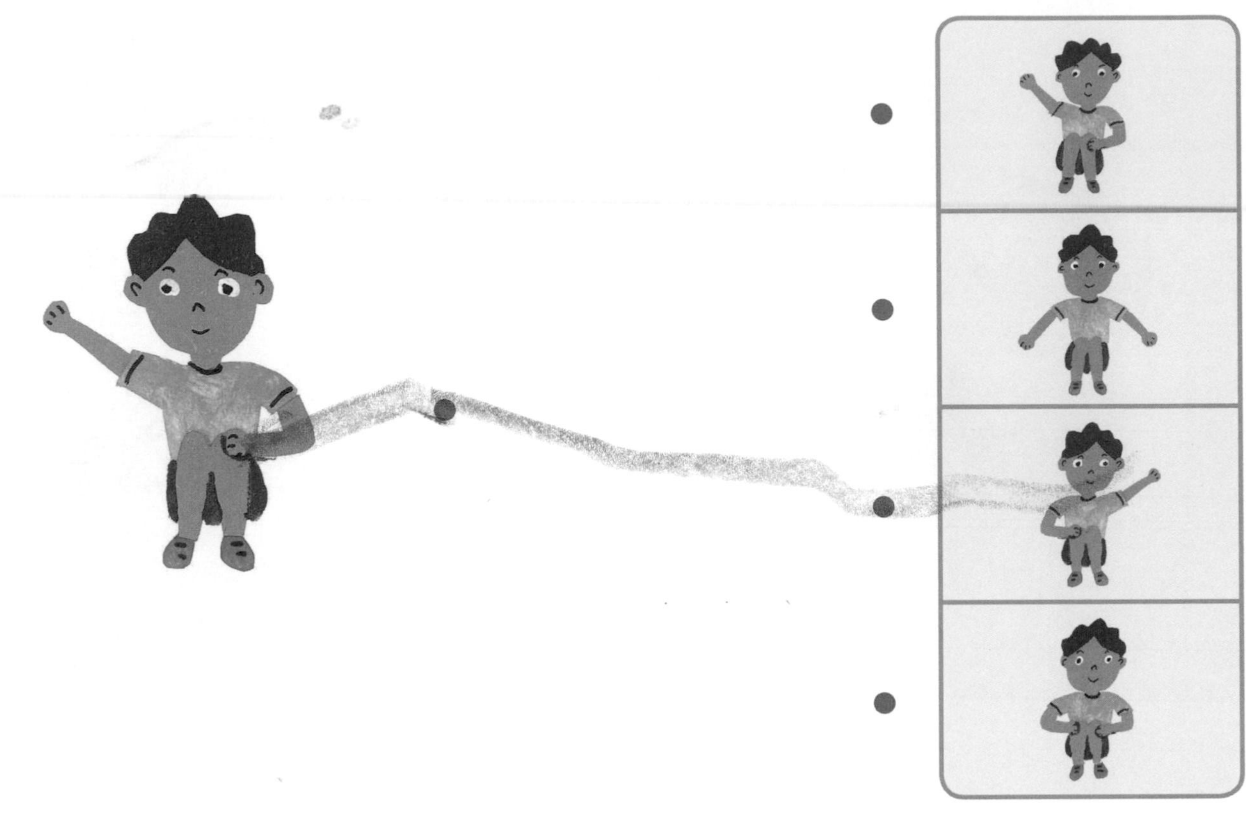

Matching Mirror Images
Level Three

Name

Date

■ Draw a line to the mirror image.

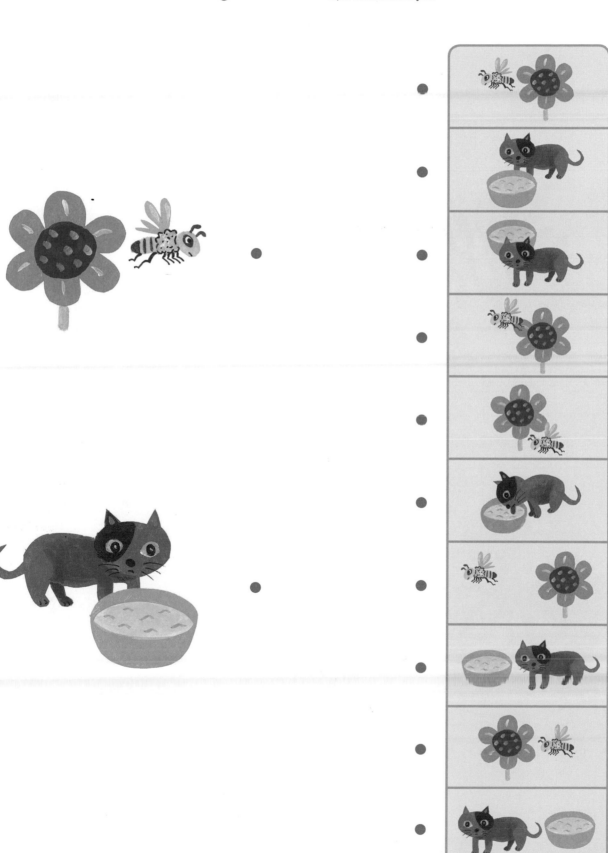

To parents
Help your child notice whether the animal is beside, in front of, or behind the object.

■ Draw a line to the mirror image.

Differentiation

Level One

Name

Date

To parents

If your child has difficulty, ask him or her to describe how each object is used.

■ Write a check mark (✓) above the picture that does not belong.

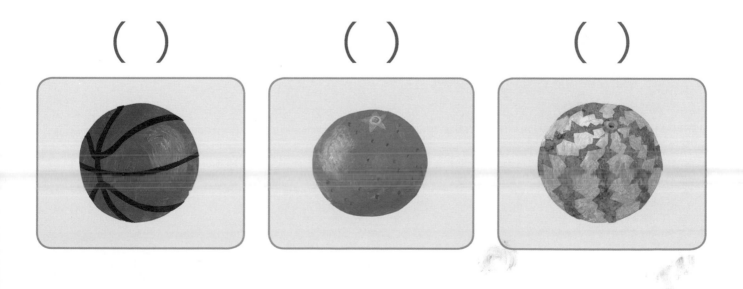

( ) ( ) ( )

■ Write a check mark (✓) above the picture that does not belong.

Differentiation
Level Two

Name

Date

To parents

There are now four answer choices. If your child has difficulty, guide him or her to identify the three objects that are in the same category.

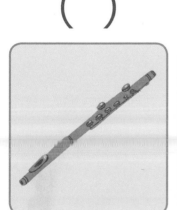

■ Write a check mark (✓) above the picture that does not belong.

( ) ( ) ( ) ( )

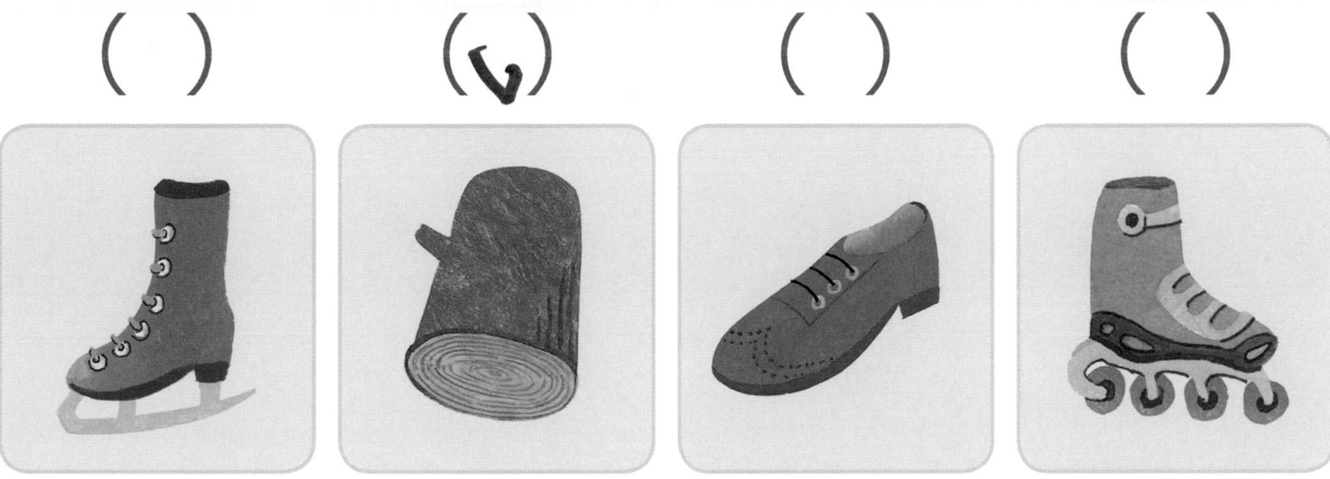

( ) ( ) ( ) ( )

■ Write a check mark (✓) above the picture that does not belong.

( ) ( ) ( ) ( )

Differentiation
Level Three

Name

Date

To parents
Now there are two pictures that do not belong. Encourage your child to look for both of them.

■ Write a check mark (✓) above the two pictures that do not belong.

( ) ( ) (✓) ( )

( ) ( ) ( ) ( )

( ) (✓)

SOAP

■ Write a check mark (✓) above the two pictures that do not belong.

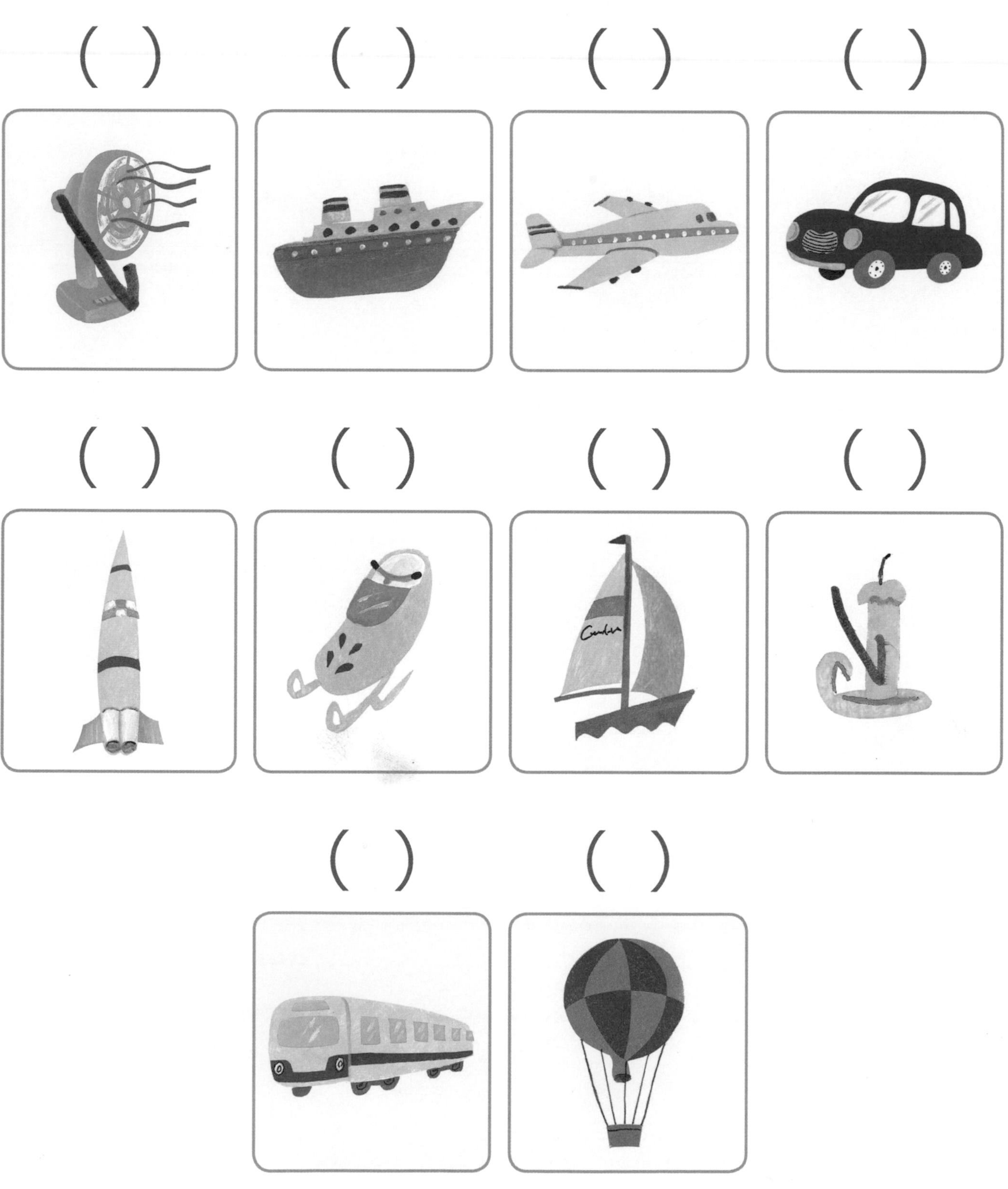

Differentiation
Level One

Name

Date

To parents
The goal of this activity is to find the two pictures that are in the same category. Help your child understand how this task differs from the previous one.

■ Write a check mark (✓) above the two pictures that are in the same category.

■ Write a check mark (✓) above the two pictures that are in the same category.

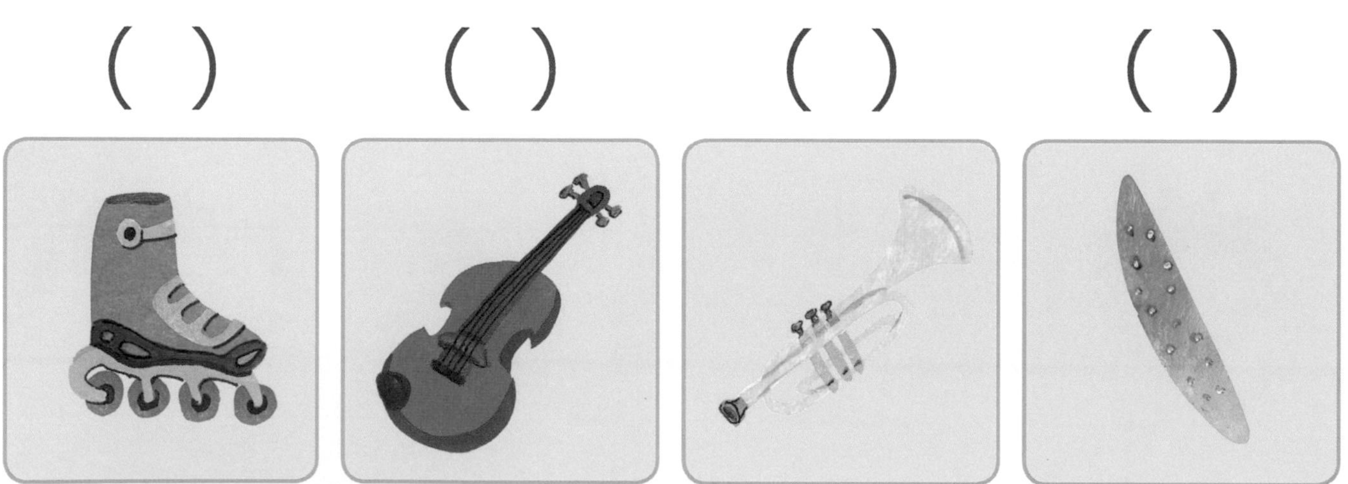

Differentiation

Level Two

Name

Date

To parents

If your child has difficulty, ask him or her to identify how each object is used.

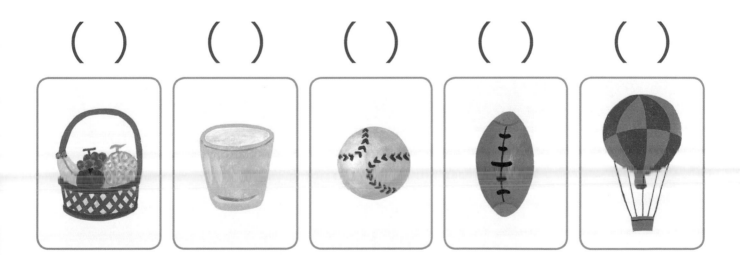

■ Write a check mark (✓) above the two pictures that are in the same category.

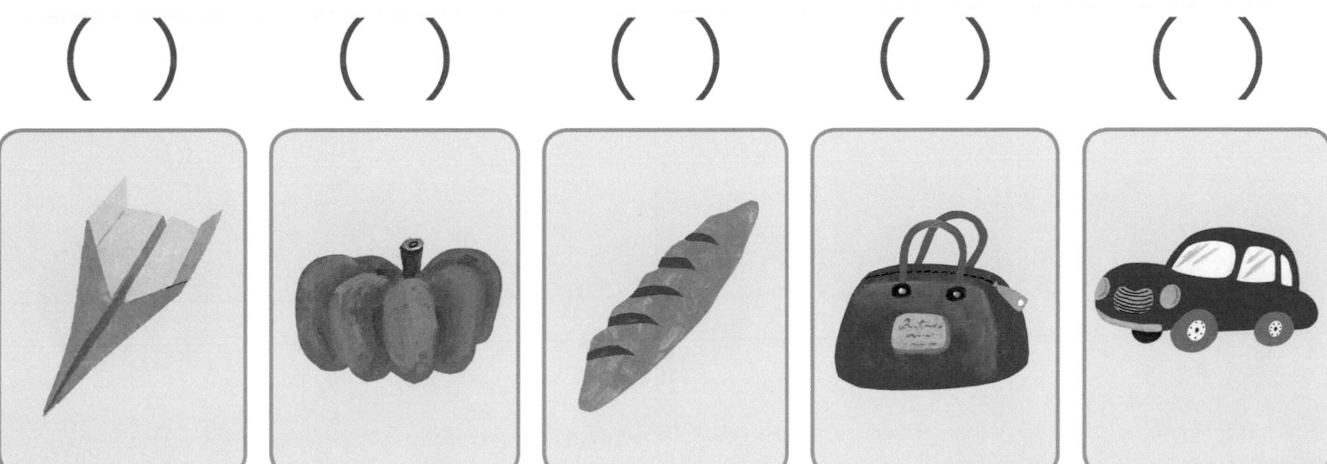

( ) ( ) ( ) ( ) ( )

■ Write a check mark (✓) above the two pictures that are in the same category.

( ) ( ) ( ) ( ) ( )

( ) ( ) ( ) ( ) ( )

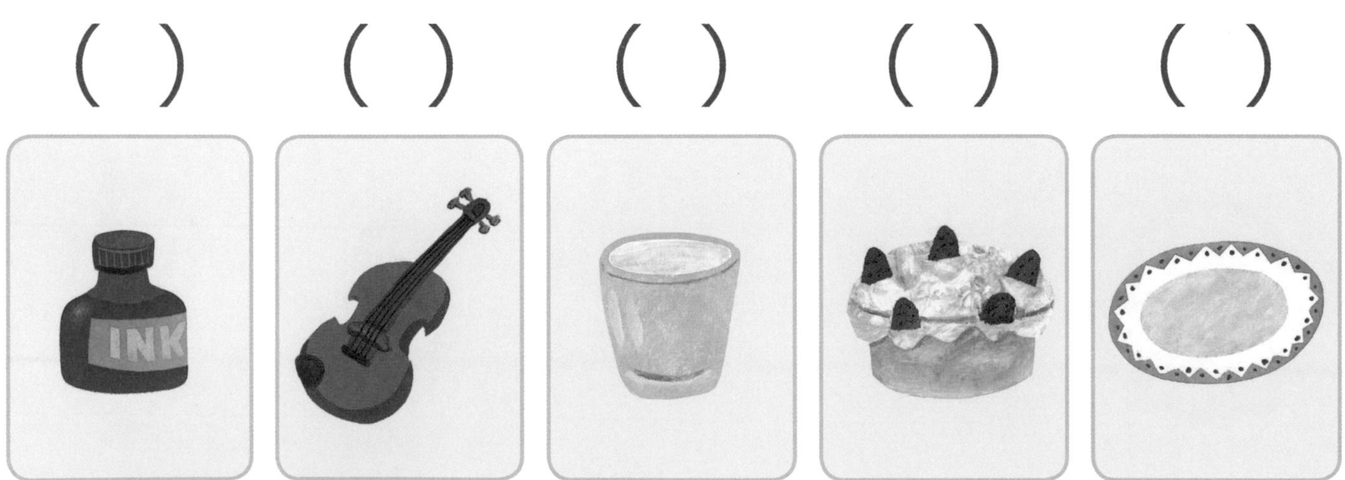

Differentiation

Level Three

Name

Date

To parents

The instructions have changed. Help your child look for the three objects that are in the same category.

■ Write a check mark (✓) above the three pictures that are in the same category.

( ) ( ) ( ) ( )

( ) ( ) ( ) ( )

( ) ( )

■ Write a check mark (✓) above the three pictures that are in the same category.

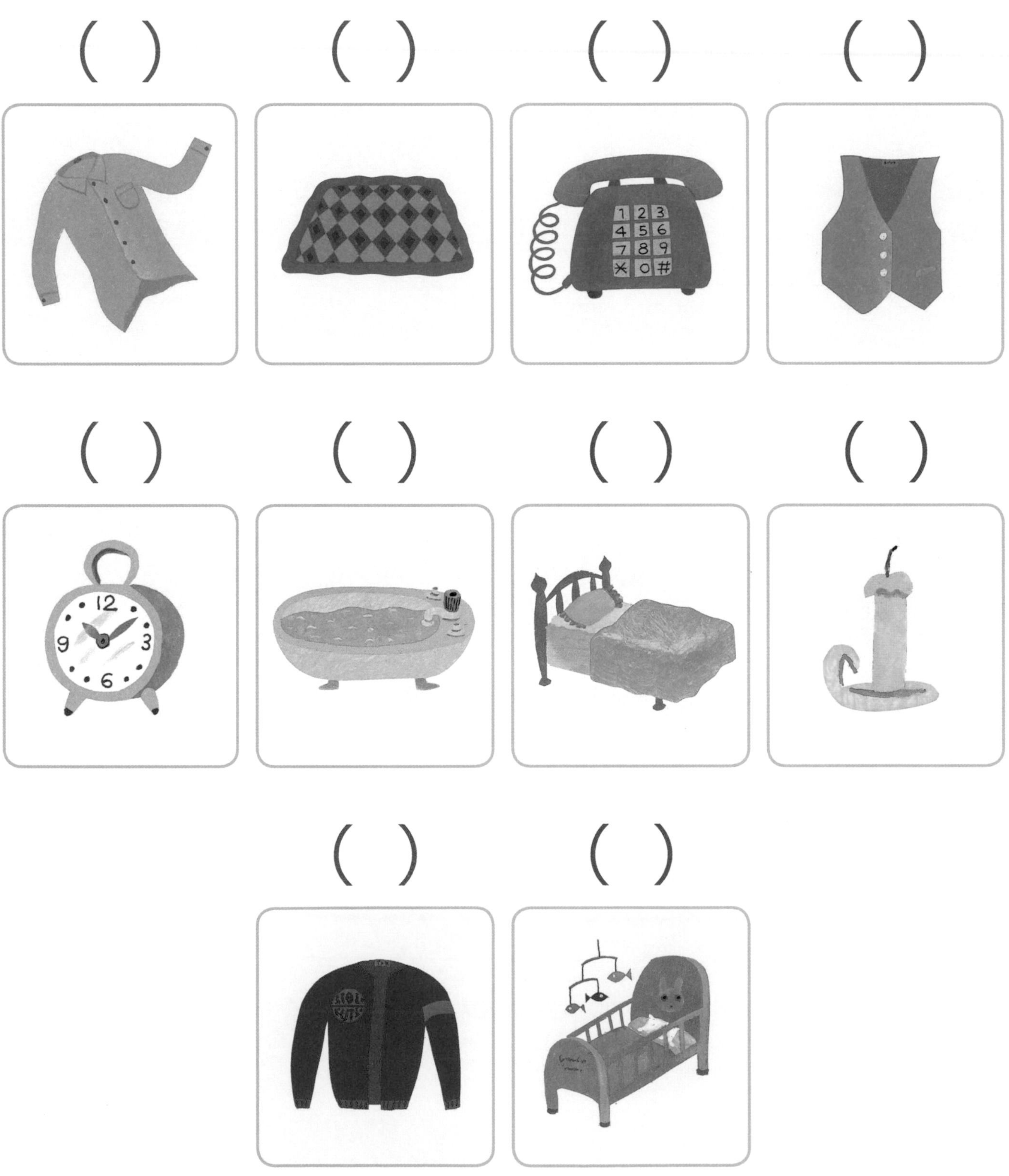

Differentiation
Level One

Name

Date

To parents

These exercises are more difficult because all three pictures are in the same general category. Help your child find the picture that does not belong with the other two.

■ Write a check mark (✓) above the picture that does not belong.

(✓) ( ) ( )

( ) ( ) ( )

■ Write a check mark (✓) above the picture that does not belong.

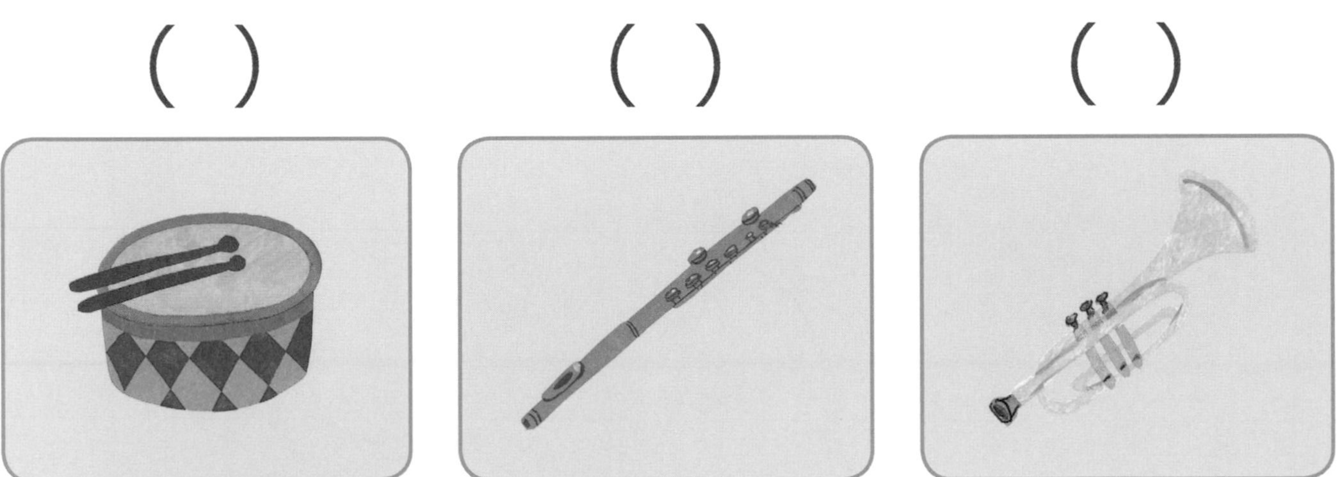

Differentiation
Level Two

Name

Date

To parents

The number of answer choices has increased. If your child has difficulty, talk together about each of the objects shown.

■ Write a check mark (✓) above the picture that does not belong.

  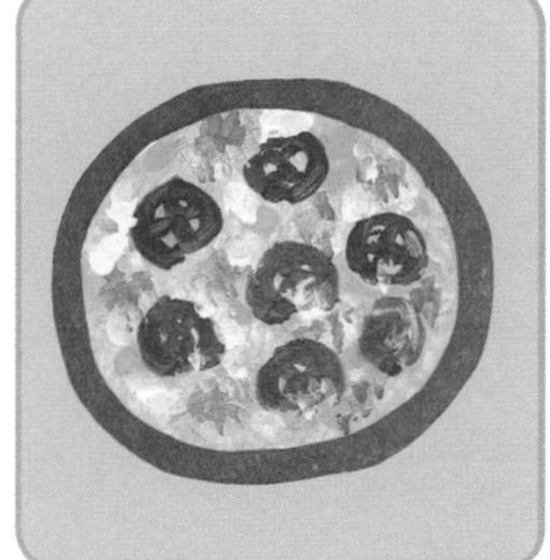 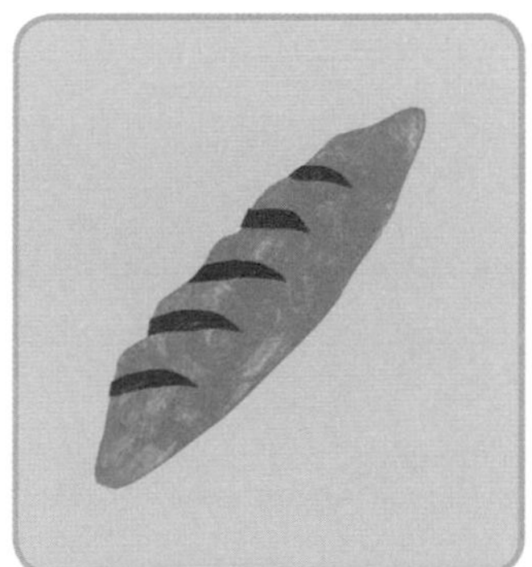

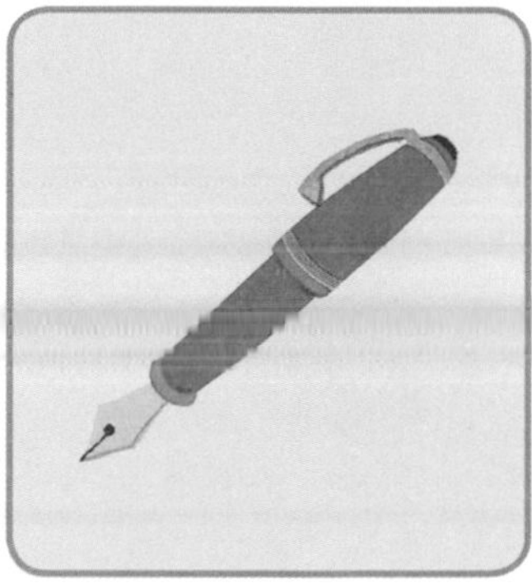

■ Write a check mark (✓) above the picture that does not belong.

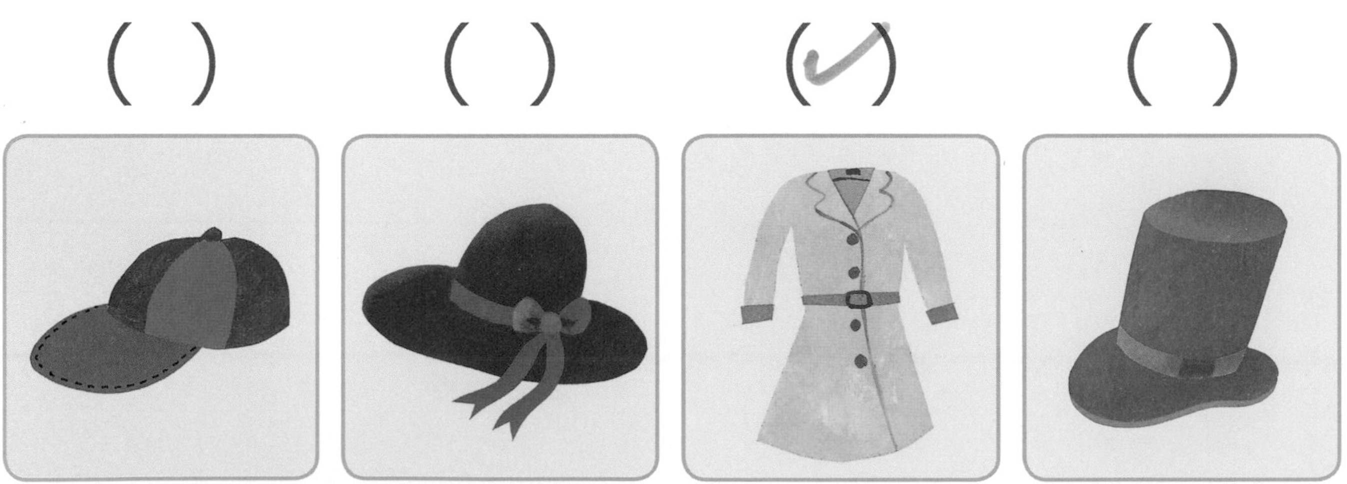

Differentiation

Level Three

To parents

Now there are two pictures that do not belong. Encourage your child to find both of them.

■ Write a check mark (✓) above the two pictures that do not belong.

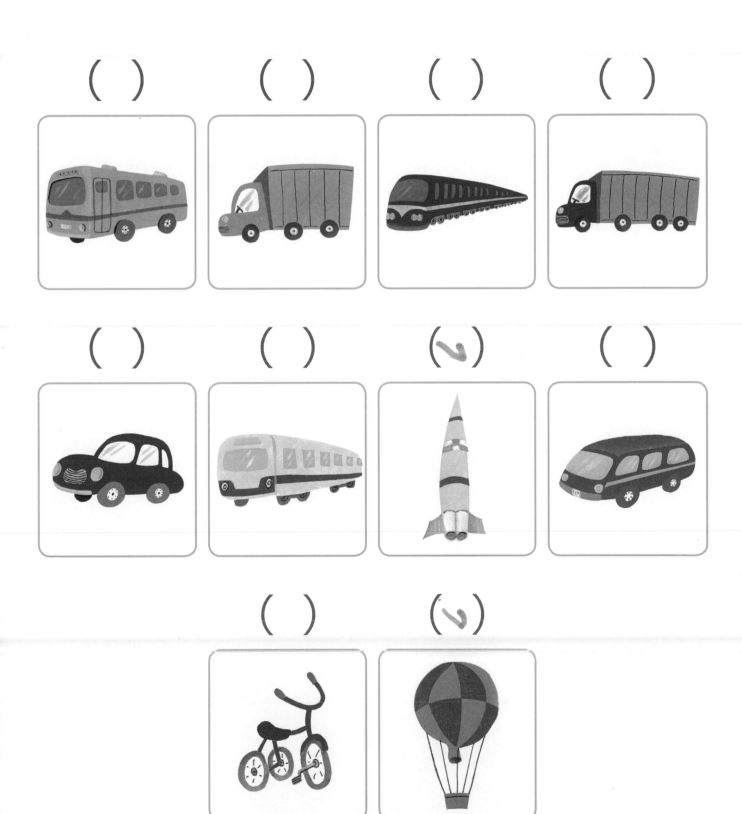

( ) ( ) ( ) ( )

( ) ( ) (✓) ( )

( ) (✓)

■ Write a check mark (✓) above the two pictures that do not belong.

Differentiation
Level One

Name

Date

To parents

All four objects are in the same general category. Help your child find the two that are the most similar.

■ Write a check mark (✓) above the two pictures that are the most similar.

( ) (✓) ( ) (✓)

(✓) (✓) ( ) ( )

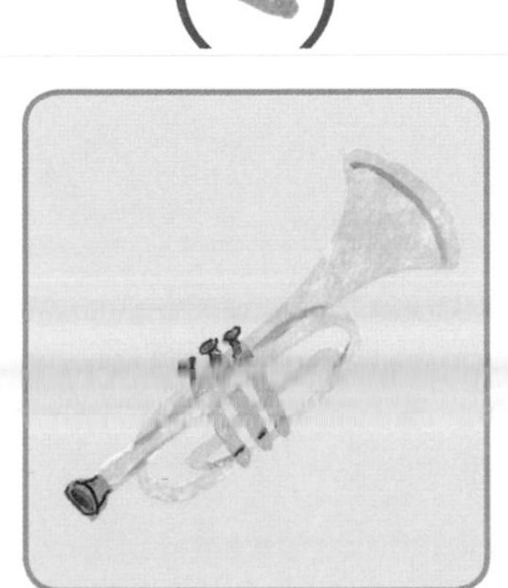
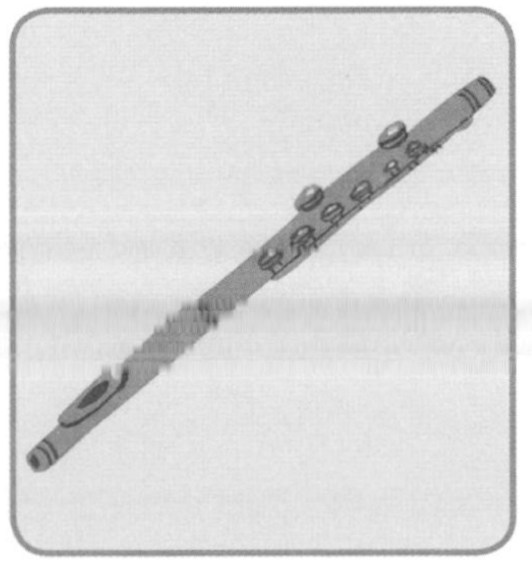

- Write a check mark (✓) above the two animals that are the most similar.

Differentiation

Level Two

Name
Date

To parents

The number of answer choices has increased. Guide your child to look carefully at each picture.

■ Write a check mark (✓) above the two pictures that are the most similar.

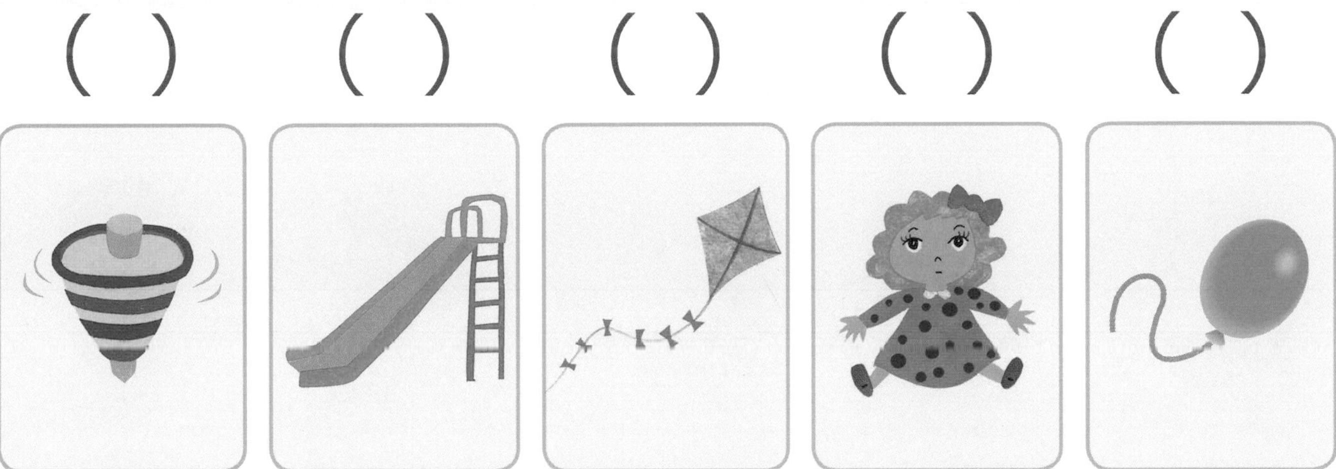

( ) ( ) ( ) ( ) ( )

■ Write a check mark (✓) above the two people who are doing something similar.

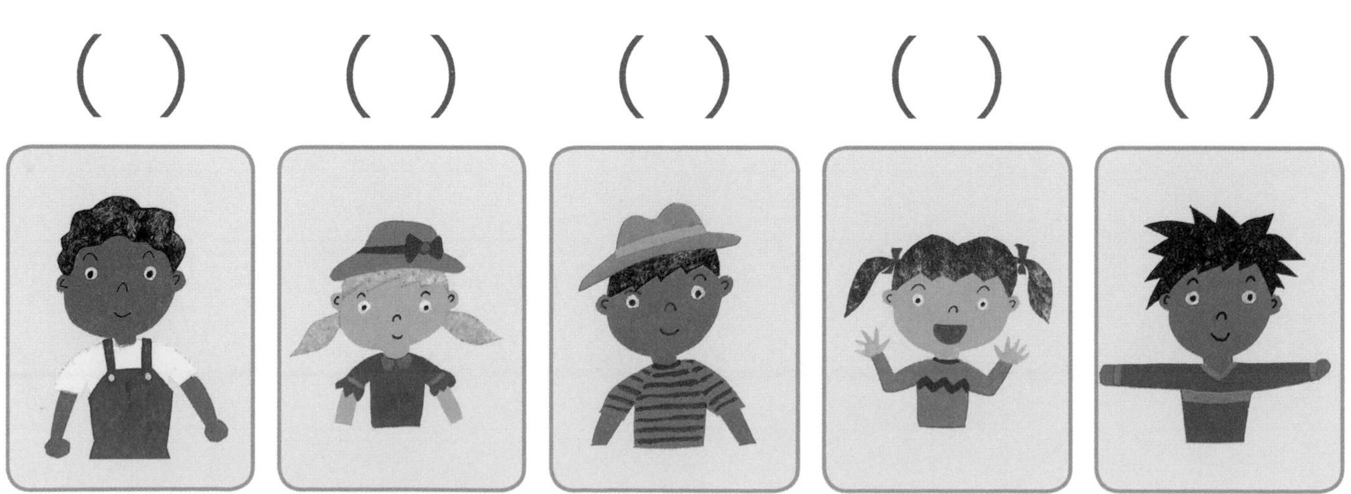

Differentiation
Level Three

Name

Date

To parents
If your child has difficulty, help him or her look for a group of exactly three objects that do something similar.

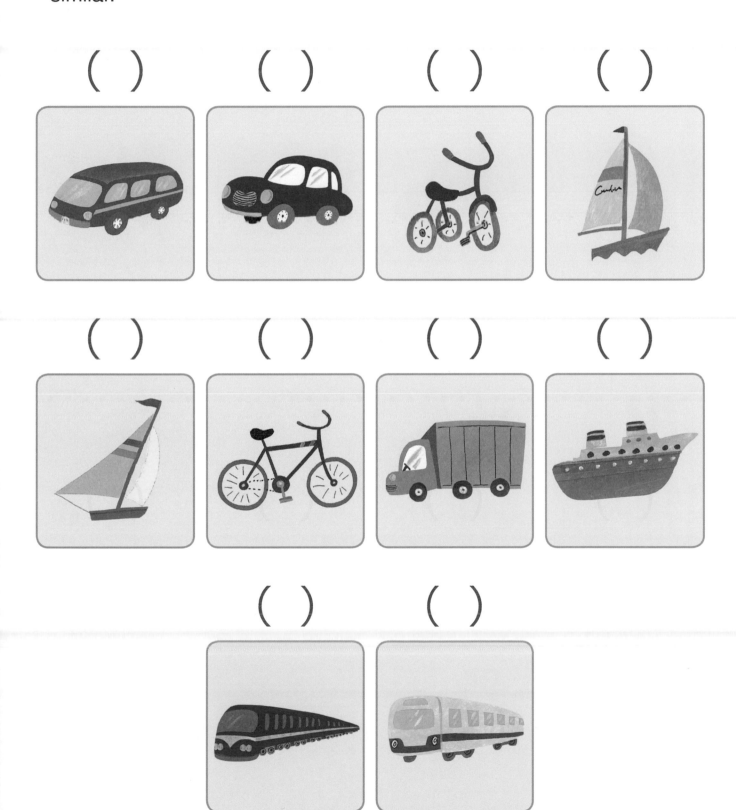

■ Write a check mark (✓) above the three objects that do something similar.

( ) ( ) ( ) ( )

( ) ( ) ( ) ( )

( ) ( )

■ Write a check mark (✓) above the three animals that are the most similar.

Matching Pairs

Level One

Name
Date

To parents

If your child has difficulty, show him or her how to eliminate answer choices by crossing off matching pairs.

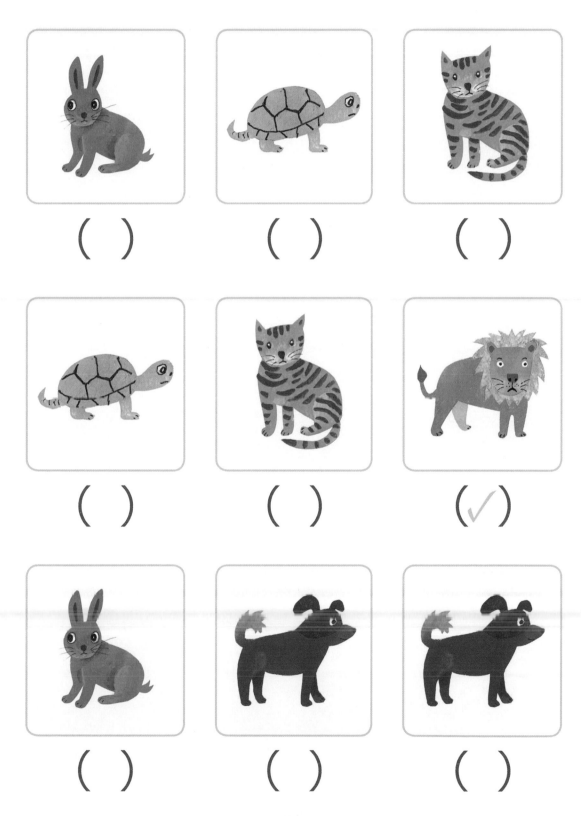

■ Write a check mark (✓) under the picture without a match.

( ) ( ) ( )

( ) ( ) (✓)

( ) ( ) ( )

■ Write a check mark (✓) under the picture without a match.

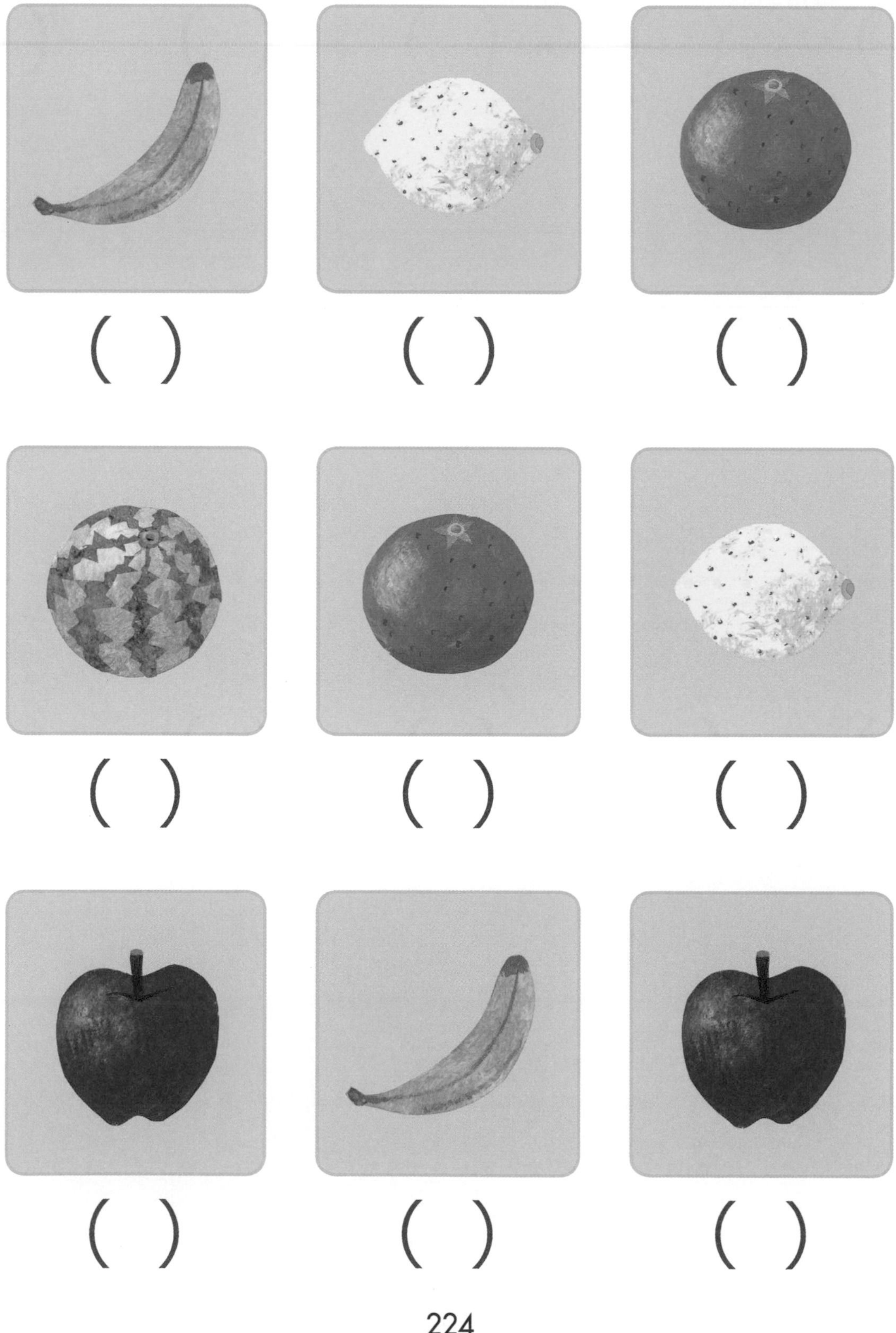

Matching Pairs

Level Two

Name

Date

To parents

You may wish to encourage your child to notice the color of the objects as a way to find matching pairs quickly.

■ Write a check mark (✓) under the picture without a match.

( ) ( ) ( ) ( )

( ) ( ) ( ) ( )

( ) ( ) ( )

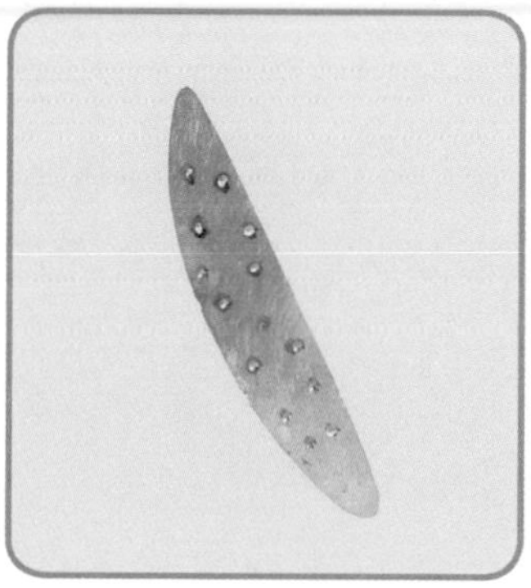

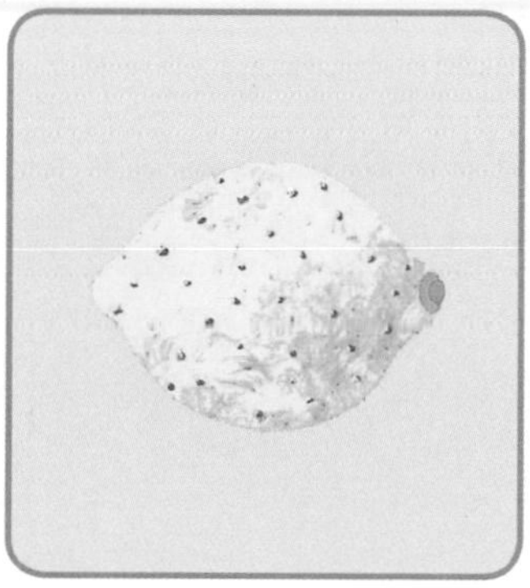

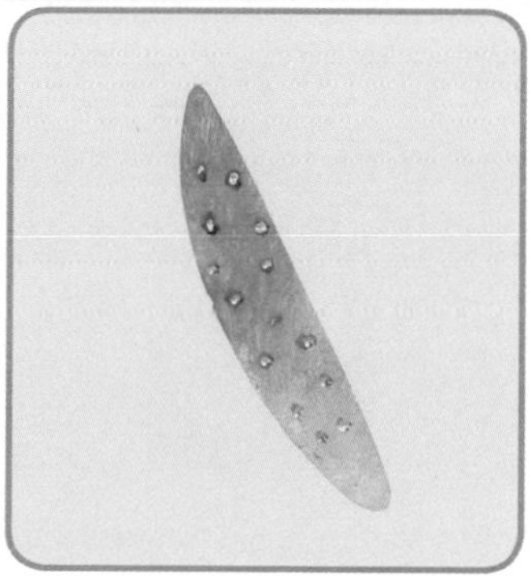

■ Write a check mark (✓) under the picture without a match.

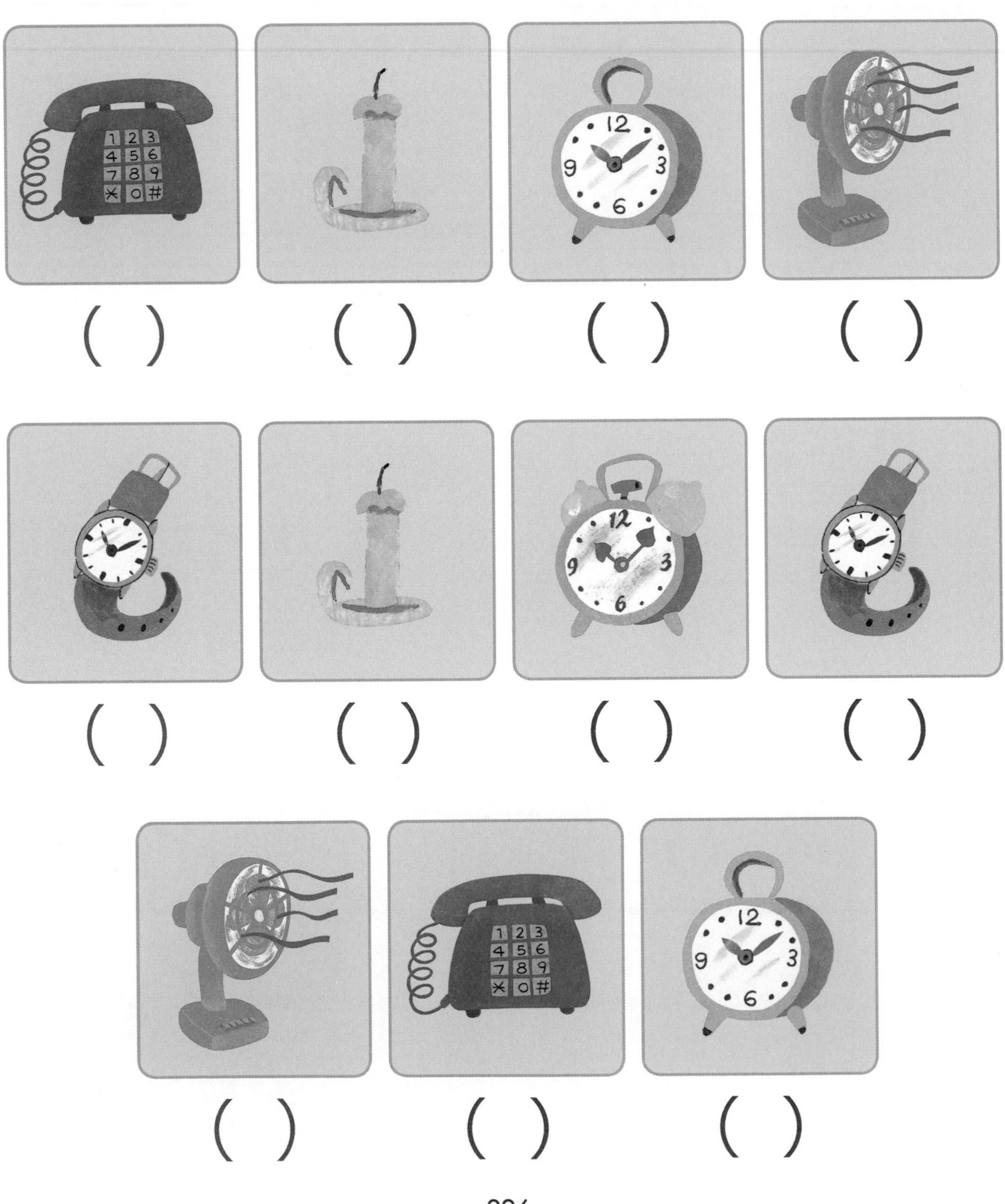

( ) ( ) ( ) ( )

( ) ( ) ( ) ( )

( ) ( ) ( )

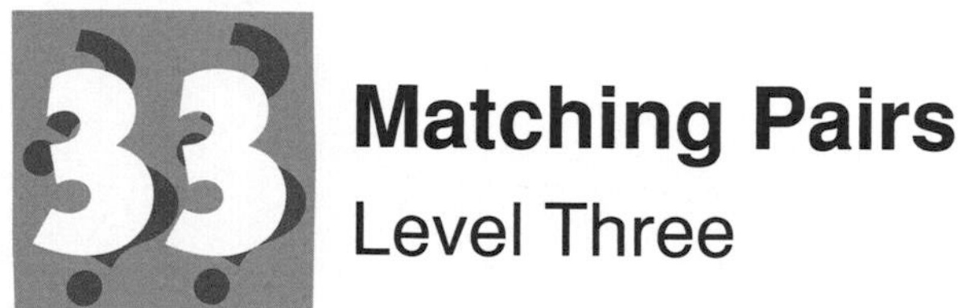

Matching Pairs
Level Three

Name

Date

To parents
If your child has difficulty, guide him or her to look at each picture one by one and check if it has a match.

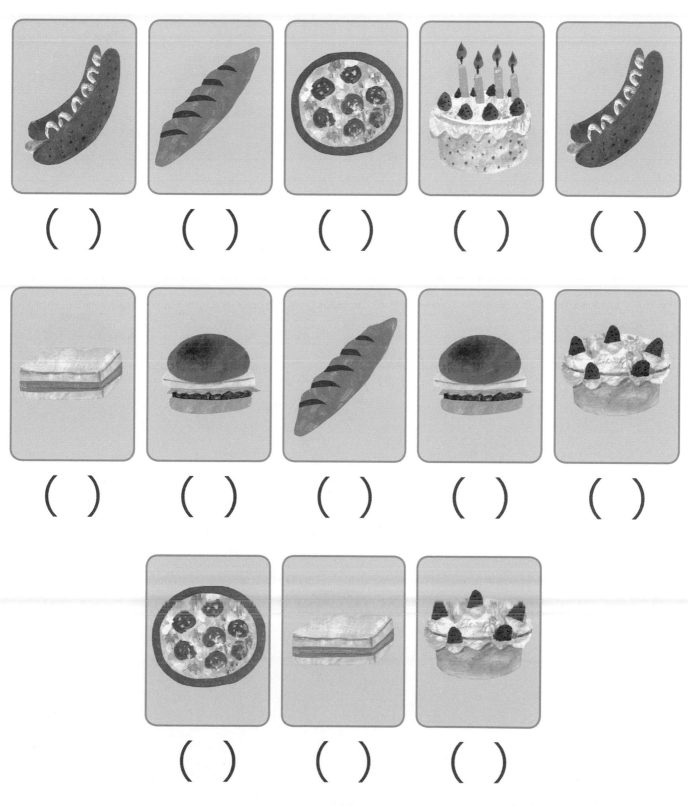

■ Write a check mark (✓) under the picture without a match.

( ) ( ) ( ) ( ) ( )

( ) ( ) ( ) ( ) ( )

( ) ( ) ( )

■ Write a check mark (✓) under the picture without a match.

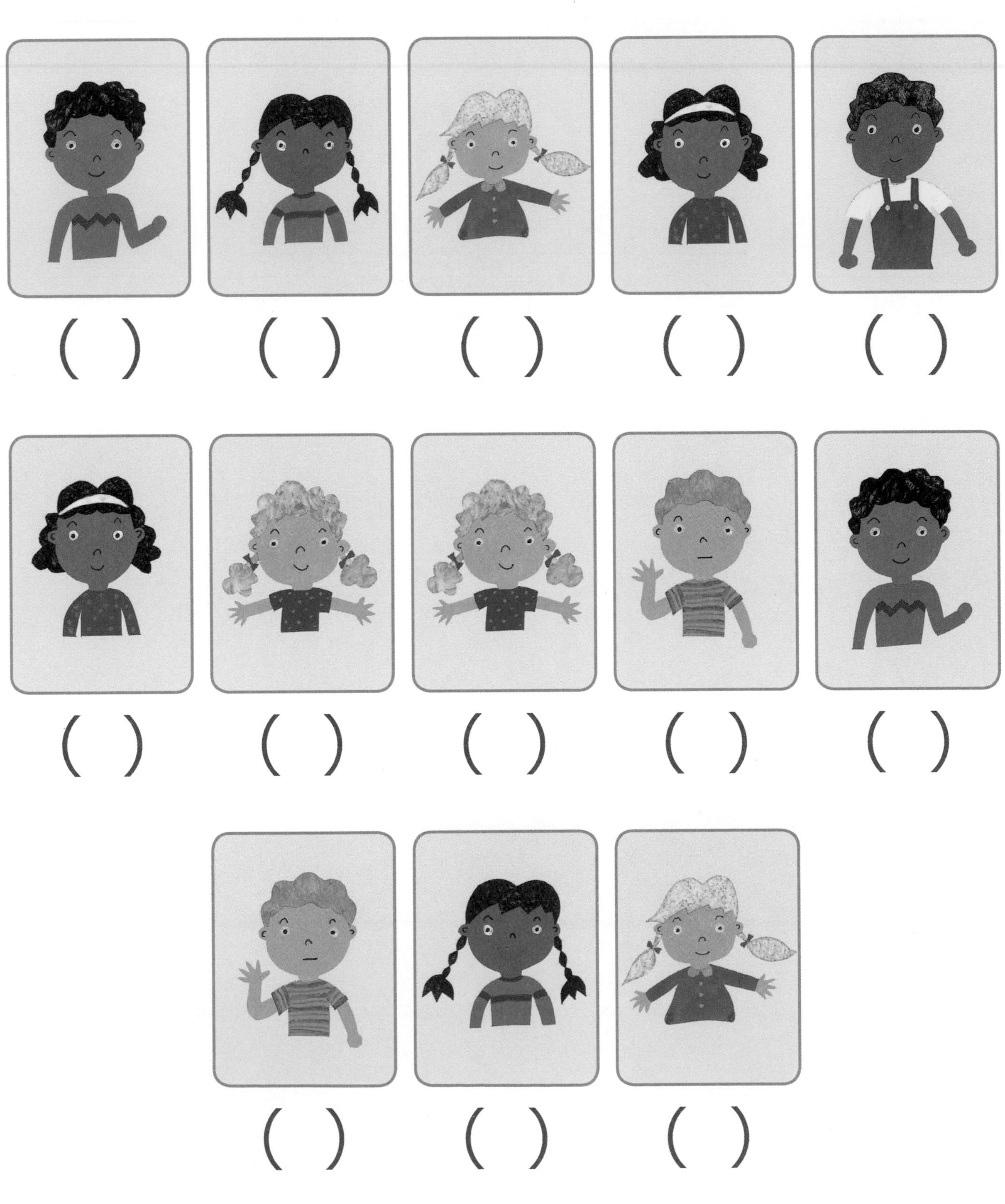

Identifying Objects

Level One

Name

Date

To parents

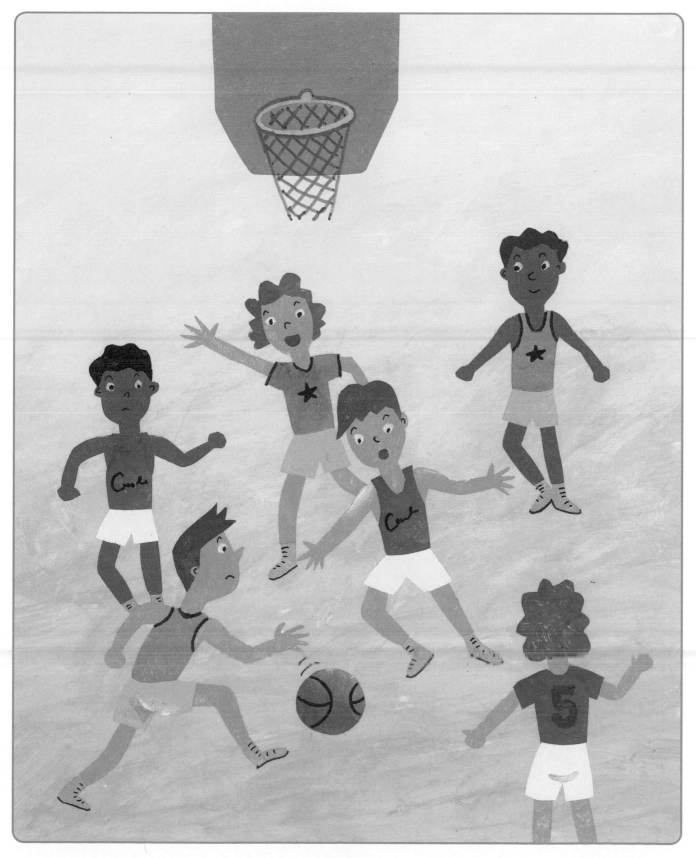

Point to the object shown in the instructions. Guide your child to find the same object in the picture below.

■ Find and circle the basketball ( ).

■ Find and circle the whisk ().

Identifying Objects
Level Two

Name

Date

To parents
If your child enjoys looking at the picture, encourage him or her to identify other objects in the scene.

■ Find and circle the hat ( ) and shovel ( ).

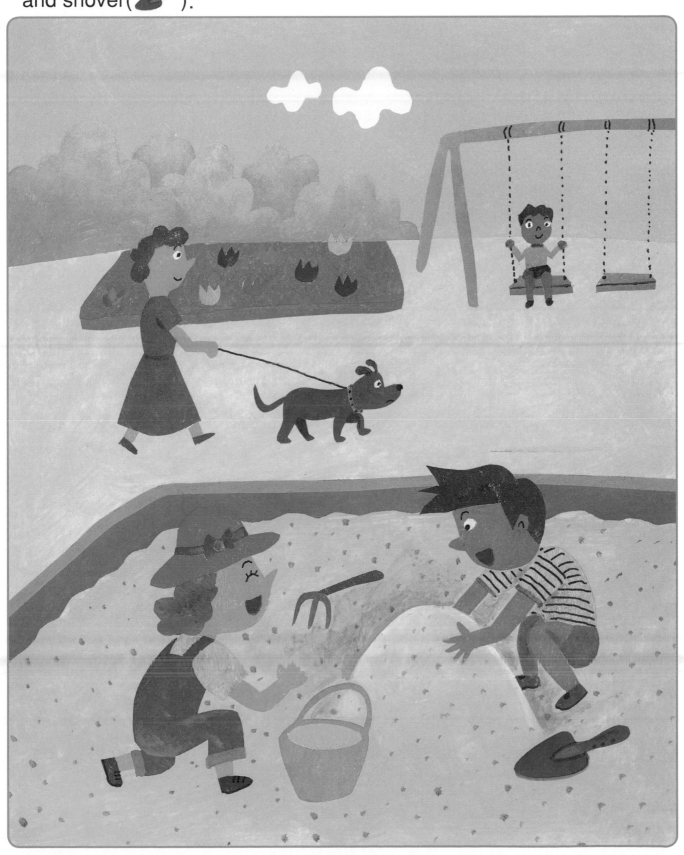

■ Find and circle the tires ( ) and the backpack ( ).

Identifying Objects
Level Three

Name

Date

To parents
The number of different objects to find and circle has increased. Encourage your child to look for all three objects.

■ Find and circle the bird (), the frog (), and the map ().

To parents

This is the last exercise of this section. Please praise your child for the effort it took to complete this workbook.

■ Find and circle the cake ( ), the bouquet ( ), and the gift ( ).

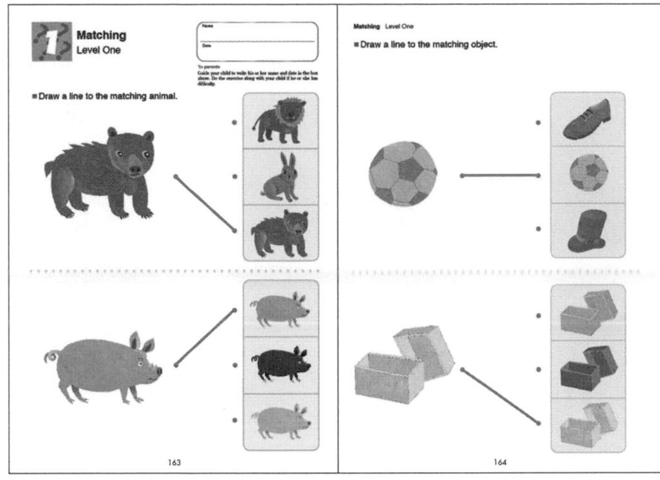

pages 163 and 164

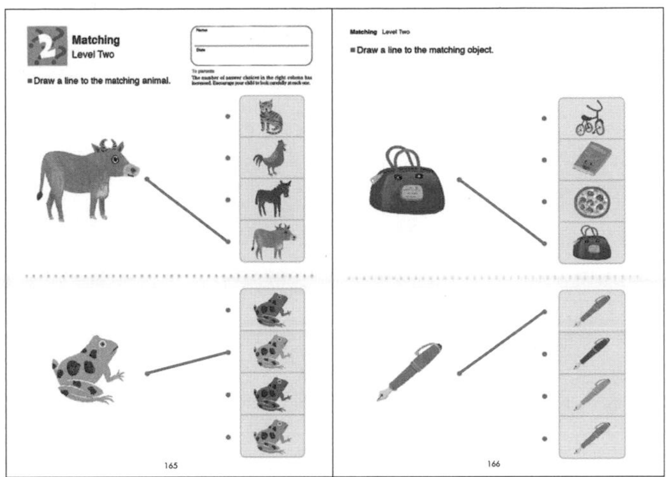

pages 165 and 166

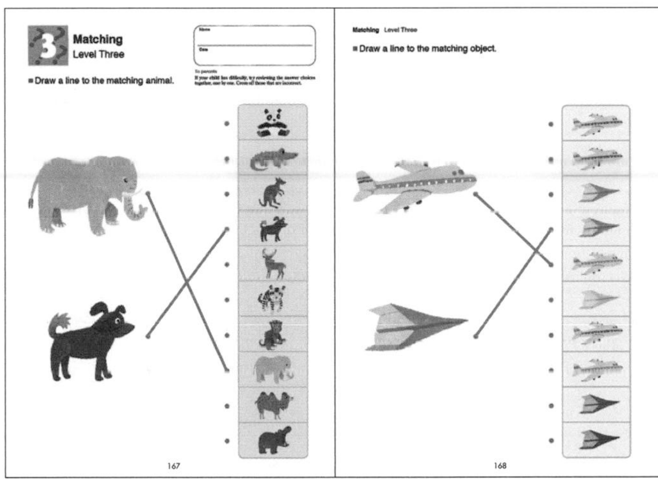

pages 167 and 168

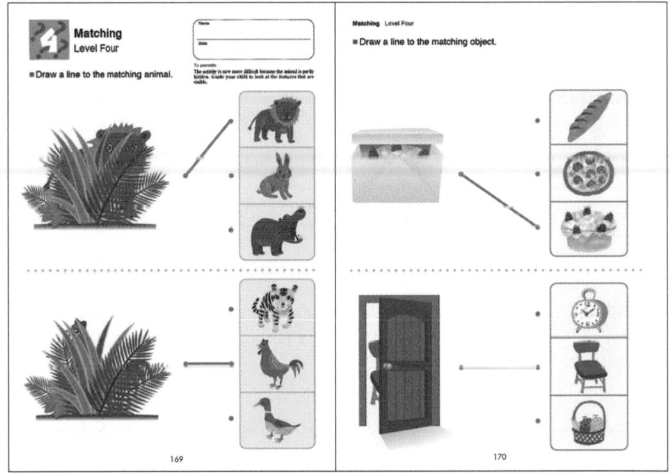

pages 169 and 170

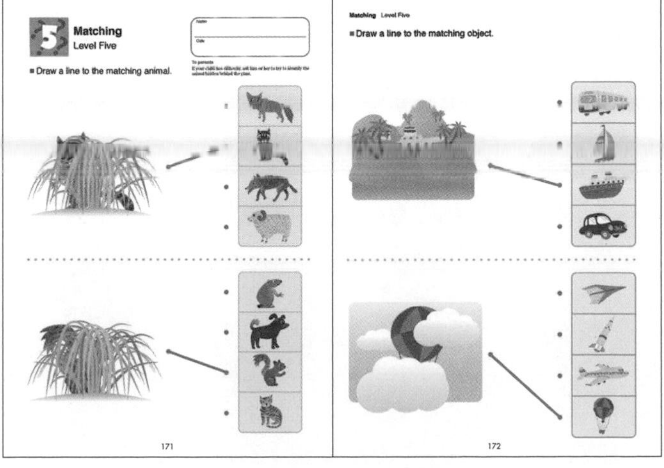

pages 171 and 172

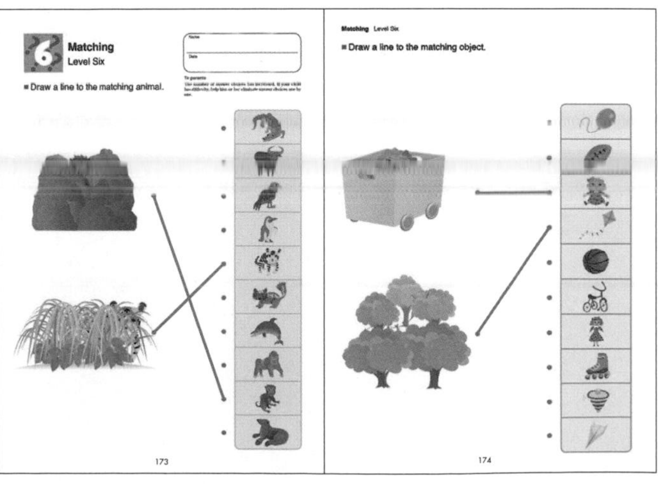

pages 173 and 174

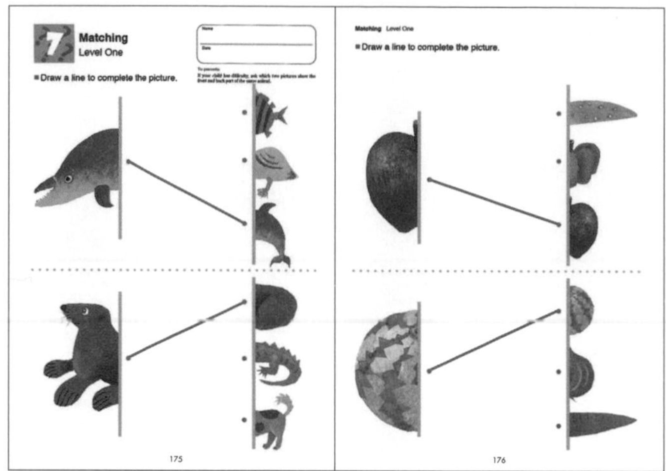

pages 175 and 176

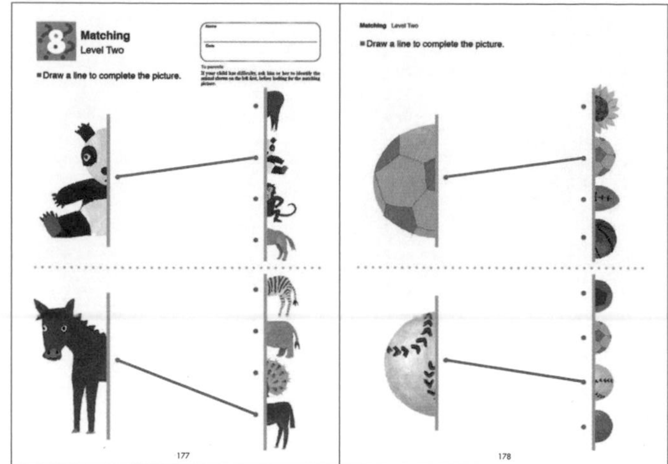

pages 177 and 178

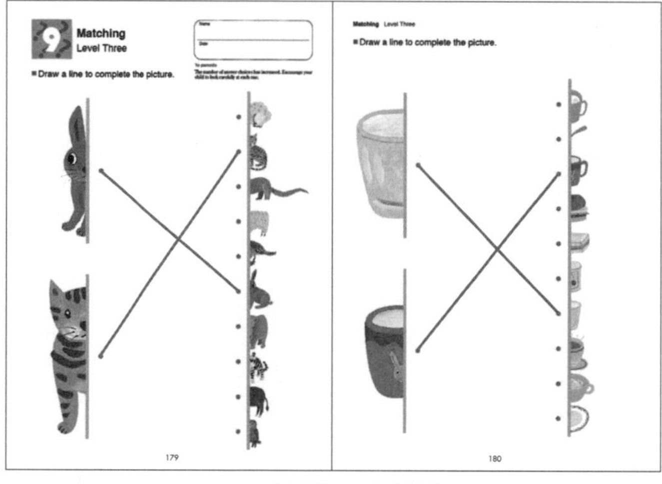

pages 179 and 180

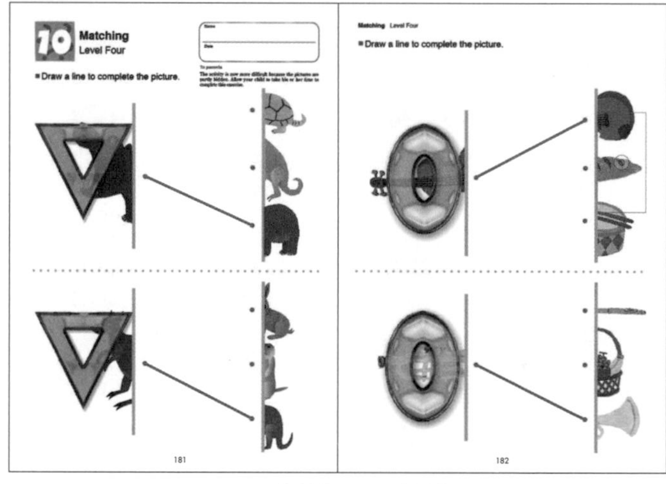

pages 181 and 182

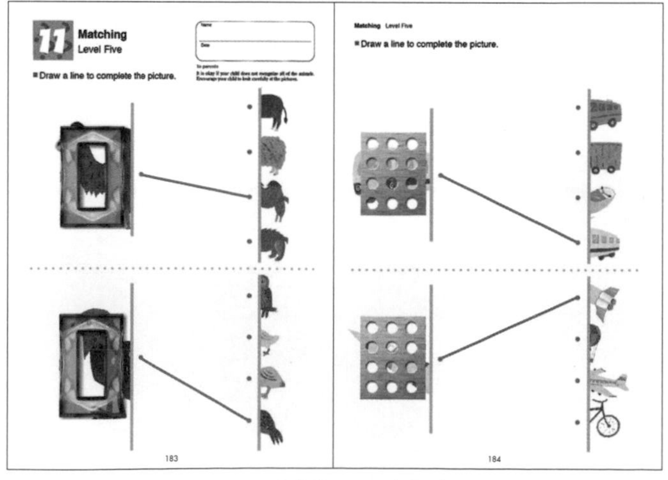

pages 183 and 184

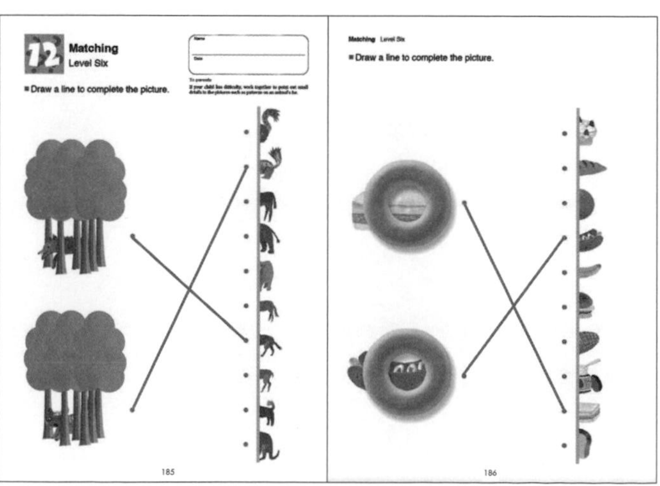

pages 185 and 186

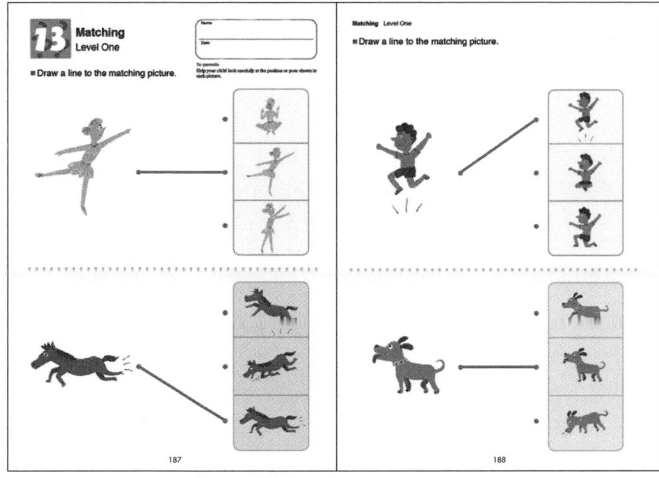

pages 187 and 188

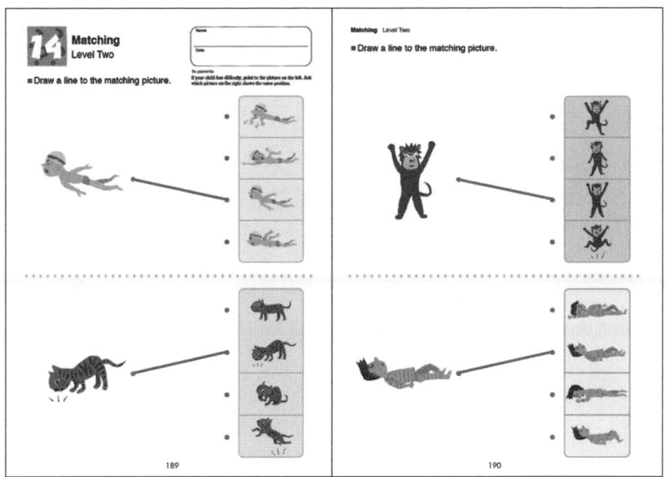

pages 189 and 190

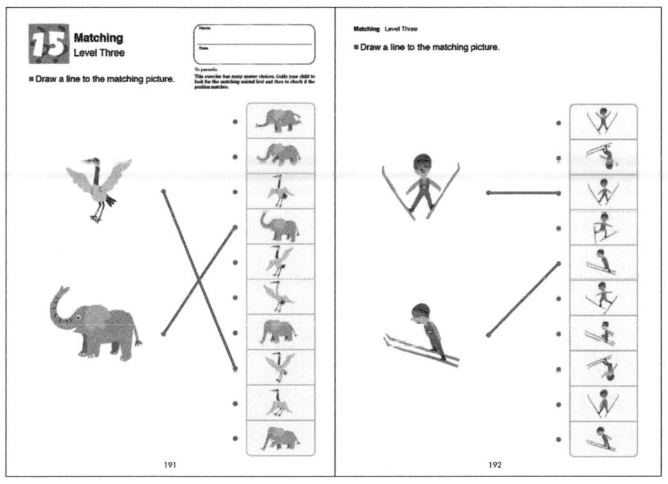

pages 191 and 192

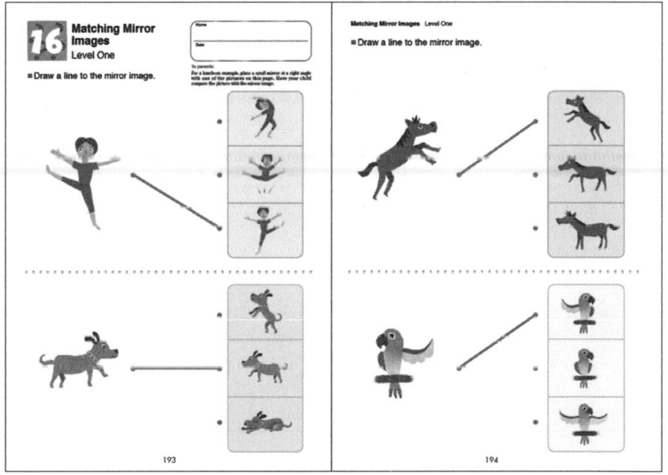

pages 193 and 194

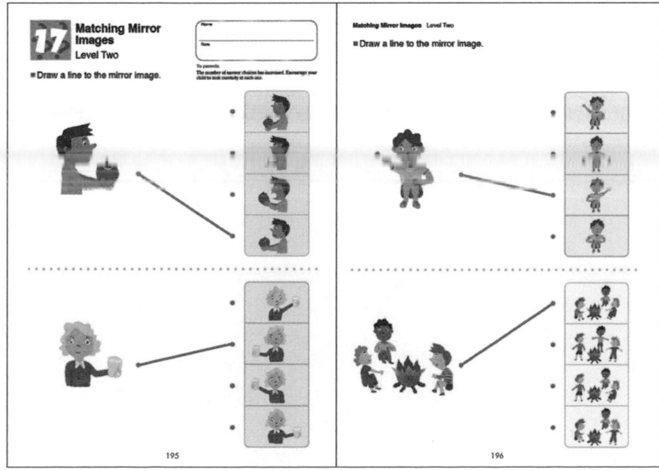

pages 195 and 196

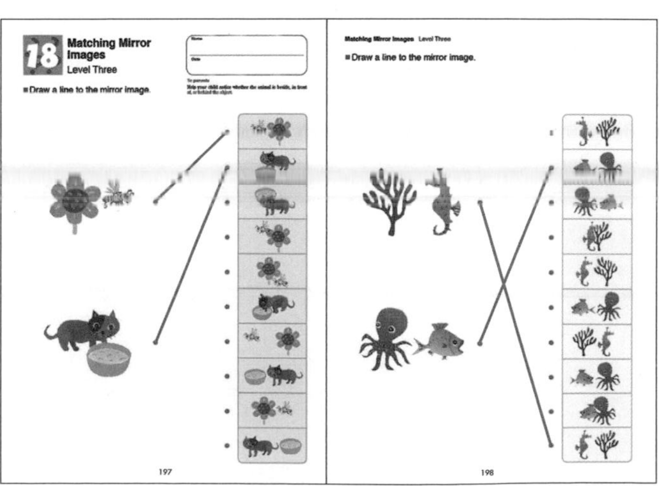

pages 197 and 198

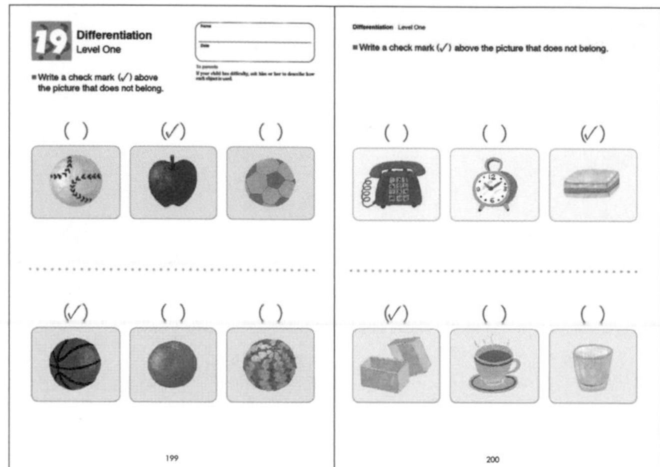

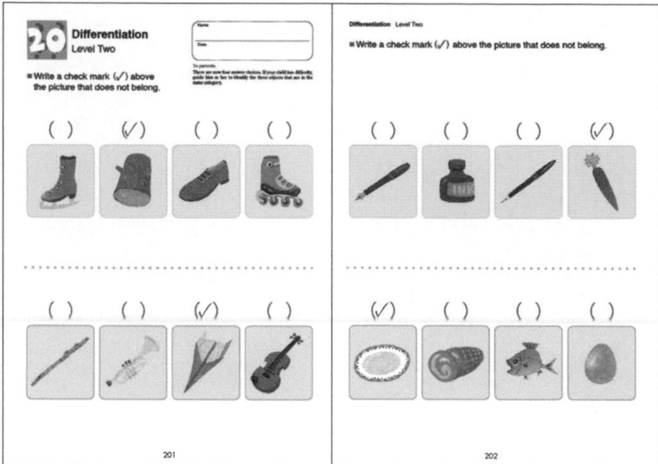

pages 199 and 200

pages 201 and 202

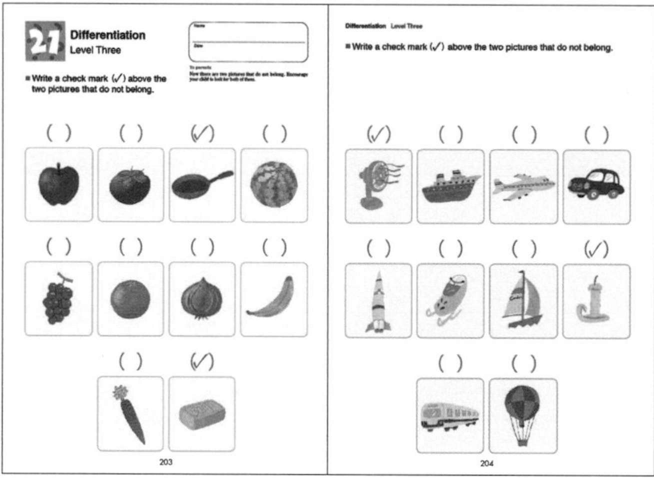

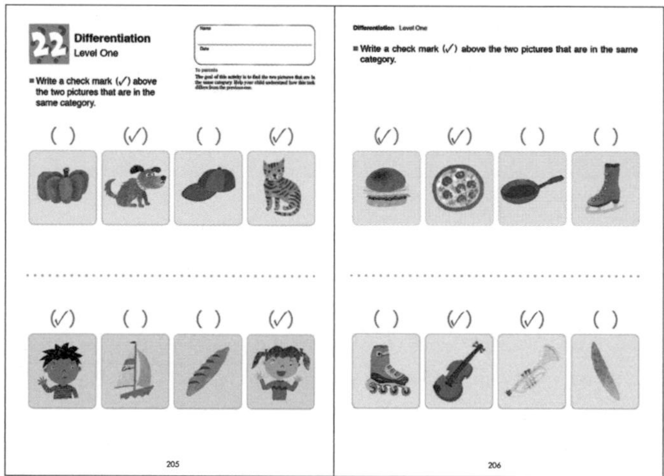

pages 203 and 204

pages 205 and 206

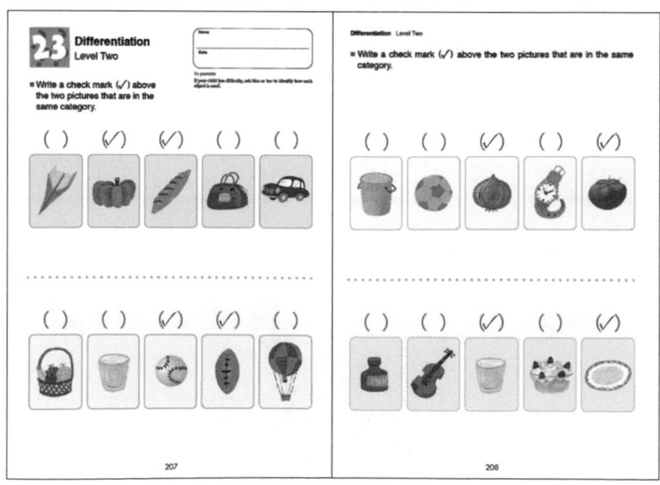

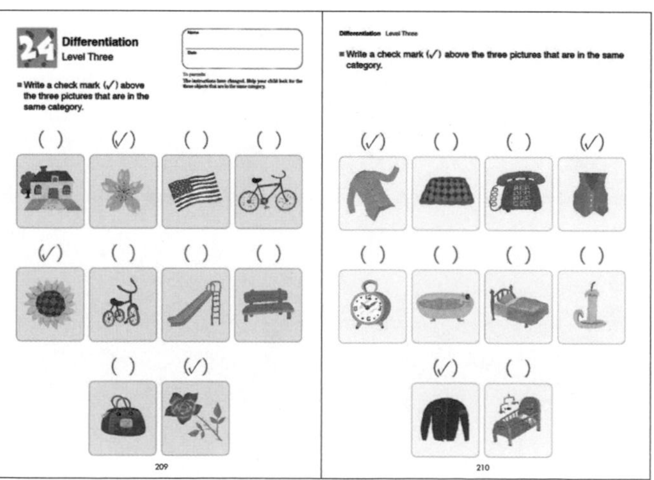

pages 207 and 208

pages 209 and 210

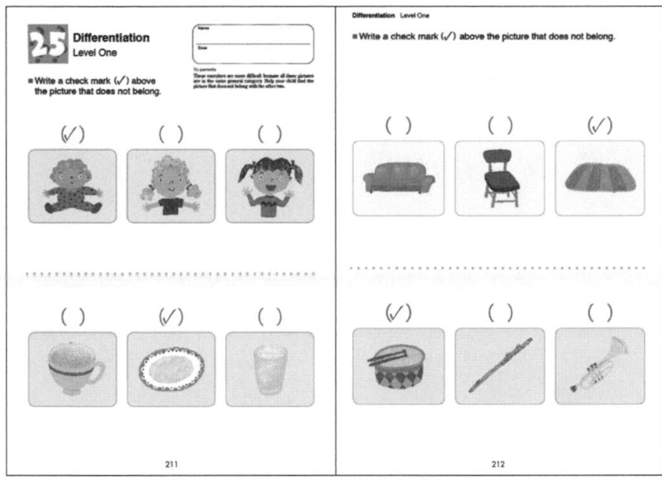

pages 211 and 212

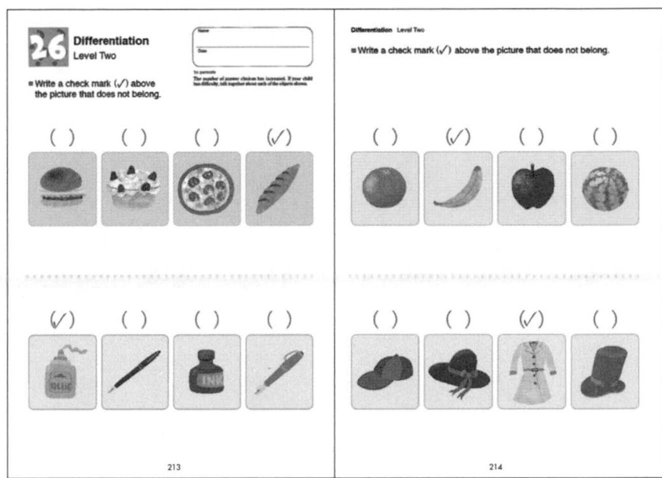

pages 213 and 214

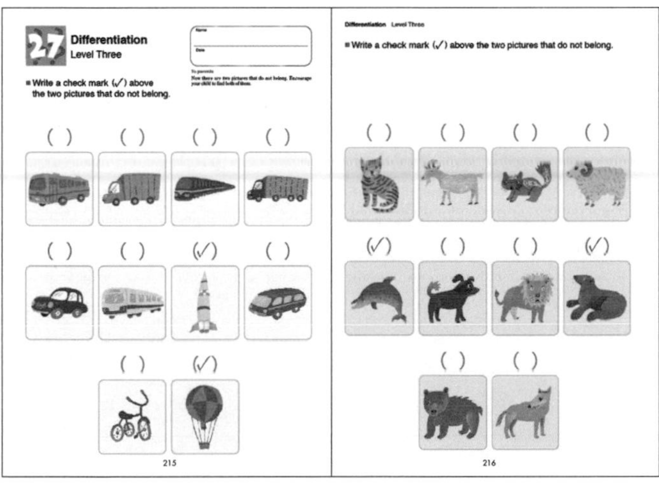

pages 215 and 216

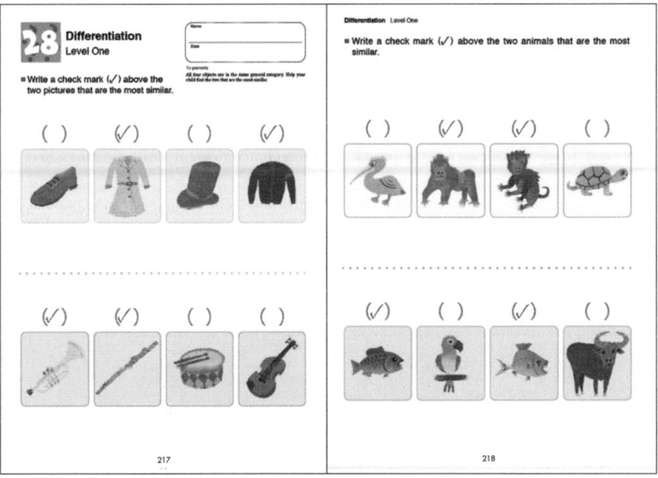

pages 217 and 218

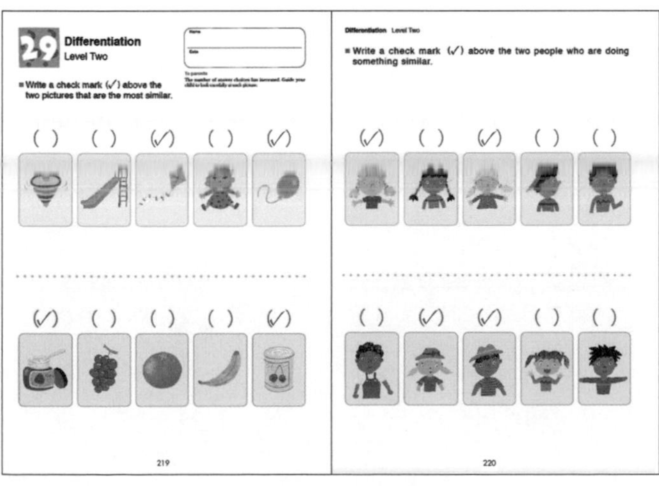

pages 219 and 220

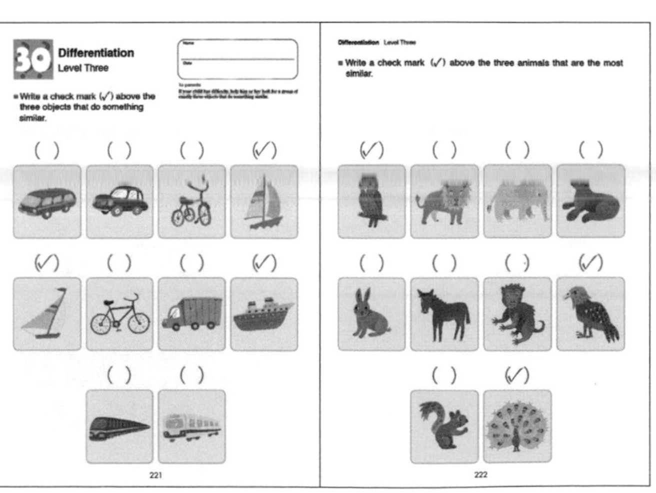

pages 221 and 222

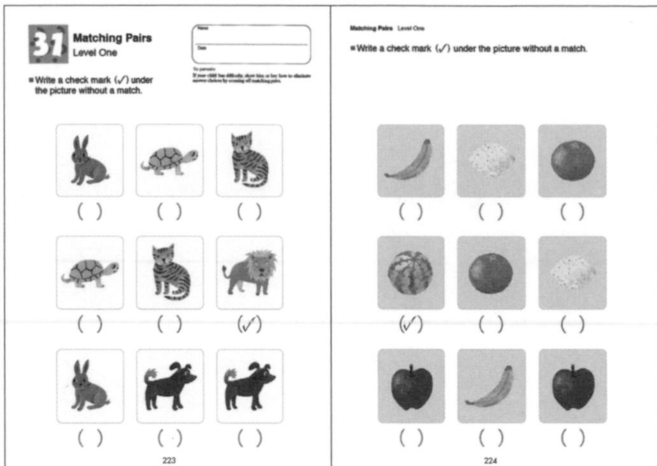

pages 223 and 224

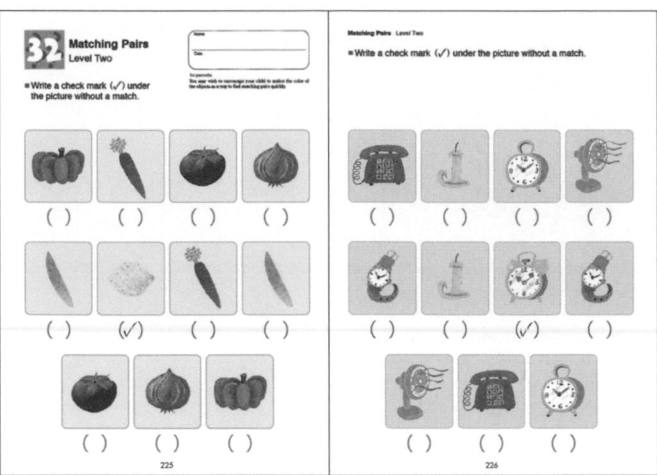

pages 225 and 226

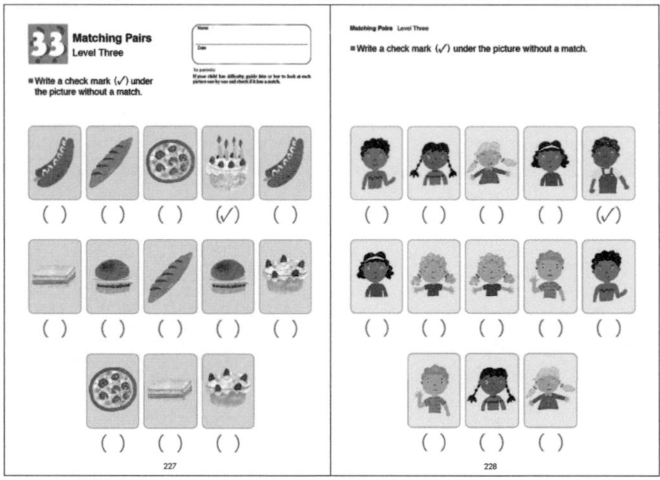

pages 227 and 228

pages 229 and 230

pages 231 and 232

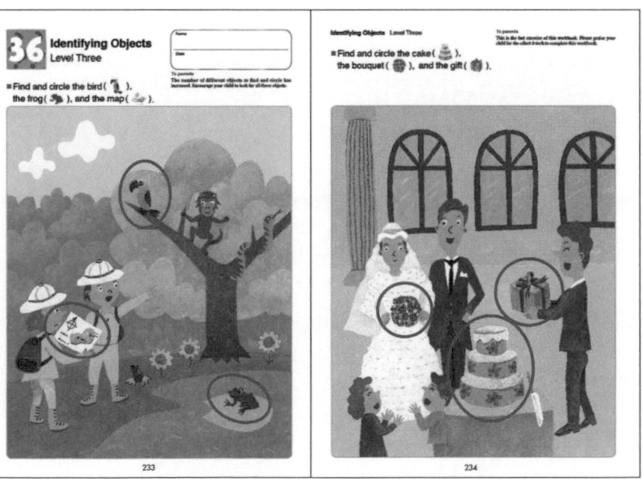

pages 233 and 234

Creativity

Table of Contents

To parents:

Creativity

Many children feel overwhelmed when given a blank page and asked to create something original. Therefore, this section uses a gradual, step-by-step approach that provides more and more opportunities for spontaneous creativity as your child progresses. This approach allows your child to develop creativity without frustration.

In this section, your child will complete activities to develop his or her creativity skills. This section contains activities such as tracing, drawing, altering pictures, and completing scenes. Each activity gives your child an opportunity to copy an example or to work more independently, so your child can progress at his or her own pace. By completing this section your child will strengthen his or her creativity ability.

Tracing
Level One

Name

Date

To parents
Guide your child to write his or her name and date in the box above. Do the exercise along with your child if he or she has difficulty.

■ Draw a line from the dot (●) to the star (★).

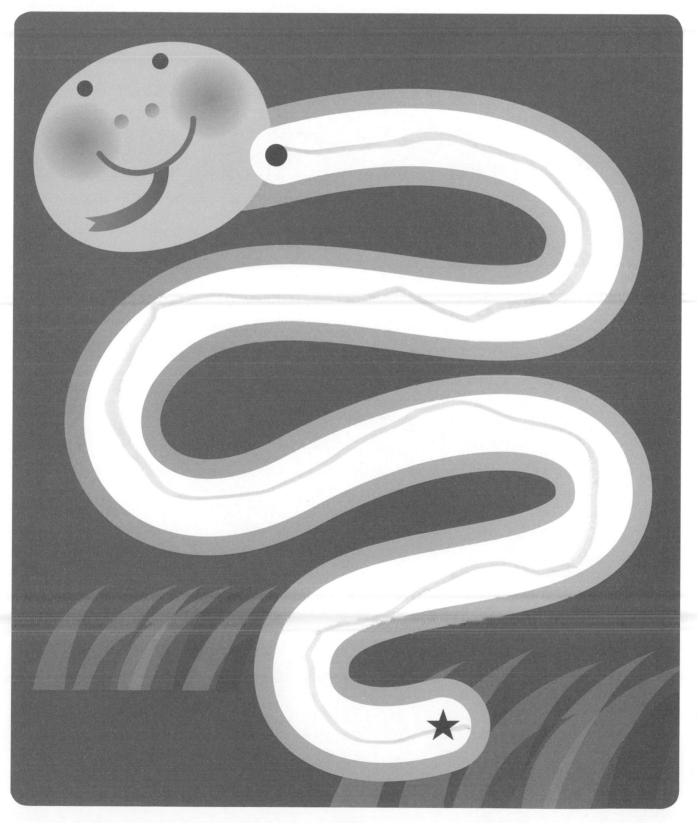

■ Draw a line from the dot (●) to the star (★).

Tracing
Level Two

Name

Date

To parents
Throughout this book, you may wish to offer your child a choice of markers, crayons, or colored pencils.

■ Draw a line from the dot (●) to the star (★).

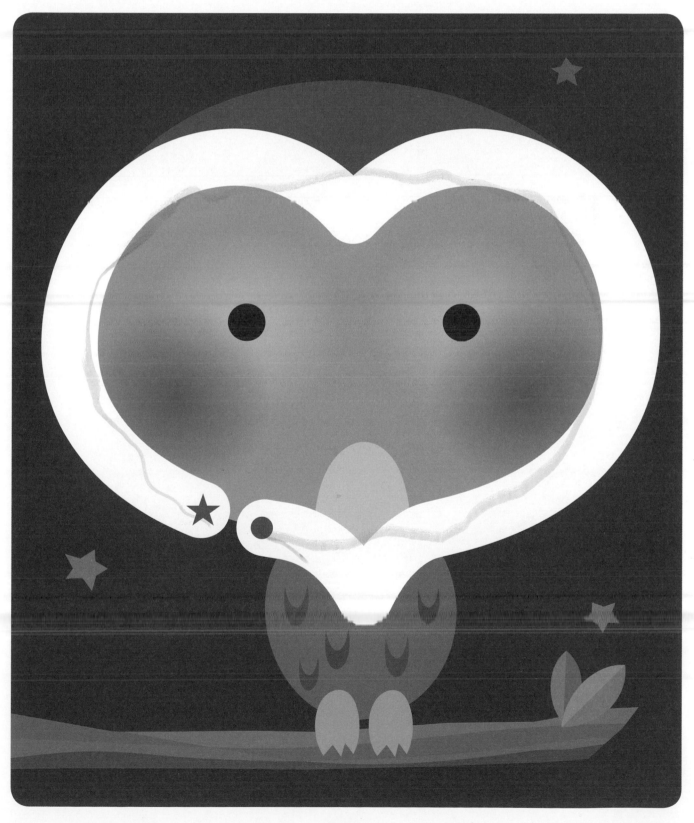

■ Draw a line from the dot (●) to the star (★).

Tracing
Level Three

Name

Date

To parents
When your child has finished, ask him or her what is shown in the picture. Color the picture for some extra fun!

■ Draw a line from the dot (●) to the star (★).

■ Draw a line from the dot (●) to the star (★).

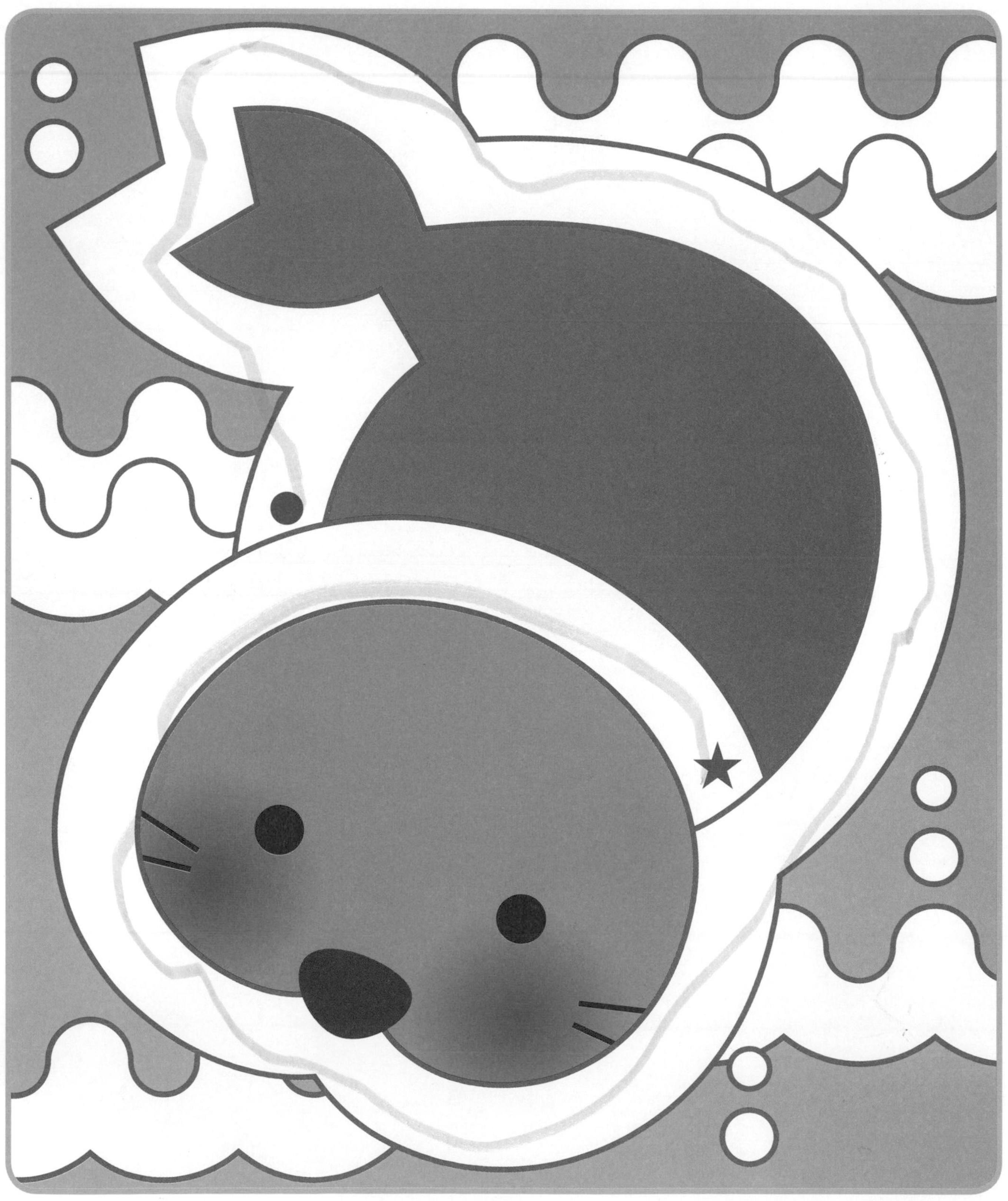

Tracing

Level Four

Name

Date

To parents
Each activity in this book is part of a gradual, step-by-step process designed to help your child develop both creativity and confidence.

■ Draw a line from the dot (●) to the star (★).

■ Draw a line from the dot (●) to the star (★).

Drawing Faces

Level One

Name

Date

To parents
Many activities in this book involve tracing followed by drawing. This helps your child build confidence in his or her ability to draw freely.

■ Look at the sample. Then trace the lines in the picture below.

■ Trace the lines. Then color the picture.

■ Trace the lines. Draw the eyes, nose, and mouth. Then color the picture.

Drawing Faces
Level Two

Name

Date

To parents
Encourage your child to use the sample as a guide if he or she has difficulty.

■ Look at the sample. Then trace the lines in the picture below.

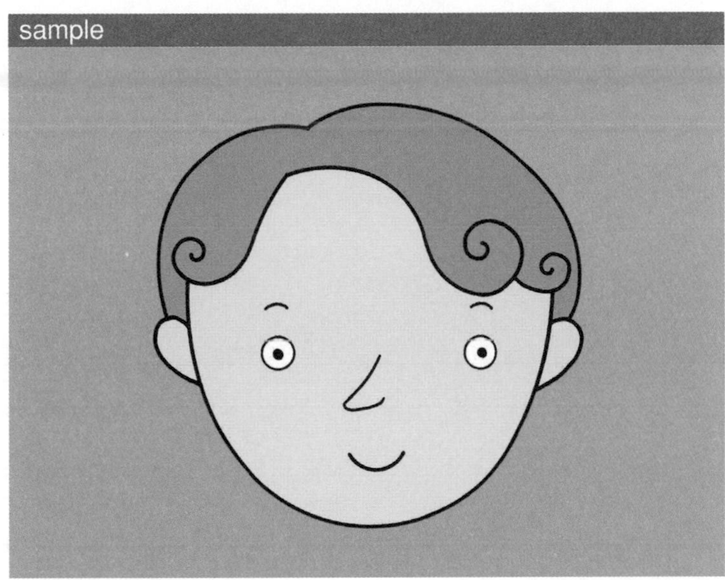

■ Trace the lines. Then color the picture.

■ Trace the lines. Draw the eyes, nose, and mouth. Then color the picture.

Drawing Faces
Level Three

Name

Date

To parents
Colored pencils may work best for tracing the lines in these pictures.

■ Look at each sample. Then trace the lines in each picture below.

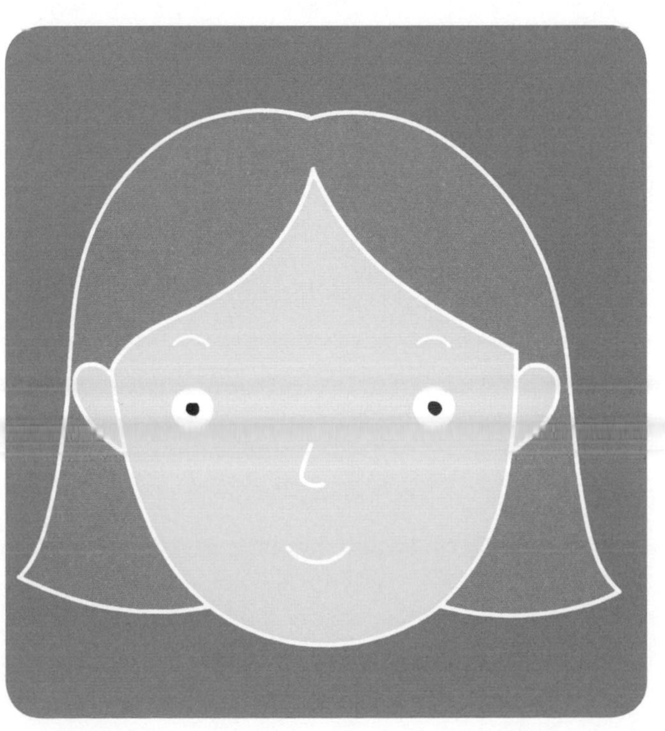

■ Trace the lines. Then color each picture.

■ Trace the lines. Draw the eyes, nose, and mouth. Then color.

Drawing Faces
Level Four

Name

Date

To parents
It is okay if your child wishes to use different colors from those shown in the sample.

■ Look at each sample. Then trace the lines in each picture below.

■ Trace the lines. Then color each picture.

■ Trace the lines. Draw the eyes, nose, and mouth. Then color.

Drawing Animals

Level One

Name

Date

To parents
Help your child notice the different facial features of each animal.

■ Look at each sample. Then trace the lines in each picture below.

sample

sample

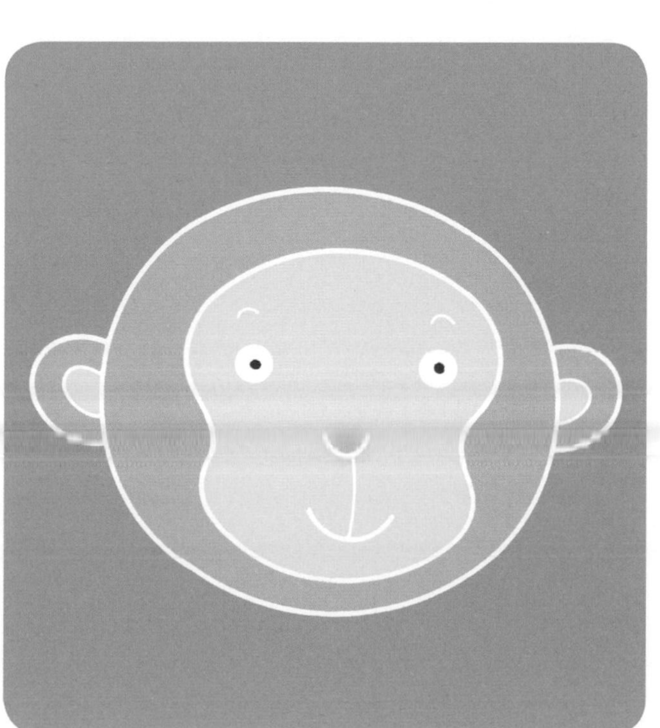

■ Trace the lines. Then color each picture.

■ Trace the lines. Draw the eyes, nose, and mouth. Then color.

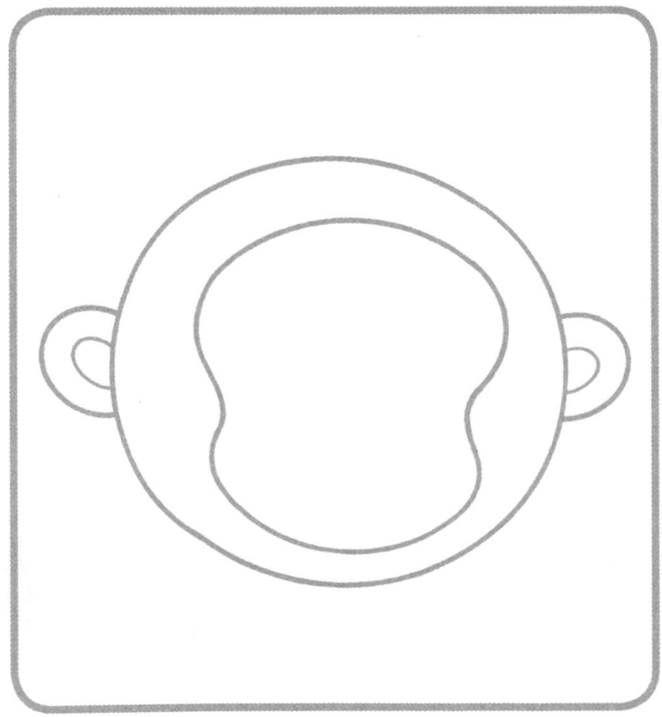

Drawing Animals

Level Two

Name

Date

To parents
As your child progresses through these activities, he or she may start to rely less on the samples and more on his or her own creativity.

■ Look at each sample. Then trace the lines in each picture below.

■ Trace the lines. Then color each picture.

■ Trace the lines. Draw the eyes, nose, and mouth. Then color.

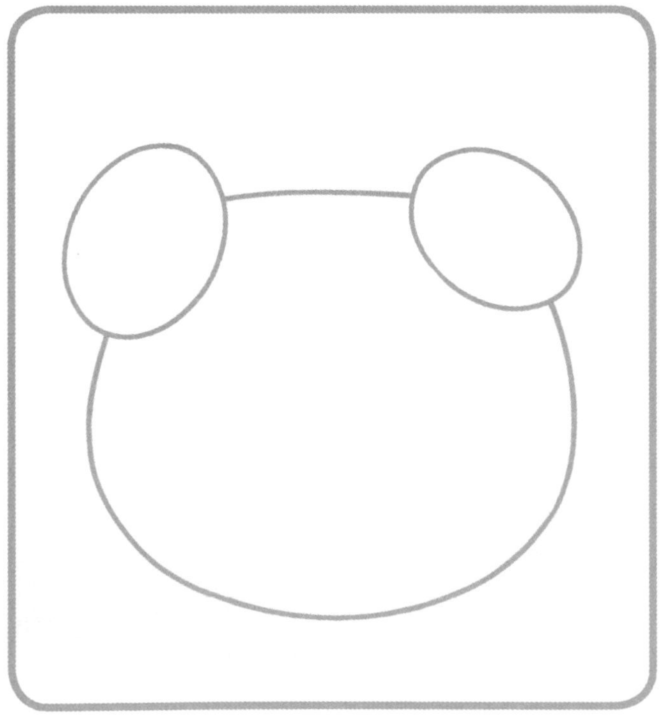

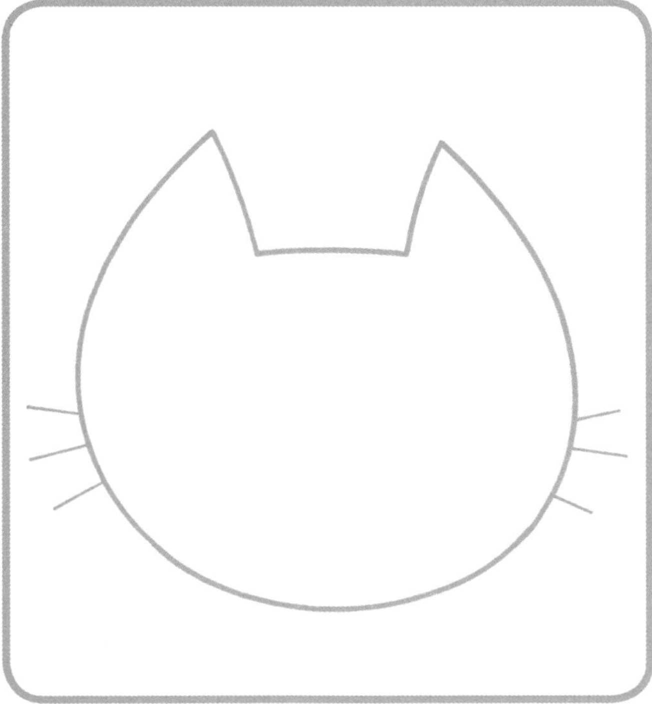

Drawing Places

Level One

Name

Date

To parents
Your child may find this activity more difficult because the picture is now more detailed. Encourage him or her to use the sample as a guide.

■ Look at the sample. Then trace the white lines in the picture below.

■ Trace the lines. Then color the picture.

■ Trace the lines. Draw the missing objects. Then color the picture.

Drawing Places
Level Two

Name

Date

To parents
If your child has difficulty, ask him or her to describe the objects in the picture before drawing.

■ Look at the sample. Then trace the white lines in the picture below.

■ Trace the lines. Then color the picture.

■ Trace the lines. Draw the missing objects. Then color the picture.

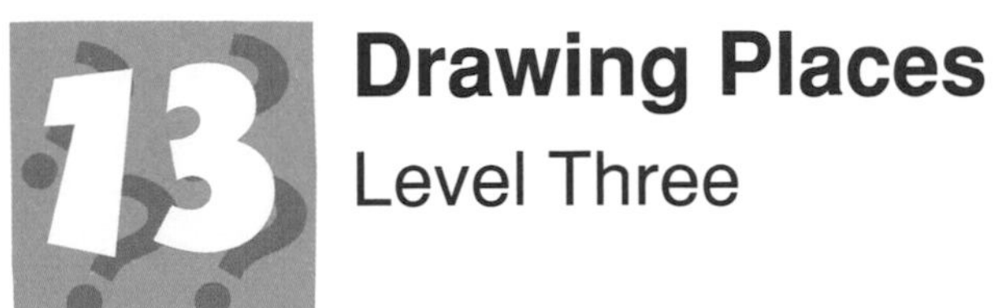

Drawing Places
Level Three

Name

Date

To parents
It is okay if your child does not trace the lines perfectly. Encourage him or her to enjoy the exercise.

■ Look at each sample. Then trace the white lines in each picture below.

sample

sample

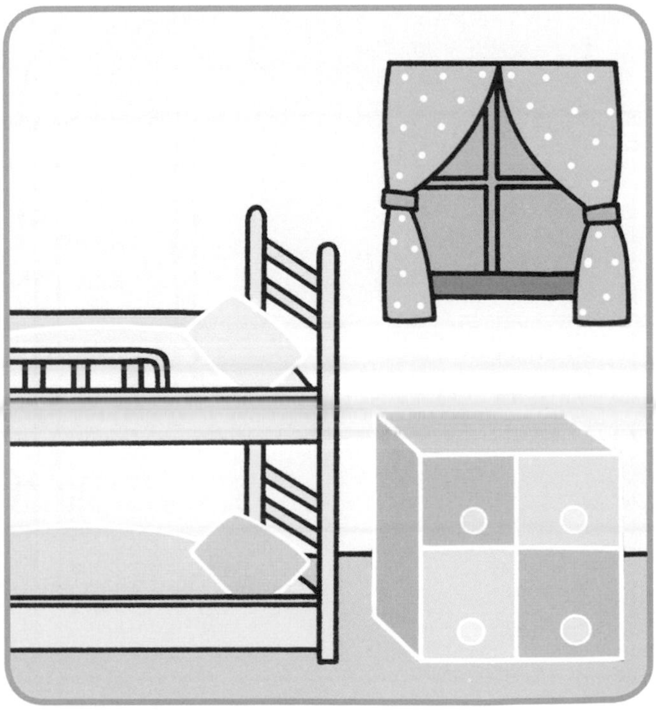

■ Trace the lines. Then color each picture.

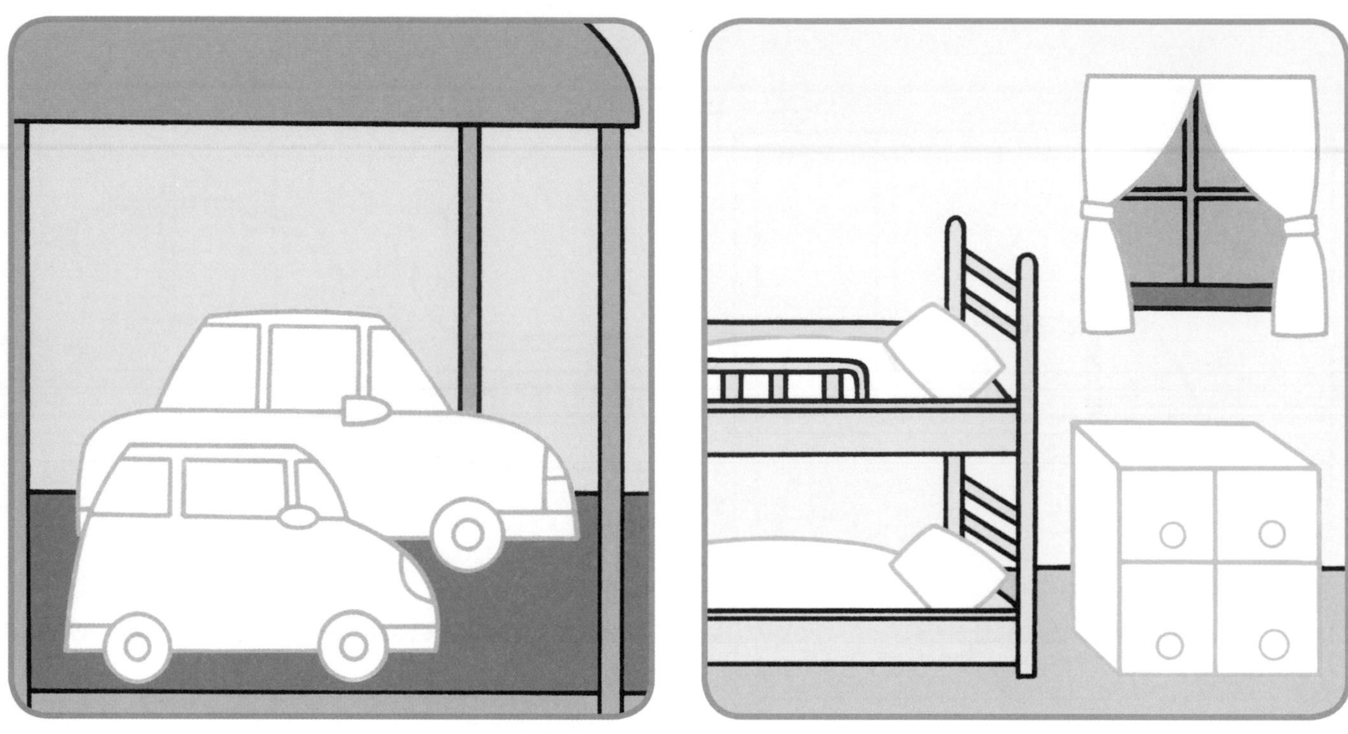

■ Trace the lines. Draw the missing objects. Then color each picture.

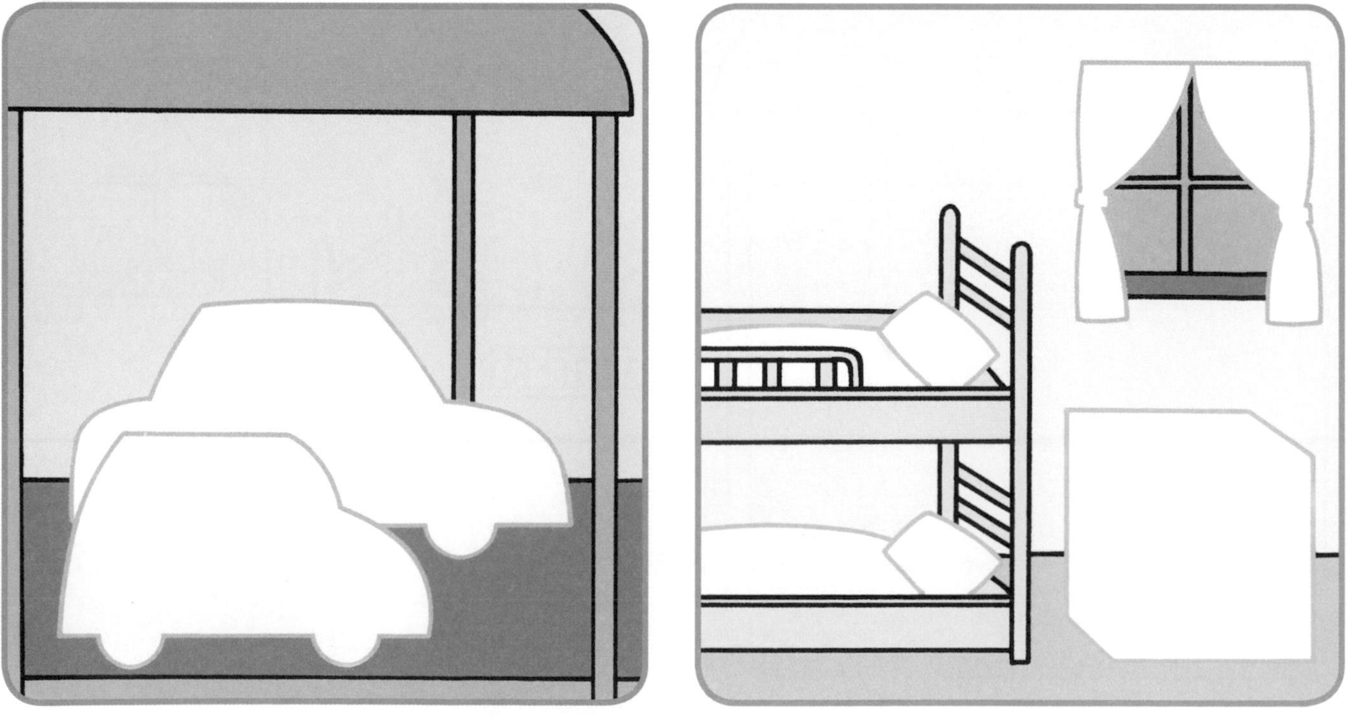

Drawing Places

Level Four

Name

Date

To parents
As your child progresses through these activities, he or she may start to rely less on the samples and more on his or her own creativity.

■ Look at each sample. Then trace the white lines in each picture below.

sample

sample

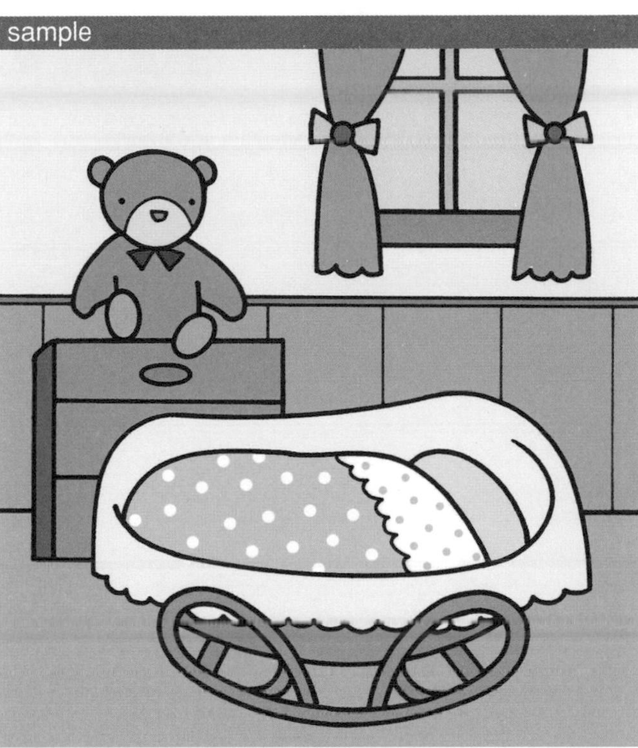

■ Trace the lines. Then color each picture.

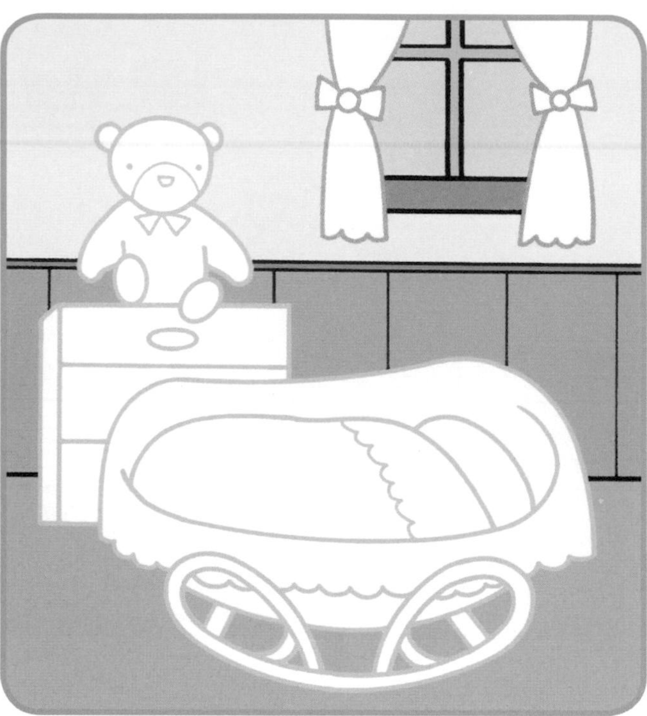

■ Trace the lines. Draw the missing objects. Then color each picture.

Drawing Scenes

Level One

Name

Date

To parents
It is okay if your child wishes to use different colors from those shown in the sample.

■ Look at the sample. Then trace the white lines in the picture below.

■ Trace the lines. Then color the picture.

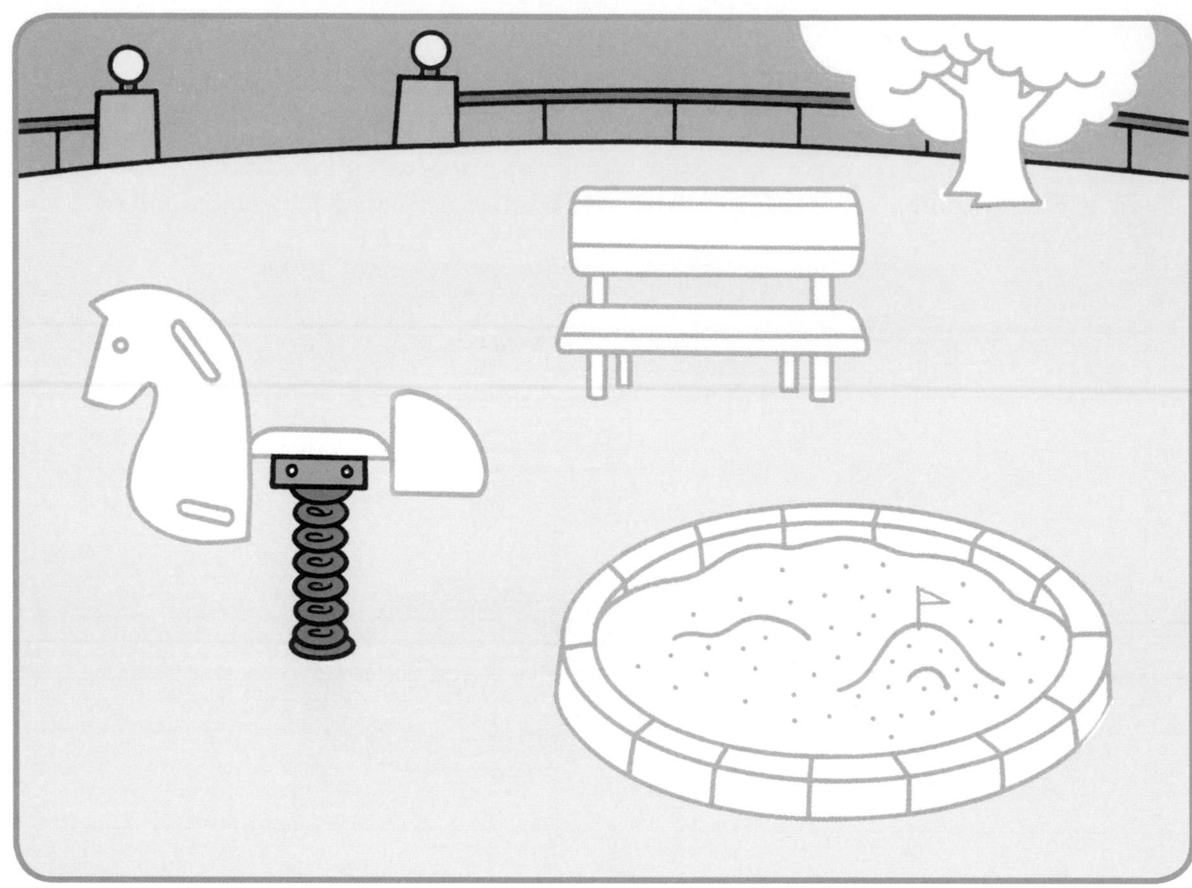

■ Trace the lines. Draw the missing objects. Then color the picture.

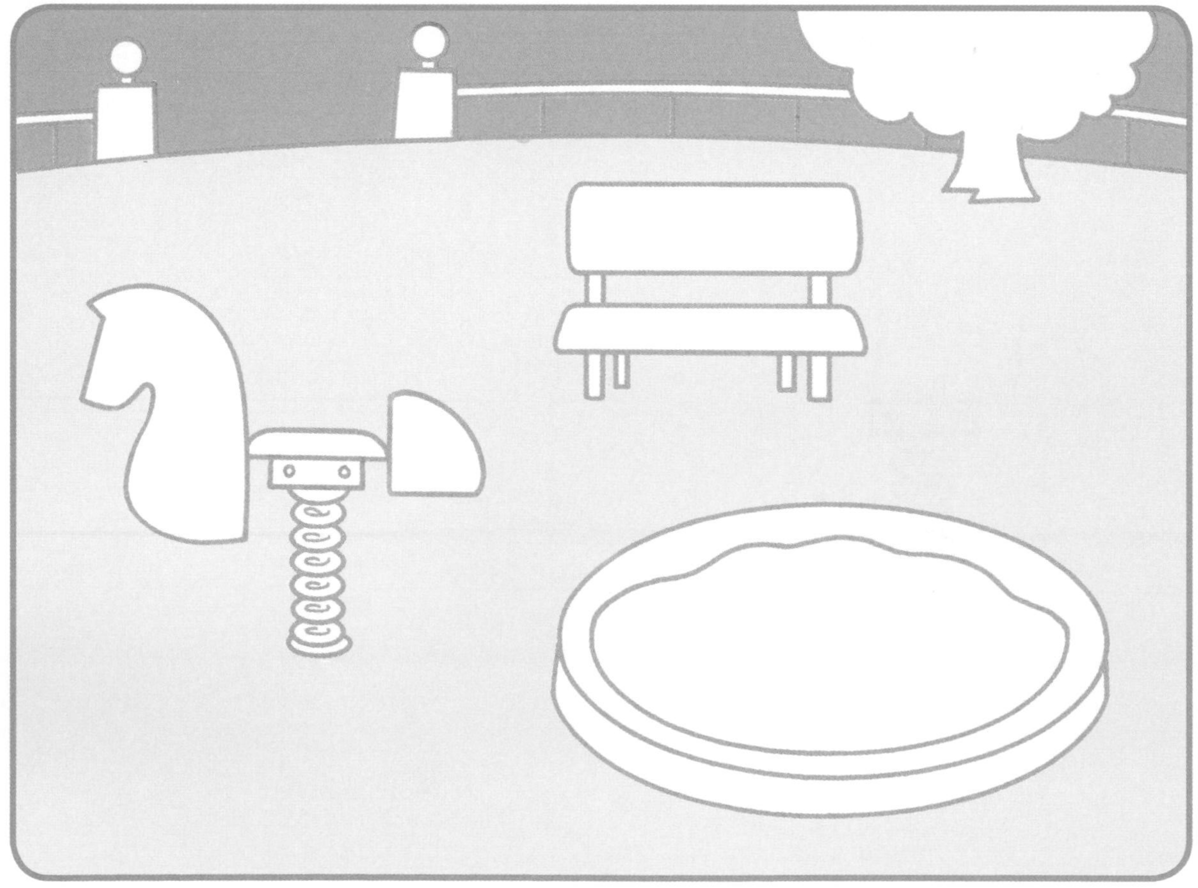

Drawing Scenes

Level Two

Name

Date

To parents
If your child has difficulty, ask him or her to describe the animals before drawing them.

■ Look at the sample. Then trace the white lines in the picture below.

sample

■ Trace the lines. Then color the picture.

■ Trace the lines. Draw the missing animals. Then color the picture.

Altering Scenes
Level One

Name

Date

To parents
Guide your child to draw rain in the picture. If he or she has difficulty, point to the sample.

■ Look at the sample. Then draw rain in the picture below.

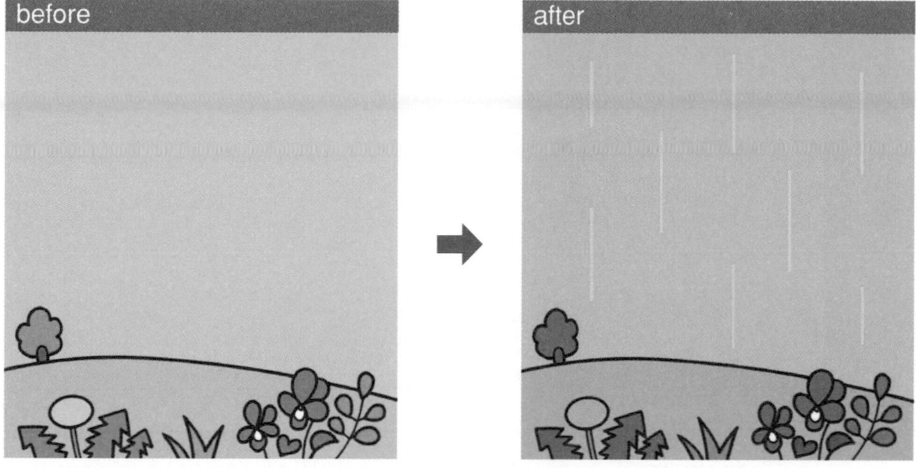

■ Draw rain. Then trace and color.

■ Draw rain. Then trace and color.

Altering Scenes
Level Two

Name

Date

To parents
It is okay if your child does not color perfectly within the lines. Encourage him or her to enjoy the exercise.

■ Look at the sample. Then draw rain in the picture below.

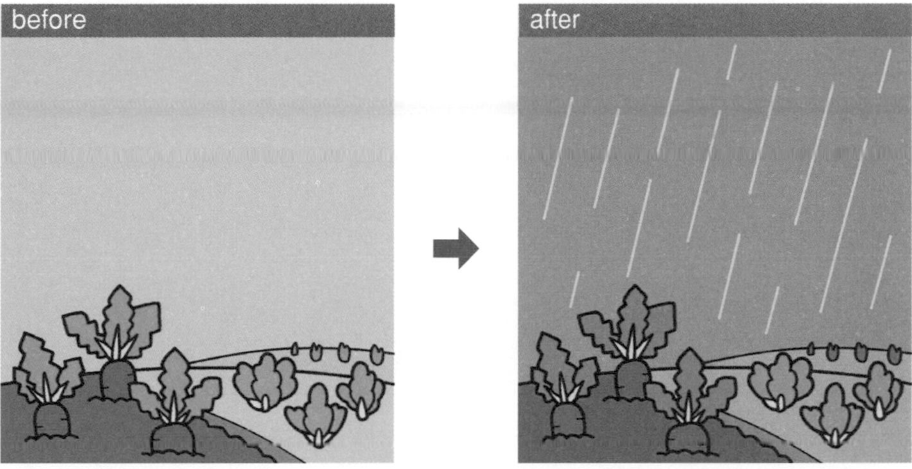

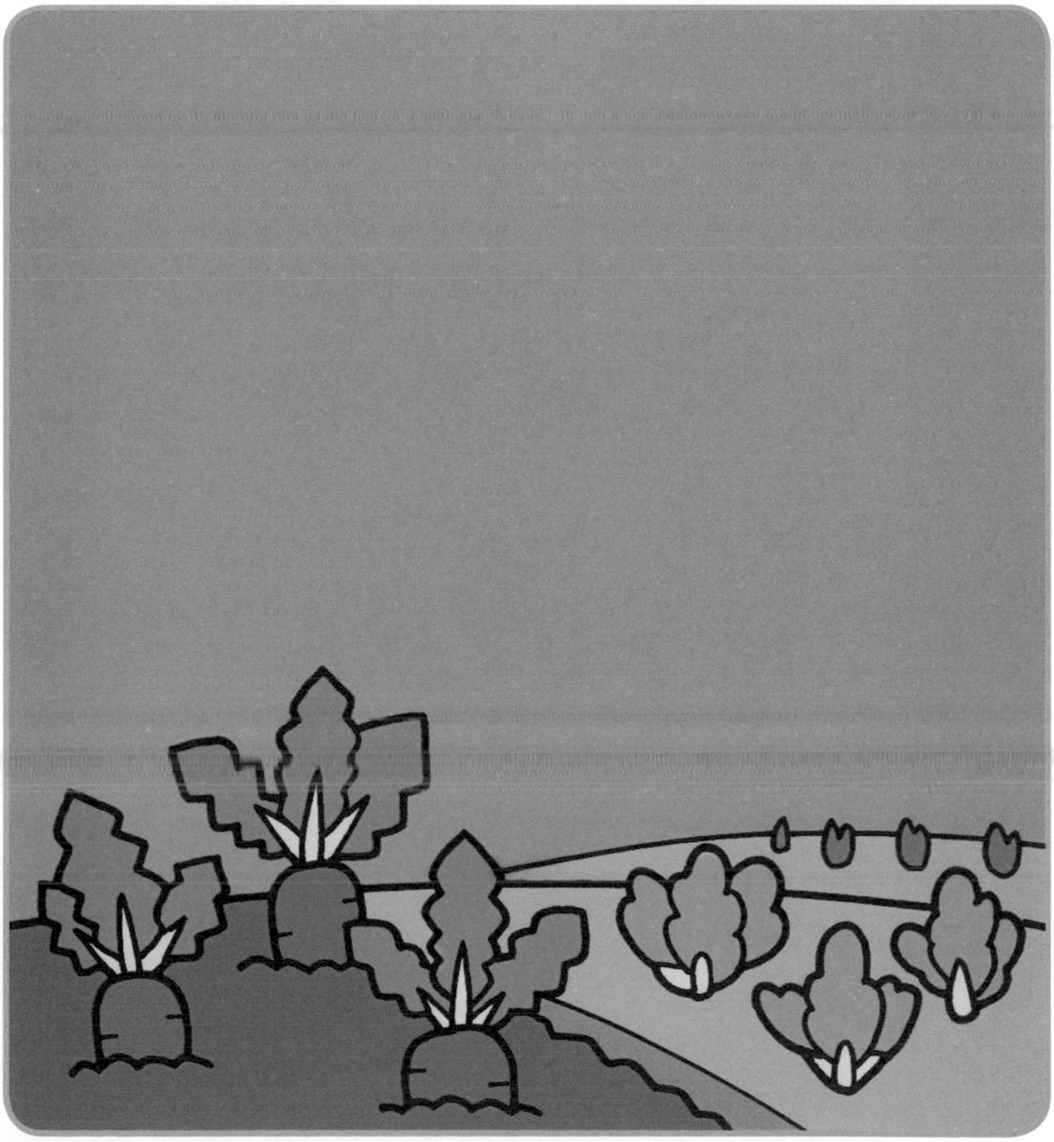

■ Draw rain. Then trace and color.

■ Draw rain. Then trace and color.

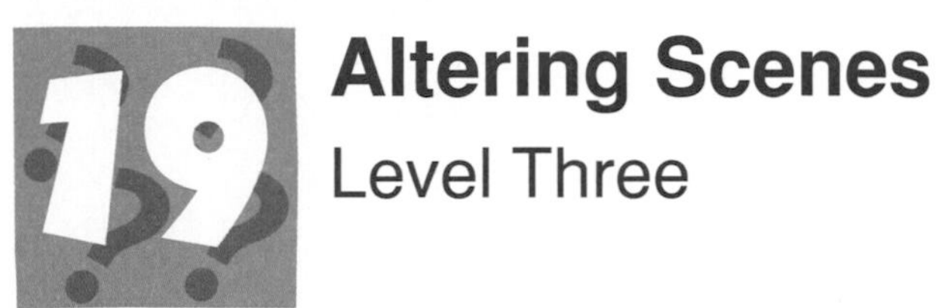

Altering Scenes
Level Three

Name

Date

To parents
You may wish to encourage your child to try different ways of drawing rain.

■ Look at the sample. Then draw rain and trace the white lines.

■ Draw rain. Then trace and color.

■ Draw rain. Draw the boy's eyes, nose, and mouth. Then trace and color.

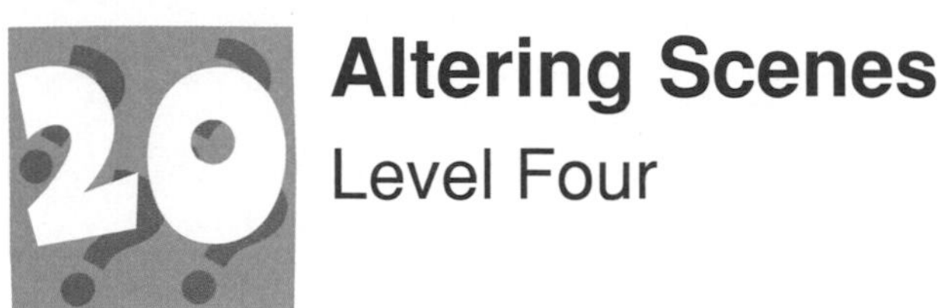

Altering Scenes

Level Four

Name

Date

To parents
This sequence of activities involves drawing facial features, which your child practiced earlier in the book.

■ Look at the sample. Then draw rain and trace the white lines.

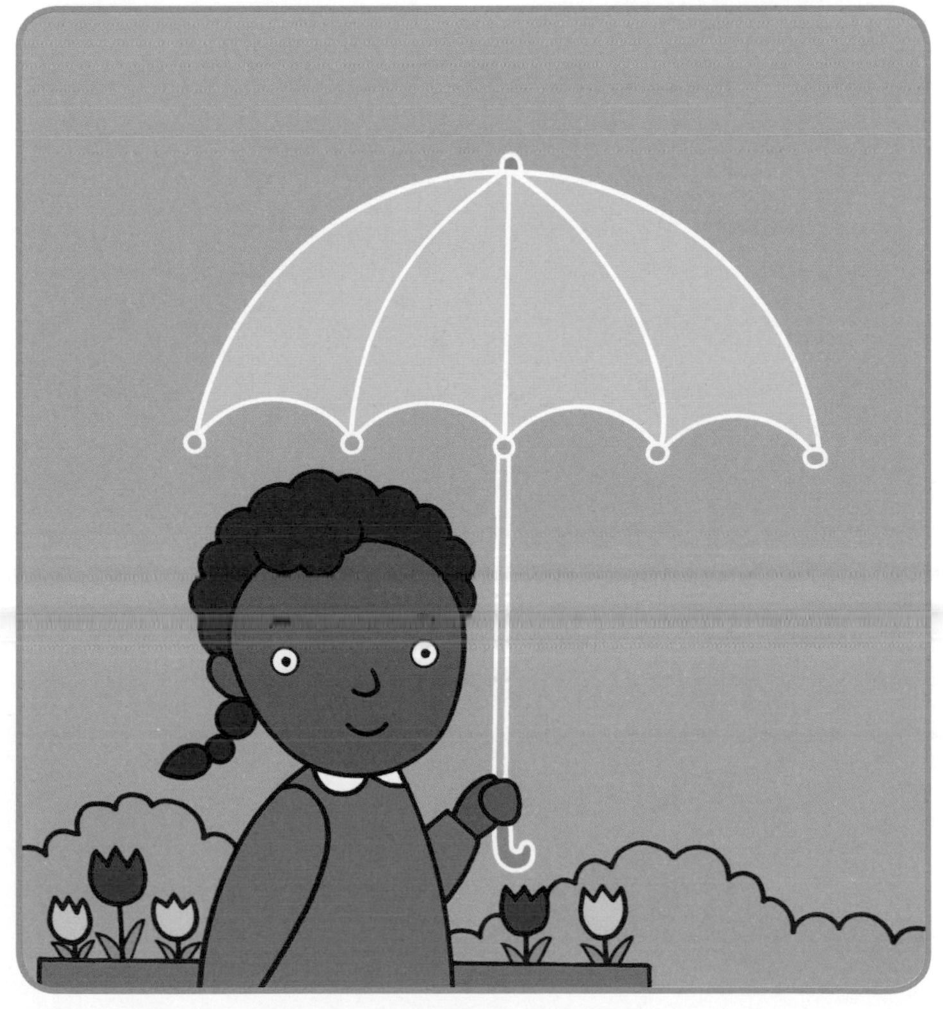

■ Draw rain. Then trace and color.

■ Draw rain. Draw the girl's eyes, nose, and mouth. Then trace and color.

Altering Scenes
Level Five

Name

Date

To parents
It is not necessary for your child to copy the sample. Your child can use it as a model if he or she has difficulty.

■ Look at the sample. Then draw rain and trace the white lines.

■ Draw rain. Then trace and color.

■ Draw rain. Draw the girl's eyes, nose, and mouth. Then trace and color.

Altering Scenes
Level Six

Name

Date

To parents
This is the last exercise in this sequence. You may notice that your child's confidence with this task has increased.

■ Look at the sample. Then draw rain and trace the white lines.

■ Draw rain. Then trace and color.

■ Draw rain. Draw the boy's eyes, nose, and mouth. Then trace and color.

Completing Scenes

Level One

Name

Date

To parents
This activity incorporates free drawing. Guide your child to draw a balloon in the last picture of the activity.

■ Look at the sample. Then trace the balloon below.

■ Trace the lines and color.

■ Draw a balloon and the boy's eyes, nose, and mouth. Then trace and color.

Completing Scenes

Level Two

Name

Date

To parents
Your child's drawing does not need to look like the sample. The sample is provided only as a model.

■ Look at the sample. Then trace the bird below.

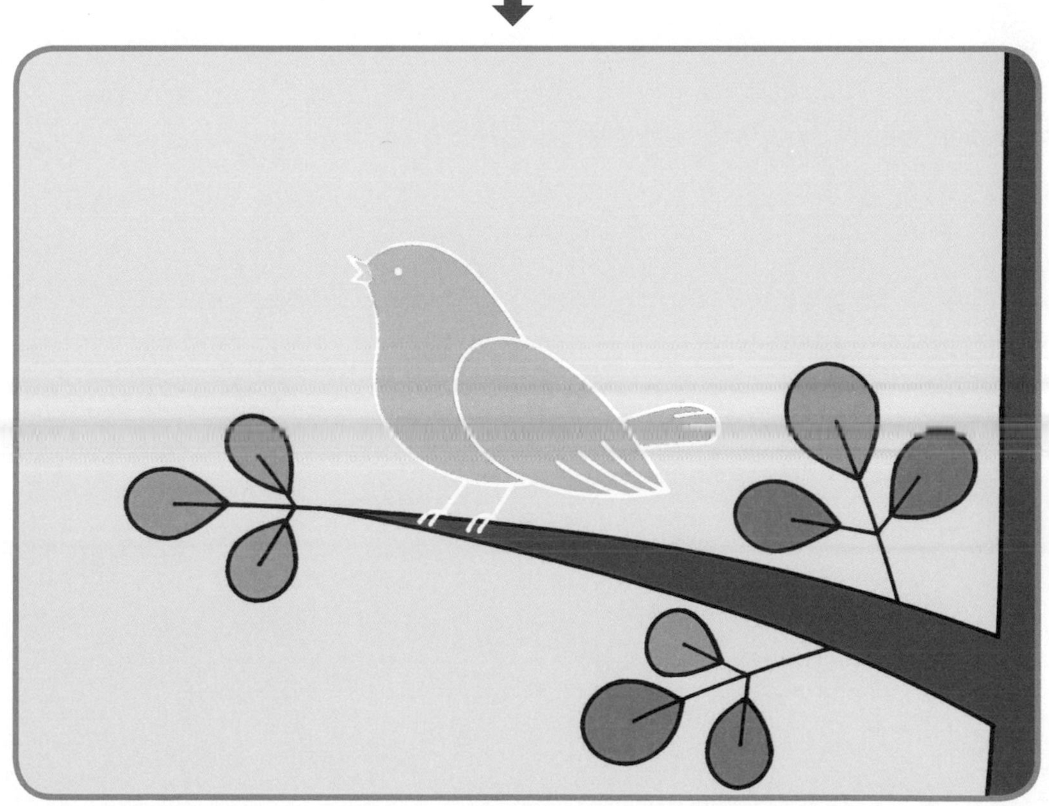

■ Trace the lines and color.

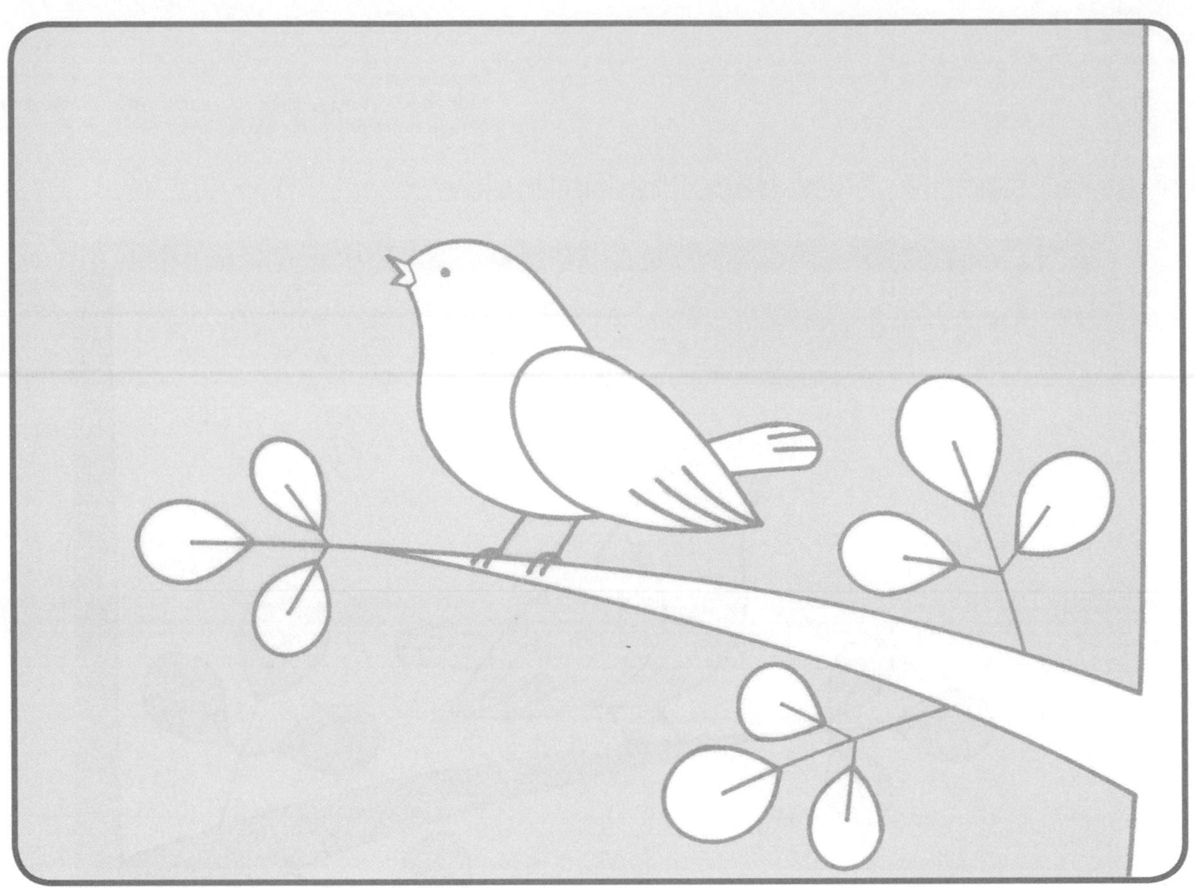

■ Draw a bird. Trace the lines. Then color.

Completing Scenes

Level Three

Name

Date

To parents
Offer your child a lot of praise for his or her drawing. This will help build your child's confidence in his or her creative abilities.

■ Look at the sample. Then trace the apple and banana below.

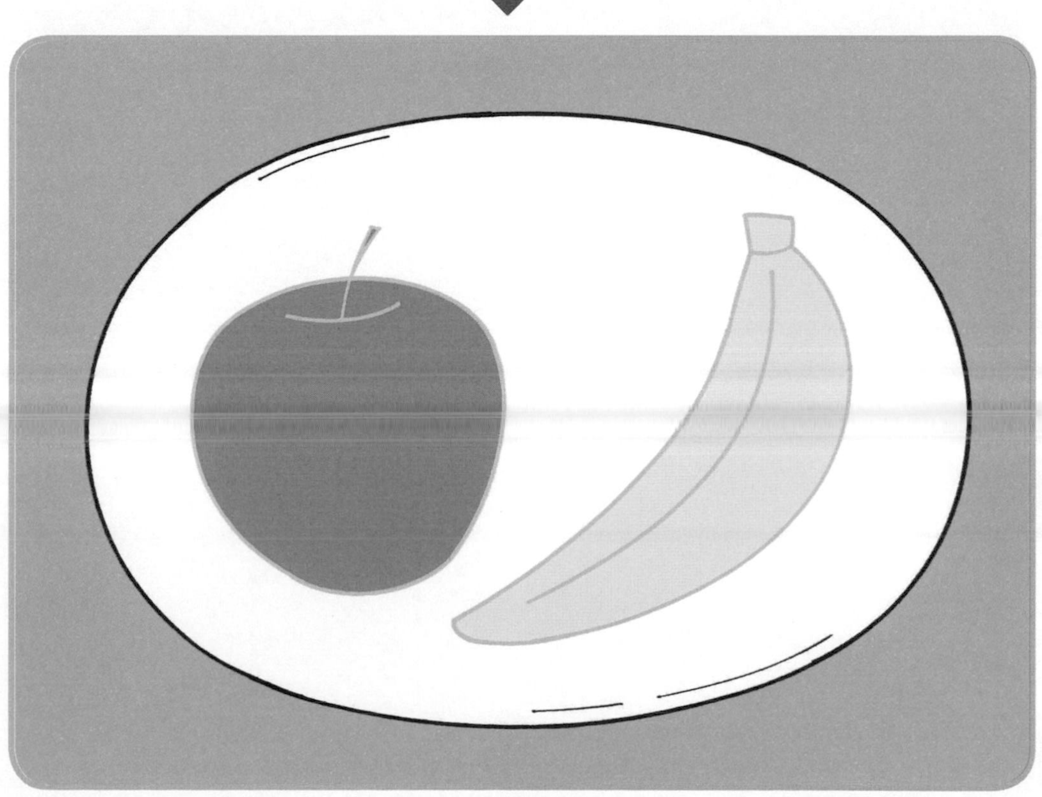

■ Trace the lines. Then color.

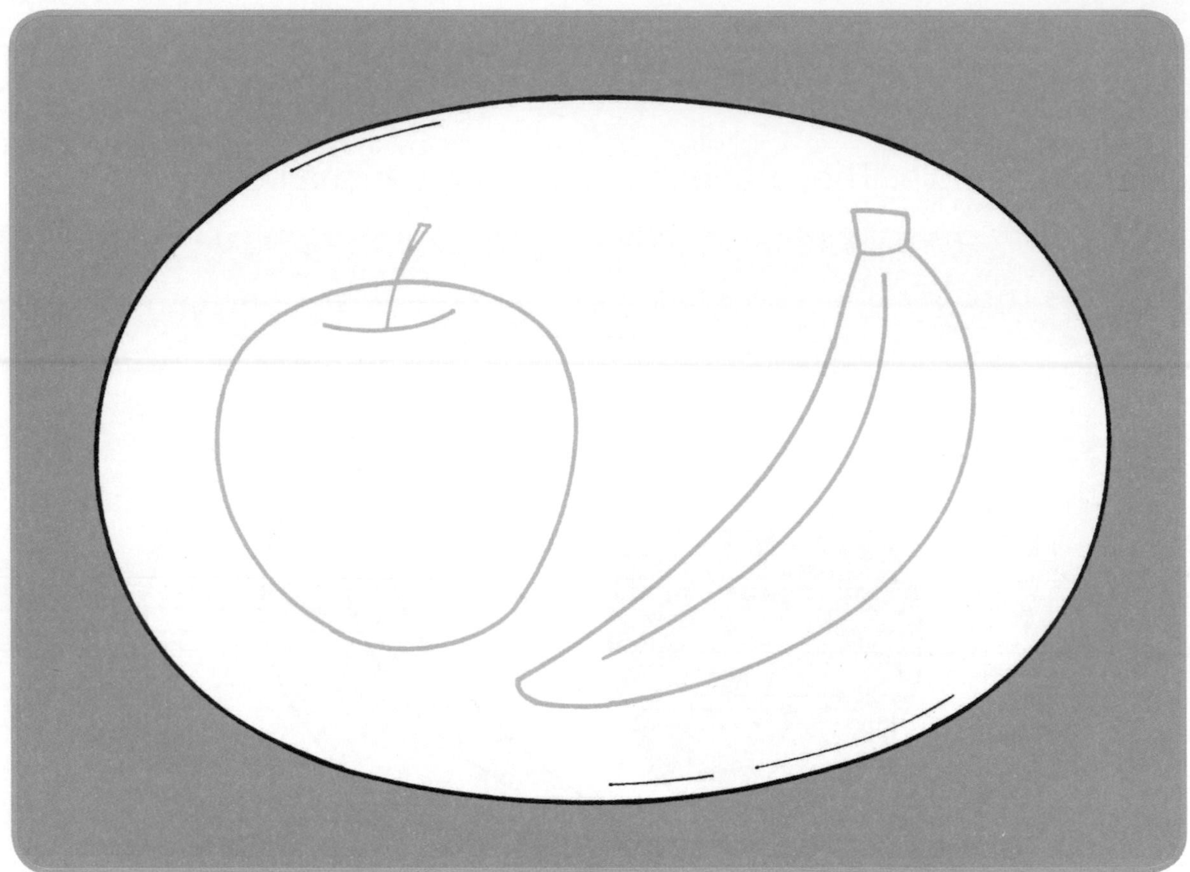

■ Draw an apple and banana. Trace the lines. Then color.

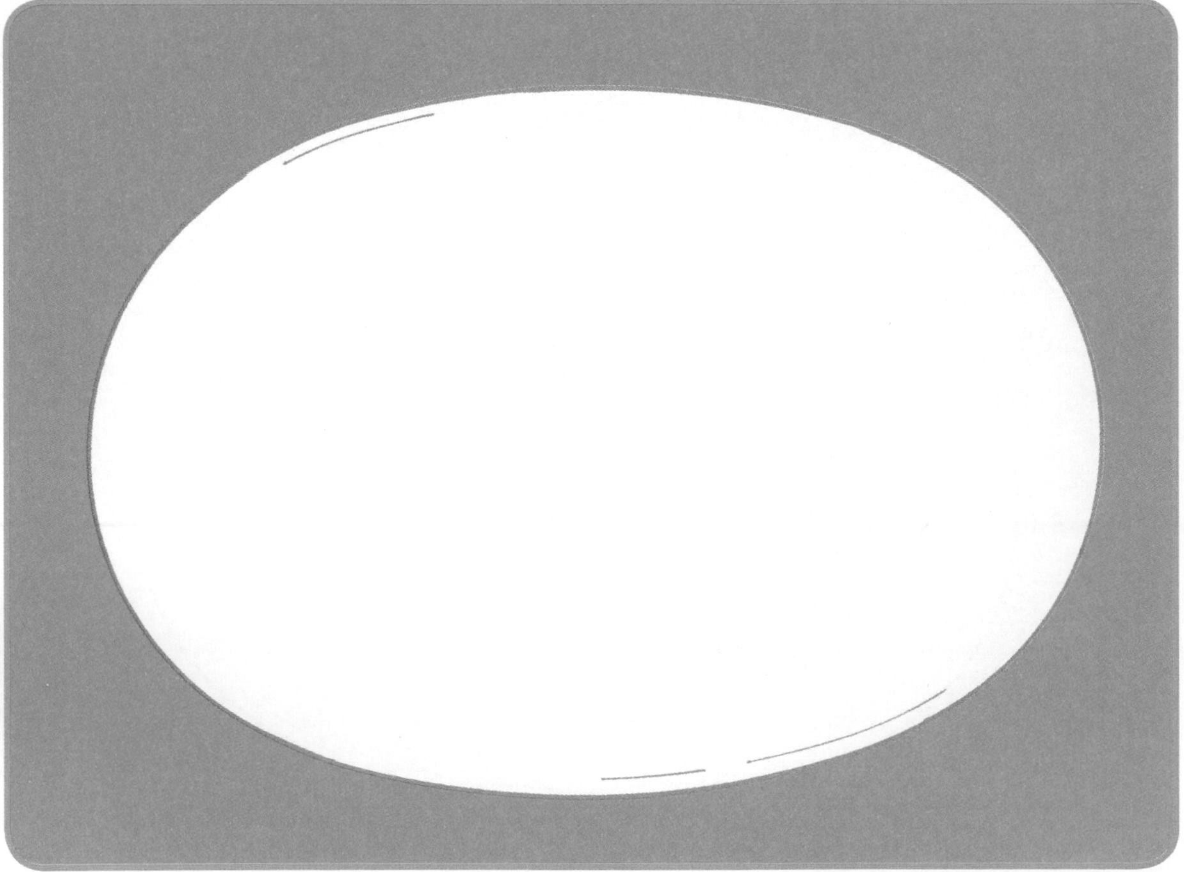

Completing Scenes

Level Four

Name

Date

To parents
The knife and fork in the sample picture have red handles. Your child may wish to draw a knife and fork differently.

■ Look at the sample. Then trace the knife and fork below.

sample

■ Trace the lines. Then color.

■ Draw a knife and fork. Trace the lines. Then color.

Completing Scenes

Level Five

Name

Date

To parents
The objects to draw are now more complex. Encourage your child to take his or her time with this activity.

■ Look at the sample. Then trace the shells below.

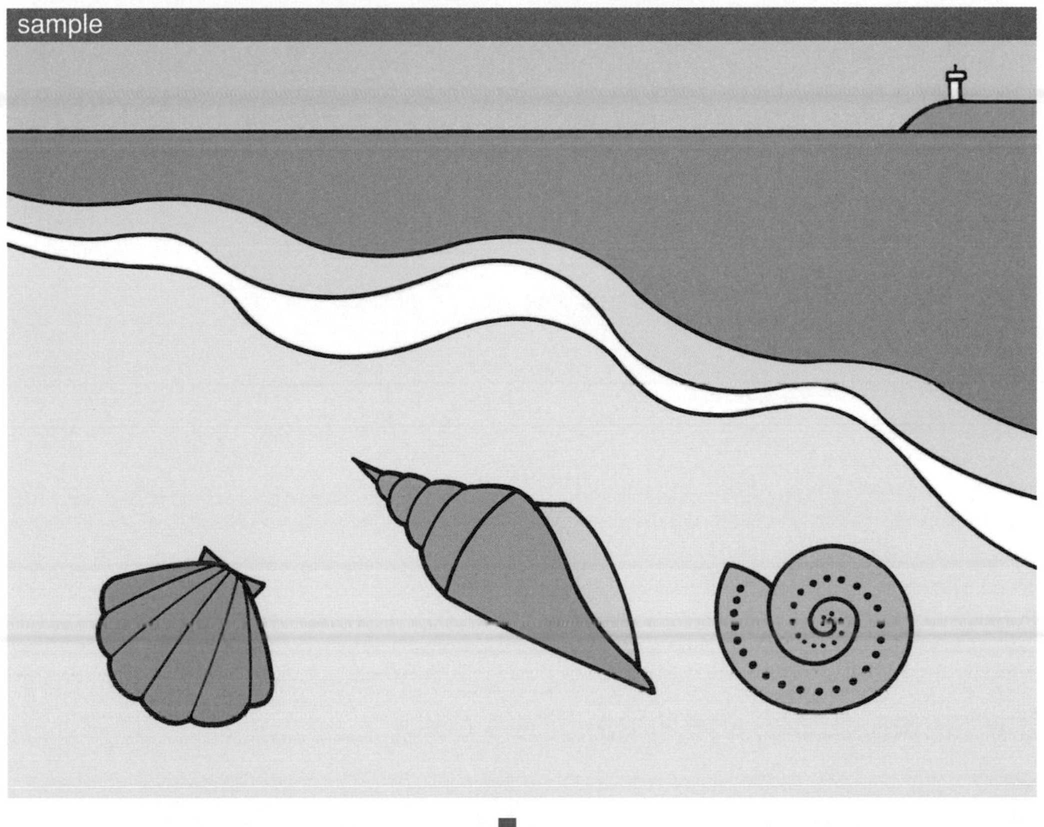

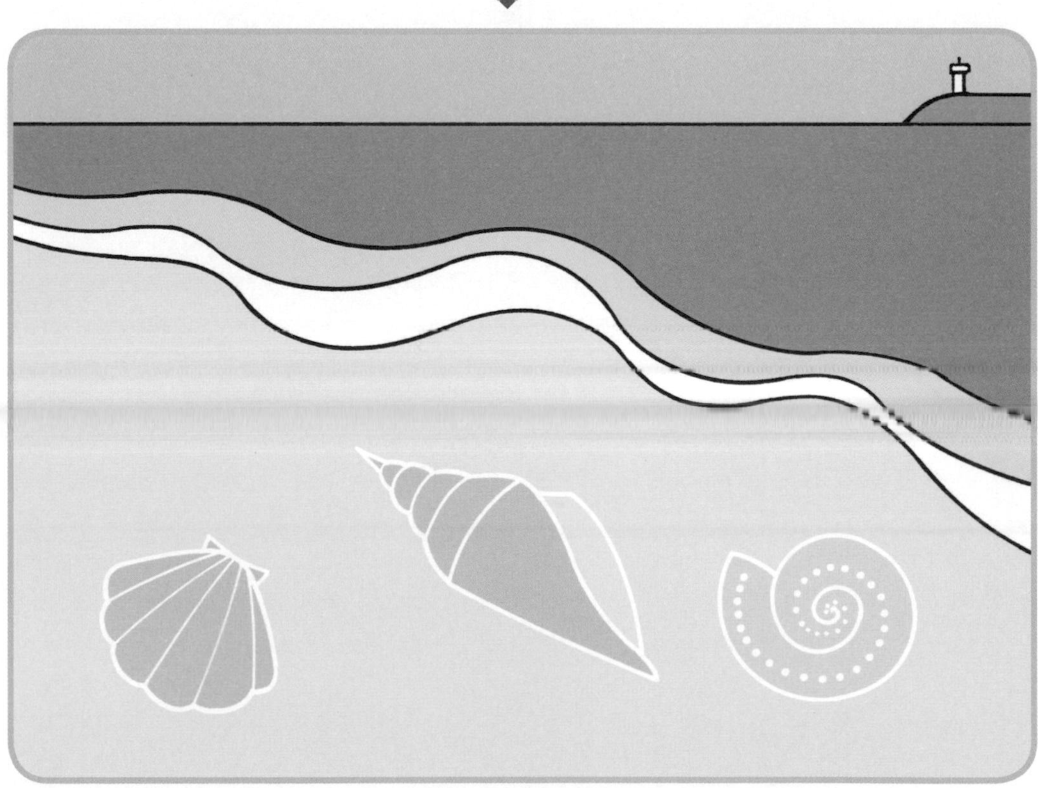

■ Trace the lines. Then color.

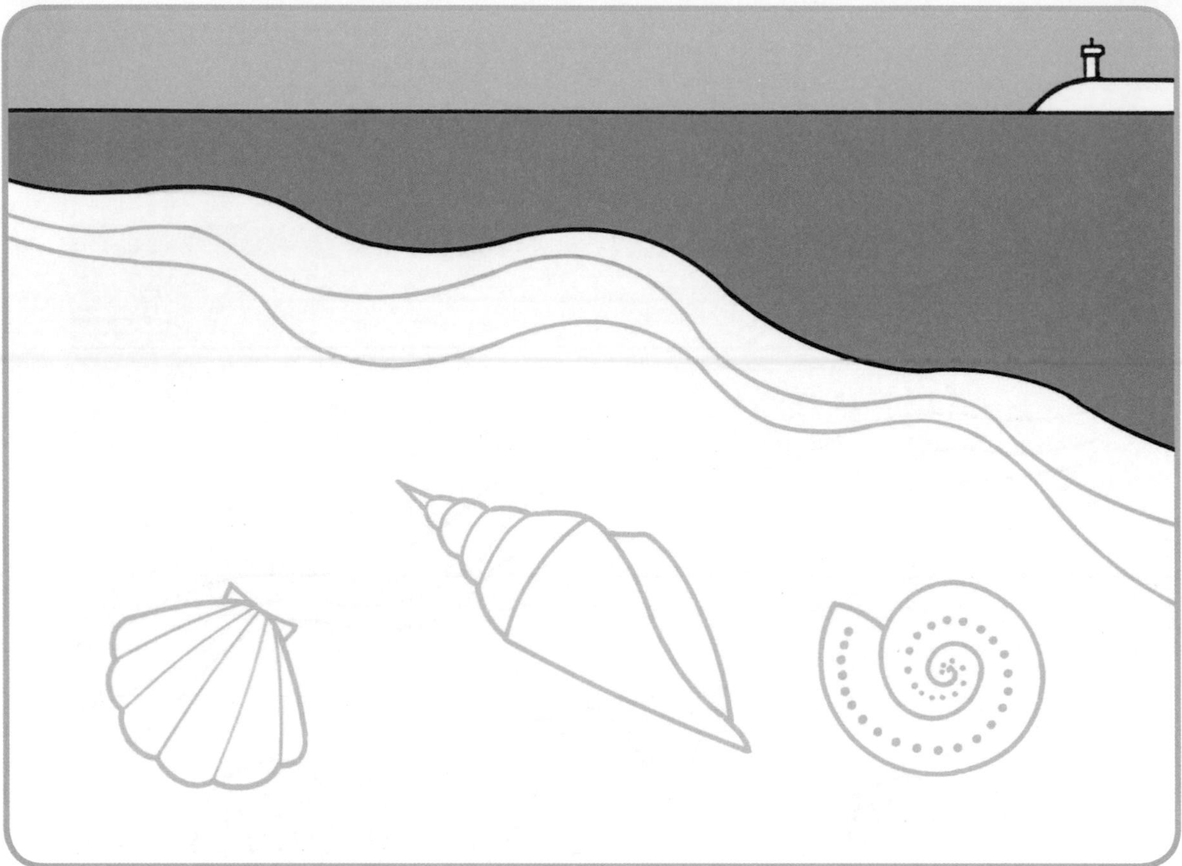

■ Draw the shells. Trace the lines. Then color.

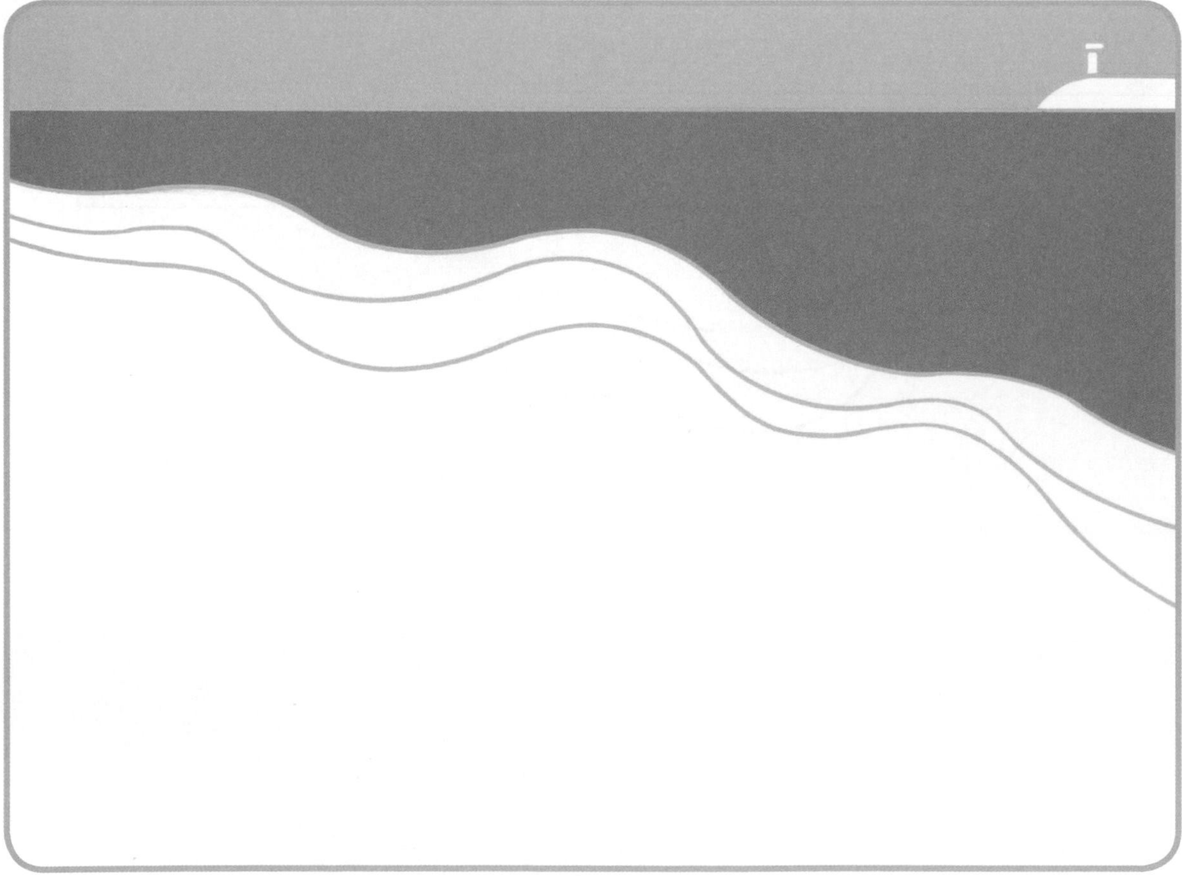

Completing Scenes

Level Six

Name

Date

To parents
If your child has difficulty, look at the animals together and describe them before your child begins drawing.

■ Look at the sample. Then trace the animals below.

sample

■ Trace the lines. Then color.

■ Draw the animals. Trace the lines. Then color.

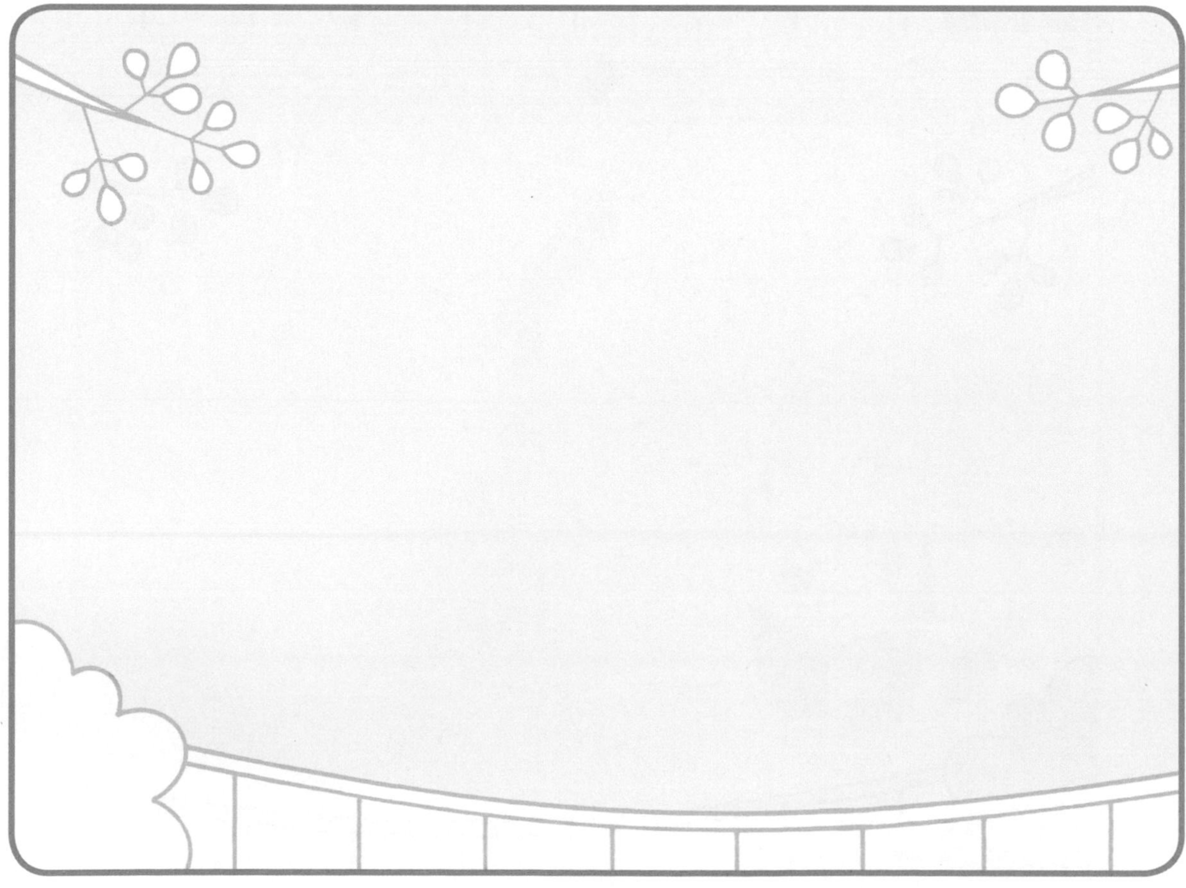

Creative Drawing

Level One

Name

Date

To parents
In the last part of this activity, your child can copy one of these samples or draw something different.

■ Look at each sample. Then trace the white lines.

sample

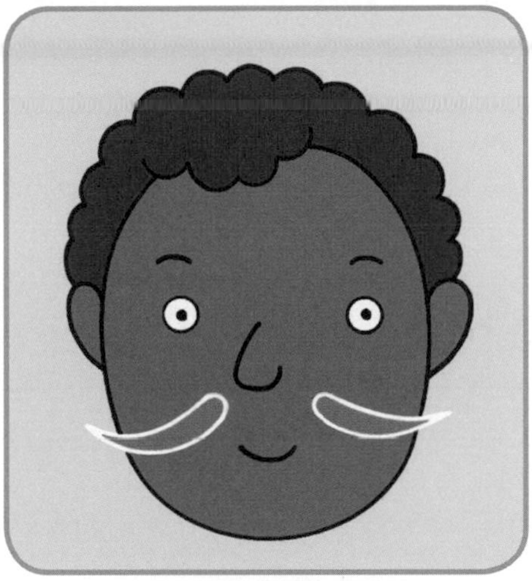

→

sample

→

sample

→

■ Trace the lines. Then color.

■ Draw a beard or mustache on the face. Then trace and color.

Creative Drawing
Level Two

Name

Date

To parents
Help your child notice how the patterns on the shirts are different from one another.

■ Look at each sample. Then trace the lines.

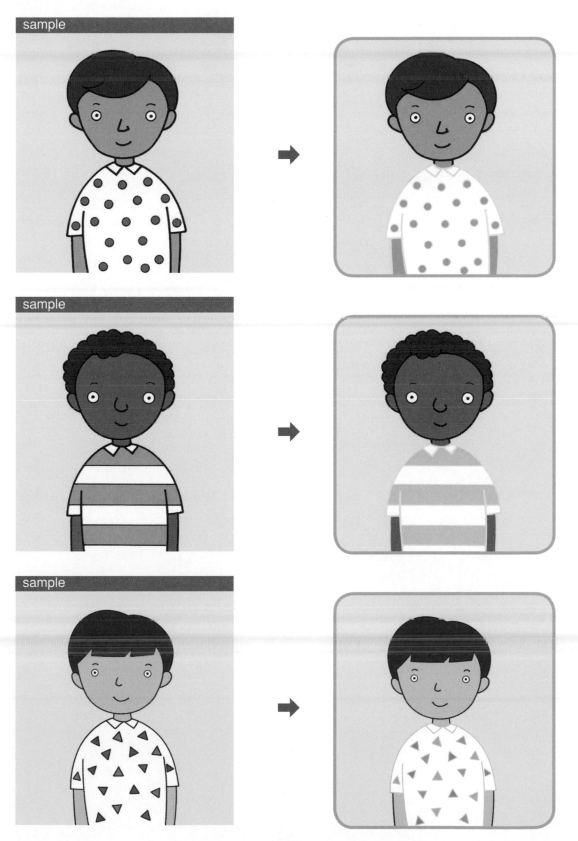

sample

sample

sample

■ Trace the lines. Then color.

■ Draw a pattern on the shirt. Then trace and color.

Creative Drawing

Level Three

Name

Date

To parents
If your child has difficulty, you may wish to guide your child to draw his or her favorite fruits.

■ Look at the sample. Then trace the white lines.

sample

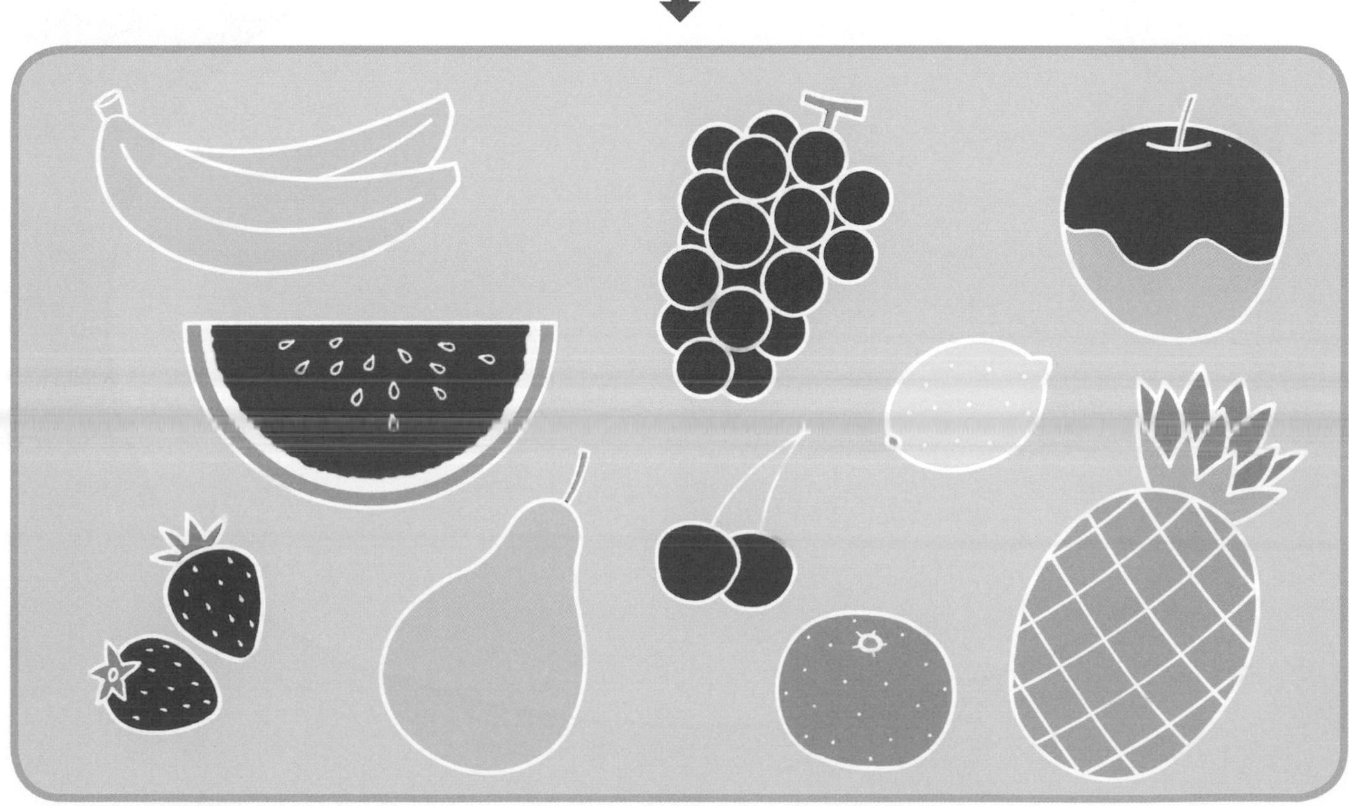

■ Look at the sample. Then draw and color three fruits of your choice.

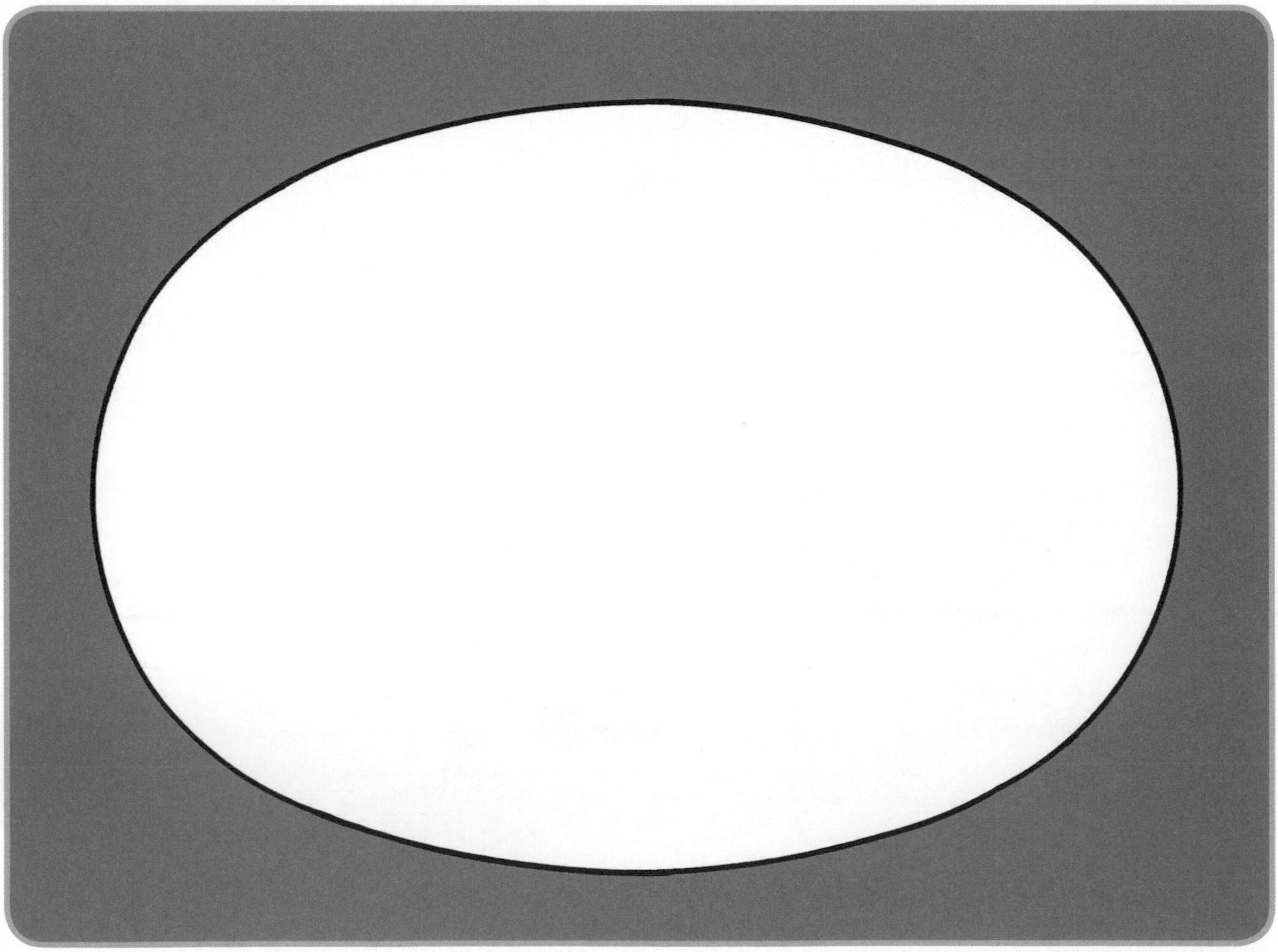

Creative Drawing
Level Four

Name

Date

To parents
Remind your child that he or she does not need to trace the lines perfectly.

■ Look at the sample. Then trace the white lines.

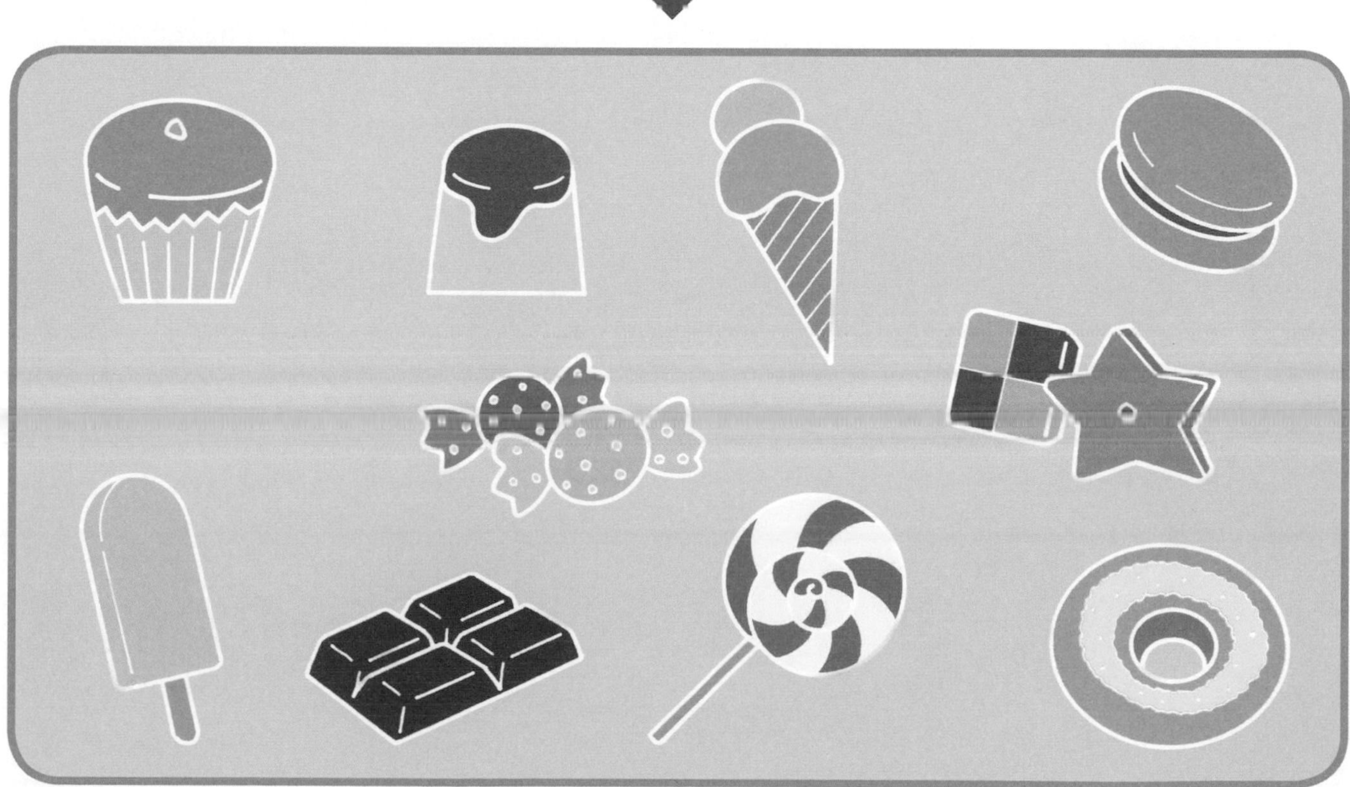

■ Look at the sample. Then draw and color three sweets of your choice.

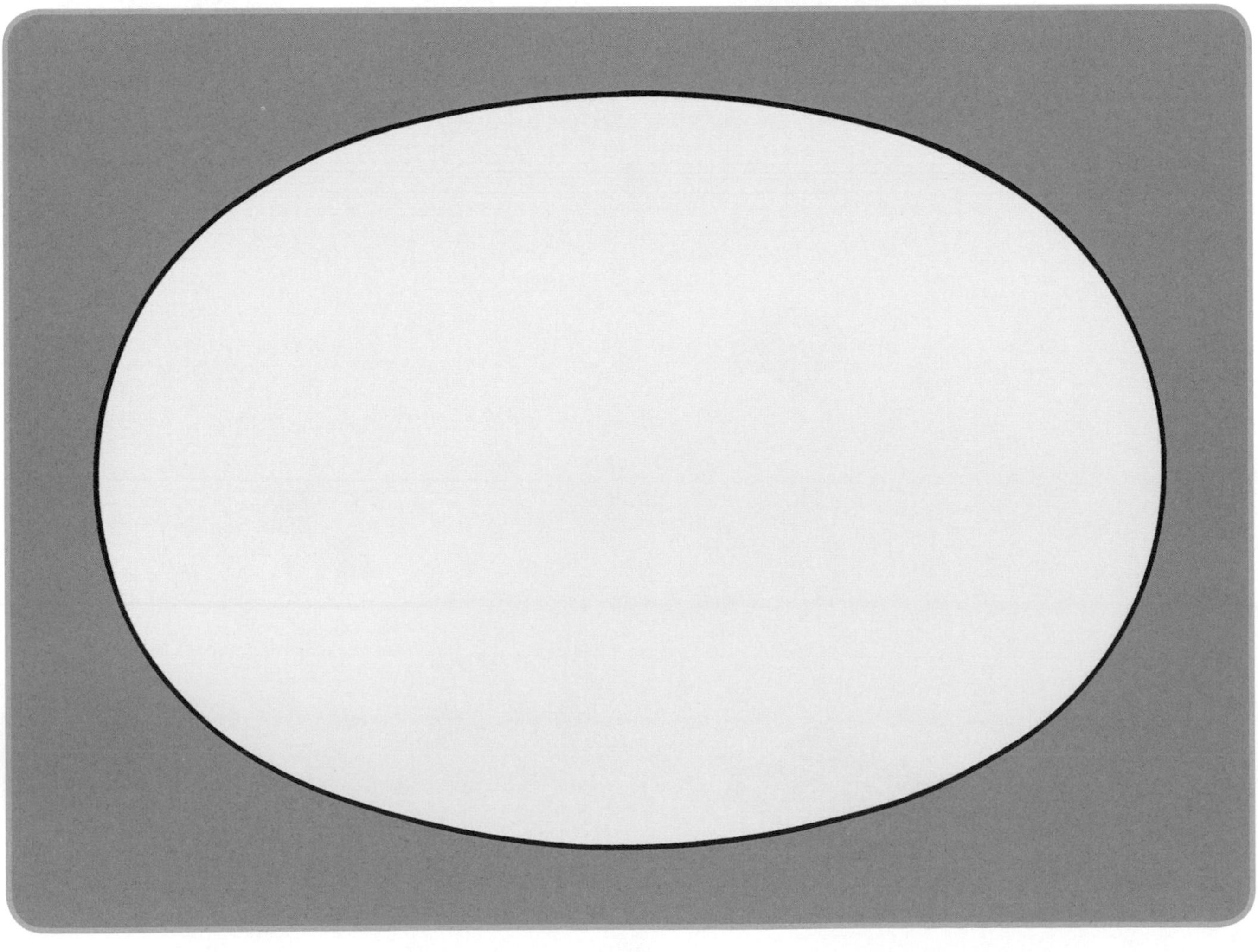

Creative Drawing
Level Five

Name

Date

To parents
Encourage your child to enjoy drawing and coloring the stars.

■ Draw and color stars in the sky. Then complete the scene as you like.

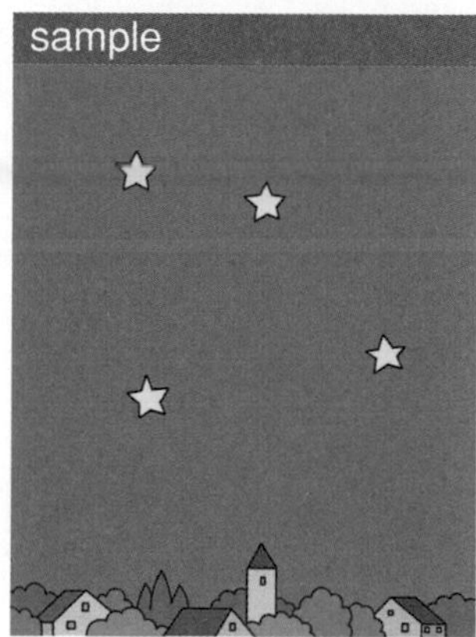

■ Draw and color leaves. Then complete the scene as you like.

sample

Creative Drawing

Level Six

Name

Date

To parents
Guide your child to draw a face on each of the jack-o'-lanterns.

■ Draw and color faces on the jack-o'-lanterns. Then complete the scene as you like.

samples

■ Draw and color pets in the yard. Then complete the scene as you like.

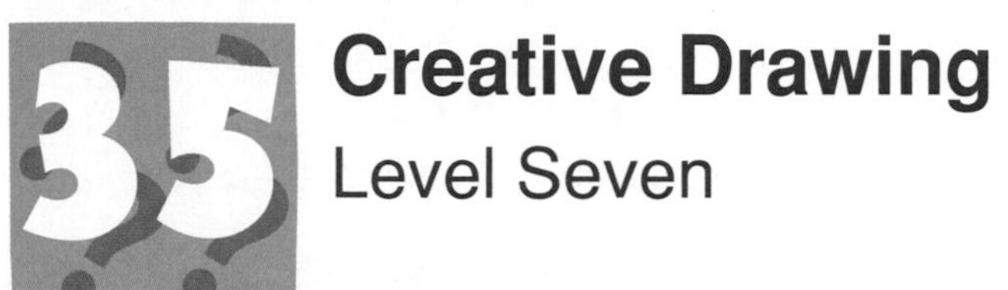

35 Creative Drawing

Level Seven

Name

Date

To parents
Point out the other objects in the scene such as the island and the palm tree.

■ Draw and color birds and planes in the sky. Then complete the scene as you like.

samples

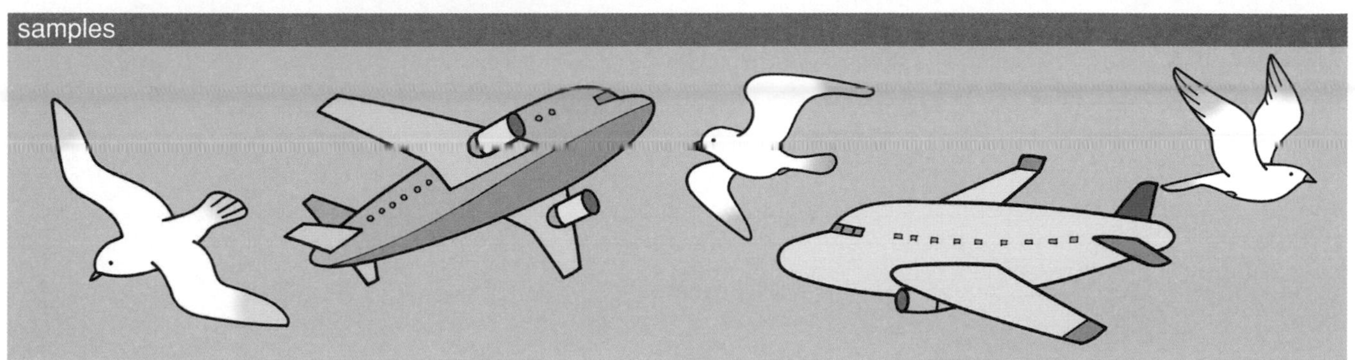

■ Draw and color animals and flowers in the field. Then complete the scene as you like.

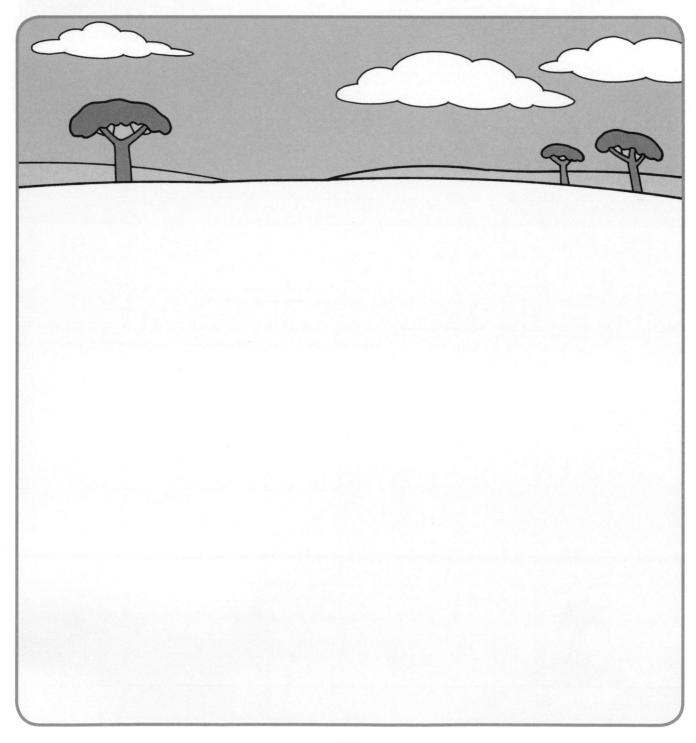

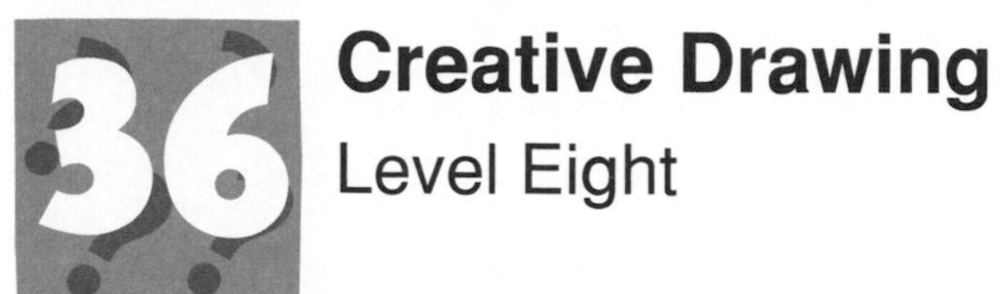

Creative Drawing

Level Eight

Name

Date

To parents
The sample pictures are examples only. Your child does not need to copy the samples.

■ Draw and color ships and fish in the ocean. Then complete the scene as you like.

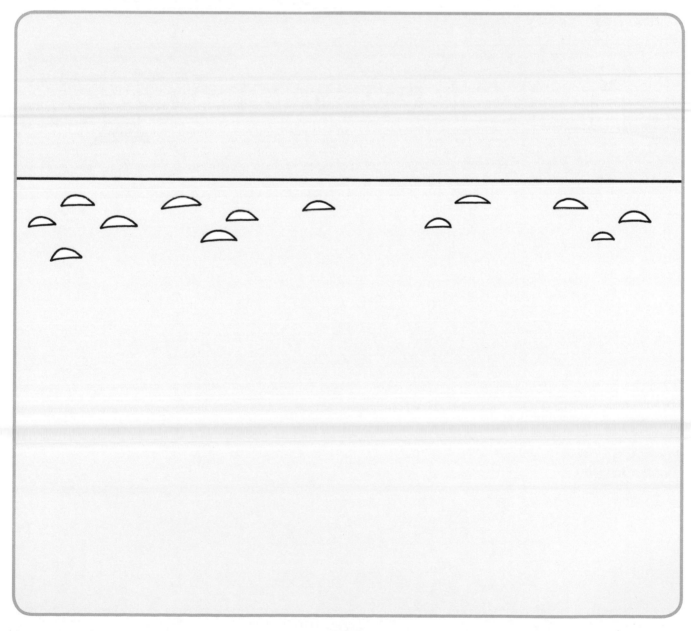

To parents
This is the last exercise of this workbook. Please praise your child for the effort it took to complete this workbook.

■ Draw and color the playground. Then complete the scene as you like.

samples

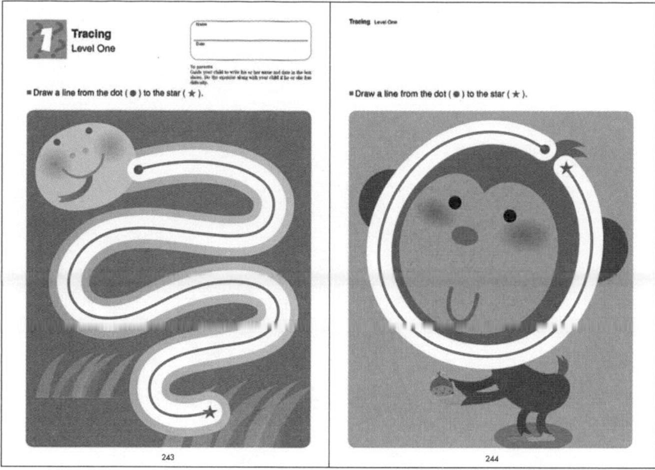

pages 243 and 244

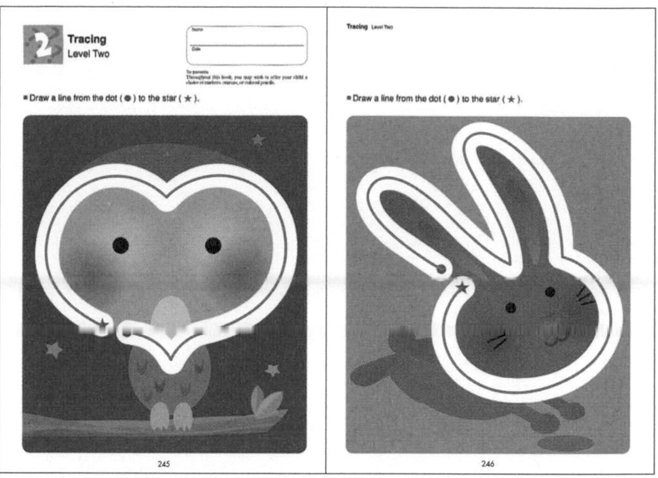

pages 245 and 246

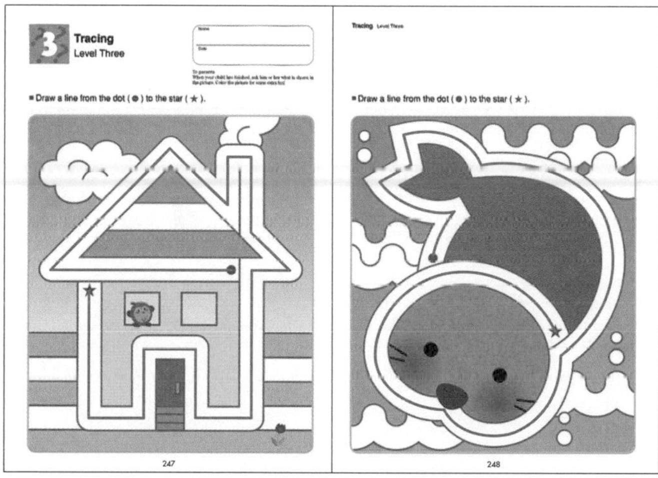

pages 247 and 248

pages 249 and 250

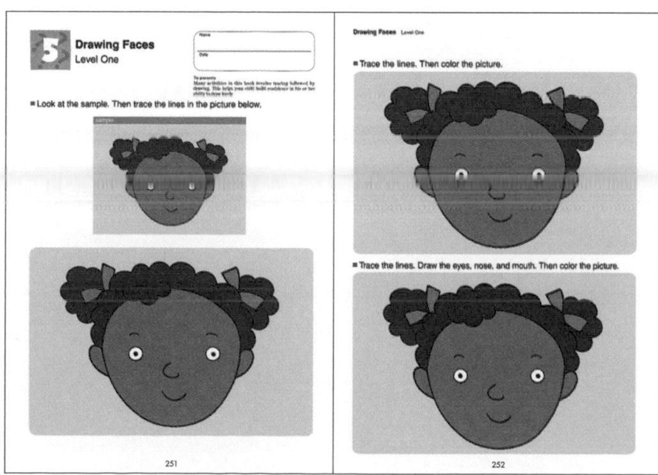

pages 251 and 252

pages 253 and 254

pages 255 and 256

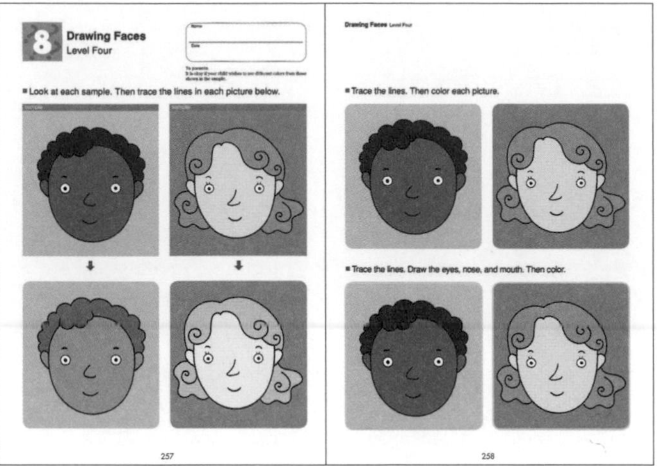
pages 257 and 258

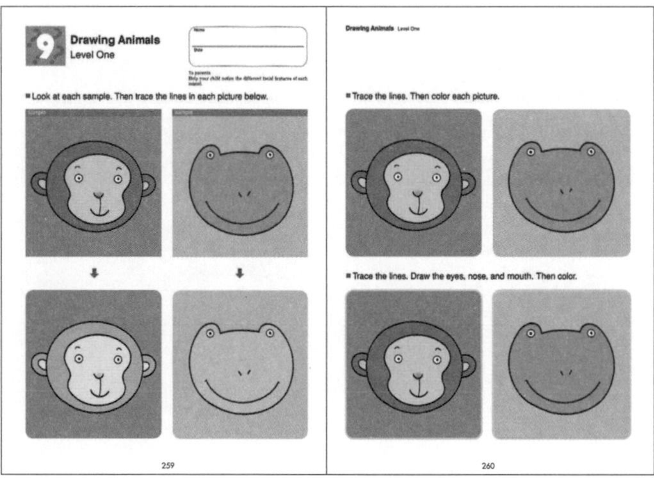
pages 259 and 260

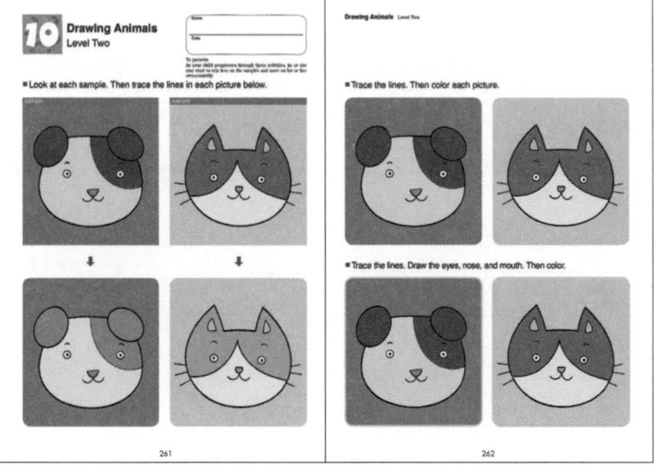
pages 261 and 262

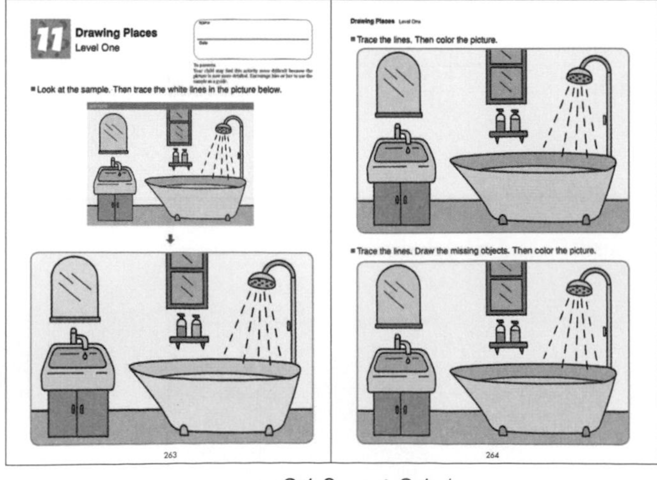
pages 263 and 264

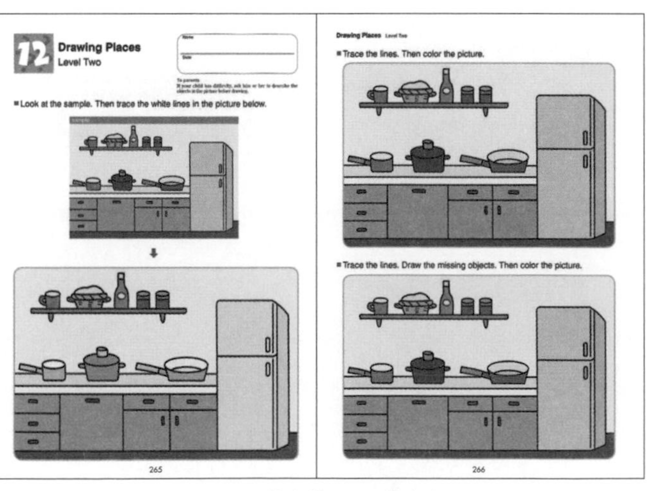
pages 265 and 266

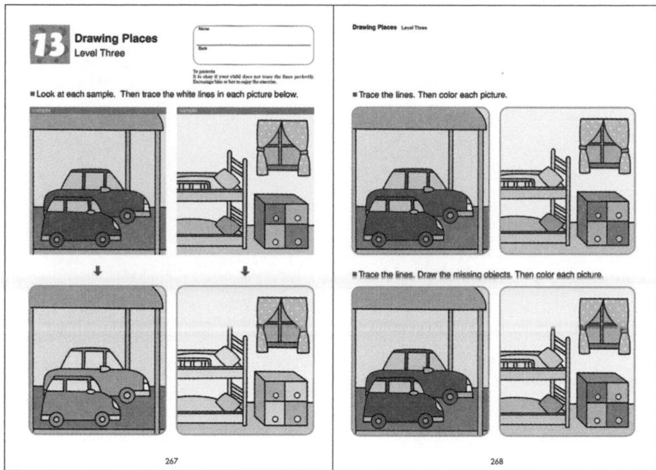

pages 267 and 268

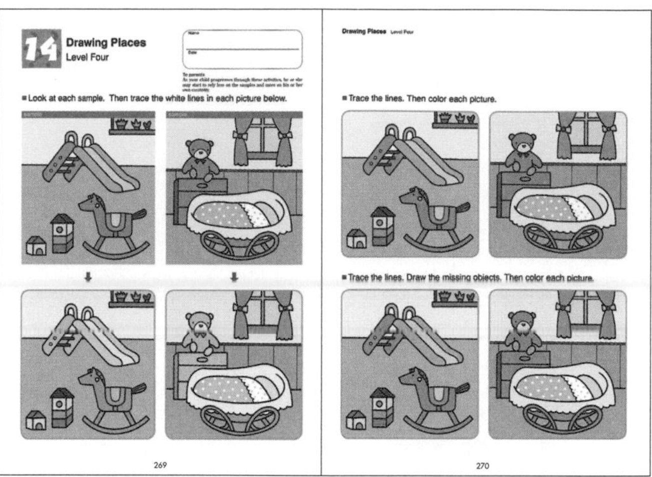

pages 269 and 270

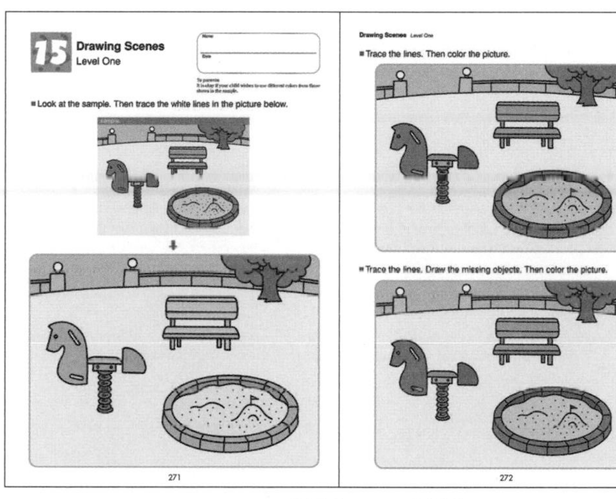

pages 271 and 272

pages 273 and 274

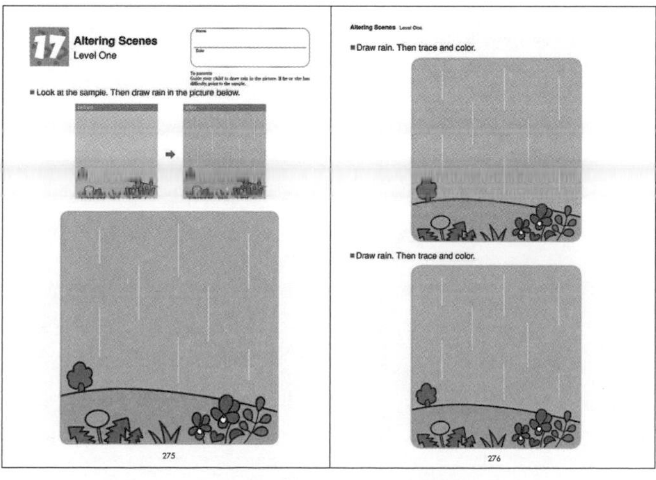

pages 275 and 276

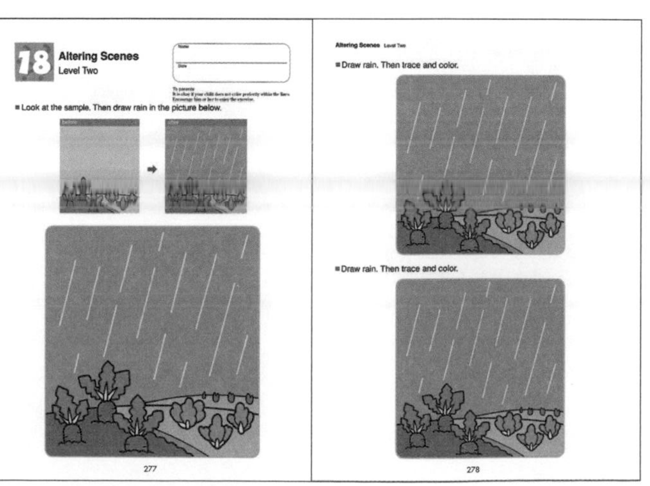

pages 277 and 278

19 Altering Scenes
Level Three
Name
Date
■ Look at the sample. Then draw rain and trace the white lines.
279
Altering Scenes Level Three
■ Draw rain. Then trace and color.
■ Draw rain. Draw the boy's eyes, nose, and mouth. Then trace and color.
280

pages 279 and 280

20 Altering Scenes
Level Four
Name
Date
■ Look at the sample. Then draw rain and trace the white lines.
281
Altering Scenes Level Four
■ Draw rain. Then trace and color.
■ Draw rain. Draw the girl's eyes, nose, and mouth. Then trace and color.
282

pages 281 and 282

21 Altering Scenes
Level Five
Name
Date
■ Look at the sample. Then draw rain and trace the white lines.
283
Altering Scenes Level Five
■ Draw rain. Then trace and color.
■ Draw rain. Draw the girl's eyes, nose, and mouth. Then trace and color.
284

pages 283 and 284

22 Altering Scenes
Level Six
Name
Date
■ Look at the sample. Then draw rain and trace the white lines.
285
Altering Scenes Level Six
■ Draw rain. Then trace and color.
■ Draw rain. Draw the boy's eyes, nose, and mouth. Then trace and color.
286

pages 285 and 286

23 Completing Scenes
Level One
Name
Date
■ Look at the sample. Then trace the balloon below.
287
Completing Scenes Level One
■ Trace the lines and color.
■ Draw a balloon and the boy's eyes, nose, and mouth. Then trace and color.
288

pages 287 and 288

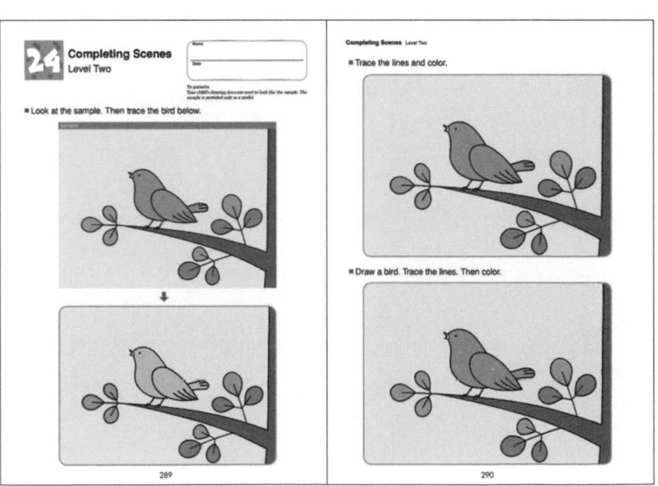
24 Completing Scenes
Level Two
Name
Date
■ Look at the sample. Then trace the bird below.
289
Completing Scenes Level Two
■ Trace the lines and color.
■ Draw a bird. Trace the lines. Then color.
290

pages 289 and 290

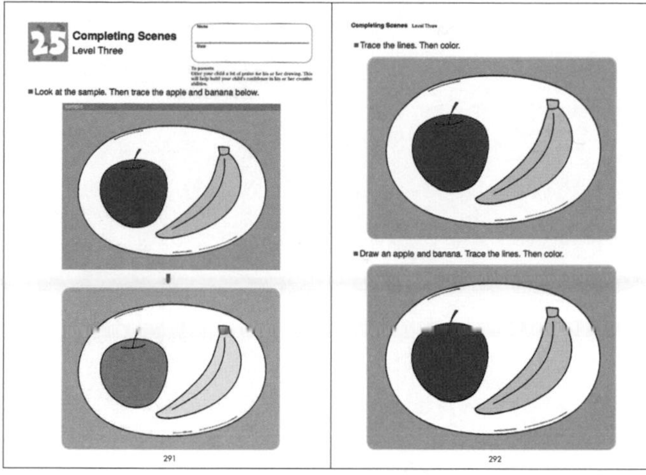
pages 291 and 292

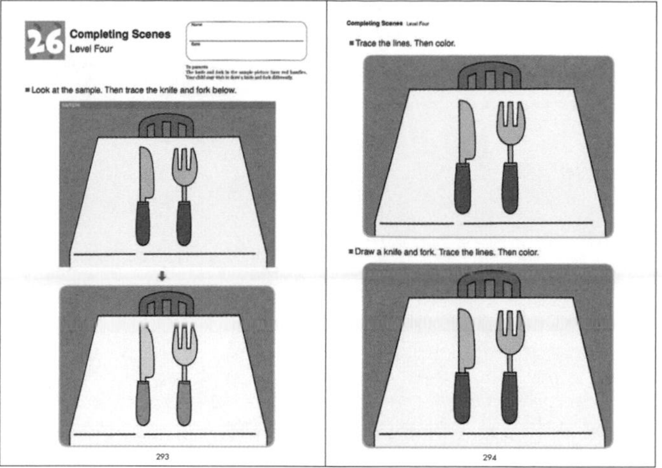
pages 293 and 294

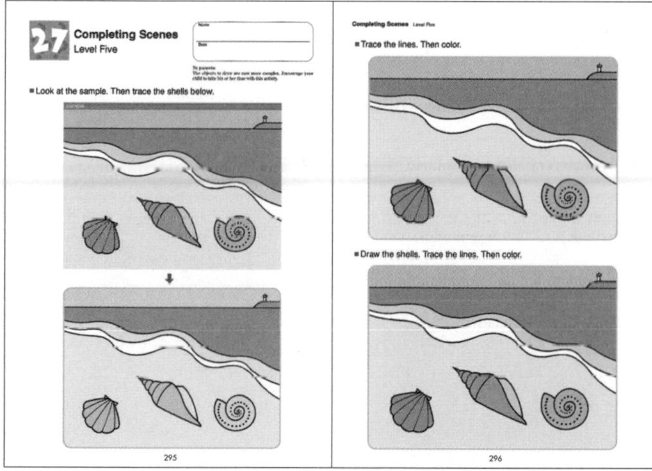
pages 295 and 296

pages 297 and 298

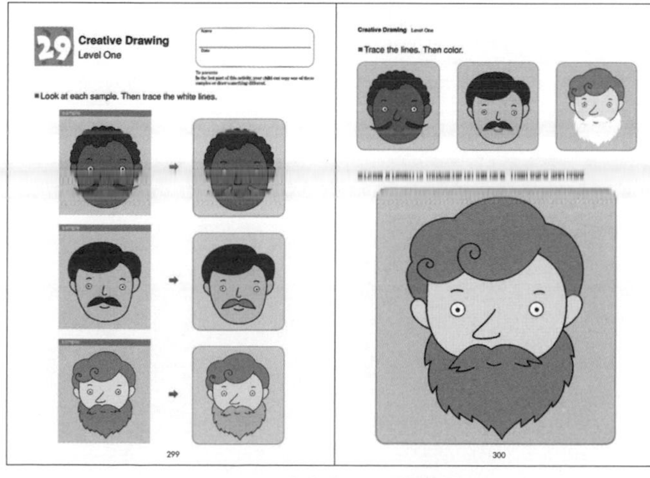
pages 299 and 300

pages 301 and 302

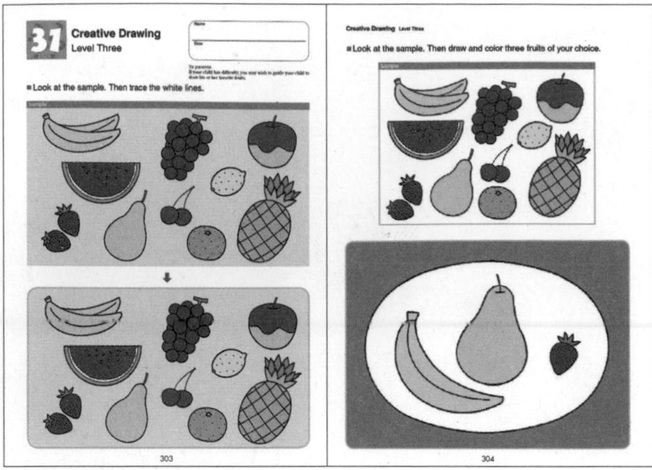
pages 303 and 304

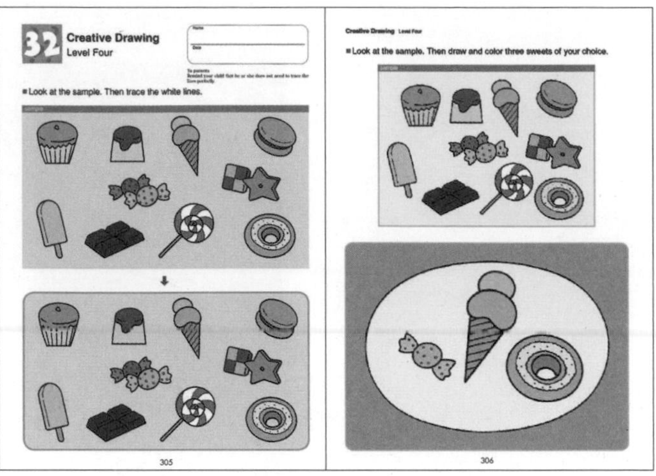
pages 305 and 306

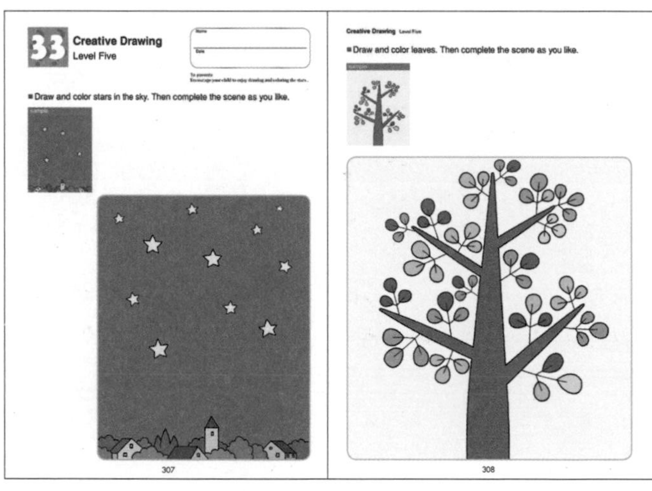
pages 307 and 308

pages 309 and 310

pages 311 and 312

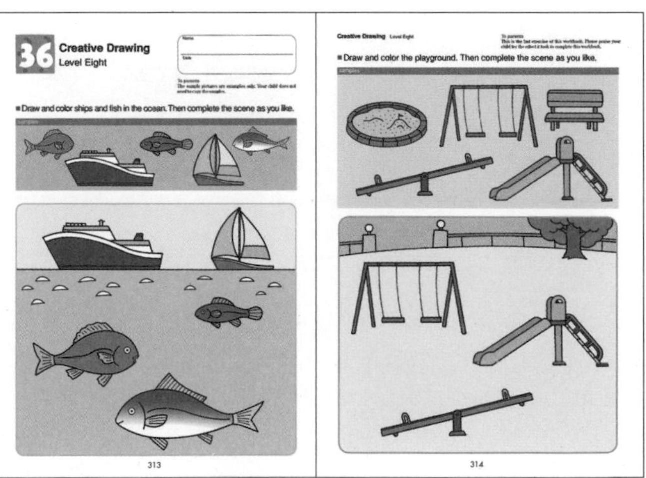
pages 313 and 314